# Managing Information Systems

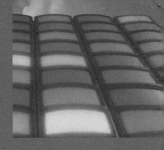

Third Edition

# MANAGING INFORMATION SYSTEMS

## Strategy and Organisation

### David Boddy
University of Glasgow

### Albert Boonstra
University of Groningen (The Netherlands)

### Graham Kennedy
Royal Bank of Scotland

**FT** Prentice Hall
FINANCIAL TIMES

*An imprint of* **Pearson Education**
Harlow, England • London • New York • Boston • San Francisco • Toronto
Sydney • Tokyo • Singapore • Hong Kong • Seoul • Taipei • New Delhi
Cape Town • Madrid • Mexico City • Amsterdam • Munich • Paris • Milan

**Pearson Education Limited**

Edinburgh Gate
Harlow
Essex CM20 2JE
England

and Associated Companies throughout the world

*Visit us on the World Wide Web at:*
www.pearsoned.co.uk

First published 2002
Second edition published 2005
**Third edition published 2008**

© Pearson Education Limited 2002, 2005, 2009

ISBN: 978-0-273-71681-5

**British Library Cataloguing-in-Publication Data**
A catalogue record for this book is available from the British Library

**Library of Congress Cataloging-in-Publication Data**
Boddy, David.
    Managing information systems : strategy and organisation / David Boddy, Albert Boonstra,
Graham Kennedy. – 3rd ed.
        p. cm.
    Includes bibliographical references and index.
    ISBN 978-0-273-71681-5 (pbk.)
    1. Management information systems.   2. Information resources management.   3. Business
enterprises–Computer networks–Management.   I. Boonstra, Albert.   II. Kennedy, Graham,
1961–   III. Title.

    HD30.213.B627  2009
    658.4′03801—dc22

                                                        2008028331

10   9   8   7   6   5   4   3   2
12   11   10   09

Typeset in 9/12 Stone serif by 35
Printed and bound by Ashford Colour Press Ltd, Gosport

*The publisher's policy is to use paper manufactured from sustainable forests.*

# BRIEF CONTENTS

# CONTENTS

**Instructor resources**
Visit www.pearsoned.co.uk/boddy to find valuable online resources

**For instructors**
- Complete, downloadable Instructor's Manual
- PowerPoint slides that can be downloaded and used as OHTs

For more information please contact your local Pearson Education sales representative or visit www.pearsoned.co.uk/boddy

# PREFACE

Modern information technologies are transforming the delivery of goods and services, but to secure an adequate return managers need to deal with issues of strategy and organisation. Information systems succeed when those responsible for implementing them take a coherent approach to both the management and the technical issues. This book draws on extensive empirical research to present a distinct organisational perspective on the management of computer-based information systems.

The book is intended for those studying towards a management qualification at universities or business schools. Undergraduate courses for which it is suitable include Level 2 and Level 3 courses with titles such as 'Information Systems Management', 'Information Systems in Context', 'Information Systems and Organisational Transformation' or 'Information Systems in Business' taken as part of degrees such as BA in Business Management, BSc in Information Systems, BSc in International Business and Management or a BBA qualification.

Postgraduate courses for which it is suitable include 'Management Systems and Organisations' as part of an MSc in Information Technology or 'e-transformation: strategy and implementation' as part of an MBA.

We offer readers the accumulating evidence of current practice, based on our research and on published studies. The book includes many case studies drawn from these sources, which will enable readers to be more confident in handling similar situations. It takes a management perspective towards information systems (IS), in that it identifies the issues of organisation and strategy that managers face as they decide how to respond to technological opportunities. Managing successive IS projects as part of a coherent organisational process (rather than as isolated technological events) will produce an information system that enhances broader strategy.

The issues will be presented within a coherent theoretical framework. This is based on the interaction between people, technology and contexts. The chapters deal with the components of the model in turn, so that readers can link to it at different points. The cases (from a wide range of sectors) illustrate aspects of the model.

This means we can draw from a broad range of technological applications – with a consistent focus on realising the business opportunities. It is not tied to a particular technological fashion. It offers a timeless framework that managers can use to consider new developments in the information revolution as they arise – in this edition we pay more attention to mobile computing and social networking.

This new edition takes account of helpful comments from staff and students who used the second edition and the suggestions of six anonymous reviewers. The book retains the content of the second edition, with the addition of a completely new chapter on the social contexts of information systems, allowing us to introduce issues of data privacy and intellectual property. The chapter on costs and benefits has been moved to the end of the book, and the two chapters on implementation have been combined into a single Chapter 9. Chapter 1 has been substantially revised to set out more fully and systematically the distinctive theoretical perspective of the book.

Eight of the Chapter Cases are new: Tesco, Google, Intel, Zara, NHS Connect, Cemex, Nokia and the BBC. The continued Siemens and RBS cases have been completely rewritten to take account of new developments – in the latter the acquisition of ABN Amro. There are many new examples and illustrations, and over 100 new references. A new pedagogical feature has been added – 'Weblinks' – that, following the Further Reading, offers suggestions of sites to visit for more information.

## ● Objectives

When they have read the book, students should be able to do the following.

- Evaluate current IS provision in an organisation, in the light of emerging technical possibilities.
- Outline how IS could support an organisation's strategy, including developing new products, services and markets.
- Propose how IS can add value to a business process and enable radical re-engineering of existing processes.
- Propose how human and structural changes should be made to gain more value from a computer-based IS.
- Evaluate how their IS function is organised and propose alternatives.
- Manage organisational and IS changes to achieve complementarity between them.
- Avoid the common pitfalls that damage many IS projects.
- Evaluate and discuss an organisation's approach to these issues and make well-grounded recommendations on actual or planned IS applications.
- Take a balanced view of how computer-based IS can benefit their organisation.

## ● Outline of the book

There are four parts in the book, dealing with foundations, strategy, organisation and implementation. Chapter 1 outlines the role of information in organisations and the components of an information system. This includes the fundamental point that information systems include people as well as technology. It also presents the central theoretical perspective of the book, that people interpret and interact with their context as they respond to an information system. These interactions shape the outcomes of a project – and identify whether these match the promoters' objectives.

Chapter 2 concentrates on recent developments in computer-based information systems, in applications to support customer relationship management, knowledge management, enterprise resource planning, inter-organisational working and community systems. It illustrates the far-reaching possibilities these enable, while indicating that the issues they raise are more to do with management than with technology.

The new Chapter 3 outlines features of the wider social context that are relevant to those managing information systems. It shows the influence of political and economic factors on aspects of information systems management and how variations in cultures between nations can affect the use of information systems. There are two sections on the legal context, dealing respectively with data privacy and intellectual property. It then shows how to consider ethical issues as part of organisational strategy.

Part 2 deals with some strategic issues. Chapter 4 examines the interaction between strategy and information systems. It begins by using established models of the strategy development process to show how companies have used information systems to change the way they compete. It then considers the concept of strategic alignment and concludes with an analysis of the practical complexities of forming an information system strategy.

Chapter 5 examines how companies have used computer-based systems to modify their business processes. Modern systems make it possible for people to link the horizontal processes of organisations more effectively, by eroding established functional boundaries. This depends on a good understanding of different approaches to business process redesign and the managerial and organisational interactions that such projects involve.

Part 3 of the book turns to organisational issues. Cultural, structural and political issues dominate Chapter 6. It is increasingly clear that the prevailing culture in an organisation affects how people react to information systems. It is equally clear that managers can use information systems to centralise or to decentralise decisions – which approach gives most coherence with wider strategy? A major issue for companies introducing an Internet venture is whether to integrate this with the existing structure or to create it as a separate business unit. The chapter ends with a consideration of the links between power and information systems.

Chapter 7 considers one aspect of structural choice, namely the place of the information function itself within the organisation. It outlines the main options – centralised, decentralised, federal or outsourcing – and the benefits and costs of each. It also considers alternative approaches to charging for information services and the problem of balancing the conflicting expectations of user, IS and corporate constituencies.

Chapter 8 examines people in relation to information systems. Theories of human motivation offer some guidance on how people will react to new systems – whether as users or customers. Staff tend to welcome those which complement valued skills and experience and reject those that do not. The chapter also considers research into distributed working arrangements – which indicates that they are more likely to bring worthwhile benefits if management creates a coherent context for the people concerned.

The first chapter in Part 4 focuses on process – how managers implement an information system in a way that achieves, or exceeds, its objectives. It outlines four complementary models of change, each of which can guide management action in a project, and then considers ways of monitoring and controlling what is happening. The chapter then moves from considering projects to the additional techniques required to manage programmes, groups of related projects, such as that undertaken by The Royal Bank of Scotland to integrate its acquisition, ABN Amro Bank.

Chapter 10 considers how to evaluate the costs and benefits of investing in information systems. The dilemma all managers face is that, while they can usually predict the costs of an information system, they are much less certain about the benefits: a dilemma facing the BBC as it decides how much to invest in digital networks, alongside its conventional broadcasting channels. The chapter outlines briefly the principles, and the weaknesses, of conventional investment appraisal methods. It then introduces some alternative methods that give more weight to non-financial criteria.

## ● Pedagogical features

The book includes these pedagogical features.

- **Learning objectives** at the start of each chapter. These serve as a focus for the chapter and a reference point for learning.

- **Cases** at the start of each chapter. Most of these relate to familiar companies and trace how, in different ways, their managements have sought to make good use of computer-based information systems. Developments in the case or additional perspectives are introduced later in the chapter. These provide a good basis for group work before or during a class.

- **Case questions** encourage students to make connections between the case and the theoretical perspectives of the chapter.

- **MIS in practice** boxes throughout the chapter illustrate the themes.

- **Research summary** boxes highlight significant pieces of research or scholarship.

- **Activities** – each chapter contains several activity features that invite readers to make connections between theory and practice. They invite them, for example, to gather some information or reflect on practice as a stimulus to thinking about the theory.

- **End-of-section summaries**. Each section concludes by summarising the topic covered, which helps students to draw the material together.

- **End-of-chapter questions**. At the end of each chapter there are at least five questions, which readers can use to test their understanding of the topics or which teachers can use as a way of structuring class discussion.

- **Further reading**. As well as extensive references to (accessible) sources, each chapter contains an annotated guide to at least two books or articles that deal with issues in greater depth or from a different perspective.

- **Weblinks** – some suggested websites as sources of further information and ideas.

- **References** – the text is fully referenced to academic sources, and this edition includes over 100 new references.

## ● Supplementary material

An Instructor's Manual is available at **www.pearsoned.co.uk/boddy** to adopters of the text. This offers:

- suggested responses to the activity (where appropriate) and chapter questions;

- additional or more recent information about some of the chapter cases and other cases;

- some additional models or diagrams, to supplement those in the text;

- suggested tutorial and/or examination questions;

- a set of PowerPoint slides for each chapter, including many of the figures.

# ABOUT THE AUTHORS

David Boddy, BSc(Econ), MA (Organizational Psychology), is Research Fellow in the Department of Management at the University of Glasgow. He teaches courses for experienced managers on the management issues raised by computer-based information systems – which has been the main focus of his research. His books include *Management: An Introduction* (4th edition) and *Managing Projects: Building and Leading the Team* (2nd edition), both with Financial Times/Prentice Hall, Harlow. He has recently published in the *Journal of Information Technology,* the *Journal of General Management,* the *Journal of Management Studies, New Technology, Work and Employment* and the *European Journal of Information Systems.*

Albert Boonstra, Bec, MBA, PhD, is an associate professor at the Faculty of Management and Organisation, University of Groningen, The Netherlands. His research focuses on the human and organisational issues of implementing and using information and communication technologies. He teaches IT-management-related courses for students as well as for experienced managers. He also consults for profit and not-for-profit organisations on the management of information systems. He has recently had articles published in the *Journal of General Management,* the *European Journal of Information Systems* and *New Technology, Work and Employment.*

Graham Kennedy holds an MBA degree from the University of Glasgow and currently works in the internal consultancy division of The Royal Bank of Scotland. He has over eighteen years' experience as a manager of change initiatives in industries as varied as financial services and engineering. A common thread throughout his career has been the application of information systems to business areas, and this has provided him with many insights into the opportunities – and problems – which new technologies present to users.

More information is available from **www.pearson.co.uk/boddy**.

# ACKNOWLEDGEMENTS

This book is the result of several years' cooperation between the authors in teaching an MBA elective on the topic. They have delivered this to managers taking the Executive MBA programme at the University of Glasgow, and also to managers on Executive MBA programmes from around the world who have attended the European Summer School for Advanced Management or the Asian Intensive School for Advanced Management as part of their MBA studies. The managers attending these Executive MBA programmes are too numerous to mention, but they have contributed beyond measure to the development of our thinking in this area.

## Publisher's acknowledgements

We are grateful to the following for permission to reproduce copyright material:

**Table 2.4** This material is taken from *Case Studies in Knowledge Management* (1999) written by Scarbrough, H. and Swan, J., with the permission of the publisher, the Chartered Institute of Personnel and Development, London (www.cipd.co.uk); **Table 4.2** from Six IT decisions your IT people shouldn't make, by Ross, J.W. and Weill, P., *Harvard Business Review* 80(11) p. 87, copyright 2002; and **Table 6.3** from Get the right mix for bricks and clicks, by Gulati, R. and Garino, J. *Harvard Business Review,* 78(3) p. 114, copyright 2003 by the Harvard Business School Corporation, all rights reserved; **Table 5.1** from *Process management, creating value along the vale chain,* by Wisner, J.D. and Stanley, L.L., (2008), Thomson Publishing/Cengage Learning; **Table 5.2** from *Open Innovation: The New Imperative for Creating and Profiting from Technology*, by Chesborough, H.R., p. 121, copyright 2003; **Table 5.3** from Pre-conditions for BPR-success by Markus, M.J., *Information Systems Management* 11(2) pp. 7–14, copyright 1994 Taylor & Francis Informa UK Ltd; **Table 6.1** from *Organizational Culture: Mapping the Terrain.* Martin, J., 2002, Sage Publications Inc.; **Table 7.1** Reprinted from *Corporate Information Systems Management: Text and Cases,* Applegate, L.M., McFarlan, F.W. and Kennedy, J.L., Irwin/McGraw-Hill, p. 420; and **Table 7.3** from *Corporate Information Systems Management: Text and Cases*, by Applegate, L.M., McFarlan, F.W. and Kennedy, J.L., Irwin/McGraw-Hill, p. 445, copyright 2007, McGraw-Hill Companies, Inc.; **Table 7.6** from Technochange management: using IT to drive organizational change, by Markus, M.L. 2004, *Journal of Information Technology*, 20(1) p. 7, Palgrave MacMillan; **Table 10.3** reprinted from The Impact of inadequacies in the treatment of organisational issues on information systems development projects, by Doherty, N.F., King, M. and Al-Mushayt, O., *Information and Management* 41, pp. 49–62, 2003 with permission from Elsevier Limited.

**Figure 3.1** from Graph of internet subscribers by region and access type 2006, www.itu.int/ITU-D/ict/statistics/, reproduced with the permission of the International Telecommunication Union; **Figure 3.2** from Variation in demographic characteristics of UK Internet users, *eMori Technology Tracker*, Ipsos MORI; **Figure 3.3** reprinted from Table of Privacy Policy Assessment Matrix, K.S. Schwaig et al., *Information and Management* 43, pp. 805–820, 2006, Table 10; **Figure 3.4** from Graph showing Downloads share of singles sales in the UK by week 2004–2006, British Phonographic Industry/OCC; **Figure 3.6** from Ethical decision-making in organisations: a person–situation interactionist model, *Academy of Management Review,* (11)3, pp. 601–617; Trevino's model of ethical decision making; **Figure 4.2** Reprinted from *Competitive Advantage: Creating and Sustaining Superior Performance* by Porter, M.E., with the permission of The Free Press, a Division of Simon & Schuster Adult Publishing Group, copyright 1985, 1998 by Michael E. Porter, all rights reserved; **Figures 4.7** from Strategy and the Internet, by Porter, M.E., *Harvard Business Review*, 79(2) pp. 63–78, copyright 2001; and **Figure 10.3** from The balanced scorecard: measures that drive performance, by Kaplan, R.S. and Norton, D.P., *Harvard Business Review* 70(1) pp. 71–79, copyright 2002 Harvard Business School Publishing Corporation, all rights reserved; **Figure 4.10** from *The Internet Encyclopedia,* Bidgoli, H., copyright 2004, John Wiley & Sons, Inc., p. 324, reprinted with permission; **Figure 4.11** The dynamics of alignment: Insights from a punctuated equilibrium model by Sabherwal, R., Hirscheim, R. and Goles, T., 2001, *Organization Science* 12(2), pp. 179–197, reprinted by permission; **Figure 4.13** from *E-business and E-Commerce Management* 3rd edn, by Chaffey, D., 2007, Financial Times Prentice Hall; **Figure 6.1** The inertial impact of culture on IT implementation, by Cooper et al., 2003, *Information and Management,* 27(1) pp. 17–31; **Figure 6.2** from Real strategies for virtual organizing, by Venkatraman, N. and Henderson, J.C., 1998, *MIT Sloan Management Review* 40(1) p. 34; and **Figure 10.1** from New approaches to IT investment, Ross, J.W. and Beath, C.M., 2002, *MIT Sloan Management Review* 43(2) pp. 51–59, MIT; **Figure 8.3** *Organizational Behaviour* 6th edn, by Huczynski, A.A. and Buchanan D.A., 2007, Financial Times Prentice Hall; **Figure 8.6** from Distributed work arrangements: a research framework, by Belanger, F. and Collins, R.W. 1998, *Information Society* 14(2) p. 139; **Figure 9.1** from *Business Information Systems*; by Chaffey, D., 2003, Financial Times Prentice Hall; **Figure 10.2** from An expanded instrument for evaluating information system success, Saarinen, T., 1996, *Information and Management*, 31, pp. 49–62, with permission from Elsevier Limited.

  **MIS in Practice p. 224** from The flowering of feudalism, *The Economist* 27 February 1993, copyright 1993 The Economist Group, all rights reserved.

We are grateful to the Financial Times Limited for permission to reprint the following material:

**Chapter 10** Knowing when to take the giant leap, Financial Times, 3 October 2003, copyright *Financial Times*, 3 October 2003.

In some instances we have been unable to trace the owners of copyright material, and we would appreciate any information that would enable us to do so.

**Table 2.3** from Alavi, M. and Leidner, D.E. (2002), Knowledge management and knowledge management system: conceptual foundations and research issues, *MIS Quarterly*, 25(1) pp. 107–136 Table 3, p. 125 and **Table 6.2** from Leidner, D.E. and Kayworth, T. (2006) A Review of culture in information system research: Towards a theory of information technology culture conflict, *MIS Quarterly* 30(2) pp. 357–399; **Table 3.1** from Variation in amount and number of purchases in Europe, EIAA, 2006; **Figure 4.1** from *The Strategy Process: Concepts, Contexts, Cases*, by Mintzberg, 2003, Financial Times Prentice Hall, p. 18; **Figure 8.2** from Venkatesh, V., Morris, M.G., Davis, G.B. and Davis, F.D. (2003) A unified theory of acceptance and use of technology, *MIS Quarterly* 27(3):

425–478, Management Information Systems Research Center; and **p. 274** from Venkatesh, V., Morris, M.G., Davis, G.B. and Davis, F.D. (2003) A unified theory of acceptance and use of technology, *MIS Quarterly* 27(3) p. 460; **Figure 9.3** from Graph showing RBS share price relative to UK banks since offer proposed.

## Reviewers' names

We would also like to thank the reviewers for their feedback in developing the new edition:

Eric Bodger
Adrienne Curry
Chris Kimble
Niki Panteli
Syed Nasirin
P.E.A. Vanderbossche.

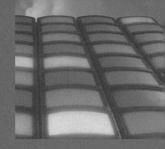

# PART 1

# Foundations

In this part we set the scene by examining the links between information systems and organisations. Chapter 1 considers what we mean by 'information' and why it is essential to organisational performance. It also describes the components of an information system (IS) and introduces the central theme of this book: that information systems include people as well as technology. It presents the idea that the outcomes of an information system depend on the interaction between people, technology and organisational contexts, which the rest of the book develops in more detail. The Chapter Case (Tesco) shows how the company has used information systems to improve its performance and gain a competitive advantage, by relating the technology very closely to the strategy and the organisation as a whole.

Chapter 2 illustrates the growing power and reach of information systems, and classifies them in terms of their formality, reach, purposes and complementarities. It presents examples of major business applications of IS: enterprise systems, knowledge systems, customer relationship systems, inter-organisational systems and community systems. The Chapter Case is about Siemens, which as well as being a major supplier of advanced technologies uses them to support all aspects of the business – though here the focus is on managing customer relations and knowledge.

Chapter 3 (for which Google is the case) outlines some features of the wider social context that are relevant to those managing information systems. It shows the influence of political and economic factors on aspects of information systems management, and how variations in cultures between nations can affect the use of information systems. There are two sections on the legal context, dealing respectively with data privacy and intellectual property – both areas where long-standing arrangements are struggling to cope with the power of modern technology. It then introduces some models to help people think about ethical issues that arise in using IS, and how to consider ethical issues as part of organisational strategy.

# CHAPTER 1

## Information systems and organisations

### Learning objectives

By the end of your work on this topic you should be able to:

- Explain why people need data, information and knowledge to add value to resources

- Outline the reasons for organisations' increased dependence on IS

- Give examples of how companies of all kinds use computer-based IS to add value

- Explain and illustrate how context affects the outcomes of computer-based IS

- Outline an interaction model of IS and context

- Use the interaction model to analyse an IS project in an organisation

# Tesco and the power of information systems

## www.tesco.com

In 2008 Tesco was the UK's leading chain of super-markets, with 31 per cent of the grocery market, and steadily rising profits. The UK business accounted for 80 per cent of total sales, employing over 250,000 people in 1800 stores.

To continue growth, the emphasis is on developing the range of non-food items, such as clothes, fur-nishings, entertainment and health products. Tesco Personal Finance (a joint venture with The Royal Bank of Scotland – see Chapter 9 case) offers loans, credit cards, mortgages and other financial products to retail customers. Since the mid-1990s the company has been investing in markets overseas, and by 2008 it was active in 12 countries outside of the UK.

The Chief Executive, Terry Leahy, has said:

> If we are to meet our objectives, the Tesco team needs to work together. Because we need to focus on every aspect of what Tesco does, we use a management tool we call the Steering Wheel to bring together our work in all areas and measure our performance. It helps us manage Tesco in a balanced way, by covering every-thing we do, and allows us to plan for the future by setting targets for years to come. The Steering Wheel literally guides us through our daily running of the company, while allowing us to change to meet cus-tomers' demands.

In 1994 it launched the Tesco Clubcard scheme, which has over 11 million active holders. Shoppers join the scheme by completing a simple form with some personal information about their age and where they live. Their purchases earn vouchers based on the amount they spend. Every purchase they make at Tesco is scanned electronically at the checkout, and the company analyses this data (from over 10 million transactions each week) to identify customers' shopping preferences. This information determines a package of special offers that are most likely to appeal to that customer, which Tesco mails to customers four times a year. Each mailing brings a large increase in business.

The data is also analysed to identify the kind of person the Clubcard holder is – such as if they have a baby, young children or they like cooking. Each prod-uct is ascribed a set of attributes such as expensive or cheap, ethnic recipe or traditional dish, own-label or upmarket brand? The information on customers and product attributes is used to support all aspects of the business – identifying possible gaps in the product range, assessing the effect of promotional offers, and noting local variations in taste.

The information is also sold to suppliers, who use it when planning to launch new products. Within hours of a product going on sale, or of launching a promotional offer, brand managers can track who is buying their products or responding to promotions. The company is keen to stress that no data on indi-viduals is ever released – the analysis is based on categories of consumers, not individuals. The data-base is believed to be the largest collection of personal information about named individuals within the UK. It has also shaped a series of strategic decisions, such as the move into smaller store formats, and the launch of the Internet shopping site. It also influenced the development and sale of Tesco mobile phones, pet insurance and the Finest food range.

*Source*: Published information and the Tesco website.

## CASE QUESTIONS 1.1

Visit the Tesco website and find out about recent developments in the company's use of information systems.

- What evidence is there on the shopping pages about how the company uses IS in dealing with customers?
- How will information help managers to use the 'Steering Wheel' in managing operations?
- In what specific ways does the Clubcard support the company's competitive position?
- Use Figure 1.5 to identify examples of management issues that the company may have faced in using computer-based information systems to support the business?

# Introduction

Tesco is clearly a successful retailer, meeting the expectations of a growing number of customers in the UK and increasingly overseas. On financial measures it is adding value to the resources it uses, in large part because it has invested heavily in systems that provide staff at all levels with accurate and timely information. These help it to make internal processes efficient, integrate the many functions within the business, and create electronic links with suppliers. The company has also designed the Clubcard scheme, which gives it information about individual customers' spending patterns, allowing it to shape promotional offers that will most appeal to the customer. The case illustrates how information systems support the competitive position of the business, and how they affect the work of people at all levels.

Managers in most organisations depend on a similar flow of accurate and timely information, so a primary management responsibility is to create high-quality information systems (IS) to provide this. There are examples of this throughout the book – Siemens, in Chapter 2, depends heavily on modern IS to link the many separate businesses in the group to each other, and to the company's many customers. The Royal Bank of Scotland (Chapter 9) shows how companies in financial services have become ever more dependent on modern IS to manage internal operations efficiently, and to offer new services to customers. Other examples include Google, Nokia and Intel: in all of these, managers depend on information to manage the business. They do not delegate the task of designing such systems to IS staff, and use whatever system they advise. Rather, managers work with IS staff to ensure they develop or acquire systems that serve the needs of the business and the people within it.

This responsibility has become more widespread as computer-based information systems have moved from the background to the foreground of organisations. Technological developments mean that managers throughout an enterprise are expected to shape the information systems that affect their performance. Companies in manufacturing or transport need IS to *support* their core business. For those in media, communication or financial services the information systems *are* the business, since they depend on customers paying for information, not physical products.

The chapter begins by outlining the role of information, and how converging technologies are transforming how many people access information. It then outlines the model that provides the structure for the book, and introduces the elements which later chapters develop.

## 1.1 A dependence on information

We all depend on information. Medical staff treating a patient need information about their condition, history, and the likely effects of alternative treatments. Those managing a unit need information about (amongst other things) the demand for services, available capacity or the cost and effectiveness of alternative treatments. As you manage your work on an assignment you need information – what your teacher requires, the due date, advice from previous assignments, and theories and evidence you may choose to use.

### ● Why people need information

The need for information reflects the fact that organisations are open systems, interacting with their environment. They draw resources from the external environment (inputs), transform them into outputs and pass them back to the environment. These outputs can be in a tangible, physical form (a Nokia handset) or in an intangible, informational form (a text message or a video clip received on a handset). Figure 1.1 illustrates the flow, and shows that the value the organisation obtains for their outputs (money, reputation, goodwill, etc.) enables them (shown by the feedback arrow from output to input) to continue attracting resources. If the outputs fail to generate sufficient new resources, the enterprise cannot continue.

Information about inputs could include the cost and availability of materials or staff; information about transformation could be about delivery schedules or quality; output information could show sales or customer satisfaction. Figure 1.1 shows how information systems support these business activities.

**Figure 1.1** The role of information systems in organisations

### Activity 1.1 Collecting examples of information

Arrange a short discussion with someone who works in an organisation (or use your experience). Ask them to give examples of information that is used regularly by:

(a) a senior manager

(b) a departmental manager

(c) a professional specialist.

Also ask them how they receive that information and how it helps them in their work.

## ● Data, information and knowledge

We need to clarify the terms 'data', 'information' and 'knowledge'.

● **Data** refers to recorded descriptions of things, events, activities and transactions – their size, colour, cost, weight, date and so on. It may or may not convey information to a person.

● **Information** is a sub-set of data that means something to the person receiving it – which they judge to be useful, significant or urgent. It comes from data that has been processed (by people or with the aid of technology) so that it has value for the recipient. Information is subjective: one person may see value in a report that another sees as worthless data.

● 'Knowledge builds on information that is extracted from data' (Boisot, 1998, p. 12). While data is a property of things (size, price, etc.), **knowledge** is a property of people that encourages them to act in a particular way. Knowledge embodies prior understanding, experience and learning, and is confirmed or modified as people receive new information.

The significance of the distinction is that we use knowledge to make better use of resources. Knowledge allows us to react to information and data differently from those without it. Someone with accurate, relevant knowledge of a market will use that to interpret information about, say, current sales. They use their knowledge to identify patterns or trends, so that the information means more to them. They can use that insight to make decisions (such as where to concentrate resources) that are more likely to meet their objectives than someone without that knowledge. Figure 1.2 shows this relation between data, information, knowledge and information systems.

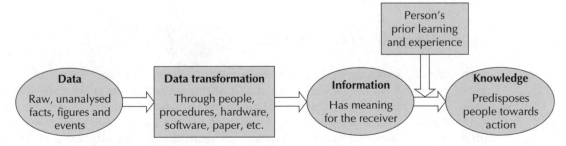

**Figure 1.2** The links between data, information and knowledge

Having distinguished the three terms, we also recognize that people use them interchangeably – as if they meant the same thing. We follow this convention by generally using the term 'information', unless in the specific context one of the other words is more suitable.

## ● Information systems

An **information system** is a set of people, procedures and resources that collects data which it transforms and disseminates. Human societies have developed successively more powerful ways of communicating with one another over space and time. The earliest humans communicated through sign language, painting or drawing and speech. The development of writing and numeric symbols, and especially the development of printing technology, enabled people to record data on paper, transform it into information and (some time later) present it to someone in another place. **Computer-based information systems** significantly lowered the cost of processing data and information. Linking computers with telecommunication systems made it even quicker and cheaper to exchange information with little regard to distance. The development of mobile telecommunications, liberating the computer from the desktop, continues the historic process of making information (and data and knowledge) available more widely and more cheaply.

This does *not* mean that all communication becomes electronic. For all the power of computing and telecommunications systems to handle internal and external data, organisations have infinite informal communication networks, which people use to pass on gossip, rumour and information. These informal systems exist alongside the computer-based (often called 'digital') information systems that are the subject of this book.

## ● Summary

- People depend on information to manage inputs, transformation processes and outputs.

- Raw data is transformed into information that has meaning.

- People use their knowledge (based on experience and learning) to interpret information in a way that makes better use of resources.

- Human society has developed a succession of technologies that make information available more widely and more cheaply.

## 1.2 The technology infrastructure

Many daily activities depend on infrastructures that support the flow of information – between individuals (an exchange of e-mails), within an organisation (an order passing from sales to production), between organisations (an order for materials passing from a manufacturer to a supplier) or between organisations and individuals (a special offer sent to a mobile phone). This information technology infrastructure, shown in Figure 1.3, has five linked components – computer hardware, computer software, data

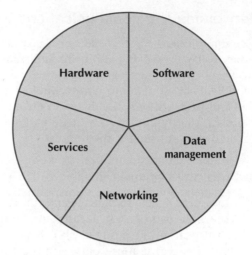

Figure 1.3 Components of the IT infrastructure

management technology, networking and telecommunications technology, and technology services (Laudon and Laudon, 2007a).

## ● Computer hardware

**Computer hardware** is the technology for processing and storing data, and for gathering and delivering it as output. Data is processed in all kinds of computers, from large mainframes to handheld **personal digital assistants (PDAs)**, and in mobile devices that access data from a phone network or the Internet. Data can be held in primary storage (within the computer itself) or on secondary devices such as optical disk (e.g. CD-ROM, DVD). Input devices include keyboard, mouse, joystick, scanner, touch screen, camera, microphone, sensor and many more. Output devices include printers, screens or sound systems.

## ● Computer software

**Computer software** is a set of instructions that controls the operation of the computer. System software manages the resources of the computer, such as the processing, storage or output devices – Windows, Unix and Linux are examples of system software. Application software enables users to apply the computer to specific tasks such as e-mail, word-processing or stock control.

## ● Data management technology

Recognising its value, many systems capture the data that each customer transaction generates, and pass (or at least make available) relevant parts of it to people who can use it. They do so by creating **databases** – a group of files of data that are related to each other. Distributed databases are stored and updated in more than one location, yet the data remains consistent. When a database is designed around major business subjects, such as customers, vendors or activities, it may be called a **data warehouse**. Using such data to discover trends or patterns of behaviour is called **data mining**.

9

## ● Networking and communications technology

Rapid communication across distance once depended on voice transmission over the telephone. Today networking and communications technologies enable data in digital form to pass between users who are physically distant – whether in organisations or as private individuals. Communication technologies combine hardware and software that can send and receive information between linked computers. They can be local area networks (LANs), usually limited to a single building, or wide area networks (WANs) that cover great distances – such as the Internet.

## ● Technology services

Organisations need people to manage and run the components of the IS infrastructure. Often these will be part of an IS department, but there may also be local experts in the various departments of the business who are able to provide users with immediate help and advice. Other organisations outsource this function, so another company provides the IS service: Chapter 7 presents options in this area.

---

### Activity 1.2  Collecting examples of information technology

Consult one or more business magazines, newspapers or websites (such as the BBC or the *Financial Times*) to identify reports of ONE new development in EACH of the five technology infrastructure components (such as an announcement of some new computer hardware).

- State in one sentence what the item is called, and what it does.
- What effects do those introducing the development expect it to achieve?
- In what areas of economic activity do they expect it to be used?
- Who are the expected customers for the product?

---

## ● Convergence of voice, image and data technologies

The most dramatic changes in managing data, information and knowledge come from the convergence of three technologies that developed independently.

> the telephone was invented in 1876, the first television transmission occurred in 1926, and the electronic computer goes back to 1946, if not earlier. For much of that time the pace of change was slow, but began to gather pace in the late 1980s. (Cairncross, 2001, p. 27)

### The telephone

The ability to send signals along glass fibre-optic cables greatly increased capacity and reduced the cost of carrying additional calls: it is virtually zero, irrespective of distance. This has encouraged people to use the telephone network not only for speech but also for passing data and pictures between fixed computers and between them and mobile devices. The cost of long-distance communication continues to fall, with major implications for managing businesses around the world.

| MIS in Practice | Apple – from computers to phones to film rental . . . |
|---|---|

Apple Computers has evolved from a company manufacturing personal computers to one that also sells music players and mobile phones – especially the sophisticated iPhone. This caused concern at Motorola, the world's second largest mobile phone maker. It is also planning to launch a film download service, which would allow users to download and rent films, and to move them from their computer to one other device – such as their iPhone. This would allow Apple to compete against the cable companies which offer video on demand services.

*Source*: *Financial Times*, 28 June 2007.

### The television

Although consumers rapidly adopted television, the technology changed little for many years. A breakthrough came with the development of communications satellites, which enabled viewers to see that they were in some respects part of a global community. The other big change was when broadcasters began to transmit programmes in digital form, increasing the capacity of available channels and foreshadowing the convergence of televisions and computers.

### The networked computer

By fitting more power into the microchips that are at the heart of a computer, engineers are able to roughly double computing power every two years. As the power of each microchip multiplies, so the price of computing falls, leading to smaller computers and greater capacity. From being standalone calculators, computers are now embedded in many other gadgets – such as games and video cameras.

### The Internet

The **Internet** is the world's largest and most widely used network. It uses a set of rules that specify the format in which data to be sent over the Internet must be packaged. These rules enable computers all over the world to communicate with each other, so connecting not only computers but also telephone and television services. Linking mobile phones to the Internet has led to the 'Wireless Internet', enabling information to pass readily between people wherever they are. Integrating previously separate computing and telecommunications technologies means that computing increasingly takes place over the network – mobile phones perform computing functions, with successive models able to send and receive more voice, image and data signals.

### ● Summary

- The technology infrastructure that supports information provision consists of hardware, software, communications and networking, data management and technology services.
- The convergence of previously separate technologies has steadily reduced the time and cost of transmitting data and information, giving many people unprecedented access to data and information.

# 1.3  Using IS technology to add value

These technical developments only have business value if people use the data and information they provide to improve the use of resources required to supply physical or information products.

## ● Using IS to add value to physical products

Organisations that make and deliver physical products and services need to coordinate people and other resources, often in many separate places. Direct human contact to exchange information – face-to-face meetings, telephone calls, letters and faxes – is a good way to do this when the operation is small. It also works when people are dealing with new or unforeseen problems where the solution is unclear, so they need to share ideas rapidly with colleagues. As organisations become bigger, informal methods may cause more problems than they solve, and people begin to look to computer-based IS. Technical developments make it possible to perform many business tasks (such as ordering, production planning or payment) electronically, especially when the information is routine. Modern IS enable much business communication to be conducted almost entirely by electronic means.

Early systems dealt with isolated aspects of the transformation process – such as orders, salaries or payments – so there were often many separate systems in an organisation. These can be brought together within single, enterprise-wide systems. As an example, BP, the global energy company, maintains all human resource information on a single electronic database, which any authorised staff can access. They can check their records and company policies online, enabling everyone to work on the same, up-to-date information. They can deal with, say, overseas postings more efficiently than when they used manual systems or unconnected computer systems. Other companies use IS to link widely dispersed functions so that, for example, marketing, engineering, manufacturing and design units can exchange information electronically in designing new products.

Many organisations now extend such systems to link their internal processes electronically with suppliers' and customers' systems. Customer orders are automatically processed to work out the implications for raw materials or other inputs, and these orders are then automatically passed to relevant suppliers. They in turn send invoices and receive payment electronically.

Companies offer both physical and information products. Online bookstores provide information such as reviews and notices of similar books that may interest a customer: their primary book-selling business, while conducted online, has physical elements – supplying a book ordered online still requires the production and delivery of a physical product. Conversely, many firms with a physical output offer additional electronic services – selling information, music or videos through a website, or encouraging customers to pay utility bills electronically.

## ● Using IS to add value to information products

Some organisations provide customers with information and knowledge rather than physical manufactured products – companies like Bloomberg or Reuters that provide online financial information to businesses, or social networking sites like MySpace. Such information-intense companies depend on being able to capture, create and distribute information to, or amongst, their customers – who are themselves widely dispersed. Information-intense sectors include financial services, software, media, reservation services, commodity trading and social networks. Familiar examples of information-intense companies and activities include the following.

● *Financial Times* (like most newspapers) offers online as well as print subscriptions: the online version gives subscribers access to, amongst other things, frequently updated news, video presentations and online discussions.

● Ryanair, in addition to selling all tickets online, invites customers to use the website to book hotels, care hire, travel insurance – and to gamble online.

● Apple's website offers computers, iPods and other devices, and also the ability to download videos to rent.

● Virgin's website offers access to all the services offered by the company, from long-established travel ticket sales to the resources of Virgin media, such as mobile phone services and a range of film and video services.

● Facebook and similar social networking sites enable people to share interests and exchange personal information with large numbers of other people.

---

| MIS in Practice | easyGroup   www.easy.com |
| --- | --- |

From the day that Stelios Haji-Ioannou launched easyJet as a low-cost airline, the company had a strategy centred on meeting customer needs efficiently, using technology wherever possible and adapting processes to suit market conditions. When it began to operate it took reservations on the telephone, so paid no commissions to travel agents. The company's emphasis on technology meant that as the Internet became available it rapidly adapted its business model to offer online reservations. easyJet took its first online reservation in April 1998. By April 2001 over 85 per cent of reservations were made online – probably the highest proportion of total sales for any established business. Soon that became the only way to book with the airline – making huge savings in the cost of printing and distributing tickets.

Its success in using the Internet led to the launch of more online services, such as easyCar (car rental) and easyMoney (financial services). Stelios then created easyGroup as a private holding company that creates new ventures based around the easyJet model of efficient, low-cost ventures. In late 2004 it reached an agreement with Deutsche Telekom's T-Mobile business to launch a low-cost mobile service – renting air-space from T-Mobile.

*Sources: Financial Times*, 24 November 2004; published information and company websites.

---

## ● Adding value depends on technology AND organisation

Figure 1.4 shows that a computer-based IS includes people and processes as well as hardware and software.

The simple example of a computer-based student record system illustrates the elements in Figure 1.4. The hardware consists of computers and peripherals such as printers, monitors and keyboards. This runs the record system, using software to manipulate the data and to either print the results for each student or send them electronically – which they see as information. The system also requires people (course administrators) to enter data

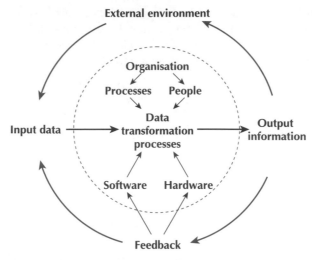

**Figure 1.4** The elements of a computer-based IS

## Activity 1.3 Collecting examples of computer-based IS

Identify two new examples of IS that have been introduced to add value to the delivery of:

a) a physical product and

b) an information product.

Make notes about the system such as:

● the companies making or using it
● what it does
● who uses it
● whether or not it is successful.

(name and other information about students and their results) following certain processes – such as that one person reads from a list of grades while another keys the data into the right field on the student's record. Managers of the department might use the output to compare the pass rate of each course – so the record system is now part of the university's management information. Staff will use their knowledge (based on learning and experience) to interpret trends and evaluate the significance of any patterns. **Information systems management** is the term used to describe the activities of planning, acquiring, developing and using IS such as this.

Figure 1.4 also shows that the hardware and software is part of a wider system, which we call the organisational or internal context. This includes, amongst other things, people and working processes. An information system does not consist only of hardware and software, but also of identifiable elements of the organisation. These affect the outcomes of an IS project, for better or worse, just as much as the design of the technological elements of hardware and software. The interaction between IS and their context is the distinctive focus of this book. The following section introduces a model that helps explain the success or failure of investments in IS.

## ● Summary

- Information systems enable companies to add value to resources whether they produce goods or services or both.

- Computer-based information systems consist not only of hardware and software, but also of people and working processes.

- These are themselves part of wider organisational contexts. The distinctive theme of this book is that projects will only add value to resources if those managing them (whether in making products or supplying information services) recognise their interdependence with these wider contexts.

## 1.4 Managing IS in context: an interaction model

To understand why IS projects succeed or fail we need a provisional model (or theory) to organise the evidence, and which we can develop in the light of new evidence. Figure 1.5 sets out the interaction model that reflects our interpretation of the evidence from experience and formal research, and provides the structure for the book.

Figure 1.5 represents the situation within which someone promoting an IS project will be working. Such projects begin their life when a sufficiently powerful **stakeholder** perceives a gap between desired and actual outcomes of an activity, and believes that a better computer-based information system is part of the solution. They decide to create an **information system project**, ranging in scale from strategic moves – such as the BBC's decision to invest in digital media – to more operational ones – such as a retailer's decision to upgrade their online shopping service. Following the previous discussion this project will embody changes in technology (hardware and software) as well as in people or working processes.

This broad decision is accompanied by moves to start an **implementation and learning process** to turn the idea into practical reality: when Tesco's board approved the

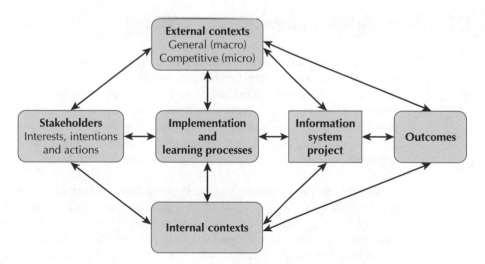

**Figure 1.5** An interaction model for managing information systems

15

proposal to launch the Clubcard, they will have begun such a process. Figure 1.6 shows that stakeholders manage that implementation process within **internal** and **external contexts**. Elements within these help or hinder the project, and are themselves changed by the outcomes – the new contexts provide the starting point for future change. Some stakeholders will be promoting the idea, and seeking to implement their vision: others will be reacting to the proposals, either positively or negatively. How stakeholders design, and how others react to, this implementation process affects the **outcomes** – success, failure or something in between. Managers (stakeholders) at Tesco implemented the Clubcard system successfully, and this outcome affected its competitive position (external context).

Managers can use this model to guide their approach to an IS project. As they become aware of a possible project, they can assess potential threats and opportunities in the external context – such as technological developments, changing customer demands or possible moves by competitors. Their analysis can also include an assessment of strengths and weaknesses in the internal context – will the culture support the change? do we have the financial resources? They can use that analysis to shape a project and an implementation process.

The following sections elaborate and illustrate the elements in this model, which should enable you to observe and analyse current IS developments in an informed way. Use these to test your understanding of the model and to identify new elements that may make it more useful in relation to a specific application. Later chapters examine each element in greater detail.

## ● Summary

- ● The interaction model represents the situation when someone tries to turn their vision of change to a computer-based IS into reality.

- ● Managers can use this model to guide their approach to such projects, and as a way of learning from their experience.

## 1.5 Stakeholders in information systems

Figure 1.5 requires a motor – a theory of what drives and sustains stakeholders' actions in relation to an information-system project. Mitroff (1983) defined stakeholders as 'all those parties who either affect or who are affected by an organisation's actions, behaviours and policies'. Some stakeholders are outside the firm, possibly in competing businesses; others are within the organisation. The task is to understand stakeholder actions – why some initiate and promote proposals, while others develop positive or negative attitudes towards them (Lyytinen and Hirschheim, 1987; Sauer, 1993; Boonstra, 2006).

Stakeholders are motivated to act by their combination of human needs – ambition, power, loyalty, security, a desire to do a good job, and all the rest – and by their perception of the organisation and its wider context. They initiate an IS project when they perceive that the current organisation is not producing the outcomes they desire or when they see some external threat or opportunity. If they see that new technologies or social trends are affecting how people spend their time, they consider how to respond:

managers at the BBC saw people using websites to access news, and decided to offer material on the BBC website, as well as in broadcast form. If managers observe that poor communication between departments is causing delay, they seek a solution – such as installing a more advanced order processing system.

An action by one stakeholder is likely to prompt a reaction by other external and/or internal stakeholders. Apple's entry into the mobile phone market is watched with great interest by operators like Vodafone and by handset suppliers like Nokia. Fearon and Philip (2005) related the low adoption of electronic trading systems in the insurance industry to the different expectations of relevant stakeholders. Boonstra and Harison (2008) show how a project failed because stakeholders with a strong interest in it lacked the power to implement, while those with power to block had low interest.

Internal stakeholders will also react to a proposal – some with enthusiasm and commitment, others with indifference, scepticism or opposition. Such attitudes may relate to the system itself and/or to its wider context (Fitzgerald and Russo, 2005) – we cannot understand human intentions unless we examine the settings in which they develop.

---

**CHAPTER CASE: PART 2**

# Tesco
**www.tesco.com**

---

The Clubcard scheme was devised by the founders of a company called Dunnhumby, who showed senior managers of Tesco how to turn the vast quantities of data in the business into useful information. Dunnhumby takes the data from Tesco's systems, and processes it as described earlier. As well as aiding decisions within Tesco, Dunnhumby also sells summaries of the data to Tesco's main suppliers, which Tesco encourages.

Tesco has continued to grow the business, often in joint ventures with companies already established in sectors into which it wants to expand. One early venture was Tesco Personal Finance, which is a joint venture with The Royal Bank of Scotland – see Chapter 9 case – through which it offers loans, credit cards, mortgages and other financial products to retail customers. It offers a travel service in association with lastminute.com, and the BBC provides the news service on its Internet access site.

Every purchase a Clubcard member makes from Tesco, whether in store or online, is recorded on the database, enabling the company to build a very full picture of the individual's shopping habits – and perhaps of their lifestyle. The system is linked to other databases such as the list of electors and the Land Registry (which holds information on every house that is sold), so probably contains more current information about named individuals in the UK than any other source. The company protects this carefully, and confirms that no other party has access to personal names and addresses.

*Sources: Financial Times Magazine*, 11/12 November 2006, pp. 17–22; company website.

---

## CASE QUESTIONS 1.2

- Who are likely to be the main stakeholders in Clubcard?
- Select one who will probably gain from the system, and one who may lose.
- How is the system likely to affect them, and will they favour or oppose it?

## 1.6 The contexts of IS

Pettigrew (1987) showed the significance of analysing the context within which stake-holders operate, a context that has external, internal and historical dimensions. The external context refers to political, economic, technological and other features of the society within which an organisation works. The internal context refers to features of the organisation itself (such as its structure or culture) within which an IS project evolves, while the historical dimension shows that the past influences how people interpret, and react to, the present. Figure 1.6 shows these contexts.

### ● External contexts

The outer circle in Figure 1.6 shows the **general context (or environment)**, sometimes known as the macro-environment – political, economic, social, technological, (natural) environmental and legal factors that affect all organisations. The more immediate part of the external context is the **competitive context (or environment)**, sometimes known as

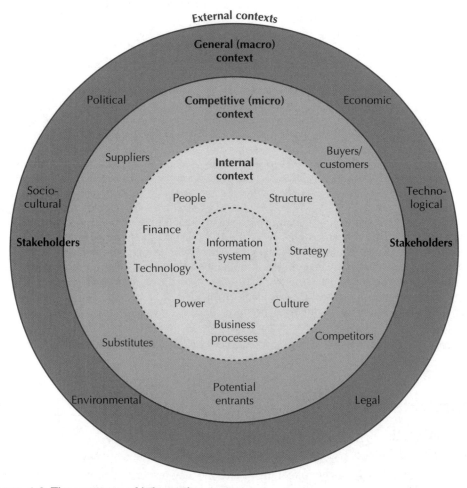

**Figure 1.6** The contexts of information systems

the micro-environment. This is the industry-specific environment of suppliers, customers, competitors, substitutes and potential new entrants.

The general (macro) environment influences how managers develop IS. The rise of social networking sites – a new feature of the social context – has implications for advertisers and the media through which they traditionally reach young audiences – see the MIS in Practice feature. Online communities are another external development to which managers are responding. Chapter 3 examines these changes in the macro context, including those affecting data privacy and intellectual property.

| MIS in Practice | Changing times for radio? |
| --- | --- |

The radio industry has for many years depended heavily on a young audience, and this has attracted advertisers targeting that group of consumers. Advertisers now perceive that young people spend more time on social networking sites such as MySpace, and assume therefore that they are not listening to radio programmes – so radio companies' advertising revenue is falling.

Television companies have also noted new opportunities. As well as buying the TV rights to sporting events they now also seek the digital rights. This allows them to broadcast the event on their website, from where customers can download it to their PCs. This brings additional revenue, as advertisers buy space beside the event on the website.

Managers pay particularly close attention to changes in their more immediate competitive environment, as moves by competitors or customers can affect their performance very directly. For example, if Yahoo's advertising revenue falls because advertisers are finding it more profitable to advertise on social network sites, then Yahoo's management will need to work out a response. This may include, for example, acquiring other companies as a way to gain access to potentially valuable technology. There are many examples of this, such as:

- Google's purchase of YouTube;
- eBay's purchase of Skype; and
- NewsCorporation's purchase of MySpace.

Chapter 4 shows how managers can systematically analyse changes in IS technologies as threats and opportunities for the business, and how they can use that to develop a coherent strategy. Their views on the strengths and weaknesses of the internal context will also shape proposals.

### ● Internal context

The internal context is the immediate environment within which people work, and into which they introduce IS projects. The centre of Figure 1.6 shows the elements of this internal context; Table 1.1 gives an example of each element and the chapter(s) in which we discuss them.

A stakeholder who initiates an IS project to improve internal operations will initially focus on one or more of these elements – aiming, say, to implement a system to improve working processes or to give people more information about current performance. As they do so they will find that other elements help or hinder progress. Effective managers

**Table 1.1** Elements of the internal context of an IS project

| Element | Chapter | Description and specific example |
|---|---|---|
| Technology | 2 | Type and location of physical facilities, machinery and information systems that people use to transform inputs into useful outputs. |
| Strategy | 4 | The wider strategies and desired future state of the organisation or project. |
| Business processes | 5 | The activities that people and technologies perform on materials and information to meet the strategy – such as designing products or receiving orders. |
| Culture, structure (incl. the position of IS) and power | 6, 7 | How an organisation's culture, structure and power relations influence how people interact with IS, and whether they help or hinder IS projects. Alternative ways to position IS in the organisation. |
| People and relationships | 8 | How to understand human reaction to IS, and to ensure that the design of IS satisfies both human and organisational needs. |
| Financial resources | 10 | Assessing what financial resources to use on IS projects when organisational and external factors make the future so unpredictable. |

realise that managing an IS project is not just a technical challenge but also an organisational one – as they aim to change parts of the context, the context will itself help or hinder that attempt.

All the elements in the internal context of Figure 1.6 will be present as the project begins, and some of these will influence how people react. For example, the prevailing culture influences how people view change – they will welcome a project that fits their culture, and resist one that threatens it (see Jones et al., 2005, for evidence of how

# Tesco – early success in online shopping

### www.tesco.com

The company responded to the Internet by creating an online shopping division, www.tesco.com, which rapidly established a leading position in that segment of the market. One factor in the rapid success may have been the way managers established it. While some competitors set up online operations as separate business units with their own warehouses and staff, Tesco integrated the online business with the physical stores. Staff assemble orders from stock in the stores, which reduced the investment and enabled the company to launch the new business quickly.

In 2006 the company launched Tesco Direct, which enables customers to order non-food items online – either having them delivered or calling at the store to collect their purchases.

*Source*: Company website and other published information.

**CASE QUESTIONS 1.3**

● If you have not already done so, visit the Tesco website as if you were a customer.

● Identify the main issues that managers would have had on their agenda when designing and launching the online shopping venture. Use the ideas in the section on the internal context to guide your answer.

● What does your list imply for the management skills required to make such innovations a success?

culture affected the acceptance of a new computer system). Managers who occupy influential positions in a structure will review a proposal from the perspective of their career, as well as of the organisation.

The context represented by this model occurs at several levels of the organisation: operating, divisional and corporate. Acting to change an element at one level will have effects at this and other levels. Some will give consistent, supporting signals about the project, others will not. There is no certainty that events elsewhere in the business provide a coherent context to help the IS project.

**Activity 1.4  The context of an IS**

Think of an information systems change you have observed or about which you can collect some primary data from people who were involved. You may want to combine this work with Activity 1.3.

● What was the new system intended to achieve?

● Consider each element of the internal context in Figure 1.6/Table 1.1 and make notes on whether, and how, each of these elements was changed during the project.

● Which, if any, elements of the internal context did they try to change as part of the project?

● How did other people see (interpret) and react to those changes?

● Did the project achieve what those promoting it intended?

● **The historical context**

An IS project takes place within historical and contemporary contexts. Promoters implement an IS against a background of events that have shaped the business as it is today and the readiness of people to change – they work within an inherited structure and culture, in which people remember successes and failures, affecting how they respond to current proposals. They also look to the future, questioning present systems and seeking improvements. The context reflects past events and is the focus of future uncertainties.

Some internal contexts support change, in the sense that people are receptive to new ideas and keen to try them (Pettigrew et al., 1992). Elsewhere people are unreceptive, being reluctant to accept and use new systems. The promoter's task is to manage the context to ensure that people are willing to accept and use the technology. As they work to change the context, they are at the same time working within the context. Balogun et al. (2005) show how internal change agents adapted practice to suit aspects of their context, such as the degree of local autonomy, senior management preferences, rewards systems and financial reporting systems. The outcomes of an IS project depend on whether or not changes made to the context encourage people to act in a way that supports the project.

● **Summary**

● An information system is part of a wider context, made up of the elements in Figure 1.6/Table 1.1.

● This context has both hierarchical and historical dimensions.

● Those introducing an IS may or may not change the context to support the change.

● Since organisations are systemic in nature, changes in one element affect others.

## 1.7 Interaction between IS and context

Major IS projects are likely to lead to unexpected outcomes – sometimes achieving less than expected, sometimes a great deal more (for examples see Lucas, 1975; Sauer, 1993; Drummond, 1996; Kennedy et al., 2006). Promoters are dealing with internal and external contexts, both of which will change during the project – which itself will change in response to new circumstances. McLoughlin (1999) observed that:

> *Implementing a new information system is best seen as a* process *with indeterminate outcomes.* (p. 73)

The accumulating evidence from research into IS projects of all kinds (Walsham, 1993; Orlikowsky, 2002; Boddy and Paton 2005) is that what we refer to as an interaction approach best expresses what happens during implementation. It reflects the idea that people are influenced by, and can themselves influence, the context.

Referring again to Figure 1.6, people (stakeholders) interpret their contexts and act to change it to promote personal, local or organisational objectives. Someone in (say) an established news organisation sees a change in the way some people prefer to receive their news, and also becomes aware of emerging technologies – such as ways of publishing online (external contexts) – that may offer a solution. They respond by advocating an information systems project (technology), together with changes in other aspects of the internal context, such as people, reporting relationships (structure) or working processes. When people plan and implement a change they are creating new 'rules' (Walsham, 1993) that they hope will guide the behaviour of people involved in the activity.

Others interpret this proposal in the light of *their* perspective, and try to influence decisions in a way that suits their interests – perhaps by adapting new systems in some way. As people become used to working with the new system their behaviours become routine and taken for granted, and part of the informally created new (internal) context. These interactions change the internal context – which now provides the historical background to future action. The essential idea is that the relation between the manager and the context works both ways. People shape the context, and the context shapes people.

> ### Research Summary     The scope for human adjustment to IS
>
> Some systems offer little scope for people to alter in the light of experience, as users must use them as designers intended. Others have more scope for local interpretation. Intranets are a good example, as their content depends on human action. People have to enter and maintain information to make the site worth using. If the site (part of the new context) contains little of value, staff will not use it. The more flexibility that is possible, the less useful it is to consider technology as an objective, fixed entity with predictable effects:
>
> *Technology does not impact on its social environment or vice versa but, over time, each shapes the other.* (Kimble and McLoughlin, 1995, p. 58)

Taking an interpretive perspective encourages us to consider how stakeholders vary in their attention to contextual factors and in the meanings they attach to them. Designers physically construct a technology in the light of what they believe management expects. Others socially construct the technology when they decide whether to use it, and how to adapt it to their circumstances: they experiment and improve.

## ● Summary

- The interaction model emphasises that those implementing an IS project will interpret the context and react to it, while in turn the project will shape the context.
- The context shapes people, and people shape the context, in a continuing cycle.
- This implies that the outcomes of major IS projects are hard to predict and are likely to vary significantly from the promoters' original objectives.

# 1.8 Implementation and learning processes

Implementation and learning processes are the actions, reactions and interactions of the stakeholders as they seek to move their organisations from the present to a future state.

## ● The challenges of implementing IS

Implementing IS systems raises four challenges. The first arises from the complexity of the change required. Implementation depends on complementary internal changes, which will themselves affect the change process. The systemic nature of organisations means that a change in one aspect of the context has implications for others. When Tesco introduced its Internet shopping service alongside its established retail business the company needed to create a website (technology). In addition, managers needed to decide issues of structure and people (would it be part of the existing store business or a separate business unit with its own premises and staff?) and about working processes (how exactly would an order on the website be converted to a box of groceries delivered to the customer's door?) They had to manage these ripples initiated by the main decision.

# Tesco
## www.tesco.com

While many companies have introduced loyalty schemes similar to the Clubcard, few have been as successful. Management decisions that helped this included those to:

- work with a carefully chosen specialist company to develop and manage the system;
- support the project with a strong commitment from senior management;
- involve staff in the design and implementation of the project;
- invest heavily in supporting systems and in staff training and development;
- support the Clubcard with many other changes across the business.

*Source*: Company website and other published information.

A second challenge arises from the dynamic nature of the context of most IS projects. The technology itself is rapidly changing, with systems being changed and enhanced even as they are being implemented. At the same time, the business context is changing, as competitors, suppliers or governments alter aspects of the wider context.

A third challenge arises from Mitroff's observation that stakeholders do not generally share the same definition of an organisation's problems, and hence do not share the same solutions. This implies that:

*approaches to organizational problem solving, which pre-suppose prior consensus or agreement among parties . . . break down. Instead a method is needed that builds off a starting point of disagreement.* (Mitroff, 1983, p. 5)

A final challenge is to enable people to learn from implementing systems, so increasing their capacity to work effectively. How people manage an IS project affects the immediate outcomes, and what they and the organisation learn about developing a long-term competence. Chapter 9 sets out many ideas on change, including the complementary planning, emergent, participative and political perspectives.

## ● Organisational learning

Many consider that the ability of an organisation to learn from accumulating experience affects its ability to develop competences and hence strategic capabilities. The term 'learning organisation' is used to describe an organisation that has the capacity to continuously learn, adapt and change. In a learning organisation the focus is on acquiring, sharing and using knowledge to encourage innovation (Nonaka and Takeuchi, 1995). In a learning organisation members share information and collaborate on work activities since managers have created a structure and culture that encourage the flow of ideas and information.

Argyris (1999) distinguishes between single-loop and double-loop learning – the former being the ability to correct errors, while the latter is the more difficult task of learning how to learn. This involves challenging assumptions, beliefs and norms, rather than accepting them and working within their limitations. Developing the competence to deliver the benefits of computer-based information systems depends on the skills of double-loop learning. Chapter 9 examines the processes of implementation and learning.

# 1.9 Assessing the outcomes

People invest in IS for a purpose – they expect to achieve something of benefit. These may relate to outcomes such as costs or quality or to aspects of the transformation process itself, such as (in healthcare) the extent to which a system has become embedded into routine clinical practice, and is taken for granted as part of normal professional work (May, 2006).

Interest groups use different criteria to assess the effectiveness of a project. Some see it as a success because it is on time and within budget. These are valuable achievements, and are easy to measure. But they are essentially internal and short term. A system may be efficient, but may not satisfy the customers. Conversely, a system may do little to improve immediate efficiency, but may provide valuable long-term experience in a new technology.

Table 1.2 describes eight dimensions that people can use to measure the success of an information system. People will view them differently, with some favouring an efficiency measure, others a customer satisfaction measure. Views may change with time. During the project, and in its immediate aftermath, the efficiency criterion may dominate. As time passes, it becomes easier to assess the contribution of the project to the other dimensions.

The initial objectives of an IS project usually change – either explicitly or by being quietly forgotten or given a lower priority as others become more prominent. Part of the reason is that projects often incorporate recent, and often incomplete, hardware or software. More can be done than seemed possible at the start. Another is that the change is usually introduced into a business with a volatile environment, so what needs to be done changes. Finally, interest groups will continue to nudge the project in ways that are favourable to their view of what is best for the organisation. If their support is vital to the project, their view will influence project design.

Chapter 10 shows that outcomes can be expressed in many ways, and that there are many ways of assessing how well the benefits correspond to the costs and/or to the expected benefits.

**Table 1.2** Measures of information system success

| Dimension | Description |
| --- | --- |
| Project quality | Whether project was completed on time and in budget. |
| System quality | System's reliability, features, functions, response time. |
| Information quality | Is the information relevant, clear, timely, accurate? |
| Information use | Regularity and duration of use, number of enquiries. |
| User satisfaction | Overall satisfaction, enjoyment, meets expectations. |
| Individual impact | Productivity, work satisfaction, improved decisions. |
| Organisational impact | Return on investment, contribution to performance, service effectiveness, accepted as part of normal professional practice. |
| Preparing for the future | Building organisational and technological infrastructure for the future. Is the firm more prepared for future opportunities? |

---

| MIS in Practice | Pensco – interpreting success |
|---|---|

In their study of the implementation of an IS into an insurance company, Knights and Murray (1994) noted that, in a culture which valued success and achievement, senior management were keen to stress the success of the system. They formally launched the new system, and the new products, at a high-profile presentation. This ignored the fact that many of the original objectives had not been achieved, substantial software work had still to be done and costs were higher than expected. Customer Services staff were overwhelmed by having to process policies manually, and IS staff were demoralised by the fact that they were continually moved from one part of the project to another, to deal with the current crisis. The researchers quote a senior IS manager who had attended the public presentation:

*There are two pensions projects: the one I heard about yesterday at the presentation and the one I normally hear about.* (p. 161)

*Source*: Knights and Murray (1994).

---

## ● Summary

- People evaluate IS projects on several measures.
- Interest groups will pay most attention to those objectives that benefit their position.
- Changing technology and business conditions ensure that the outcomes of a project differ from the original intention.

## 1.10 The management challenges of IS

It will be clear by now that implementing an information system raises both organisational and technical challenges. Successive chapters of the book examine these, which we note briefly here to provide an overview.

## ● Foundations

Organisations invest substantial sums in information systems, many do not secure an adequate return on this expenditure. Successive anecdotal reports, studies of failed projects, and the work of writers such as Strassman (1999) and Brynjolfsson and Hitt (2000) combine to give a picture of unrealised opportunities. This lack of convincing evidence about the benefits of IS investment has become so pervasive that several leading suppliers of information systems (including Microsoft, Cisco, Hewlett Packard and IBM) have funded an academic study into the problem. Founded in 2003 at the Sloan School of Management at the Massachusetts Institute of Technology, research is conducted on how to measure and improve the productivity of information work.

The director of the project (Eric Brynjolfsson) indicated the likely cause:

*companies need to look at the complementary changes in work practices that accompany successful IT investment . . . You can't just buy the technology and expect it to generate productivity benefits.* (*Financial Times*, 21 April 2003, p. 8)

Another participant in the initiative commented:

*Technology requires changes in the way humans work, yet companies continue to inject technology without making the necessary changes. Why? It's easier to write a cheque than change the way you work.* (*Financial Times*, 21 April 2003, p. 8)

These conclusions are scarcely new, as numerous academic studies reached the same point many years ago and continue to do so (see, for example, Markus and Robey, 1983; Sauer, 1993; Boonstra and Harison, 2008). It is also clear that many practitioners are aware that systems will be more successful if organisational issues are dealt with during the development process (Doherty et al., 2003). The challenge is to turn this awareness into action during an IS project.

## ● Strategy

Chapter 4 examines how IS projects have been able to support broader organisational strategies and the benefits of trying to align the two. There are many examples of managers who have been able to develop the business successfully with the aid of computer-based IS. Identifying and implementing applications that will support the business is another management challenge. The challenge is to be clear about the specific applications that will have most effect in a particular business. Identifying those is not easy, as different interests will press for investments that will best meet their concerns and priorities. While arguments for and against a project will inevitably be presented as being 'what is best for the business', other players may well interpret these as at best a partial view of the situation.

## ● Organising

It is clear that adapting the organisation to support a new information system remains as neglected an area as it has always been. The evidence presented in Part 3 shows clearly that companies who attempt to make at least some degree of complementary change are more likely to have a successful project than those who consider only the technology. Each chapter is intended to outline the management tasks of adapting that contextual element, in the light of emerging technological possibilities, to help people design effective IS systems.

## ● Implementing and learning

While powerful interest groups may try to shape an IS project to enhance their local position, those managing the project (the promoter or someone responsible for implementation) also need to maintain their support. They provide resources, support, ideas, means of influence and various other resources needed to move the project forward. Other groups need to support the project by being willing to change the way they work or by taking on new tasks.

Making changes on the scale implied by the widening agenda will usually be beyond the scope of the individual or even a competent project team. Creating appropriate structures to manage these projects is a key to success, and an example of this is examined in Chapter 9.

## ● Summary

Using the interaction model highlights four challenges in IS management:

- identifying where best to secure business value from IS, when interest groups may have different interpretations of contextual developments;
- aiming to secure an acceptable degree of coherence between the elements of the context;
- maintaining the support of interest groups, especially those who interpret the project as a threat to their position;
- managing implementation through an appropriate set of mechanisms and structures to support individual action.

Subsequent parts of the book provide ideas, theories, examples and tools that help people deal with these issues.

## Conclusions

Organisations have always depended on human and technical information systems to help conduct their business. Technological developments have greatly increased this dependence, as applications have moved from essentially background tasks to include customer-centred foreground tasks. Most organisations depend heavily on computer-based IS, and most managers depend on accurate and timely information.

The discussion has also emphasised that while technology is central to modern IS, it is only part of the story. Figure 1.4 (p. 14) showed that information systems include people and processes as well as hardware and software. Throughout the chapter we have shown that information systems raises wider management and organisational issues. Smaller and more portable systems encourage changes in working arrangements. Advances in communication technology erode boundaries between functions and organisations. The capacity of the new technologies is such that they raise major questions of strategy – about the kind of business that a company is in, about the internal changes that technology may imply and about the processes of implementation.

## Chapter questions

1. Consider your work and/or your studies. What information are you missing that might be harming your performance? How should this information be generated?
2. Use one or more of the models in the chapter to explain why organisations of all types depend on information.
3. Give examples of the use of IS in a business you know or have read about – preferably distinguishing between those with physical or information products. What were the main reasons for implementing them?
4. Use Figure 1.6 to identify which factors in (a) the internal and (b) the external context were probably important to Tesco in launching the Clubcard.
5. Explain the interaction model in your own words, and what it means for those managing an IS project.

6. Explain how the historical context affects an IS project – preferably with an illustration from a case study or other example.

## Further reading

Two books that present detailed case studies of major IS projects illustrating the themes of the book:

Drummond, H. (1996) *Escalation in Decision-making: The Tragedy of Taurus*, Oxford University Press, Oxford.

Sauer, C. (1993) *Why Information Systems Fail: A Case Study Approach*, Alfred Waller, Henley-on-Thames.

Two recent empirical studies developing themes from the chapter:

Doherty, N.F., King, M. and Al-Mushayt, O. (2003) 'The impact of inadequacies in the treatment of organisational issues on information systems development projects', *Information & Management*, **41**(1), 49–62.

Fitzgerald, G. and Russo, N. (2005) 'The turnaround of the London Ambulance Service Computer-Aided Despatch System (LASCAD)', *European Journal of Information Systems*, **14**(3), 244–57.

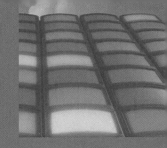

# CHAPTER 2

## Emerging technologies for information systems

### Learning objectives

By the end of your work on this topic you should be able to:

- Explain the changing role of information systems

- Compare information systems in terms of formality, purpose, reach and complementarities

- Discuss the management issues of IS applications that are especially relevant for organisations:

  - enterprise systems

  - knowledge systems

  - customer relationship management systems

  - inter-organisational systems and

  - customer participation systems

# Siemens' e-strategy

## www.siemens.com

Siemens, a German company, is the world's fourth largest electrical and electronics manufacturer, with operations in almost every country. Its activities are grouped into 15 divisions, which themselves are part of 3 business sectors – industry, power and healthcare. In 2008 it employed about 400,000 people, many of whom work in scientific research laboratories linked with universities around the world.

Mr von Pierer, who was for many years the CEO, was well aware of the need for the company to develop what he called an 'e-mindset':

*for me the Internet has two parts. One is technology and the other is the mindset – how we view our business.*

He developed a vision of how Siemens, as well as making and selling advanced technologies in its products, would use these information technologies to transform the way Siemens itself worked. His vision had four elements.

The first is knowledge management – through its ShareNet system. The second is online purchasing – e-procurement. He expected this to bring large administrative savings, mainly from economies of scale by pooling the demands of several purchasing departments, using a company-wide system called click2procure. The third part of the strategy is to improve internal administrative processes – such as by handling 30,000 job applications a year online or expecting employees to book their business travel arrangements over the Internet. There is more to this than paperless administration. The idea is to make sure that the whole supply chain – from customers, through Siemens, and then on to its suppliers – runs smoothly. Different bits of Siemens have developed e-business applications independently, which has caused problems:

*it was almost impossible to connect all these different systems in order to get information to flow from your customer to your supplier.*

The fourth element is Siemens' dealings with its customers, most of whom are other companies. An early application was an Order and Request System (ORS) that provided the (then) Fujitsu-Siemens Computers division with a simple way of presenting its configurable products for sale via the Internet. This reduced the time a customer had to spend to place an order, and also reduced the number of incorrect orders. All sales executives and customers were able to place orders online at any time and track their progress. To simplify ordering, major customers had dedicated pages showing the products and configurations they ordered most frequently. Access was by passwords, which controlled the areas of the site any individual could reach.

They also believed that they needed to develop their information systems so each customer had a single view of the company. Being so large, it was likely that several business units could sell something to a major customer. A manager commented:

*That is a big advantage of the company's wide range of activities. But I don't think that in the future such a customer will tolerate four or five different views of Siemens. They want one view of our capabilities. Even if a customer is buying from several divisions, they should deal directly with only one, which should act as a sort of lead manager within the company. Inside Siemens, the customer should be identified by only one code.*

Of the four elements of this strategy, von Pierer expected e-procurement to yield the quickest returns. However:

*If you want to transform a company to an e-business company, the problem is not so much e-procurement and the face to the customer. All this can be done rather fast. What is truly difficult is to reorganise all the internal processes. That is what we see as our main task and where the main positive results will come from.*

*Sources*: *The Economist*, 31 May 2001; www.siemens.com and www.my-siemens.com; company website.

# Introduction

Siemens is an example of a company that both supplies and uses advanced information systems. A successful global player by any standards, managers are well aware of the competition, and of the need to improve performance continually. Senior managers have identified four main ways in which modern IS can support the business – and acknowledge how human issues and organisational structures can help or hinder that transformation.

Information systems are influenced by three forces: relentless business pressures, fast-changing technology and rapidly evolving organisations that need to manage information of all kinds more effectively to add value to resources. This chapter illustrates the evolution of such systems and shows how, if properly managed, they enhance the competitive ability of an organisation.

The chapter begins by outlining the evolution of computer-based IS from **back office systems** to **customer-facing systems**, and from there to systems that transform value chains and industries. It outlines alternative ways of classifying IS and then describes five applications with significant management implications:

- enterprise integration;
- knowledge management;
- customer relations;
- inter-organisational working; and
- customer participation.

Together these illustrate the expanding role of information systems.

---

## CASE QUESTIONS 2.1

### IS and the Siemens business

Visit the Siemens website to gain an understanding of the main activities and the breadth of its geographical spread.

- What are its main products, and how would you broadly describe the nature of its businesses?
- Identify three ways in which you would expect modern IS to be used in the company.

---

# 2.1 The evolution of information systems

Between 1965 and 1975 managers concentrated on automating those functions where they could make large efficiency gains. These typically included those that processed many routine transactions, such as payroll, stock controls and invoices. Department managers often delegated responsibility for information management to an emerging IS department, which became very skilled at running large, routine and usually centralised systems. This function became very influential as managers of the main operating departments left IS matters to the specialists. The technologies did not yet affect many smaller organisations.

In the following decade automated systems spread widely. Technical developments made smaller systems possible and more attractive to managers in other parts of the organisation. Departmental managers discovered many new uses for information technology and so became familiar with issues of budgeting for hardware, requesting support, defining requirements and setting priorities. Suppliers developed systems for smaller organisations.

Since the mid-1980s technical developments have brought IS to the foreground of corporate policy. Systems that for decades have supported core business functions, such as finance, manufacture and distribution, continue to develop and employ more modern technology. Computer-based systems have now been extended to serve many other business functions and are used to support business processes in more integrated ways. Software suppliers have expanded product lines to support functions as diverse as production forecasting, supplier rating and project management. Information systems now support managers and professional staff directly in most business areas.

The rise of the Internet since the mid-1990s has further stimulated these developments. It challenges traditional organisations to innovate their processes and to integrate them with those of suppliers and customers. This clearly leads to corporate transformation, reinvention of value chains and new ways of doing business. Developments in mobile phone technology have freed the Internet from the desktop, allowing people to access information for business or social purposes almost wherever they are.

These developments affect most, though not all, established organisations and have led to the creation of many new services and industries, such as social networking, online gambling and interactive entertainment. Many markets are becoming more transparent and customers show new buying patterns and behaviours. Many commentators interpret this as a fundamental change from an industrial economy to a global network economy where companies can only survive if they are agile, flexible and adaptive to these new technologies.

## 2.2  Classifying information systems

There are several ways of classifying information systems and, although not definitive, such schemes help to understand and compare examples in a complex field. Here we use the criteria of formality, purpose, reach and the complementarities they require.

### ● Classifying IS by their formality

Information systems range from informal human or paper-based ones to those which are highly automated and computer based. Many begin as human systems, become paper based and then computer based. In small firms, the owner determines the price of a product depending on (say) the specification and the customer – a human information system. If the business grows the owner will usually find it useful to make a price list on paper to guide pricing decisions: even if it is scanned and available on computers, it is basically paper or document based. At the other extreme, large businesses usually include all aspects of the sales process in their computer software together with customer data, inventory, production schedule and purchasing functions. This would clearly be a computer-based system.

## Human information systems

These are informal information systems. Everyone uses sense organs to receive impulses from the environment; the brain interprets these impulses, leading to decisions on how to respond. From this perspective everyone is an information system. People observe events and use this information as they manage their responsibilities. Managers who believe that the best way to manage is to communicate directly with subordinates and to see for themselves what is happening 'manage by walking around' – they realise the value of human information systems.

Studying is also a human information process. The study material available is data, but the student has to remember relevant information and use it in tutorials and written examinations.

## Paper-based information systems

People still use many paper-based systems as they are cheap to implement and easy to understand. Paper systems have some virtues, and the genuinely paperless office is rare. Companies often define their procedures on paper, and staff are confident with information on paper. They can file a hard (paper) copy and use it easily for audit purposes. They often use paper systems when it is important to be able to trace all stages of a transaction, and when responsibility is high. Hospital staff keep most patient records on paper, sometimes alongside computer-based systems. The format of paper information systems is often a piece of A4 paper with printed instructions or boxes to complete. It may be a label attached to a part being routed through a shopfloor with instructions on what work to do. A manual, paper-based attendance list kept by a lecturer is another example, as is a paper address book or a diary.

## Computer-based information systems

Most information systems beyond the smallest now use electronic means to collect data and to provide information. Electronic devices often now collect the initial data – such as the barcodes and scanners that capture product details in shops. Thereafter electronic systems process, manipulate, distribute and record the data, providing paper output when required. Examples are the till receipt for the customer or a summary report on the pattern of sales. Table 2.1 lists some examples.

**Table 2.1 Examples and descriptions of computer-based information systems**

| Sector and example | Description |
| --- | --- |
| Retailing: electronic point-of-sale (EPOS) terminals. | Provide faster customer checkout, identify customer preferences and improve inventory control by direct links with suppliers' computer systems. |
| Financial services: automated teller machines (ATMs), telephone or online banking. | Support 24-hour banking services and enable customers to make transactions without visiting a branch. |
| Travel: computer-based reservation systems. | Enable customers to check fares and availability, and to make and pay for reservations without working with an agent. |
| Manufacturing: computer-aided design and manufacturing. | Linking design and manufacturing increases the speed of introducing new products, especially when there are electronic links to suppliers and customers. |

> ### Activity 2.1  Information systems you use
>
> Identify two formal but paper-based information systems that you use or affect you.
>
> - What are their advantages and disadvantages?
>
> Identify two computer-based information systems that you use or affect you.
>
> - What are their objectives?
> - Could you achieve those objectives without using a computer?
> - What are their advantages and disadvantages?
> - Are computer-based systems always better?

## Classifying IS by their purposes

Information systems can serve many purposes, four of which are: operational, monitoring, decision support (including knowledge) and communication.

### Operational

Early computer systems were **operational** in the sense that management introduced them to process routine transactions. This is still a major function as they rationalise and standardise transactions in an efficient, reliable and uniform way. If a student informs the university administration that they have a new address, they expect the change to apply quickly and to all the relevant files. The university would use a transaction processing system to do this. Banks and other financial institutions use operational systems to process millions of transactions such as payment instructions. Other examples are payroll and order entry systems.

Operational (or transaction processing) systems also exchange data between organisations. They help retailers to control stock and to manage the supply chain. The attraction of **electronic point-of-sale systems (EPOS)** is that they instantly record each sale, using a laser scanner that reads the barcode on the product. There is a direct link between the shops and the supplier so that stock can be reordered automatically in line with actual sales.

Staff in operating theatres can use barcoding or RFID tags to 'check in' and 'check out' all the tools used during an operation to prevent any being left inside the patient. **Radio frequency identification (RFID)** technology is an automatic identification method that stores and retrieves data remotely, and is widely used to keep track of goods and materials in a production process.

### Monitoring

**Monitoring systems** check the performance of activities, functions or people at regular intervals. The factor being monitored can be financial, quality, departmental output or personal performance. Being attentive to changes or trends gives the business an advantage as it can act promptly to change a plan to suit new conditions.

Universities in the Netherlands use student trail systems that monitor the academic progress of students. These systems link to the national institution that provides scholarships. This information enables this institution to stop or reduce the scholarship when results are below the required standard.

## Decision support

**Decision support systems (DSS)**, sometimes called expert or knowledge systems, help managers to calculate the likely consequences of alternative actions. A DSS incorporates a model of the process or situation, and will often draw data from operational systems. Knowledge systems also support decision-making by incorporating human knowledge. A knowledge engineer works with experts in the domain to learn how they make decisions, and incorporates this into that part of the software known as the knowledge base. Here are some examples.

● Businesses use DSS to calculate the financial consequences of investments.

● Universities use them to optimise room allocation and lecturer times.

● Banks use knowledge systems to analyse proposed loans. These incorporate years of lending experience and enable less experienced staff to make such decisions.

● NHS Direct in the UK uses an expert system to enable nursing staff in a call centre to deal with calls from patients who would otherwise visit their doctor. The system proposes the questions to ask, interprets the answers and recommends advice.

Computer-based systems are not as good as people at interpreting new knowledge and experience. Many people now use the term 'knowledge systems' rather than 'expert systems' (Balch et al., 2007) for systems that support people in their work. While knowledge systems can replace the experts to some extent, most only provide support to them (Balachandra, 2000; Voelpel et al., 2005) – they make suggestions to the human experts, but do not make decisions.

## Communication

People design **communication systems** to overcome barriers of time and distance. They make it easier to pass information around and between organisations. E-mail enables people to communicate electronically, irrespective of time or place, as does the World Wide Web. A third type of communication system is groupware (Artail, 2006; Cormican and O'Sullivan, 2007), also known as a 'workflow system', which supports cooperation among people working in physically separate teams. Multinational companies use virtual teams to develop new products, and the Research Summary overleaf describes a project to develop a groupware system to support them.

Companies often integrate these IS purposes – as when their website combines communication with customers with operational features which manage online purchase and delivery processes.

---

### Activity 2.2 Information on new applications

The media regularly report new applications of computer software.

● Collect examples of new systems that seem to have implications for how people manage their organisations.

● Try to find one example for each of the four purposes identified in this section.

● Compare notes with others and decide which of these systems is likely to be of greatest significance over the next two years.

**Research Summary**   **Developing groupware modules**

Cormican and O'Sullivan (2007) worked with ten multinational manufacturing companies to design a groupware system that would meet the particular communication challenges of teams developing new products. This is a knowledge-intensive process, so managers need a method that enables information from all members of the group (usually located at sites around the world, and including customers and suppliers) to be captured and used. The researcher team designed and tested a web-based groupware system with seven modules.

*Customers*: structured forms capture customers' views, complaints and statistics, and can be linked to customer relationship management (CRM) systems (see Section 2.5).

*Goals*: identifies and communicates stakeholders' requirements, and sets measures of team performance.

*Ideas and Problems*: These modules encourage members to communicate problems and to generate ideas towards their solution.

*Projects*: Clarifies the processes for creating and resourcing projects.

*Teams*: Helps teams to monitor and review their performance and suggest improvements.

*Results*: Incorporates tools such as project reviews and reporting systems that enable teams to measure their results.

*Source*: Cormican and O'Sullivan (2007).

## ● Classifying IS by their reach

Computer-based IS vary in the geographic reach of their operation and this affects their influence on organisations.

### Individual systems

Common examples of **individual systems** are word-processing, spreadsheets and database systems to manage individual professional work, perhaps downloading data from company-wide systems as required. The advantage is that the individual decides what to use the system for and can control the way they work. The disadvantages are that the software may not be compatible with that used by other staff, and the data from the corporate database may date before someone uses it.

### Local or departmental systems

If separate units or departments in companies have a distinct task to perform, management can create a **local IS** to support this. They have the same advantages and disadvantages as individual systems and there is usually pressure to integrate them into organisation-wide systems. A university may use a system that provides information about courses and assessments on the local departmental network, which students can access.

### Company-wide systems

**Company-wide systems** integrate departments and people throughout the organisation. Units in hospitals can use centralised patient data systems to retrieve or update information about a patient, as these make it easier for all staff to work from the same information. If managers want to implement a hospital-wide system they will discourage standalone systems, such as a doctor's list of patients held on a spreadsheet that she or he considers the definitive list.

### Inter-organisational systems (see also Section 2.6)

Many systems link organisations electronically by using networks that cross company boundaries. These inter-organisational systems (IOS) enable firms to incorporate buyers, suppliers and partners in their business processes, in the hope of enhancing productivity, quality, speed and flexibility. New distribution channels can be created and new information-based products and services can be delivered. In addition, many IOS radically alter the balance of power in buyer–supplier relationships, raise barriers to entry and exit and, in many instances, shift the competitive position of industry participants.

| MIS in Practice | Electronic links at Albert Heijn |
|---|---|

Albert Heijn, a Dutch chain of retailers belonging to Ahold, requires 100 per cent electronic data interchange with all suppliers. This 'continuous inventory replenishment system' captures data through scanning at the checkout to control inventory and to transmit orders to restock automatically. Amand Schins, manager of data optimization, comments: 'new regulations, customer expectations and the ever increasing need for cost reductions make it necessary to have full electronic links'.

This IOS gives managers at Albert Heijn, and their suppliers, an immediate insight into the process performance, and hence into profitability.

*Source*: *Food Magazine*, 29 May 2006.

### Community systems

A topical example of **community systems** is the growth of social network sites such as MySpace or YouTube. **Blogging** is one major use, as well as exchanging music and videos amongst people with similar interests. Although not related to an organisation (apart from those that own the site), they are significant for managers, since customers can use them to exchange positive or negative information about the company.

Combining the purposes of systems with their reach leads to Figure 2.1, which gives a systematic way of distinguishing IS. A spreadsheet application in Excel developed and used by one employee would fit in box O1 while a computer-aided design system used by engineers in a company and its suppliers would probably fit boxes O3 and O4. Systems such as e-mail or groupware extend beyond the company, so they would be C4 or C5 if, for example, it was a corporate blog that supported communication with customers. Customer relationship management systems (CRM) would be in areas D3 to D5.

The significance of this is that the organisational implications of systems vary across the figure. Those in the top left-hand area – largely individual, operational – will be easy to implement and affect few staff. Those towards the lower right-hand area raise increasingly complex technical and organisational issues.

| Purpose | Reach | | | | |
|---|---|---|---|---|---|
| | Individual | Local/departmental | Organisational | Inter-organisational | Community |
| Operational | O1 | O2 | O3 | O4 | O5 |
| Monitoring | M1 | M2 | M3 | M4 | M5 |
| Decision support | D1 | D2 | D3 | D4 | D5 |
| Communication | C1 | C2 | C3 | C4 | C5 |

**Figure 2.1  Purposes and reach of IS combined**

## Activity 2.3  Electronic links at Albert Heijn

- What is the reach and what are the purposes of the system at Albert Heijn?
- What benefits may the company gain from this?
- The manager claims that the system helps the company to respond more effectively to changing customer demands. How does it do that?

## Classifying IS by their complementarities

The implications of Figure 2.1 are illustrated by McAfee (2006), who classifies IS according to the extent of complementary organisational changes they require. Some information technologies (functional) can deliver results without the complements being in place; others (networks) allow the complements to emerge over time; and still others (enterprise) impose the complements they need as soon as companies deploy the technologies. The significance of this is that it helps managers to understand the scale of the organisational changes they are likely to need to make to benefit from the investment. It can also indicate which projects will be relatively easy to implement.

### Functional systems

**Functional systems** help people to perform standalone tasks more efficiently – word processors and spreadsheets are common examples. Designers, accountants, doctors and many other specialists use these technologies in the normal course of their work. As they work individually with a high degree of professional independence, they can use the technology as a standalone system, with few if any complementary changes required elsewhere in the organisation. An R&D engineer may be able to use a computer-aided design (CAD) program without requiring changes in how the rest of the department functions:

> Furthermore, [functional systems] don't bring their complements with them. CAD software, for example, doesn't specify the processes that make the most of its power. Companies must identify the complements that [functional systems need]. (McAfee, 2006, p. 144)

### Network systems

**Network systems** help people to communicate and include e-mail, instant messaging, blogs and **groupware** such as Lotus Notes. These allow people to interact, but do not define how they should do so: people can experiment. These systems bring some complements with them, but allow users to implement them gradually, and to modify them. They allow people to work together, but do not specify who should send or receive messages. Their effective use will probably depend on some complementarities – such as rules on who can access which parts of the system or who is responsible for responding to customer comments on a blog – but users can modify these in the light of experience.

---

### CASE QUESTIONS 2.2

#### Classifying IS at Siemens

Consider the types of business Siemens is in, and the kinds of IS it is using.

- Where would you place them in these classification schemes? Either from the case or from the Siemens website, identify at least one system they are using that would be an example of each category.
- Can you suggest which of these systems may have been the most difficult to implement?

---

### Enterprise systems

Enterprise systems allow companies to restructure interactions amongst groups of employees or with business partners. Applications that structure entire business processes or enable data to pass between organisations fall into this category. Unlike network technologies, which percolate from the bottom, enterprise technologies are top-down; they are purchased and imposed by senior management.

> *Companies can't adopt enterprise systems without introducing new interdependencies, processes, and decision rights. Moreover, companies can't slowly create the complements to enterprise systems; changes become necessary as soon as the new systems go live.* (McAfee, 2006, p. 145)

Enterprise systems allow companies to redesign business processes, and to ensure that employees follow the correct procedures. They also enable companies, once they have identified complementary business processes, to implement them widely and reliably throughout the organisation. They also enable close monitoring of what is happening around the enterprise, bringing a high degree of management control.

The value of McAfee's analysis is that it alerts managers to the organisational implications of different systems. Functional systems raise few organisational issues, as the professionals themselves decide whether or not and how to use them. Network systems require more organisational decisions (such as who can have access to a system, and on what conditions), but these can emerge with experience. Enterprise systems require significant organisational changes if the company is to benefit, and will be correspondingly difficult to implement.

---

### Activity 2.4 Listing IS by complementarities

Identify and list five information systems that you use, such as e-mail, intranet or electronic learning environment.

- To which of McAfee's three categories does each most closely correspond?
- What might that have implied for those managing or implementing the system?

In the following sections we illustrate the evolution of IS by discussing four widely used systems that support, respectively:

● enterprise resource planning (ERP);

● knowledge management (KM);

● customer relationship management (CRM); and

● inter-organisational systems (IOS).

Each section describes one of these systems and introduces the management issues they raise.

## ● Summary

● IS can be classified by their formality, purpose, reach and complementarities.

● The formality of IS ranges from human, paper to computer-based systems.

● Purposes include operational, monitoring, decision support and communication.

● Reach can be individual, departmental, organisational, inter-organisational and community.

● Combining the classifications by purpose and reach gives some clues about the relative difficulties of implementing different systems.

● McAfee (2006) reflects this in distinguishing between systems in terms of the complementary organisational change that they require, depending on whether they are functional, network or enterprise systems.

## 2.3 Managing information flows with enterprise-wide systems

Fulfilling a customer order requires people in sales, accounting, production, purchasing and so on to cooperate with each other to exchange relevant information. However, the IS on which they depend were often designed to meet the needs of a single function or organisational level. They were built independently and cannot automatically exchange information. Manufacturing might not know the number and types of product to make because their systems cannot easily obtain information from the systems that process orders. A common solution is to use **enterprise systems (ES)**, also known as enterprise resource planning (ERP) systems. These coordinate activities, decisions and knowledge across many different functions, levels and business units in the hope of increasing efficiency and service.

Enterprise systems aim to create an integrated platform to coordinate internal processes. Discrete functions become integrated into company-wide business processes that flow between levels and functions, as shown in Figure 2.2.

At the heart of an enterprise system is a single database that draws data from and feeds data to applications throughout the company. Table 2.2 shows examples of business processes and functions supported by enterprise systems. These 'modules' can be implemented separately, but promise greater benefits when they are linked to exchange information continuously through the database.

ERP systems give management direct access to current operating information enabling them to:

- integrate customer and financial information;
- standardise manufacturing processes and reduce inventory;
- improve information for management decisions across sites;
- enable online connections with suppliers' and customers' systems with internal information processing.

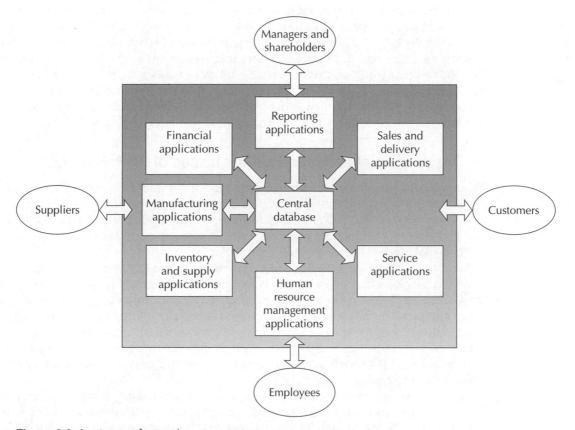

**Figure 2.2** Anatomy of an enterprise system

**Table 2.2** Examples of business processes supported by enterprise systems

| Business function | Enterprise system |
|---|---|
| Financial | Accounts receivable and payable, asset accounting, cash management and forecasting, executive information system, general ledger, product-cost accounting, profitability analysis, profit-centre accounting, financial reporting. |
| Human resources | Payroll, personnel planning, travel expenses, benefits accounting, applicant tracking. |
| Operations and logistics | Inventory management, material requirements planning, materials management, plant maintenance, production planning, project management, purchasing, quality management, routing management, shipping, vendor evaluation. |
| Sales and marketing | Order management, pricing, sales management, sales planning, billing. |

Leading suppliers of ERP systems include SAP, PeopleSoft, Oracle and J.D. Edwards, each tending to specialise in particular industries – some of which have themselves standardised on a particular vendor (McKeen and Smith, 2003).

ERP systems are semi-finished products that user organisations must tailor to their needs, called **configuration**. For example, financial software must be configured so that it knows which companies exist, which companies are subsidiaries of which other companies, the currency for each subsidiary, the sales tax regimes for each subsidiary and so on. Adding non-standard features to the software by adding or changing program code is usually called **customisation**. This ranges from relatively simple changes such as developing a new report, to major changes that require work on code in the software. Customisation is costly and risky, and new software releases may require recustomisation. Companies can avoid this by changing their processes to match those supported by the software – but the risk then is that the processes embedded in the system software may not suit the company. Changing an organisational process is itself difficult.

## ● Organisational and management issues of ERP systems

There is controversy about whether adopting an ERP system gives a competitive advantage or not (McKeen and Smith, 2003). A company may not benefit if using the generic models provided by standard ERP software prevents it from using unique business models that had given it a competitive edge. ERP systems promote centralised coordination and decision-making, which may not suit a particular firm.

Another problem is inflexibility. Some analysts argue that ERP systems lock companies into rigid processes that make it hard, if not impossible, to adapt quickly to changes in the marketplace or in organisation structure. A study by Markus et al. (2000a) shows that many ERP problems relate to a misfit between the system and the characteristics of the organisation. Enterprise systems are completely intertwined with corporate processes and it may take years to implement them all. It is difficult to change integrated systems because a change in one part affects the others, so that the company may become inflexible and hard to change.

ERP systems are expensive to install, and few companies build enough post-implementation costs into their budgets, and frequently underestimate training costs. ERP implementation should be viewed and managed as an organisational change process, rather than as the replacement of a piece of technology. It impacts strategy, structure, people, culture, decision-making and many other aspects of the company. The MIS in Practice feature, right, illustrates these issues.

Chapter 5 discusses ERP systems further from a business process perspective.

---

### Activity 2.5 Researching ERP systems

Read this section on enterprise systems, including the Invacare example – and also the FFC dairy food example in Chapter 5 – and compare the descriptions of ERP use and implementation. You could also use sources from the Internet (e.g. Wikipedia and ERP user communities).

● Gather specific examples showing the opportunities and advantages of such systems, and also their disadvantages and limitations.

● If possible, compare your conclusions with others in your class.

| MIS in Practice | Invacare struggles with ERP |
| --- | --- |

Invacare is the world's leading manufacturer and distributor of non-acute healthcare products, including wheelchairs, motorized scooters, homecare beds, portable compressed oxygen systems and skin and wound care products. It conducts business in over 80 countries, maintaining manufacturing plants in more than 12 countries.

In 2004 Invacare began to replace a collection of legacy systems with modules from Oracle's E-business Suite. Invacare had been using Oracle database software and had implemented the financial modules four years earlier with no significant difficulties. However, it experienced significant problems when it went live with an 'order-to-cash' module, which let the company receive an order, allocate the supplies, and enable customers to track the status of their order.

Amongst the problems were that call centre staff were unable to answer customer queries promptly, and delivery performance declined rapidly, leading to a loss of sales. It also affected the company's internal financial reporting controls, so it had to take special steps to validate the figures used in financial statements.

Invacare had expected implementation problems, but not on this scale. According to the financial officer, the problems were not caused by the software, but by the way the company had configured the software and linked it with its business processes. He also believed that the company should have done more testing.

*Source*: Laudon and Laudon (2007), p. 287.

## ● Summary

- ERP systems are software packages that enable the integration of transactions-oriented data and business processes throughout an organisation.

- Such systems have to be configured and can be customised to create a fit with the organisation. Organisational processes can also be adjusted to fit with the system.

- ERP implementation is an organisational change process, rather than the replacement of a piece of technology. It impacts strategy, structure, people, culture, decision-making and many other aspects of the company.

## 2.4 Knowledge management systems

Developments in IS are of great interest to those who want to improve their organisation's ability to create and mobilise knowledge. Many businesses depend on the skill with which they are able to create and acquire knowledge and ensure that people use it throughout the organisation. Knowledge is vital to innovation and many see it as the primary source of wealth in modern economies. People often believe that the knowledge they need to improve performance is available within the business – but they cannot find it.

**Knowledge management** (KM) refers to attempts to improve the way organisations create, acquire, capture, store, share and use knowledge. This will usually relate to customers, markets, products, services and internal processes, but may also refer to knowledge about relevant developments in the external environment.

**Table 2.3 Knowledge management processes and the potential role of IS**

| Knowledge management processes | Knowledge creation | Knowledge storage/retrieval | Knowledge transfer | Knowledge application |
|---|---|---|---|---|
| Supporting information technologies | Data mining. Learning tools. | Electronic bulletin boards. Knowledge repositories. Databases. | Discussion forums. Knowledge directories. | Expert systems. Workflow systems. |
| IT enables | Combining new sources of knowledge. Just-in-time learning. | Support of individual and organisational memory. Inter-group knowledge access. | More extensive internal network. More communication channels. Faster access to sources. | Knowledge can be applied in many locations. More rapid application of new knowledge through workflow automation. |
| Platform technologies | Groupware and communication technologies. Intranets and sometimes extranets. | | | |

*Source*: Based on Alavi and Leidner (2002), p. 125.

Managing knowledge is not new – the Industrial Revolution occurred when people applied new knowledge to manufacturing processes. What is new is the degree to which developments in IS make it easier for people to share data, information and knowledge irrespective of physical distance. This has encouraged many managers to believe that implementing knowledge management will enhance performance and some studies, such as that by Feng et al. (2004), claim that companies adopting KM systems perform better than non-adopters. Three common purposes are to:

- code and share best practices;
- create corporate knowledge directories; and
- create knowledge networks.

Table 2.3 illustrates how IS can potentially support each element of knowledge management – these subdivisions are of course arbitrary, and systems typically support several.

Echikson (2001) outlined how the oil company BP uses advanced IS to enable staff in this global business (including those in recently acquired companies) to share and use information and knowledge. These include a web-based employee directory (an intranet) called 'Connect', which contains a home page for almost every BP employee. Clicking on someone's name brings up a picture, contact details, interests (useful for breaking the ice between people who have not met) and areas of expertise. When a manager in a BP business needed to translate their safety video into French, he used Connect to identify French-speaking employees who could do the work, rather than an external translation service. At the core of the business, decisions on where to drill are now informed by an Internet system that brings geological data to one of several high-tech facilities. Engineers view the images and make, in hours, decisions that used to take weeks – and help reduce the danger of expensive drilling mistakes.

It is important to recall the distinctions made in Chapter 1 about data, information and knowledge – in which we referred to knowledge as 'embodying prior understanding, experience and learning' (p. 7). Many systems that people refer to as 'knowledge' management systems appear on closer examination to deal with data and information rather than knowledge. While computer-based systems are effective at dealing with (structured) data and information, they are much less effective at dealing with (unstructured) knowledge. As Hinds and Pfeffer (2003) observe:

> systems [to facilitate the sharing of expertise] generally capture information or data, rather than knowledge or expertise. Information and information systems are extremely useful but do not replace expertise or the learning that takes place through interpersonal contact. (p. 21)

Nonaka and Takeuchi (1995) distinguish **explicit** from **tacit knowledge**. Explicit knowledge is that which people have codified, structured, perhaps written down – formulae, instructions, historical trends – and which can be identified, extracted and passed on to other users. Tacit knowledge is inherent in individuals or groups, and is not written down – it is a sense about the way to do things, how to relate to each other and to situations. Because it is personal and specific to the context it will often be the most useful kind of knowledge – yet the hardest to transmit by even the most sophisticated technology.

# Siemens' ShareNet

**www.siemens.com**

Voelpel et al. (2005) describe what they call one of the few success stories in creating global knowledge-sharing systems – Siemens' ShareNet. The company's customers increasingly expect it to provide complete solutions to complex engineering problems and staff had, by the mid-1990s, become aware that managing the company's knowledge was vital to continued success.

ShareNet began as an initiative in the (then) Information and Communication Networks (ICN) Division, with a system linking the 17,000 sales and marketing employees. In addition to providing a database containing all project results, it enabled employees at ICN to communicate and exchange their know-how, experience and comments. An example of its value was when staff were bidding for a telecommunications project in China. Sales staff using ShareNet found out that similar systems had already been implemented in Thailand and Chile, which meant that their colleagues in those countries could give them valuable information about the hardware and software features that would be needed.

However, getting people to contribute to, and use, ShareNet was a significant challenge. Managers realised that the hierarchical structure within isolated business units discouraged collaboration:

> there were always excuses. People said, 'I don't have the time to spend on this.' Others were reluctant to share. [Some said] 'Sure, we have knowledge, but it's for sale, it's not for free'. (Voelpel et al., 2005, p. 15)

The project team responded by introducing incentives to motivate employees to use the knowledge network. Posting of queries and suggestions steadily increased, and was adopted by other businesses within the group. Although the project faced challenges over its cost, and the difficulty of demonstrating a business benefit, Voelpel et al. (2005) conclude that ShareNet shows:

> the thoughtful implementation of a knowledge-sharing system enhances the transfer of knowledge within a global organisation, and can therefore create value.

*Sources*: Voelpel et al. (2005); article 'Heading for Knowledge-Guided Networks' on company website, Spring 2004.

CHAPTER CASE: PART 2

| MIS in Practice | Problems with KM in a consultancy |
|---|---|

The company is one of the leading global management consultancies, with over 75,000 consultants in over 40 countries. As do most such firms, it considers the knowledge of its staff to be a core capability for achieving competitive advantage. To ensure that this knowledge is widely shared it has spent large sums on KM systems, especially Knowledge Exchange (KX) – a repository of internally generated knowledge about clients, topics, best practices and so on – to which consultants were expected to contribute ideas as they completed projects for clients.

Paik and Choi (2005) found that few East Asian consultants contributed, and identified three reasons: 1 a perception amongst East Asian consultants that others did not appreciate their regional knowledge; 2 a requirement to provide ideas in English (East Asian consultants were conversant in English, but found it difficult and time consuming to translate documents into English before submitting them); 3 cultural differences (staff in some countries were not motivated to contribute if there was no direct personal incentive – which the global reward system did not take into account).

They conclude that global companies seeking a common approach to knowledge management need to make allowances for local cultural differences.

*Source*: Paik and Choi (2005).

Scarbrough and Swan (1999) also note that, while technological systems deal well with data and information (explicit knowledge), tacit knowledge cannot be processed and passed around as people continuously create and re-create it as they work together. They interact with each other and their work, creating new knowledge and shared understandings that are unique to that situation. While a 'cognitive' model of knowledge management is appropriate for dealing with explicit knowledge, a 'community' model is a more suitable perspective from which to consider tacit knowledge. Table 2.4 contrasts these features.

**Table 2.4 Two views of the knowledge management process**

| Cognitive model | Community model |
|---|---|
| Knowledge is equated with objectively defined concepts and facts. | Knowledge is socially constructed and based on experience. |
| Knowledge is transferred through text, and information systems have a crucial role. | Knowledge is transferred through participation in social networks including occupational groups and teams. |
| Gains from KM include the recycling of knowledge and the standardisation of systems. | Gains from KM include greater awareness of internal and external sources of knowledge. |
| The primary function of KM is to codify and capture knowledge. | The primary function of KM is to encourage knowledge-sharing between groups and individuals. |
| The dominant metaphor is human memory. | The dominant metaphor is the human community. |
| The critical success factor is technology. | The critical success factor is trust. |

*Source*: This material is taken from *Case Studies in Knowledge Management* (1999) written by Scarbrough, H. and Swan, J., with permission of the publisher, the Chartered Institute of Personnel and Development, London (www.cipd.co.uk).

## ● Organisational and management issues of KM systems

Presenting the community model alongside the cognitive model helps to identify the issues in the success or failure of KM projects:

> whilst it might be relatively easy to share knowledge across a group that is homogenous, it is extremely difficult to share knowledge where the group is heterogeneous. Yet it is precisely the sharing of knowledge across functional or organisational boundaries . . . that is seen as the key to the effective exploitation of knowledge. (Scarbrough and Swan, 1999, p. 11)

Systems with a technical, cognitive perspective typically fail to take account of structures and cultures that represent people's beliefs and values about what needs to be done and what should be rewarded. They are likely to inhibit people from sharing knowledge in the way intended.

KM tools can be valuable in exploiting knowledge about previous projects, technical discoveries or useful techniques. But reusing existing knowledge may do less for business performance than creating new knowledge to suit the situation, which depends on creative interaction between people. Since most managers receive too much information it does not follow that providing them with more will improve performance. That depends not just on knowledge, but also on insight and judgement – which an information system cannot provide (Walsham, 2001, 2002).

Gupta and Govindarajan (2000) observed that:

> effective knowledge management depends not merely on information technology platforms but . . . on the social ecology of an organisation – the social system in which people operate [made up of] culture, structure, information systems, reward systems, processes, people and leadership. (p. 72)

People will be more likely to use a knowledge management system if the culture recognises and rewards the benefits of sharing knowledge. For tacit knowledge, a focus on encouraging effective communities of practice will be more effective than a focus on technology. We return to these issues in Chapters 6 and 8.

---

### Activity 2.6 What knowledge do you need for a task?

- Identify for an employee (perhaps yourself) what knowledge they create, acquire, capture, share and use while doing a task.
- Identify examples of explicit and tacit knowledge in this example.
- Discuss to what extent a computer-based knowledge system could be useful in managing that knowledge.
- Would such a system be in your interests and/or the interests of the organisation?

---

## ● Summary

- Knowledge management systems aim to improve an organisation's ability to create, acquire, capture, store, share and use knowledge.
- KM systems include data mining, bulletin boards, expert systems and workflow systems.

● Information systems can easily deal with explicit knowledge, but are mush less suited to tacit knowledge.

● Implementing useful KM systems depends on also dealing with organisational issues, including the homogeneity of the group, and organisation structure and culture.

## 2.5  Managing customer processes with CRM

It is more expensive to attract new customers than to retain existing ones, so many companies try to use the power of IS to improve the way they manage their relationship with profitable customers. Marketing staff aim to retain them, and to earn more revenue from them.

**Customer relationship management (CRM) systems** are intended to build and sustain long-term business with customers. They represent a move from mass markets and mass production to customisation and focused production. CRM software tries to align business processes with customer strategies to recruit, satisfy and retain profitable customers (Rigby et al., 2002). Figure 2.3 shows three approaches to customers. The first treats all customers in the same way by sending impersonal messages in one direction. The second sends one-directional but different messages to customers, depending on their profile. The third personalises the messages, which may lead to real interaction, in the hope of increasing customer loyalty.

In many businesses the key to increasing profitability is to focus on recruiting and retaining high lifetime value customers. So the promise of CRM is to:

● gather customer data swiftly;

● identify and capture valuable customers while discouraging less valuable ones;

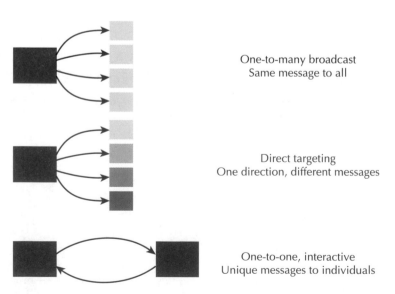

One-to-many broadcast
Same message to all

Direct targeting
One direction, different messages

One-to-one, interactive
Unique messages to individuals

**Figure 2.3 Communications methods and message**

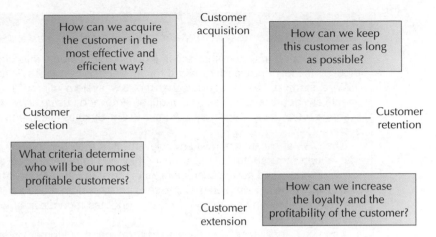

**Figure 2.4 Questions with respect to customer selection, acquisition, retention and extension**

- increase customer loyalty and retention by providing customised products;
- reduce costs of serving customers;
- make it easier to acquire similar customers.

CRM systems consolidate customer data from many sources and try to answer questions such as these.

- Who are our most loyal customers?
- Who are our most profitable customers?
- What do these profitable customers want to buy?

Firms can use these answers in their policy of customer selection, acquisition, retention and extension, as shown in Figure 2.4.

A common objective for a CRM system is to increase the lifetime value of customers, as measured by recency, frequency and monetary value – the **RFM model**. This model is based on three empiric principles:

- customers who purchased recently are more likely to buy again compared with customers who have not purchased in a while;
- customers who purchase frequently are more likely to buy again compared with customers who have made just one or two purchases;
- customers who spend the most money in total are more likely to buy again.

Using this approach, each customer is assigned an RFM score based on recency, frequency and monetary value. Customers with high scores are usually most profitable, the most likely to purchase again and the most highly responsive to promotions. Using the RFM scores, companies can determine the lifetime value of a customer – the expected profit a customer will contribute to a company as long as the customer remains a customer. Once a company knows who their most valuable customers are, they can concentrate their efforts on satisfying those customers. Figure 2.5 illustrates the model.

| MIS in Practice | CRM at The Royal Bank of Scotland |
| --- | --- |

RBS developed a system that scans incoming documents into digital images and distributed these to processing staff through electronic 'queues' – an Image & Workflow (I&W) system. It was recognised that the I&W system offered an opportunity to more effectively address CRM service requirements and, using I&W as a basis, two new systems were developed: the Customer Event System (CES) and Concerns & Queries system (C&Q).

The CES application allows any relevant staff member to view progress with recent transaction requests for any customer. They can retrieve images of recently submitted forms or letters and advise customers as to the stage their request has reached, and any issues with it being completed. Customers can therefore make a telephone call to any of the central telephony centres and receive updates regardless of where their request is being processed.

The C&Q application was developed to manage customer complaints in a way that clearly assigns ownership to a staff member, ensures that the complaint is addressed within agreed timescales, and enables RBS to comply with regulatory requirements for complaints handling. When the bank receives a complaint by telephone or letter it is entered into the C&Q system with all relevant details (including images of any written correspondence). The complaint enters an electronic queue and is picked up by the appropriate department. Progress with investigating the complaint is recorded in C&Q, which also provides prompts to ensure that staff meet the agreed time targets.

CES and C&Q are examples of systems developed on top of a back-office processing system (I&W) to provide front-end CRM services.

*Source*: Information supplied by the company.

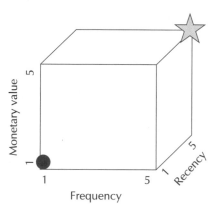

**Figure 2.5  Recency, frequency and monetary value of customers**

## ● Mobile CRM

CRM can also be practised by using customers' mobile phones. There are 2.5 billion mobile phones around the world and CRM experts believe that these are potentially a more efficient way to reach customers than through their personal computers. Especially in poorer countries the use of mobile phones is growing more rapidly than that of computers, and marketers hope to use this for 'relevant mobile ads'. Advertisers believe that much traditional advertising does not reach the right audiences, but that using text messages to a person's mobile phone will be much more accurately targeted. They aim to use the customer profiles of a mobile phone company's customers to tailor advertisements to match subscribers' habits (*The Economist*, 6 October 2007). The possible downside of this approach is that many consumers consider their phones as personal and may not welcome more advertising – though this would vary by country and type of customer.

## ● Organisational and management issues of CRM systems

CRM projects result in high failure rates. A study by the Gartner group found that 55 per cent of all CRM projects fail (www.gartner.com). In Bains' survey of management tools, CRM ranked third from bottom in terms of users' satisfaction (Bains, 2001). CRM initiatives not only fail to deliver profitable growth but can also damage long-standing customer relationships, according to a survey of 451 senior executives (Rigby et al., 2002). According to CRM-forum, only 4 per cent are software problems and 1 per cent bad advice; 87 per cent pinned failure of CRM programmes on the lack of adequate change management.

Implementing successful CRM depends more on strategy than on technology. Without a clear customer strategy a CRM system lacks direction and may disrupt relations with important customers. A customer acquisition and retention strategy has to be implemented and a segmentation analysis has to be made.

If a customer strategy is established, other dimensions, such as business processes, other systems, structure and people, have to be adapted to make the CRM system work. If a company wants to develop better relationships with its customers it needs first to rethink the key business processes that relate to customers, from customer service to order fulfilment. Such adaptations may also include job descriptions, performance measures, compensation systems, training programmes and so on. If consumers have a choice of channels – such as e-mail, web and telephone – marketing, sales and service can no longer be treated separately. A customer may place an order by phone, use the website to check the status of the order and send a complaint by mail. Multi-channel interactions pose considerable challenges if the company is to maintain a single comprehensive and real-time view of each customer.

For companies focused on products or services, this means recentring on the customer – which can be a radical change in a company's culture. All employees, but especially those in marketing, sales, service and other customer contact functions, have to think in a customer-oriented way. For example, in some call centres, employees have been measured and rewarded on how fast they resolved a customer's problem. This reflected management thinking that shorter telephone calls lowered costs. A CRM approach would concentrate efforts on customer satisfaction per call, not just call-handling efficiency (Mahieu, 2002).

An important reason for the failure of CRM projects lies in narrow and poor change management. Much time, effort and money have to be spent exclusively on managing the organisational issues. It is a struggle to move from a conventional customer strategy to a CRM philosophy. CRM projects are cross-function undertakings: IT, marketing and production have to operate on the same wavelength, yet they have different orientations and cultures. Successful CRM depends on coordinated actions by all departments within a company rather than being driven by a single department.

## ● Summary

- CRM systems are customer-facing systems for customer care and management supporting a CRM philosophy.

- CRM is primarily a customer-centric philosophy, and can be perceived as a move from mass market and industrial production to customisation and focused production.

- CRM can only be implemented successfully by managing a range of organisational issues, including establishing a strategy on which customers should be treated in particular ways. It also depends on adapting business processes, structure and skills.

## 2.6  Using IS beyond organisational borders

Networked information systems allow companies to coordinate joint processes with other organisations across great distances. Transactions such as payments and orders can be exchanged electronically, thereby reducing the cost of obtaining products and services. Organisations can share all sorts of business data, such as catalogues or mail messages, through networks. Many such systems use web technology, with labels such as extra-organisational systems, e-commerce systems, m-commerce, e-business systems and supply chain management systems. Since these systems cross organisational borders we refer to them as **inter-organisational systems (IOS)**.

These inter-organisational systems can create new efficiencies and new relationships between an organisation and its customers, suppliers and business partners, redefining organisational boundaries. Firms are using these systems to work jointly with suppliers and other business partners on product design and development, and on scheduling the flow of work in manufacturing, procurement and distribution: 'Streamlining cross-company processes is the next great frontier for reducing costs, enhancing quality, and speeding operations' (Hammer, 2001, p. 84). Inter-firm collaboration and coordination can increase efficiency, value to customers and competitive advantage.

IOS includes two commonly used terms:

- **e-commerce**, the process of selling a product or service to the customer (whether a retail consumer or another business) over the Internet; and

- **e-business**, the integration, through the Internet, of all an organisation's processes, from its suppliers through to its customers.

Figure 2.6 shows how the systems within a company can be linked with external parties by electronic networks.

Many businesses have used the Internet as an information system to support their distribution processes. Such **business-to-consumer (B2C) systems** offer products, especially banking, publications, software, music or tickets, to individual retail customers. Another way of using the Internet is to change the production system. Some companies use a website to manage information about sales, capacity, inventory, payment and so on – and to exchange that information with their suppliers or business customers. They use such **business-to-business (B2B) systems** to connect electronically all the links in their supply chain, so creating an integrated process to meet customer needs.

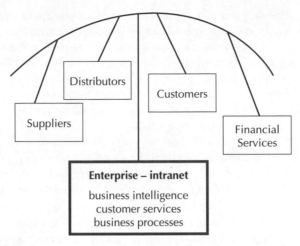

**Figure 2.6** E-business: electronic linkages within the companies and in the supply chain

## ● E-business models

When organisations use IS to communicate with business partners they have to decide which e-business models best suit their goals. A business model is defined as the organisation of product, service and information flows, and the source of revenues and benefits for suppliers and customers. The concept of an **e-business model** is the same but used for the online presence. Examples of common business models are (Li, 2007):

- e-shops: Internet shops, e.g. Amazon;
- e-procurement: the sale of supplies and services on the Internet;
- e-malls: department stores on the Internet;
- e-auctions or online auctions: the business model where participants bid for products and services over the Internet, such as eBay;
- virtual communities, also called e-communities or online communities: a group of people who interact via the Internet rather than face to face;
- information brokers: deliver requested information over the Internet, such as Google.

Roughly dividing the world into providers/producers and consumers/clients one can classify e-businesses into the following categories:

- business-to-business (B2B), e.g. ordering a product electronically through e-procurement;
- business-to consumer (B2C), e.g. a company publishing ticket prices and availablity;
- business-to-employee (B2E), e.g. using a corporate intranet to give information about rules for claiming travel expenses;
- business-to-government (B2G), e.g. licence applications;
- government-to-business (G2B), e.g. government buying office furniture;
- citizen-to-government (C2G), e.g. passport application;
- consumer-to-consumer (C2C), e.g. auction for private individuals;
- consumer-to-business (C2B), e.g. booking a ticket.

The simplest IOS applications provide information, also called 'web presence'. In B2C applications, customers can view product or other information on a company website. In B2B, business customers can place their requirements on the Internet, inviting potential suppliers to seek more information. Conversely, suppliers can use their websites to show customers what they can offer. Internet marketplaces are developing in which groups of suppliers in the same industry operate a collective website, making it easier for potential customers to compare terms through a single portal, providing links to many other sites (Hackbarth and Kettinger, 2000).

A further form of Internet use is for interaction. Customers or suppliers enter information and questions about (for example) offers and prices and the system then uses the customer information to show availability and costs. In B2B applications, a buyer can see a supplier's offer and ask further questions about optional features, volumes or delivery.

A third use is for transactions, when customers buy goods and services through a supplier's website. Conversely, a supplier who sees a purchasing requirement from a business (perhaps expressed as a purchase order on the website) can agree electronically to meet the order. The whole transaction, from accessing information through ordering, delivery (in some cases) and payment, can take place electronically.

The fourth use is integration when it links its own information systems and (within limits) links them in turn to customers and suppliers. As customers place an order, this information moves to the systems that control the seller's internal processes and those of its suppliers.

Finally, a company achieves transformation when it uses IOS to transform its internal operations as well as the value chain. It may integrate its business processes with those of suppliers and customers or use the Internet to reach the customer in more direct ways. Figure 2.7 shows these stages.

The relationship between a company and its channel partners can be changed by the Internet or by other applications of inter-organisational systems, because electronic networks can help to bypass channel partners, also called **disintermediation**. Figure 2.8 shows how a manufacturer and a wholesaler can bypass other partners and reach customers directly.

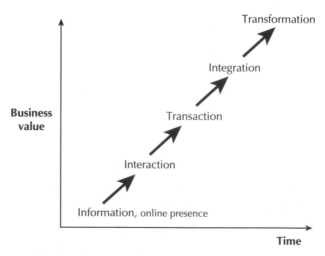

**Figure 2.7 Inter-organisational systems in five phases**

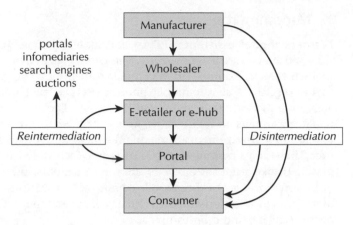

**Figure 2.8 Reinventing the supply chain**

The benefits of disintermediation are that transaction costs are reduced and it enables direct contact with customers. This also makes it possible to increase the reach of companies, for example from a local presence to a national or international presence. On the other hand, the Internet also creates the possibility for parties to reintermediate. **Reintermediation** is the creation of new intermediaries between customers and suppliers by providing (new) services such as supplier search and product evaluation (Chaffey, 2007). Portals that help customers to find the best price and offer to meet specified needs are examples of electronic reintermediators. The portal performs price evaluation and helps users to link automatically to suppliers. Internet-based reintermediators (also called **infomediaries**) include search engines, malls, virtual resellers, financial intermediaries and evaluators (who provide comparisons).

| MIS in Practice | E-government applications at the City of Amsterdam |
| --- | --- |

The City of Amsterdam aims to be an e-government city that seeks to serve its citizens with as many e-services as possible. Relations with citizens, with companies, and with tourists are facilitated with e-services but Amsterdam also tries to support the democratic processes with information technology. Here are some examples of e-services on the Amsterdam City Portal (www.iamsterdam.com).

● **Information** – latest news such as the plan to build a new stadium and business news.

● **Interaction** – citizens can give their opinions about what's going on in Amsterdam and file complaints about services of the city. It is also possible to chat with politicians and civil servants.

● **Transaction** – citizens can order new passports and driving licences. It is also possible to make theatre and hotel bookings.

● **Integration** – Amsterdam integrated a number of its web services with its own business systems. The City Portal is also connected with the systems of the Tourist Board and with the IT systems of main tourist attractions.

*Sources*: websites www.iamsterdam.com and www.amsterdam.nl

## ● M-commerce

**Personal digital assistants (PDAs)** and mobile phones have become so popular that many businesses are beginning to use m-commerce as a more efficient method of serving their customers. Examples of m-commerce are in ticketing and travel. M-ticketing means that tickets can be sent to mobile phones. Users are then able to use their tickets immediately by presenting their phones at the venue. The travel industry uses m-commerce to update customers on flight status, notify them when this information changes and offer to make new arrangements based on present user preferences requiring no input from the user. Therefore, a customer's entire trip can be scheduled and maintained using a mobile device. Unlike a home PC, the location of the mobile phone user is an important piece of information used during mobile commerce transactions. Knowing the location of the user allows for location-based services, such as local maps, local offers, local weather and people tracking and monitoring.

## ● Organisational and management issues of IOS

Feeny (2001) emphasises that existing customers should not be the only focus, since IOS may make it possible to reach new customers with new products. This is consistent with Porter's (2001) view that implementing IOS and Internet applications is not a substitute for strategy. Once most companies have embraced the Internet, the Internet itself will be neutralised as a source of advantage; companies will not survive without a website, but they will not gain any competitive advantage. That comes from traditional and sustained strengths such as unique products, excellent operations, product knowledge and relationships. IOS should be used by companies to strengthen and 'fortify' those advantages.

A major concern of companies using IOS is whether or not they can handle the associated physical processes. These include handling orders, arranging shipment, receiving payment and dealing with after-sales service. This gives an advantage to traditional retailers that can support their websites with existing fulfilment processes. Given the negative effects of failure once processes are supported by IOS, it seems advisable to delay connecting systems to the IOS until robust and repeatable processes are in place.

Another important issue is the change management associated with e-business (Boonstra and de Vries, 2005) since the move to e-business affects many processes and people, as the MIS in Practice feature, right, shows.

Kanter (2001) found that the move to e-business for established companies involved a deep change. She found that top management absence, short-sightedness of marketing people and other internal barriers are common obstacles. She quotes an executive:

*We have internal opposition from parts of the organisation that are threatened by the Internet. The sales force is obviously not keen on deploying the Internet with channel partners, which means reduced sales to them.* (p. 92)

Her research in over 80 companies showed 'deadly mistakes' as well as some lessons, including:

- create experiments and act simply and quickly to convert the sceptics;
- create dedicated teams and give them space and autonomy, sponsoring them from the wider organisation;
- recognise that e-business requires systemic changes in many ways of working.

## MIS in Practice    The electronic patient file

Computer systems are widely used in healthcare to support clinical and administrative procedures, but they are typically isolated systems, unable to pass information about an individual patient to other systems. This means that the different providers of healthcare (general practitioners, hospitals, pharmacies, etc.) do not have online access to all of a patient's records with their medical history, currently prescribed drugs and perhaps any problems they have had with particular drugs.

Such access is important in many clinical situations, such as: during clinical care, doctors and nurses in hospitals need full patient records; when patients leave the hospital, pharmacies and GPs need medical information from the hospital to complete their files; when patients visit hospitals for outpatient care, the hospital and the pharmacist need patients' information from GPs. All agree that patients will benefit if they are treated by people with access to one consistent medical record that includes information from the laboratory, X-rays, pharmacy, GP, etc. Software and hardware suppliers have developed such systems, which they actively promote.

The management of the main hospital in a region proposed that all relevant parties, especially GPs and pharmacies, should enter medical data into an Electronic Patient File (EPF) that would be managed by the hospital's IS-department. Within the hospital, medical staff would enter details about treatments and drugs prescribed. Traditionally hospital doctors entered this on to a paper file (one for each patient) that all staff then used when treating that patient. The new system would involve entering and retrieving information through a computer terminal; some doctors expected that nurses would do this work for them.

Most general practitioners in the region (independent businesses who also value their professional autonomy) had already invested in patient record systems to meet their needs. They have traditionally resisted attempts by government to control their expenditure on drugs, arguing that this would reduce their professional status.

The pharmacies had also invested in computer systems, and these were integrated in networks linking pharmacy businesses across the region. They enabled pharmacies to control and manage supplies of medicines in line with demand, and to track what drugs patients were buying, wherever they did so.

*Source*: Boonstra and Harison (2008).

## Activity 2.7  Considering the electronic patient file

An important issue in IOS is change management, since they affect many processes and people. Review the account of the Electronic Patient File and make notes on the following issues.

● What are the main elements of this system?
● How would you categorise this system in terms of functions and reach?
● Who are the potential users of this system?
● What are the possible benefits of implementing it?
● What organisational difficulties might arise?
● Identify the three main issues that hospital management should be considering if they want the proposed system to be a success.

## ● Summary

- A major management issue is the extent to which the Internet provides opportunities to improve or expand the existing business, while at the same time threatening that business by opening it to new competitors.

- When management has decided to use the Internet to develop e-commerce or e-business, strategies have to be developed as to how this will be realised. Such a strategy will have external elements (e.g. customers, suppliers, competitors) and internal elements (e.g. how to redesign the business process and the organisational structure) to support this new strategy.

---

### Activity 2.8 A research project

If you have the opportunity in an assignment or a project, you could identify:

- current main information systems used for the operational processes;
- trends and possible future changes with respect to IS use;
- the familiarity with and the relevance of ERP, KM, CRM and IOS systems.

You can obtain this information by interviewing different people, including users, managers and IS staff. Ask also about the degree of satisfaction with current IT use and familiarity with new IT and change.

---

## 2.7 Digital search and customer participation

We are now entering what some have called a digital culture, in which traditional boundaries between producers and consumers are eroding. Wikipedia (www.wikipedia.org), the online encyclopaedia written by volunteers, became in a few years the largest encyclopaedia in the world. YouTube (www.youtube.com), a site for video exchange, was taken over by Google 14 months after its foundation for $1.6billion. Second Life (http://secondlife.com), a virtual world of Linden Lab, has also received a lot of media coverage. These are examples of **user-generated content (UGC)** – electronic platforms that are created, maintained and developed by users.

This goes beyond new ways of using technology and has many legal, social, economic and business implications. **Wikinomics**, a term introduced by Tapscott and Williams (2006), refers to this changed business culture, which sees customers no longer as consumers but as co-creators and co-producers. Amazon and Google use this principle of **co-creation**. Amazon uses customer reviews to exchange information between readers and uses the buying patterns of customers to suggest books to others with similar interests. Google analyses search requests to develop profiles and make advertisements available to searchers with certain profiles. In both cases, customers create their own content and value, while increased use leads to multiplication of value. This principle is based on **Metcalfe's law**: 'the value of a network increases with the square of the number of users connected to the network'. In other words, the more people have phones, the more useful phones become. This 'network effect' leads to rapid adoption and creates barriers for new entrants. A network effect is a characteristic that causes a good or service to have a value to a potential customer which depends on the number of other customers who

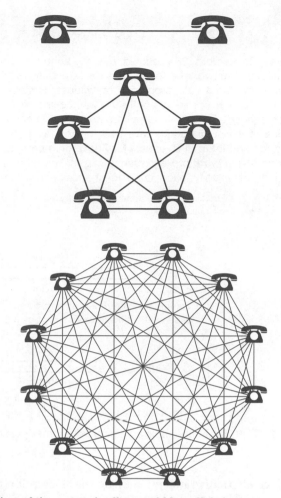

**Figure 2.9 Illustration of the network effect and Metcalfe's law**
*Source*: Metcalfe's law (26 March, 2008). Reproduced from *Wikipedia, The Free Encyclopedia*.
Retrieved 14 April 2008 from http://en.wikipedia.org/w/index.php?title=Metcalfe%27s_law&oldid=201140098

own the good or are users of the service. In other words, the number of prior adopters is a term in the value available to the next adopter (see Figure 2.9).

**Open source** initiatives, such as the development of Linux software (www.linux.org), is another example of this principle of creating value by sharing and interaction. Jenkins (2006) argues that digital technology plays an important role in the growth of a so-called 'participation culture', where people contribute actively to the development, production, consumption and assessment of products.

These new systems of producing digital products can be illustrated by the interaction model. In a traditional setting of production and consumption, producers create products or services that are ordered by and delivered to customers, who pay for that in return (see Figure 2.10a). The alternative way is that companies, such as Google, Wikipedia or Linux, provide a platform that customers use to retrieve information or software. By doing so they add to the value of the platform as more requests lead to better information and a better platform. Consumption does not lead to value reduction, but to value creation (Figure 2.10b).

---

**MIS in Practice     Social graphiti**

Mark Zuckerberg, 23 years old, recently announced that he was opening up Facebook, the social network he founded at Harvard University, to outside programmers. Anyone can now build little programs, or 'widgets', into the network. To illustrate his idea, Mr Zuckerberg projected on to the wall behind him a 'social graph', a pattern of nodes representing Facebook users and the links between them. Since then Facebook and the idea of the social graph have become the favourite conversation among venture capitalists and Internet investors. Mr Zuckerberg compares his graphing of human connections to the work of Renaissance mapmakers. Facebook is growing furiously and may catch up with MySpace, the biggest social network.

*Source*: *The Economist*, 20 October 2007.

---

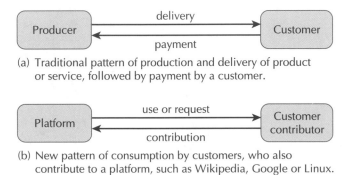

(a)  Traditional pattern of production and delivery of product or service, followed by payment by a customer.

(b)  New pattern of consumption by customers, who also contribute to a platform, such as Wikipedia, Google or Linux.

**Figure 2.10  Traditional delivery versus customer participation**

Such alternative systems build on the assumption that the voluntary contributions of many contributors can create more value than the products of professionals. This principle can be used in various situations. A physician in the field of fertility treatments at the University Hospital Nijmegen, the Netherlands, spent a lot of time telling couples about the pros and cons of treatments and also provided emotional support. As an experiment he started an electronic chat platform that could be used exclusively by his clients to share information and emotions. The platform was also used for the provision of medical information on fertility treatments. From time to time, the doctor and other staff members also joined in the chat sessions. The 'electronic fertility platform' partially replaced the time spent on providing and supporting clients. Clients contributed anonymously to the platform, and these contributions helped others, who contributed in their turn.

There are successful platforms of customer participation and peer production working on both a profit and a not-for-profit basis. Amazon, Google and YouTube are for-profit peer production companies. Wikipedia, on the other hand, is a not-for-profit company that uses only a small staff to manage this concept. There are also many platforms that can be used by customers to share information on products and by doing so create market transparency and quality rankings that influence customer preferences. Organisations have to be aware of these developments and respond effectively, for instance by creating their own customer platforms or by contributing actively to other platforms.

## Activity 2.9 Customer participation in various industries

- Choose an industry and find out how customers participate in and contribute to technology platforms. Possible industries are: financial services, education, government, consumer products, news and publishing, healthcare.
- Provide specific examples and reflect on the implications, the advantages but also the problems that may arise for companies within that industry.

## MIS in Practice      New business models in the music industry

How can the music industry make money online? Record labels are following diverging strategies. Leading record makers, in particular, have long insisted that songs sold online should be wrapped in virtual envelopes that prevent fans from e-mailing them to friends or uploading them to a file sharing network. However, this system, called 'digital rights management' (DRM) software, is eroding and many record companies as well as retailers have started selling songs without software that prevents copying. Now record companies have to develop new business models that are profitable for music makers and the music industry.

*Source*: Based on 'Online Music: The slow death of digital rights', *The Economist*, 13 October 2007.

## ● Organisational and management issues of customer participation

These developments raise new management questions for almost any company, about how it can use the ideas and experiences of its customers. Here are some examples.

- How can the company facilitate customers sharing their experiences with each other and with the developers, producers and sales staff?
- Is the organisation able to respond to these ideas and comments in adequate ways?
- Will customer participation and co-creation lead to new business models that may be hard to implement?

## ● Summary

- Wikinomics refers to the change in business culture that sees customers no longer as consumers but also as co-creators and producers.
- Co-creation is based on Metcalfe's law (network effect), which says that the value of a network increases with the square of the number of users connected to the network.
- Platforms of customer participation and peer production can work effectively on a profit as well as on a non-profit basis.

# Conclusions

Organisations have always depended on information systems to help conduct their business. Technological developments have greatly increased this dependence, as applications have moved from essentially background tasks to include foreground, customer-centred tasks. Most organisations depend heavily on computer-based information systems. For many, such systems are the basis of their business. Equally, most managers depend on accurate and timely information. We have outlined several perspectives on information systems and shown how some modern technological developments have increased the power and versatility of information systems.

The discussion has also emphasised that, while technology is central to modern information systems, it is only part of the story. Figure 1.4 showed that information systems include people and procedures as well as technology. Throughout the chapter we have shown that each perspective on information systems raises wider management and organisational issues. Smaller and more portable systems encourage changes in working arrangements. Advances in communication technology erode boundaries between functions and organisations. The capacity of the new technologies is such that they raise major questions of strategy – about the kind of business that a company is in (Chapter 4). Although the cost of the basic technology is falling, the cost of implementing new systems continues to rise. How can managers decide if the investment is worth the cost (Chapter 10)?

Looking inward, modern systems encourage companies to consider redesigning the processes through which they deliver their strategies (Chapter 5), with significant implications for the human side of organisations (Chapter 8). There are structural questions too – since information can flow more freely, it breaks down established boundaries (Chapter 6) and raises questions about the place of the information system's function itself in the organisation (Chapter 7). Finally, in Chapter 9 we examine many of the implementation issues that people have to manage in projects and programmes.

# Chapter questions

1. Which functions of information systems are becoming more important? Explain your answer by giving examples.

2. Information systems are increasing their reach. What are the reasons for this and what are the consequences for businesses?

3. What are the advantages and disadvantages of local systems?

4. What are the main motives for organisations in implementing knowledge systems, enterprise systems, customer relationship management systems and inter-organisational systems?

5. What are the limitations and possible pitfalls of knowledge systems, enterprise systems, customer relationship management systems and inter-organisational systems?

6. How can organisations benefit from the popularity of search engines like Google? Can it also be a threat? What should be an appropriate management action to deal with the development towards customer participation?

7. Give an example of the use of the network effect in an organisation that you know.

# Further reading

Chaffey, D. (2007) *E-business and E-commerce Management*, Financial Times/Prentice Hall, Harlow. A book that uses a wide range of informative case studies to cover the management issues raised by the Internet.

Gartner Group's website contains regular updates of developments in IS applications discussed in this chapter. Visit it at www.gartner.com.

Below are several empirical studies on the themes of the chapter:

Alavi, M. and Leidner, D.E. (2002) 'Knowledge management and knowledge management systems: conceptual foundations and research issues', *MIS Quarterly*, **25**(1), 107–36. Accessible introduction to knowledge management from an IS perspective.

McGinnis, T.C. and Huang, Z. (2007) 'Rethinking ERP success: a new perspective from knowledge management and continuous improvement', *Information & Management*, **44**(7), 626–34. A study of the relation between ERP and knowledge management.

Rigby, D.K., Reichheld, F.F. and Schefter, P. (2002) 'Avoid the four perils of CRM', *Harvard Business Review*, **80**(2), 101–9. Discusses the pros and cons of CRM and the pitfalls of relationship management systems.

Voelpel, S.C., Dous, M. and Davenport, T.H. (2005) 'Five steps to creating a global knowledge-sharing system: Siemens' Sharenet', *Academy of Management Review*, **19**(2), 9–23. Gives more information on the chapter case.

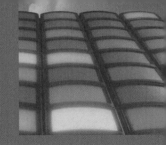

# CHAPTER 3

## Social contexts of information systems

### Learning objectives

By the end of your work on this topic you should be able to:

- Give examples of how political, economic, cultural and legal forces affect IS

- Analyse each of these factors systematically to assess their relevance for a project

- Outline how modern systems affect data privacy and how governments react to this

- Outline how modern systems affect intellectual property and how governments react to this

- Give examples of stakeholders with an interest in how organisations use information

- Evaluate systematically the ethical issues raised by the use of IS

# Google

## www.google.com

Sergey Brin and Larry Page founded Google in 1999 and by 2008 it was the world's largest search engine – 38 per cent of Internet searches in the United States were made on Google.

Its founders' mission is 'to organise the world's information and make it universally accessible and useful'. The demand for search services arose as the World Wide Web expanded, making it progressively more difficult for users to find relevant information. The company's initial success was built on Brin and Page's invention of a new approach to online searching. The details of this remain secret, but the principle is that the **PageRank** algorithm (with 500 million variables and 3 billion terms) identifies material relevant to a search by favouring a page to which another page has been linked. These links were called 'votes', because they showed that the webmaster of another page had decided that the focal page deserved attention. The importance of the focal page is determined by counting the number of votes it has received.

The Google software uses thousands of linked computers to conduct a series of simultaneous equations in a fraction of a second. Having determined which web pages are most important it then analyses their content to decide which are relevant to the current search. By combining overall importance and query-specific relevance, Google claims to put the results most relevant to a search at the top of the list.

The company generates revenue by enabling advertisers to deliver online advertising that is relevant to the search results on a page, appearing next to the search results. Advertisers pay Google a fee each time their ad is viewed, with the rate depending on how much they bid for keywords that link their advert to the search: the more they bid the nearer the top of the page their ad will be. In October 2006 Google took 31 per cent of US online advertising revenue.

When the company offered shares to the public in 2004, Page warned potential investors that Google was not a conventional company and did not intend to become one. In the interests of long-term stability the founders would own about 30 per cent of the shares, but control 80 per cent of the votes.

The company's expansion has sometimes caused controversy. The agreement it reached with the Chinese government in 2006 allowing it to offer search services in that country contained terms to which many Western commentators objected. When Microsoft launched a bid in 2008 to buy Google's main competitor, Yahoo!, Google appealed to the US regulatory authorities to block the deal.

*Sources*: Based on Harvard Business School case 9-806-105, *Google Inc.*, prepared by Thomas R. Eisenmann and Kerry Herman; company website; *Business Week*, 9 April 2007.

# Introduction

Developments in IS mean that people constantly see opportunities to add value by acquiring and processing information in ever more imaginative ways. Google is a prominent example in which two talented people saw a growing demand in society to search the Internet for information, and created a tool that would do this efficiently. That tool – PageRank – was a valuable asset, protected by intellectual property law. The business idea was an immediate success in societies that value free access to information, and whose laws and customs encourage it. In countries with different beliefs some users have been punished for downloading material of which powerful interests disapproved. Some European governments have launched a competing service to Google Library, fearing US dominance of their cultural heritage.

## CASE QUESTIONS 3.1

Before reading on, make notes on the contextual issues that you think Google may have had to deal with to enable it to spread so widely.

Apart from building ever larger technical systems, what issues in the wider social context will it have had to anticipate and manage as it expanded?

Keep your notes and add to them as you work through the chapter.

Wipro, an Indian-based global technology company, took advantage of changes in business regulations to enter the computer business – and has made similar strategic moves as circumstances changed. Microsoft is frequently engaged in lawsuits with competitors or governments that object to what they regard as uncompetitive practices by the company or for alleged breaches of copyright. Website designs vary by country, to take account not only of languages but also of deep cultural differences in the features that people value on a site.

These and many other examples (like the Google case) illustrate the theme of this chapter – that managing information systems depends on being aware not just of factors in the immediate competitive environment (which we examine in Chapter 4) but also of the wider social context. The enduring lesson of managing IS is the link between project and context. While the technology may have the same features wherever it is used, local circumstances vary. Those promoting an IS project need to be aware of the contexts in which they are working, respond to them as they design and implement a system, and recognise that their work will change the context. Such awareness makes it more likely that the IS will complement its context, and so be accepted and used to add value.

Distinctive social arrangements in nation states (and amongst groups within a state) develop as people conduct their personal and professional lives – and in doing so create unique social and legal relationships. These reflect local circumstances, sometimes emerging from invisible processes within the society and sometimes being the result of powerful people protecting their interests. Such human creations – customs, laws, business arrangements – are the social context that shapes how people who are subject to them add value to resources (as producers) and how they value the outputs of others (as consumers).

The chapter outlines in turn the political, economic, cultural and legal dimensions of the social context, showing how each has affected, and been affected by, computer-based IS. It pays particular attention to data protection and intellectual property. It outlines the expectations of stakeholders in relation to IS, leading to a consideration of the links between ethical issues and an organisation's strategy.

## 3.1 Political contexts

Countries' political systems shape what managers can and cannot do. Government regulations may specify which companies can operate within their jurisdiction and how they should do so. Political decisions sometimes affect the pattern of competition quite directly – perhaps obstructing new entrants, but protecting them once they are established.

## ● Rules on market entry

Wipro, based in India, is one of the world's leading IT companies, providing increasingly sophisticated services to companies around the world. It was originally in a different business but Azim Premji, the son of its founder, wanted to diversify, though he had no fixed plan about the direction in which to go. In 1977 the Indian government set rules that required foreign companies to operate through local, Indian-owned partners. IBM, then the world's dominant computer company, left the country, creating an opportunity for Indian companies to enter the market for computer hardware. Premji recalls: 'When IBM left, it created a vacuum. So we decided to zero in on info tech.'

By 1981 the company was designing and selling computers, leading the market for several years: later it moved into software with spreadsheet and word-processing packages. In the early 1990s the Indian government liberalised business regulations, allowing the world's top computer companies to move in again. Their large R&D resources and high sales would soon defeat Wipro if it operated only in India – but the head of the IT unit, Sridhar Mitta, had the idea of selling the company's expertise: 'We saw that while the door was open for others to come in, it was also open for us to go out. So we decided to become a global company' (Boddy, 2008, p. 207).

Rules on market entry still apply in most countries – for example Research in Motion, the Canadian manufacturer of the BlackBerry family of wireless e-mail devices, wished to begin selling the devices in China: with 500 million mobile phone users, the company saw the country as a valuable market. To enter it managers needed permission from the Chinese government – which, after eight years of trying, it received in 2007.

## ● Rules governing how companies operate

In 2004 the European Commission fined Microsoft almost 500m euros for abusing its market dominance, by including valuable software features within the operating system, so limiting the market available to specialist software providers. The Commission later launched two new competition enquiries against the company. A further example of the EU affecting the way companies compete occurred in 2008 when the Competition Commissioner warned Europe's mobile phone operators to cut the cost of texting and Internet access while customers are overseas – otherwise the EU would introduce regulations to fix prices. The new generation of phones had made it easier to surf the Internet and e-mail, and was popular with consumers – but the EU believed that companies were charging too much to users who used the service when they were away from their home country.

Governments at both national and international levels become involved in takeovers – especially in politically visible areas like the Internet – see Chapter Case, Part 2.

## ● Actions on specific markets

Government policies can directly affect the use of the Internet by citizens and businesses. They can, for example:

- encourage or discourage citizens' use of the Internet;
- enact legislation to protect data privacy and intellectual property (see Sections 3.4 and 3.5);
- create regulations that affect competition between Internet companies;

# Microsoft, Yahoo! and Google

In February 2008 Microsoft announced that it was bidding to buy Yahoo!, a rival search engine to Google. Microsoft claimed that the merger of the two companies would create more competition, by creating a stronger rival to Google, which now had about 75 per cent of the search market. The company also insisted that it was committed to openness, innovation and the protection of privacy on the Internet.

Google disagreed with this view, arguing that Microsoft might attempt to exert an inappropriate degree of control, and pressed the industry regulators (and initially the US Congress Judiciary Committee) to investigate the proposed deal. Google expressed fears that the Microsoft–Yahoo! link could limit the ability of consumers to access competitors' e-mail and instant messaging services.

*Source*: *BBC News*, 4 February 2008.

- offer training and incentives to people to acquire relevant IT skills;
- encourage the online delivery of government services;
- create companies to offer online services.

An example of the latter is the initiative taken by the French government to create an online digital library as a rival to Google. That company announced in 2004 it had reached agreement with some leading US and UK libraries to digitise millions of printed books that were no longer protected by copyright, which users would then be able to access over the Internet. French librarians (Jeanneney, 2007), and their government, acknowledged the potential benefits of such a scheme to make access to part of the world's published knowledge more readily available, but expressed deep concern about aspects of the proposal. These concerned the perceived bias towards American, or at least English language, works; the danger of overlooking works in the other 25 major European languages; and the market-centred nature of the Google proposal. These anxieties led the Bibliothèque nationale de France (BnF) to create a new portal, Europeana, which plans to digitise some 100,000 items a year. This is matched by linked initiatives in other European countries to create the European Digital Library, which will ensure multilingual access to Europe's cultural heritage.

| MIS in Practice | Governments aim to compete with Google |
| --- | --- |

*The [Japanese] government, alarmed at the dominance of Google and other online services, is launching a project to encourage companies to develop new search technologies. It hopes to use Japan's strength in developing devices such as mobile phones and car navigation systems to create proprietary search and information retrieval functions. But some question whether a state-led project is capable of [overtaking] Google. France and Germany have also launched a plan to seed development of a 'next generation' European search engine, although Germany then pulled out of the plan.*

*Source*: *Financial Times*, 5 September 2007, p. 1.

### Activity 3.1  Gathering information about political contexts

Identify one new example of a government action affecting use of the Internet.

- What was the action?
- What had led to the intervention?
- What were the implications for those affected?
- Is there any evidence about how those affected reacted?

## ● Summary

- The political context affects the management of business information systems as it reflects the interests of powerful players and vested interests in a country. These are often expressed in regulations governing business activity, including those based on the Internet.
- It includes the ability to grant or withhold permission to operate in a country.
- It may also affect the freedom with which individuals can use the Internet.
- Political interests also launch business activities as rivals to commercial interests.

## 3.2 Economic contexts

One of the main factors affecting decisions on IS investment is the pattern of customer usage in potential markets. Ideally managers need to know, for each type of customer and for each digital channel (Internet, mobile phone, digital TV, etc.), the proportion of customers who:

- have access to the channel;
- are influenced by using the channel;
- purchase using the channel.

The following sections illustrate this with information about Internet access.

### ● Internet access

The International Telecommunications Union (ITU) estimates (see Figure 3.1) that in 2006 about 400 million people were Internet subscribers – of whom 180m were in the Asia-Pacific region, 120m in Europe, 90m in the Americas and only 10m in Africa. Such figures are of course very approximate, and count the number of *subscribers*: the number of users will of course be higher (because of families). Some believe that lack of access to modern IS hinders economic development and advocate policies to make it more available to people in poorer countries. Mobile phone usage in Africa is growing rapidly, allowing those nations to avoid costly investment in fixed-line telephone systems.

There will be similar variations in access within a country. While the Office for National Statistics in the UK estimates that in 2006 over 58 per cent of households have access to the Internet, the proportion will vary according to demographic characteristics

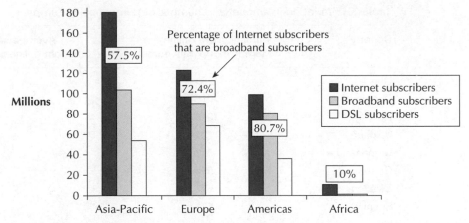

**Figure 3.1 Internet subscribers by region and access type, 2006**
*Source*: ITU (www.itu.int/ITU-D/ict/statistics/).

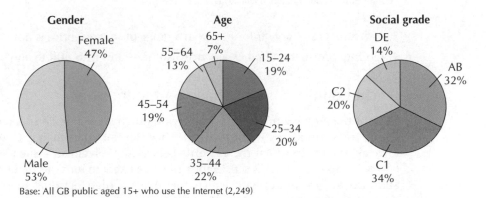

Base: All GB public aged 15+ who use the Internet (2,249)

**Figure 3.2 Variation in demographic characteristics of UK Internet users by gender, age and social class**
*Source*: eMori Technology Tracker.

– such as social class, gender, age and income. Figure 3.2 shows how Internet use varies on these demographics.

## ● Customers who are influenced by using the Internet

Those wishing to develop an effective online service need to understand their customers' online buying behaviour. Finding information online is a popular activity, but companies need to know more about the specific actions of their target group. A study quoted in Chaffey (2007, p. 155) found the following.

1. The Internet is a vital part of the research process with 73 per cent of Internet users agreeing that they now spend longer researching products. The purchase process is considered and complex.

2. The Internet is used at every stage of the research process from the initial scan to the more detailed comparison and final check before purchase.

**Table 3.1  Variation in amount and number of purchases in Europe**

| Country | Amount spent online per Internet shopper (in euros) | Average number of items bought online per Internet shopper |
|---|---|---|
| UK | 1285 | 12 |
| Denmark | 1078 | 9 |
| Norway | 1074 | 7 |
| Belgium | 701 | 4 |
| Netherlands | 612 | 3 |
| Germany | 594 | 10 |
| Sweden | 577 | 5 |
| Spain | 521 | 2 |
| Italy | 449 | 3 |
| France | 373 | 6 |

*Source*: EIAA (2006), quoted in Chaffey (2007, p. 158).

**3.** Consumers are more informed from a range of sources; price is not the primary driver.

**4.** Online information and experience also translates into offline purchases.

## ● Customers who purchase on the Internet

Most of the growing number of people who purchase online do so after gradually building up their confidence in the medium. They typically start their online purchasing with low-value items in which there is little personal involvement – such as travel tickets or books. If this experience is satisfactory, they are likely to move to higher-value purchases, and also to buy things with which they have a high personal involvement, such as expensive electronic products. Table 3.1 also shows significant differences between European countries in the value and number of Internet purchases.

The European Interactive Advertising Association (EIAA) conducts regular surveys of online purchasing – the Activity encourages use of the site to find up-to-date information.

---

**Activity 3.2  Latest trends in online shopping**

Visit the EIAA website (www.eiaa.net/news/).

● Have they provided more recent data than that shown in Table 3.1?

● If so, what are the main differences in the pattern, if any?

● What other information can you find on the site about recent trends in online shopping?

---

## ● Summary

● Significant aspects of the economic environment that affect management decisions about IS investment include the number with access to the technologies, how they use them and how much they buy.

- We illustrated these factors in relation to Internet usage, but similar data is available for other technologies.
- Internet access varies by country and demography.
- How customers use the Internet varies by demographic, such as age and gender.
- Internet purchase behaviour varies according to experience and demographic.

# 3.3 Cultural contexts

Cultures influence the way people live and work together, and vary between places and social groups. It affects, for example, how people use social networking sites and their attitudes to online information.

## ● What is culture?

**Culture** is distinct from human nature (features that all human beings have in common) and from an individual's personality (their unique way of thinking, feeling and acting). It is a collective phenomenon, shared with people in the common social environment in which it was learned. Hofstede and Hofstede (2005) describe it as the unwritten rules of the social game:

> the collective programming of the mind which distinguishes one group or category of people from others (in which 'group' means a number of people in contact with each other, and a 'category' means people who have something in common, such as people born before 1940). (p. 4 and p. 377)

While humans share common biological features, those in a particular society, nation or region develop a distinct culture.

Tayeb (1996) distinguishes between high- and low-context cultures. A **high context culture** is one in which information is implicit, and can only be fully understood in conjunction with shared experience, assumptions and various forms of verbal codes. High context cultures occur when people live closely with each other, where deep mutual understandings develop that then provide a rich context within which communication takes place. In a **low context culture** information is explicit and clear. These cultures occur where people are typically psychologically distant from each other, and so depend more on explicit information to communicate:

> Japanese, Arabs and Mediterranean people, who have extensive information networks among family, friends, colleagues and clients and who are involved in close personal relationships, are examples of high context cultures. Low context peoples include Americans, Germans, Swiss, Scandinavians and other northern Europeans; they compartmentalise their personal relationships, their work and many aspects of day-to-day life. (Tayeb, 1996, pp. 55–6)

## ● Culture and social networking

Many people use the Internet to meet new people, which encouraged entrepreneurs to launch **social networking sites** – some of which are now the most popular sites on the web. They allow people to communicate interactively with others who share their interests, and millions of people use them enthusiastically for social purposes. MySpace is launching locally targeted sites, and now has 24 local language sites in 20 countries, including French, German and Japanese. In 2008 it was the biggest social networking site across Europe as a whole, but in France the local Skyrock dominated, with about 70 per cent of the social networking market. In the UK Facebook recently had more users.

Businesses are seeking ways of using the social networks' ability to bring people with similar characteristics together. Bands use MySpace (owned by News Corporation) to promote their work, and the MIS in Practice features below give examples relating to sales and recruitment. Poynter (2008) reports on how consumer products companies use Facebook to supplement conventional market research methods.

---

### MIS in Practice    BurdaStyle    www.burdastyle.com

Burda, an established German publisher of sewing patterns, has launched an English language website to boost sales in the US. Each week it publishes a different pattern online as a PDF document that visitors can copy or print and modify to make new designs. As soon as each pattern is posted, the BurdaStyle online community springs into action. Members swap tips and post photographs in the forum, and exchange blogs on how to alter the designs. They create guides on how to alter the posted design – which some users then make into clothes they sell commercially: one said that 'having the community makes it so easy to figure out how to make different alterations'.

In 2008 the site had 29,000 members, and received 1.65 million page views a month. Burda makes no profit from the designs it publishes on the site, but hopes that word-of-mouth recommendations will boost sales of its other patterns.

*Source*: *Business Week*, 14 January 2008.

---

### MIS in Practice    Recruiting on social networking sites    www.facebook.com    www.myspace.com

Large employers who wish to recruit the most able graduates from around the world are exploring how best to respond to the user-led boom in social networking sites. The ability of sites such as Facebook and MySpace to gather people together could create opportunities for companies to reach young adults who might not otherwise come their way. They see that social networks are central to the way in which young adults move between business and leisure, with many organising much of their life through online communities.

So if a company wants to talk to them about professional opportunities, they may need a presence on the site. One option is to create a sponsored group on, say, Facebook for anyone interested in a career with the company. This enables the company to present corporate information, and potential applicants to hold online discussions and to ask current employees about their experience.

*Source*: *Financial Times*, 10 July 2007, p. 16.

## Activity 3.3 Reflecting on social networking sites

Reflect on how you use social networking sites, and make notes on these questions.

● Which sites do you use, and are you using them more or less than you did three months ago, and one year ago?

● What are the main benefits you obtain from using them?

● How does the fact that information you share on the site will be visible for many years affect what you post?

● Do you consider yourself to be in a high context or low context culture? Does that affect how you use these sites?

Compare your answers with others on your course, and explore if any differences in use reflect membership of high context or low context cultures.

## ● Technology as tool or fashion?

One of the reasons behind Nokia's dominance of the mobile phone market (as well as its mastery of the logistics of getting millions of phones to customers around the world) was that its managers were quick to recognise that mobile phones were not a commodity but a fashion accessory. By offering smart designs, different ring tones and coloured covers Nokia became the cool mobile brand for fashion-conscious people. In personal computers, Apple has for many years delivered distinctive stylish designs, which were part of its appeal to the market. PC makers are now:

*focusing as never before on turning utilitarian machines into fashion statements, and not just for the young and hip. Lenovo, the world's No. 3 PC maker is . . . expanding from commercial into consumer markets. The company is introducing three splashy notebooks – super-svelte and colorful, with textured covers that make them easy to grip. The lightest, at 2.3 pounds, is aimed at sophisticated, globe-trotting professionals. . . . And Netherlands-based Tulip Computers is showing off ultra-high-end notebooks that look like expensive purses and are pitched at wealthy, middle-aged women.* (Business Week, 14 January 2008)

## ● Producing and consuming

Modern information systems are changing the relationship between production and consumption. Alvin Toffler (1980) observed three distinct phases in human history. In the pre-industrial wave most people consumed what they produced – within their families or isolated village communities. Very little was traded. Industrialisation changed that, creating a situation in which most goods and services were produced for exchange, with people specialising in distinct aspects of the process:

*industrialism broke the union of production and consumption, and split the producer from the consumer. The fused economy of the First Wave was transformed into the split economy of the Second Wave.* (p. 53)

He went on to point out that now, in what he termed the Third Wave, that distinction is breaking down in many spheres of life. More people do more things for themselves, rather than rely on professionals – seeking advice on medical problems from the Internet or engaging in small-scale craft production (see BurdaStyle in the MIS feature) in community enterprises that enable a greater degree of self-sufficiency from the market economy.

Modern IS enable this shift, making it easier for 'producers' and 'consumers' to contribute to the product or service. Online reservation and ordering systems have long allowed consumers to perform some of the work previously done by the producer, and many manufacturers offer customers the chance to specify the features of their product online before ordering. More radical developments in the media sector include encouraging customers (as readers, listeners or viewers) to contribute to online discussion groups that include professional broadcasters or public figures – see MIS in Practice feature below. Figure 2.10 on page 62 illustrated this.

---

**MIS in Practice    The BBC – 'Have your say'    www.bbc.com**

The British Broadcasting Corporation (BBC) is one of the world's largest broadcasting organisations, with a staff of thousands delivering its output on radio, television and now in digital formats. Aware of the increasing tendency of younger people to contribute to blogs, and to be active rather than passive news consumers, the corporation now hosts many online discussion forums to which members of the public contribute. Through the BBC website they can suggest topics for discussion and/or take part in those already under way, by posting their e-mail comments on the website, which then appear as part of the discussion. As licence-payers they have paid an annual fee to receive programmes, but now choose to help make them for no financial reward.

*Source*: BBC website.

---

## ● The Internet and national differences

While the Internet as a communication technology transcends national boundaries, societies vary in how their citizens respond to values such as:

- open access to information;
- freedom of expression;
- individual privacy;
- individual security;
- democratic and transparent governance.

A culture that values freedom of expression, for example, will generate a regulatory context supporting freedom of information at the expense of protecting individual rights to privacy.

## ● Summary

- ● Some societies are characterised as high context cultures, and others as low context: this is likely to affect how people in those cultures use forms of IS, such as social networking sites.

- ● Although social networking sites are used primarily for social communications, organisations are beginning to use this new contextual factor for commercial purposes.

- ● Some forms of IS, such as mobile phones and personal computers, meet both fashionable and functional needs.

- ● Some applications of IS are altering the boundary between producer and consumer, as media companies in particular involve consumers in the production process.

# Google in Europe

**www.google.com**

CHAPTER CASE: PART 3

In some countries, such as Russia, Google has struggled to compete against local rivals such as Yandex and Rambler: 'Our support for the Russian language was not great, so we opened an office in Russia and got Russian engineers to look at the problem' (Nelson Mattos, Google's head of engineering for Europe).

Meanwhile Google is launching products such as mapping services that by their nature require regional expertise. A team in Israel is leading developments that include reading Internet pages from right to left. There is also fear in the company that unless Google is sensitive to concerns voiced by European governments it could become embroiled in long legal disputes. European data protection officials, for example, question the length of time Google keeps the results of search queries, amid concern that these could compromise users' rights to privacy.

Local touches are something the company is increasingly keen to add. It is staging a recruitment drive across Europe, seeking to hire thousands of engineers to help it create products suited for markets outside the US.

*Europe is different from the US and there are certain topics that are taken a lot more seriously here. Engineers from Europe will be more sensitive to these topics.* (Nelson Mattos)

*Source*: *Financial Times*, 27 September 2007, p. 16.

## CASE QUESTIONS 3.2

Review the Google website, especially the pages headed 'Corporate Information' in order to gain an insight into the range of its activities.

*'Google succeeds because it's in tune with modern cultures'*. Evaluate this point of view by considering the following:

- ● In what ways does Google reflect the cultures in which it operates?
- ● In what ways is Google changing these cultures?

## 3.4 Legal context (1) – data privacy

Governments create the legal framework within which companies operate, most obviously in areas like health and safety, employment, consumer protection and pollution control. Two themes relevant here are data privacy and intellectual property (see Section 3.5).

### ● Technical developments and data privacy

Company websites learn the identities of visitors who choose to register on the site by using **cookies** – files deposited on a user's computer when they visit a site. When the user returns, the website searches their computer, finds the cookie, and knows what the person did on previous visits. This enables the cookie to customise the contents of the site for that person – such as suggesting products that are likely to interest them. Banks (like Tesco in Chapter 1) use personal data about customers to design promotional incentives. Companies can also share information in their databases with other sources to develop quite comprehensive customer profiles.

Technology can monitor and record online activities, including which online news-groups or files a person has visited, which websites they use, and what they have purchased. Much of this tracking and monitoring occurs in the background, without the visitor's knowledge. Electronic surveillance systems monitor the location of people and vehicles, while systems to monitor employee e-mails or Internet use can ensure they do not break company rules.

All these applications may benefit customers, employees or citizens – but may equally cause them harm if the data is used in a way that violates the privacy of their data – in terms of not acquiring, using or distributing data without the person's permission.

### ● Protecting personal data

Laws protecting personal data are stronger in the European Union (EU) than in the US or Japan (Baumer et al., 2004). In 1973 a task force at the US Department of Health Education and Welfare (HEW) developed a **Code of Fair Information Practices (FIP)**, and most developed countries have passed **data protection laws** that reflect these principles. In contrast, the US has not codified them into a comprehensive federal law, though they have informed some state law. In summary the FIP principles cover the following.

| | |
|---|---|
| Notice/awareness | Consumers have a right to know if personal information is being collected and how it will be used. |
| Choice/consent | Consumers have a choice about whether or not information collected for one purpose will be used for other purposes and they have a choice about whether or not information will be shared with third parties unless it is required by law. |
| Access/participation | Consumers have a right to access information and to correct errors. |
| Integrity/security | Organisations should protect personal information from unauthorised access during transmission and storage. |
| Enforcement/redress | Consumers have a right to ensure that organisations comply with these core privacy principles either through external regulation (audits) or certification programs. (Schwaig et al., 2006) |

Schwaig et al. (2006) examined the extent to which Fortune 500 companies adhered to these principles, by analysing their websites against the FIP requirements. They studied not only the extent to which companies met the requirements but also the extent to which they undertook 'advanced disclosure', by including factors beyond the minimum. This enabled them to construct a privacy policy assessment matrix, showing the extent to which companies in the sample complied with FIP, and the extent to which they made advanced disclosure. This gives four categories.

● Insufficient protection/no policies – sites offer little or no protection.

● Public relations policies – sites cover all the categories, including some indicating advanced disclosure, but little information about enforcement – so offering only the illusion of protection.

● Focused/narrow policies – strong protection, but only in some areas.

● Mature policies – cover most FIP areas and offer genuine protection.

Figure 3.3 shows that only 16 per cent of firms had mature policies: many more appeared unconcerned with privacy or regarded it as a public relations exercise. In general, the authors found that larger firms provided stronger protection than small, and that information-intensive companies were more likely to provide protection than less information-intensive ones. They conclude that their method of analysis, and the assessment matrix, provide useful tools that managers can use to assess their company's compliance with fair information practices.

---

### Activity 3.4  Evaluating privacy policies

Choose a website you visit regularly, go to the 'Privacy Policy' page, and read the privacy policy.

● Which of the FIP principles does it mention either explicitly or in some other way?
● Where would you place it in Figure 3.3?

---

| Advanced disclosures | HIGH | Public relations 99 (26%) | Mature policies 63 (16%) |
| | LOW | Unconcerned with privacy 174 (45%) | Limited/Focused protection 47 (12%) |
| | | **FIP compliance** **Low** | **High** |

**Figure 3.3** Privacy Policy Assessment Matrix applied to the Fortune 500
*Source*: Adapted from Schwaig et al. (2006).

**Table 3.2** Summary of the provisions of the UK Data Protection Act

| Principle | Examples of required practices |
|---|---|
| Data shall be fairly and lawfully processed | Organisation must appoint a **data controller** responsible for data protection and advise people how to contact them; a person must give informed consent before data is processed. |
| Data to be processed for limited purposes | Must make clear at point of collection why and how personal data will be used – e.g. for marketing promotions. |
| Adequate, relevant and not excessive | Specifies that only the minimum data necessary for the purpose must be collected. |
| Accurate | Not only when collected but that the organisation keeps it up to date to avoid incorrect credit rating, for example. |
| Not kept longer than necessary | May be obvious if a customer relationship has ended, but if the data is about an occasional purchaser, criterion less clear. |
| Processing recognises data subject's rights | Rights include being able to receive a copy of the personal data that is held about them, not causing distress, being able to unsubscribe from mailings. |
| Secure | Must protect against unauthorised processing and against accidental loss, damage or destruction of personal data. |
| Not transferred to countries without adequate protection | An important protection against international companies transferring data to places with weaker individual protection. |

*Source*: www.informationcommissioner.gov.uk

The Organisation for Economic Cooperation and Development (OECD) has also formulated guidelines similar to the FIP (OECD, 1980) that aim to balance commercial and private interests in privacy law. This guided the European Commission's Directive on Data Protection, which requires member states to enact data protection legislation requiring companies and public bodies to inform people when they collect information about them, and explain how they will store and use it. In the UK this requirement is met by the Data Protection Act (DPA) 1984, 1988, which is typical of the pattern throughout the EU. Any company or public body that holds personal data on computers must register with the relevant agency – in the UK this is the Information Commission. Table 3.2 summarises the data protection principles to which the DPA gives effect.

National legislation is clearly intended to protect individuals against the misuse of their data, and reflects a balance at the time it was formulated between the perceived interests of individuals and those who wish to use data about them.

## ● Summary

- Developments in IS make it possible to collect and process unprecedented amounts of personal data about people and customers.
- While many claim this enables them to offer better service, others see it as a threat to privacy, especially if misused.
- Fair Information Principles give guidance on good practice in relation to customer data, but few websites in the United States follow these principles fully.
- Legislation to protect personal data is stronger in Europe than in the United States, with member states being obliged to legislate on the matter.

- The Data Protection Act sets out requirements for UK companies in terms of acquiring, protecting and distributing personal data.

## 3.5 Legal context (2) – intellectual property

**Intellectual property rights (IPR)** is a set of rights that protects those who create ideas and information that have commercial value. They give them exclusive rights over the knowledge and information they create, to prevent others using it without permission. Most governments have developed laws that protect the owners of IP, to encourage them to create and disseminate knowledge. The guiding principle is that ideas are expensive to produce but cheap to copy. If creative people know that others can copy and use their ideas without payment, they will have less incentive to spend time and effort in creating new music, books or films. Protecting the rights of those who own IP is intended to encourage them to produce more and to make it public so that others can benefit.

### ● Protecting intellectual property

There are three main ways to protect IP – copyright, patents and trademarks.

### Copyright

**Copyright** is a legally enforceable grant that aims to protect the creators of IP from having their work copied, distributed, performed or lent without the consent of the owner. It applies to a wide range of creative outputs, including written works, films, software, paintings, radio and TV broadcasts and sculpture. Copyright comes into effect as soon as the work is created and 'fixed' in some way – on paper, film or as an electronic record on the Internet. The intent behind copyright law is to encourage creativity and authorship by ensuring that creative people receive the financial and other benefits of their work. Most industrial countries have copyright laws, supported by international conventions and agreements. There is a balance – strong property rights create monopolies that can exploit their position, while weak property rights may discourage artistic work and innovation.

### Patents

A **patent** is a set of rights that the state grants to a person for a fixed period of time (20 years in the UK) in exchange for the regulated, public disclosure of certain details of an invention. The right granted is that of preventing anyone else from using or selling the invention. As with copyright, the intention is to encourage creativity by ensuring that inventors of machines and methods receive financial rewards for their skill and inventiveness, while at the same time ensuring that business benefits from using the device in return for a payment to the patent's owner.

### Trademarks

A **trademark** is a badge of origin that distinguishes goods or services – it can be a word, name, logo, colour, shape or sound. Once registered it gives the trademark owner the right to prevent others from using the same or similar marks on similar products.

## ● Technological developments and IP

Before the advent of networked computing, printed material, films, music or computer software had to be stored in a physical form – as paper, computer discs or video, making distribution somewhat difficult. Legal protection was to some extent strengthened by the practical difficulties of breaking the law. Modern IS challenge this protection, as digital media make it much easier to copy and distribute a work, perhaps altering it to disguise its origin:

> *the UK's music and film industries lose around twenty per cent of their annual turnover through pirated CDs and illegal online file sharing.* (Gowers, 2006, p. 3)

Such protection as exists usually applies only to a single state, offering little protection in a global economy.

The number of households in developed countries with computing and broadband connections is increasing very rapidly, and is expected to exceed 12 million in the UK by 2008. Fast digital networks increase the ability of production companies to distribute films, music and games digitally, but at the same time make it easier to copy that information without the permission of the copyright owner – see Figure 3.4.

> *Downloading music and films from the Internet is now the most common legal offence committed by young people aged between 10 and 25 in the UK. Up to 80 per cent of music downloads are not paid for, even though most consumers recognize it to be illegal.* (Gowers 2006, p. 27)

The development of broadband facilitates music sharing and millions of files of copyright material being downloaded every day, of which over 60 per cent are estimated to be music (Zentner, 2006). The most popular albums are available for online sharing almost immediately after release and in some cases even before.

> *Napster (an early and very popular music-sharing website) and its successors were banned in many universities because the very fast connections induced so much file sharing that there was little bandwidth left for anything else. In the case of the University of Illinois at Urbana-Champaign, this amounted to 75 per cent of the total bandwidth.* (Zentner, 2006, p. 65)

Zentner (2006) concluded that file sharing reduced legal sales of music by about 30 per cent. File sharing is not limited to music. The development of fast connections is extending downloading to other digital goods such as movies, software, video games,

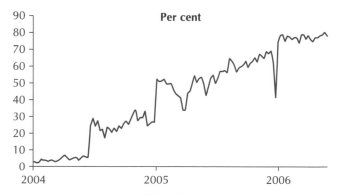

**Figure 3.4** Downloads as a proportion of singles sales in the UK, by week, 2004–2006
*Source*: British Phonographic Industry, quoted in Gowers (2006), p. 28.

and books. Some movies are available online during the opening week of theatrical release and before the authorised DVD is available.

Infringement of copyright is now common, with Gowers (2006) concluding that piracy is now a significant drag on the performance of UK creative industries:

> Total losses to the film industry in 2005 are estimated at £719 million, on industry box office and video sales of £3.5 billion. Enforcement through the civil courts is costly, and cases are difficult to prove. [Enforcement agencies] are all aware of the problem, but it remains one of many competing priorities. (p. 41)

Differences in the professional values of those working in the software industry also help to explain the growth of copyright infringement (see Research Summary feature below).

---

**Research Summary | Contrasting values of software designers**

McGowan et al. (2007) examined the varying attitudes within the IS profession towards copyright laws that are intended to protect software from being copied without paying a fee to the creator. They identified four groups within the profession, with different views about the role of law and ethics in relation to software development.

- **Proprietary Proponents**: believe that software can be protected, and that owners will compete for sales in the market. For competition to be fair, owners must be able to protect their software, or there will be no incentive to develop it.

- **Software Anarchists**: express the view that technology is critical to social progress and it is morally wrong to restrict access to the latest software developments. Use **hacking** tactics to enter and copy software that frequently breach copyright laws.

- **Open Source/Free Software Advocates**: with slight differences in tactics, both groups advocate that software should be designed so that other designers can read, modify and redistribute the underlying code within a piece of software. They believe that this is a more effective way of developing quality software, and having it widely and quickly used.

*Source*: McGowan et al. (2007).

---

## ● Summary

- Most developed countries have sought to encourage innovation by protecting intellectual property.

- Modern IS make unauthorised copying and distribution of IP easy and cheap, and illegal copying of music, software and films is widespread.

- Companies that depend on income from creative products are seeking new ways of countering this threat to their businesses.

---

# 3.6 Ethics, stakeholders and contexts

Many management issues raise ethical dimensions, and the IS area is no exception. Given rapid technological developments that make possible new products and services, and enable people to have much greater information about others, it is inevitable that new issues arise – which are not illegal, but some people believe challenge accepted ethical codes of behaviour.

## ● Ethical issues in IS

Modern systems raise new questions about the rights and obligations of people in relation to data, information and knowledge. Laws to protect data privacy and intellectual property are frequently ignored or deliberately broken. Copying music or software is both easy and often illegal – but many ignore this because, in their view, the law favours large music production companies and hinders free expression. As people consider how best to use IS, they face situations that involve a conflict between the needs of the part and the whole – the individual and the organisation, groups within the organisation or the organisation and society.

- Should a company monitor websites to check if staff are:
  - using company time and resources for private purposes;
  - downloading pornographic or paedophiliac material?
- Should an Internet search engine provide information to government about the sites an individual has visited or their contributions to an Internet discussion group?
- Should a healthcare computer system that contains information about, say, a parent's alcohol problem share that information with a social care system which holds information about his or her children?
- How carefully should companies protect individual data?
- Is it right for companies to send unsolicited messages (**spam**) to mainly vulnerable people inviting them to send money to the advertiser in return for which they will receive large sums of money (that of course never arrive)?

Often the actions illustrated are not illegal – but some believe they are unethical.

## ● Three domains of human action

Figure 3.5 identifies three 'domains' of human action. Some actions fall within the domain of codified law – they are the subject of legislation that can be enforced in the courts. Some nations have laws about data privacy and intellectual property that influence what some people choose to do.

At the other extreme is the domain of free choice – areas not covered by the law in a particular jurisdiction, so that individuals can act as they wish.

In between is the ethical domain, covering activities that laws do not prohibit, but in respect of which some people are constrained by shared principles in their society about

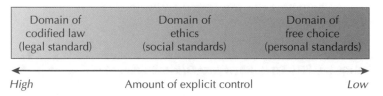

**Figure 3.5** Three domains of human action

*Source*: From Daft, *Management* (5th edition) (2000). Copyright © 2000. Reprinted with permission of South-Western, a division of Thomson Learning.

acceptable behaviour. To them, an ethically acceptable action is one that is legal *and* meets the shared ethical standards of the society. Boddy (2008) discusses alternative ethical codes more fully – see also the Research Summary below.

---

**Research Summary**     **Criteria for justifying an action**

Philosophers have identified principles that people use to justify an action – including moral principles, utilitarianism, human rights.

- **Moral principles:** This approach evaluates whether or not a decision is consistent with an accepted moral principle. Societies develop rules that members generally accept as the way to behave – such as not to steal from each other, and that people have a right to privacy. If an act would breach this principle, it would be unethical.

- **Utilitarianism:** Someone following this approach would consider the effect of an action on overall human well-being, and would see an act as ethical if it produces more pleasure than pain. If it harms some people but benefits more, then it is ethical – and vice versa.

- **Human rights:** This is the idea that people have fundamental rights, such as consent, privacy, free speech or fair treatment. Monitoring employee e-mails could violate the right to privacy, and so be unethical – unless there were good reasons to believe the e-mails were being used to harm others.

*Source*: Boddy (2008), pp. 149–50.

---

**Activity 3.5 Justifying actions**

Choose one of the ethical dilemmas posed earlier in the section.

- Identify three arguments you could use to justify a course of action, each based on one of these ethical reasons.
- Then identify three arguments, each based on one of these ethical reasons, stating why that action would be unethical.
- Compare your answers with another student's.

---

## ● Ethics and stakeholder interests

'Acceptable behaviour' is clearly a highly subjective matter, yet someone managing an IS project needs a practical way of considering ethical issues that arise. One way of doing so is to consider ethics not as an abstract set of ideas, but in relation to the organisation's stakeholders. They have interests, including views about what constitutes ethical behaviour.

Stakeholders are individuals, groups or other organisations with an interest in, or who are affected by, what the enterprise does (Freeman, 1984). Organisations depend on acquiring resources from their environment, which is made up of a network of stakeholders. Managers (whether in the private or public sector) need to ensure that they understand what other stakeholders expect and that they meet those expectations to an acceptable degree or they may withdraw their support:

*Failure to attend to the information and concerns of stakeholders clearly is a kind of flaw in thinking or action that too often and too predictably leads to poor performance, outright failure or even disaster.* (Bryson, 2004, p. 23)

### Stakeholder expectations

Stakeholders typically include customers, shareholders, employees, suppliers and the communities in which the organisation works – and in the present context that could include hackers or members of the Open Software movement. Table 3.3 lists likely stakeholders in an IS, and their possible interests – which would then shape how they see an IS-related decision.

Those responsible for IS projects need to be aware not just of stakeholder interests, but also their relative power. Boonstra and Harison (2008) studied a project to install an electronic patient record system in a region of the Netherlands. All agreed that a common record, containing up-to-date information about a patient from the hospital, GP and chemist, would benefit patient care. However, the proposed system was never implemented, because the hospital that proposed the system had no power over GPs and chemists. Doctors and chemists refused to join the project, even though all agreed it would benefit patients.

Google's experience in opening its search business in China illustrated very clearly the conflicting expectations of some stakeholders: it was very much in the interests of shareholders to expand the business, and many potential customers were keen to use the service. The Chinese government had other views, which required Google to agree to conditions to which others objected – see chapter case Part 4. What this suggests is that ethics cannot usefully be considered in isolation, but within a context.

**Table 3.3** Stakeholders and their expectations in relation to IS ethics

| Stakeholders | Expectations |
| --- | --- |
| Employees | Transparent policies about surveillance and monitoring at work. |
| IT professionals | Policies consistent with their (diverse) ethical views on (e.g.) intellectual property rights. |
| Shareholders | Acceptable return on investment. |
| Suppliers (e.g. to retailers) | Fair use of information about products from electronic point of sales systems. |
| Customers (e.g. of banks) | That companies which hold data about them respect their privacy AND ensure data is secure against fraud or financial loss. |
| Citizens | That public bodies holding data about them respect their privacy AND ensure data is secure against fraud or financial loss. |
| | That others cannot use the Internet for criminal activities. |
| Creative writers, musicians, etc. | Payment, respect for copyright, patents and/or intellectual property rights. |
| Governments | Obey laws and regulations on data security, not using the Internet for illegal purposes. |
| Open source advocates | Software code to be public, so that others can use, modify and distribute the work. |
| Hackers | Being able to gain access to computer files to alter or copy them. |

# Google in China

**www.google.com**

In early 2006 Google received unwelcome publicity in the Western media over the terms on which the company had launched its search engine service in China. To obtain permission to offer the service there, the company had acquiesced to the Chinese government's tough censorship laws, which mean that sites containing politically sensitive terms such as 'Tiananmen Square' or 'political prisoners' cannot be accessed by a search using those terms. The Chinese government's Internet censorship policy raised international concern about freedom of expression and human rights violation, in a country that has traditionally blocked the free flow of information.

Google managers defended their decision by arguing that they have to comply with local law in China, just as they would in any country. One argued that 'in an imperfect world, we had to make an imperfect decision', and recognised that the constraints Google operates under in China are inconsistent with the company's core commitments to user interests and providing access to information (Fry, 2006, p. 137).

*Source*: Fry (2006) and other published sources.

## CASE QUESTIONS 3.3

Which ethical principles appear to have guided (a) the Chinese government; (b) Google management; (c) Western critics of Google?

Would it be possible for Google to have reconciled its commercial interests with its stated ideal of making the world's information accessible to all?

## ● Ethics in context

The ethical choices people make reflect the social context, so understanding why people act the way they do may be helped by using an **ethical decision-making** framework. This examines the influence of both individual characteristics (such as personal value systems) and organisational contexts (such as its structure and distribution of power) on ethical choices. Trevino (1986) sees ethical (or unethical) action as the result of individual and situational components – shown in Figure 3.6.

## ● Summary

- Stakeholders have expectations of an organisation, and assess how an IS project will affect those interests.
- Those managing such projects are most likely to succeed if they take account of stakeholder power and interests.
- Guidelines that people use to justify their actions as ethical include:
  - moral principles – a decision is consistent with generally accepted principles within a society;

89

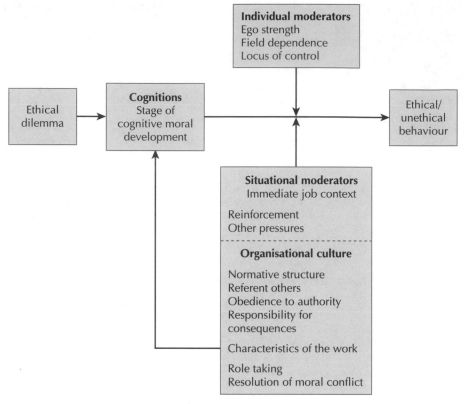

**Figure 3.6 Trevino's model of ethical decision-making**
*Source*: Trevino (1986). Reproduced with permission.

- utilitarianism – a decision that benefits more people than it harms;
- human rights – a decision that enhances or protects a person's human rights.
- Stakeholders' expectations, including those relating to ethical issues, may conflict, and a task for management is to decide which of those interests to take into account, in that context.
- Trevino's ethical decision-making model shows how a person's choice of behaviour is affected not only by personal considerations but also by their beliefs about the social context in which they work (what others do, what is acceptable).

## 3.7 Can ethical behaviour pay?

In deciding how to deal with the political, economic, cultural, legal and ethical dimensions of the context, managers relate them to what they perceive to be the interests of the business. At one extreme, some people and companies take the view that it is profitable to act illegally, and to make money quickly by evading the law – unauthorised copying, software piracy, illegally downloading music or videos. Others act in ways that do not break the law, but others see as unethical – sending junk e-mails offering non-existent prizes in return for money. Others act carelessly or choose not to spend sufficient time or money on data security. Others decide to act ethically.

It is easy to advocate ethical behaviour – but unless this contributes in some way to an organisation's performance, the business may not survive. Competitors who avoid the costs and distractions of ethical behaviour may perform better and satisfy their shareholders more fully. David Vogel suggests that in a competitive economy virtuous behaviour is only sustainable if it brings some competitive benefit to the company – see the Research Summary below.

---

**Research Summary** | **David Vogel on responsibility and strategy**

Vogel (2005) examines the claims for and against the idea that corporations should act responsibly, by analysing the forces driving the corporate responsibility (CR) movement. He concludes that ethical behaviour is only sustainable if 'virtue pays off'. He acknowledges that not every business expenditure or policy needs to directly increase shareholder value, and that many of the benefits of responsible action are difficult to quantify. But ultimately ethical action is both made possible and constrained by market forces.

Market forces encourage and also limit responsible corporate action. Encouraging forces include demand for responsibly made products, consumer boycotts or challenges to a firm's reputation by pressure groups. These lead many firms to accept that they need to be accountable to a broad community of stakeholders. Virtuous behaviour can make business sense for some firms in some areas in some circumstances:

> There is a place in the market economy for responsible firms. But there is also a large place for their less responsible competitors. (p. 3)

While some companies can benefit from acting responsibly, market forces alone cannot prevent others from acting in less responsible ways, and profiting from doing so.

*Source*: Vogel (2005).

---

Vogel's ideas are valuable because they offer some guidance as to how managers can decide between conflicting stakeholder interests, including those that involve ethical issues. Ethical beliefs are part of the context in which people introduce IS, which managers balance alongside other contextual pressures expressed by stakeholders. Ethical behaviour in relation to, say, data privacy or intellectual property is most likely to be sustainable if it contributes to corporate performance, which it may do in one of four ways – enlightened self-interest, corporate mission, negative publicity and corporate strategy.

## ● Enlightened self-interest

Shareholders expect an acceptable financial return and managers may sometimes be able to deliver that by meeting, to some degree, the expectations of other stakeholders. This may have a cost, but can also avoid negative publicity or enhance the company's reputation – it is enlightened self-interest.

*Firms with this perspective will invest in social initiatives because they believe that such investments will result in increased profitability.* (Peloza, 2006)

## ● Corporate mission

Some companies place ethical behaviour at the heart of their business, reflecting the beliefs and values of founders and senior managers. They gain media attention and increase customer loyalty with little advertising. An example is the Co-operative Bank (now known as Co-operative Financial Services), founded as a cooperative enterprise in the 1870s. It launched its present ethical policy in May 1992 and is a prominent example of this approach. Google's mission statement 'don't be evil' is an example from the online world.

## ● Negative publicity

Many companies differentiate themselves less by their products than by the ideas, emotions and images that their brand conveys. Managers who allow their brand to become associated with being indifferent to privacy issues, careless with information or unfair in dealing with copyright issues are risking their reputation. Adopting responsible practices in these areas enables a firm to imbue the brand with positive themes that coincide with the beliefs of many customers. The value of a positive reputation is:

*precisely because (developing one) takes considerable time and depends on a firm making stable and consistent investments.* (Roberts and Dowling, 2002)

## ● Corporate strategy

If customers have concerns about the use of personal information collected during an online transaction, they will be less inclined to use that medium. It makes sense for any business that wants to build an online presence to ensure customers are confident the company will handle data responsibly. Roman (2007) developed and tested an instrument to measure consumers' perceptions regarding the ethics of online retailers, which have a strong influence on repeat buying behaviour – see the Research Summary, right.

Some firms invest in educational projects to improve the social climate in which the firm operates or to ensure long-term supply of staff. In coordinating such a programme, Cisco (a supplier of switching equipment for computer networks) aligns its economic and social goals by ensuring a future supply of well-trained employees.

## ● Summary

- Ethical behaviour is only sustainable if it contributes in some way to organisational performance.
- It can do so in several ways, by developing IS policies that are ethical *and* contribute to:
  - enlightened self-interest;
  - corporate mission;
  - avoiding negative publicity;
  - corporate strategy.

| Research Summary | What factors do consumers value in online retailers? |
|---|---|

Roman (2007) observed that, while online retailing is growing rapidly, so are customers' concerns about the ethics of such retailers. Identifying, and then addressing, these concerns will affect the development of this business method.

Through a process of literature review, in-depth interviews and focus group interviews with online customers, the research team developed a set of measures that appeared likely to shape consumer attitudes to online retailing. These were then refined and tested in two large surveys, through which the researchers confirmed the validity of the measures. These were the following.

- **Security**: the safety of the financial aspects of the transactions, and the protection of credit card data from unauthorised access.

- **Privacy**: individual control over the disclosure and later use by the organisation of personally identifiable information about the consumer – for example about not selling data to other companies for marketing purposes, expressed in a clear and credible privacy policy.

- **Non-deception**: the extent to which the consumer believes the online retailer does not use deceptive practices to persuade consumers to buy things they may not want, making exaggerated claims about a product or offering services (like air tickets) at invitingly low prices, but which it is in practice almost impossible to buy.

- **Fulfilment/reliability**: relating to the accurate display and description of a product so that what consumers receive is what they thought they had ordered, as well as the delivery of the product within the promised time.

The paper concludes that the research has developed a scale to measure consumers' perceptions of the ethics of online retailers (CPEOR) made up of four measurable dimensions – privacy, security, non-deception and fulfilment. The more companies are able to meet consumers' expectations in these areas, the more likely they will buy online.

*Source*: Roman (2007).

# Conclusions

Stakeholders promoting and developing an IS do so within a context that shapes how they design it, the features they value and how they expect people to use it. As people use the system *their* social context will shape their responses – which may or may not be what the system's designers or promoters expected. The outcomes will reflect the system's technical features – which will be much the same for everyone – and the social context in which people use it. The interaction model predicts that, as people in a society come to accept and use a system as part of their normal experience, and in doing so bring about changes in that society, the change becomes embedded as normality.

Stakeholders – people and groups with expectations of the organisation – give expression to the political, economic, cultural and legal dimensions of the context. They have their distinct interests and draw upon evidence and ideas in the social context to add legitimacy to their case – seeking support in political arrangements, relating their concerns to cultural differences or calling for legal redress to solve conflicts of interest. At the same time they will be trying to change or support aspects of the context so that it serves them better – lobbying for more (or less) data privacy, for access to markets (or protection from competition), or for more (or less) protection of intellectual property.

Some stakeholders will try to influence an organisation's ethical policies regarding IS, especially in the areas of data protection and intellectual property. Vogel advises, a company that chooses to act ethically may face severe competitive challenges from those that do not. To be able to operate a sustained ethical policy, the company should aim to ensure that its ethical policies add value to the business in some way, such as by meeting the needs of a particular group of customers or being in some other way consistent with wider strategy.

Throughout the chapter we have stressed the interaction between context and organisation. While the political, cultural and legal contexts clearly affect an organisation's position and policies, managers are not passive – they can themselves aim to change the context in a way that helps their strategy.

## Chapter questions

1. Explain, with new examples, how the political context has affected a company's Internet business, and how companies seek to shape that political context.

2. The cultural context has many dimensions. Which of these are most likely to affect an information system, and how may this vary between countries?

3. Give examples of how IS can threaten individual data privacy.

4. What are the principles underlying the different approaches to data protection in the United States and in Europe?

5. What do you understand by the term 'intellectual property' and why has the Internet made this harder to protect?

6. Give examples from the chapter of specific instances in which stakeholders have affected the outcomes of an IS project.

7. Explain the three ways of justifying a decision as ethical, and give an example to illustrate your explanation.

8. What is the central theme of David Vogel's theory that there is a 'market for virtue'?

9. How can a company ensure that ethical information practices contribute to company performance?

## Further reading

Fishman, K.D. (1982) *The Computer Establishment*, McGraw-Hill Osborne Media, San Francisco, CA. One of the first books to treat computing as a serious business. The author describes a mature industry of mainframe computing that was about to be overwhelmed by the microprocessor revolution – a dramatic change in context.

Two sources with more information about Google – the first an inside story of its growth, the second a European reaction to the GoogleLibrary project:

Vise, D.A. (2005) *The Google Story*, Macmillan, New York.

Jeanneney, J.-N. (2007) *Google and the Myth of Universal Knowledge*, University of Chicago Press, Chicago.

These three empirical studies are useful for their results, and are also good examples of how to conduct research in this area from the initial idea, through developing the research instruments, analysing results and presenting conclusions:

McGowan, M.K., Stephens, P. and Gruber, D. (2007) 'An exploration of the ideologies of software intellectual property: the impact on ethical decision making', *Journal of Business Ethics*, **73**(4), 409–24.

Roman, S. (2007), 'The ethics of online retailing: a scale development and validation from the consumer's perspective', *Journal of Business Ethics*, **72**(2), 131–48.

Schwaig, K.S., Kane, G.C. and Storey, V.C. (2006), 'Compliance to the fair information practices: how are the Fortune 500 handling online privacy disclosures?', *Information & Management*, **43**(7), 805–20.

# PART 2

# Strategy

This part deals with issues of strategy and process redesign. Chapter 4 examines the interaction between strategy and information systems using established models of the strategy development process. The chapter also considers the concept of strategic alignment, and the possible impact of inter-organisational information systems on organisational strategies. It concludes with an analysis of some of the practical complexities of forming an information system strategy.

The focus of Chapter 5 is on how companies have used computer-based systems to modify their business processes. Established functional boundaries often add cost and delay to the task of delivering products and services. Modern systems make it possible for people to break down these boundaries by passing information electronically to those who need it, irrespective of their location or affiliation. However, the task is complex and depends on a good understanding of different approaches to business process redesign and being aware of organisational interactions.

# CHAPTER 4

## Using information systems to reinvent strategy

### Learning objectives

By the end of your work on this topic you should be able to:

- Describe and explain the possible strategic role of information systems

- Explain in what different ways an IS strategy can be developed

- Analyse how information systems can affect an industry and relate this to company strategy

- Explain different ways of using the Internet for strategic advantage, and assess the implications

- Outline how IS can play different roles and analyse the possible strategic advantage of IS to a business

- Explain the risks of using IS strategically

- Evaluate the options in deciding how to position e-business within an existing firm

# E-business strategies at Intel

## www.intel.com

Intel is the world's largest producer of integrated circuit chips. Incorporated in 1968, Intel supplies the computing and communications industries with chips, boards and systems building blocks that are integral to computers, servers, and networking and communications products. Its products are offered at various levels of integration, and are used by industry members to create advanced computing and communications systems.

The company has evolved from a basic component maker into a supplier of network and server hardware, Internet hosting services, and other e-business services. Its technological leadership ranges from microprocessor design to advanced manufacturing and packaging. In the mid-1990s key customers such as Dell and Cisco introduced e-procurement systems, and persuaded Intel to use this online method of doing business. Intel began to investigate the feasibility of building an e-business system of its own. Under the mandate from the chairman to make Intel an 'Internet company', Sandra Morris, Vice President of Sales and Marketing Group, and Director of Internet Marketing and E-Commerce stated: 'a lot of people feel overwhelmed by "The Task."'

With over 50 per cent of its revenues and many customers coming from outside the US, the benefits of a global e-business system for Intel were too great to be ignored. To support over US$25 billion annual sales and a worldwide network of business partners, resellers, and original equipment manufacturers Intel had to improve its efficiency by automating its business processes. These were too slow, so management decided to deploy a web-based order management system.

Intel's early mission was to use Internet technology to improve the competitive advantage of its value chain activities. The goals were to design and deploy a worldwide e-business solution for its current business, and build an infrastructure that worked with existing business processes. The intention was to integrate Internet technology into the company's overall strategy in order to gain competitive advantage in both operational effectiveness and strategic positioning.

Rather than change the entire business structure, Intel project teams used an iteration approach in building the first e-business system. They first focused on building an extranet B2B system to support direct customers online: 'We picked one thing that we could build very quickly and deploy to our customers.'

*Source*: Phan (2003).

## Introduction

Intel shows how the company uses e-business and IS to strengthen its strategic position by improving competitiveness and responsiveness to external changes. Intel sought to be innovative in technology and design in a way that clearly differentiated the company from its competitors.

Changes in the external environment in which Intel operates, especially its customers, suppliers, and in the technologies available, opened up the possibility of a new strategy. They suggested a new strategy, and would in turn support that strategy. This chapter addresses this relation between strategy and IS.

Developments in technology and competition mean that managers no longer buy IS only for background administrative support. That role remains important, but many managers also consider IS as part of their broader strategy. Tesco (Chapter 1) saw the possibilities that IS offered to build close relations with its customers, and Clubcard has become a strategic advantage to the company. Management at Google (Chapter 3) realised that social networking sites could complement the search business, so made the strategic decision to buy MySpace. The UK National Health Service saw the possibilities of using IS to improve patient care and administrative efficiency, so launched a strategic IS initiative, the National Programme for Information Technology (Chapter 6).

The significance of this for organisations and their management is that in seeing IS in this way, managers look beyond technological issues. They consider what the computer-based systems becoming available will mean for the organisation and its customers. They focus not on technical features, but on what matters to customers. They look beyond short-term matters to longer-term questions such as whether they can use IS to:

- improve quality for customers;
- reduce costs and work more efficiently;
- differentiate products or services;
- offer new or better products or services;
- lock in suppliers or buyers;
- raise barriers to market entrants;
- improve employee satisfaction.

Considering these strategic questions helps managers to avoid being driven by fashion. The technical possibilities are unlimited, and without a clear sense of strategy managers are tempted to demand the newest technology. A sense of strategic direction provides a coherent context within which to discuss technology choices.

The chapter begins with the strategy development process, and shows how managers have used IS to change the way they compete. We then examine the strategic alignment concept – the case for seeking a fit between the nature of a company and its IS. That leads to an analysis of the way companies can use the Internet to support or change their strategy. Finally, the chapter considers the practicalities of formulating an information strategy. The overall aim is to help the reader conduct a coherent analysis of the role of IS in strategy.

## 4.1 Issues in developing an IS strategy

### ● Planned or emergent IS strategies?

One theory is that managers develop strategy consciously, and that they follow a consciously **planned IS strategy**. An alternative view is that strategies only partially reflect stated intentions. Some strategies that managers intend are not implemented: the unrealised strategies. Other strategies are realised – but were unintended and followed from the cumulative effect of successive day-to-day decisions. So realised strategies combine formal plans and unplanned events (Mintzberg et al., 2003; Spil, 2003), as shown in Figure 4.1.

**Emergent strategy** expresses the idea that people have a broad long-term vision, and take only small steps towards it. They leave space to react to uncertainty, to experiment, and for participation. Since developing IS strategy is an uncertain process the emergent strategy style will often be more realistic and satisfactory than the planning style. This is

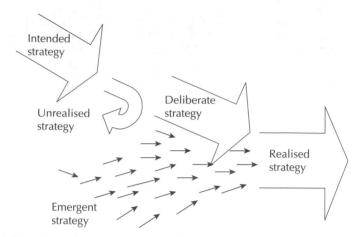

**Figure 4.1 Deliberate and emergent strategies**
*Source*: Mintzberg et al. (2003). Reproduced with permission.

especially true in relation to online business where both technology and competition change so rapidly – Google has a long-term vision, but moves towards that not by detailed planning, but by responding quickly to new opportunities, such as the decision to acquire YouTube. Equally, some aspects of Google's strategy, such as building new software development facilities around the world, require detailed planning. Realised strategy combines both planned and emergent actions.

Decisions in relation to information systems and information strategies also have emergent characteristics. Research by Boonstra (2003) indicated five issues affecting how managers make IS decisions:

● whether or not there is scope to *design* a solution;

● whether distinct alternatives have to be *searched* for or not;

● the *urgency* and *necessity* of the decision;

● whether or not it can be *subdivided* to allow a more gradual process (planned versus incremental); and

● the number and power of *stakeholders* involved.

Depending on these factors, IS-related decisions can be straightforward and planned or messy, complicated and time-consuming.

## ● IS and strategy interrelated

We use terms like 'strategy', 'strategic advantage' or 'the strategic use of IS' to describe the broad choices facing companies concerning which products to offer and which markets to target. These decisions are fundamental for their success. Competitive advantage is what a company seeks to gain from the way it positions a product or service in relation to competitors. This may emphasise, for example,

● the needs of specific customers (a niche market);

● a wide distribution network;

● a unique product in terms of price (cost leadership) or quality (differentiation).

| Competitive scope | | Competitive advantage | |
| --- | --- | --- | --- |
| | | *Lower cost* | *Differentiation* |
| | *Broad target* | COST LEADERSHIP | DIFFERENTIATION |
| | *Narrow target* | COST FOCUS | DIFFERENTIATION FOCUS |

**Figure 4.2 Generic strategies**

*Source*: Porter (1985). Reprinted with permission.

Computer-based IS can contribute to an organisation's strategy, in the same way as any other capability – human resources, finance or marketing. They are all resources that managers can incorporate into their strategic planning.

Developments in information and communications technologies have introduced a new dimension to the strategy development process. We illustrate this with Porter's well-known model, shown in Figure 4.2 (Porter, 1985; Porter and Millar, 1985; Porter, 2001). Companies can use IS to achieve a **cost leadership** strategy by using, for example,

- computer-aided manufacturing to replace manual labour;
- stock control systems to cut expensive inventory; or
- online order entry to cut order processing costs.

They can support a **differentiation** strategy by using:

- computer-aided manufacturing to offer flexible delivery;
- stock control systems to extend the range of goods on offer at any time;

They can support a **focus strategy** by using:

- computer-aided manufacturing to meet unique, non-standard requirements;
- online ordering to allow customers to create a unique product by selecting its features.

Treacy and Wiersema (1998) suggest another way to relate business strategies to IS by distinguishing three generic strategies.

- **Operational excellence**: competitive advantage lies in reliable and fluent operational processes. Effective process design and a small number of product variations are important. Organisations that follow an operational excellence strategy do not focus on developing innovative products or customer communication, but on effective, reliable and cost-controlled business processes. Examples are McDonald's and easyJet.

- **Product leadership**: competitive advantage lies in focusing on product improvement and product innovation. Product leaders try to offer the best product in their class and use new technologies to improve them. Prominent examples include Google and Apple or, in the wider economy, Mercedes and Porsche.

- **Customer intimacy**: competitive advantage lies in focusing on customers and providing a unique service for each one. The focus is on identifying and understanding customers' needs and creating an organisation that meets their expectations. Examples are Zara (Chapter 5), Fedex (see MIS in Practice overleaf) and consultants such as Ernst & Young and McKinsey.

> ### MIS in Practice   Fedex
>
> Fedex is a leader in the global transportation sector and provider of services such as express delivery, small parcel delivery, less-than-truckload delivery. FedEx spends a major part of its revenues on IS to facilitate its business processes such as operations, customer service, employee training and feedback from customers. It also integrates its internal systems with those of its clients to provide them with seamless logistic and supply chain solutions. Tracking services enable customers to know precisely where their package is at any given minute and when it will be delivered.

The Treacy and Wiersema framework is different from, but related to, Porter's model. Operational excellence is close to cost leadership, and product leadership and customer intimacy are different forms of differentiation. The main idea is that companies can use IS to strengthen or adapt their competitive advantage – indeed it is one of the main reasons why managers invest in such systems.

What is the direction of the link between strategy and information systems? One possibility is that managers shape the strategy of the firm and then ensure that their investments in information systems support that strategy. Figure 4.3 shows this.

This is a 'strategic choice' model. The information system is the dependent variable. An example of this would be when supermarkets use barcode systems to enter transaction data quickly and accurately. This supports their strategic objective of reducing costs and improving quality.

An alternative model is that information systems can themselves offer a firm new strategic possibilities. Figure 4.4 shows this possibility. This is a 'technological determinist' model (Grant et al., 2006). Strategy is now the dependent variable. An example would be when a small firm uses the Internet to sell goods or services to consumers directly all over the world. That would not be possible for such a firm if the enabling technology (the Internet) did not exist.

A third possibility is that the two affect each other – what we call the *interaction model*. That is when companies have a strategy and look for ways in which they can use IS to support that strategy. In doing so they develop their ability to manage IS, and can then use that expertise to reach a new set of customers. That has changed their context, and is the starting point for a new strategy. Figure 4.5 shows this position.

**Figure 4.3** General strategy determines the IS strategy

**Figure 4.4** IS opportunities open up new possibilities for the general business strategy

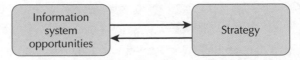

**Figure 4.5 Information systems and strategies affect each other: the interaction model**

The MIS in Practice feature, about the Dutch flower auction business below, illustrates this interaction. External developments affect the strategy and the IS in use, which in turn require changes in the supply chain and the external environment.

---

### MIS in Practice — Aalsmeer Flower Auction

Aalsmeer Flower Auction in the Netherlands offers global growers, wholesalers and exporters a central marketplace in which to trade flowers and plants. It gives them access to a range of marketing channels and financial information, storage and logistics facilities. Within the floricultural value chain, growers are the initial suppliers. Demand comes from exporters, importers, wholesalers, cash and carry stores, and retailers. Within this chain, auctions play a mediating role – they bring together suppliers and buyers and so determine prices. Sometimes these are world prices, since many parties throughout the world use them as price indicators. Another role is to increase efficiency by breaking large consignments from growers into smaller amounts for buyers.

This chain was originally dominated by growers who were able to sell what they produced in a steadily growing market. The auction was able to determine how to conduct business, and took a fairly passive role. Three developments threatened that comfortable position.

1. The emergence of alternative, electronically driven flower markets.
2. The auction met the needs of growers, not those of retailers. To satisfy changing consumer tastes the retailers asked for fresher products, more varieties, smaller quantities and multiple deliveries each week. They felt that demand should have more influence on supply.
3. Mergers and acquisitions among retailers increased their size and power. At the same time growers became more professional, which led to a more formal way of doing business and interest in new, perhaps electronic, ways of selling.

The board of the Aalsmeer Flower Auction felt that they had to react to these changes if the business was to survive. This included the possibility of using electronic networks to support its business processes and to connect with suppliers and buyers. The initial objectives of these e-business activities were to enable innovation, redefine the value chain, reduce transaction costs, strengthen the link with wholesalers and retailers, and to increase market share. The board set up a team to develop an e-business system as part of their survival strategy.

*Source*: Boonstra and van Dantzig (2005).

---

Activity 4.1 relates these ideas to the Aalsmeer case.

By relating strategic priorities and possible IS applications, management can make more informed decisions.

---

### Acitivity 4.1  Aalsmeer Flower Auction

- What are the major strengths and the main competitive advantage of the Aalsmeer Flower Auction?
- What were the strategic reasons for Aalsmeer's e-business initiatives? Relate these reasons to the Porter (1985) or Treacy and Wiersema (1998) models.
- Are the e-business initiatives (as described throughout this chapter) aligned with current strategies or do they imply changing those strategies?
- What threats may the e-business activities hold for Aalsmeer?

---

Figure 4.6 shows how companies in different industries use IS to develop their strategies. The horizontal axis shows the balance between an internal (product) and an external (market) focus. The vertical axis shows the potential competitive benefit. Those applications with the greater competitive potential are usually more expensive – so the risk is greater. The figure summarises how different IS applications relate to strategic considerations.

Early applications tended to be internally focused and of limited competitive advantage. More recently the emphasis has switched to:

- **market-centred applications**, through which companies use information systems to improve customer benefits; and

- **inter-organisational systems** that transcend organisational boundaries and connect firms electronically with suppliers, customers and other business partners.

---

**CHAPTER CASE: PART 2**

# E-business strategies for the value chain

**www.intel.com**

Intel aimed to gain competitive advantage by both operational efficiency and strategic positioning.

To improve operational efficiency, Intel helped its customers to connect to the World Wide Web to access information online. To do this the company automated its order management and information delivery system. The greatest efficiency improvement was to customers who were not already electronically connected to Intel. By providing online information Intel allowed customers to know more about Intel products and plans. Online access meant they could use more Intel resources, and so develop a closer business relationship. Electronic links to customers brought three benefits:

- more efficient use of resources;

- sales people no longer needed to deliver confidential product information by hand;

- the possibility of large increases in sales to new customers.

The strategic position was already strong, as the company had unique R&D programmes and good supply chain relationships. To further strengthen this position, Intel focused on building online relationships with large customers, including equipment manufacturers and distributors. It converted its IS from a producer-centred model to a customer-centred one. For example, the various functions within suppliers and customers all had different information needs, so Intel customised its websites to suit each customer.

Being able to deliver personalised information online allowed Intel to support the customer's staff in ways that best met the individual's needs. This makes it easier for every customer to do his/her own research and to take appropriate action. Customers visiting the Intel extranet website now find their name and specific applications available to them, based on their personal profile. This user profile allows a customer to obtain confidential information important to him or her alone.

*Source*: Phan (2003).

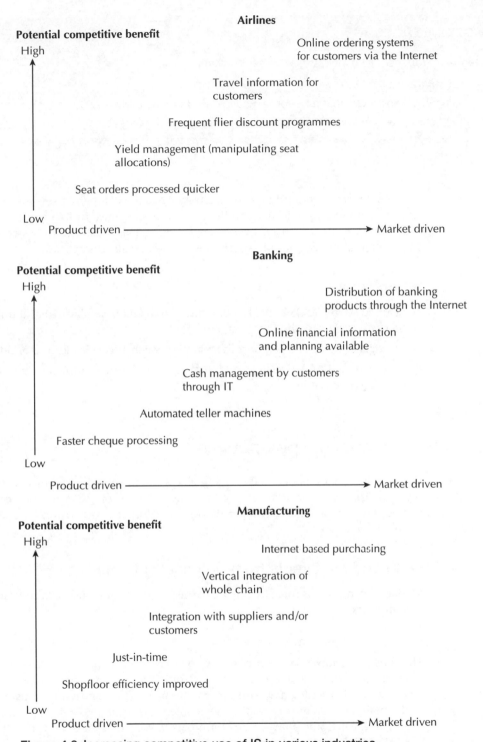

**Figure 4.6** Increasing competitive use of IS in various industries

---

**CASE QUESTIONS 4.1**

In terms of Porter's (1985) model, answer the following questions.

● What strategy is Intel following?
● What implications might that have for managing its information systems?
● Who should take part in developing and implementing the strategy?

---

The later stage of the Intel case illustrates that the company uses its e-business initiatives to combine operational excellence (1) and customer intimacy (2) as well as close relations with other partners in the supply chain. This illustrates how strategic positioning is often a refined combination of two or more value disciplines.

## ● Summary

● Realised strategies (IS as well as organisational) combine planned and unintended elements – often described as emergent.
● Managers can use IS to support their strategy (such as cost leadership or differentiation).
● The relationship between IS and strategy may be deterministic, strategic choice or interactive in nature.

## 4.2 IS from a strategic perspective

Porter's Five Forces model enables us to assess the possible impact of IS on competitiveness, as firms can use it to strengthen one or more of these forces (see Figure 4.7). Conversely it represents a competitive threat if other organisations use IS more effectively in these ways.

### ● IS and the threats from potential entrants

Managers can use this force by raising barriers to entry or by using IS themselves to enter new markets.

#### Using IS to raise entry barriers

The Aalsmeer Flower Auction is trying to strengthen its position by linking customers electronically with the auction. This electronic link makes it easier for customers to do business and harder for new entrants to compete, so strengthening Aalsmeer's position as the main auction in this field. Large retailers use computer-based systems such as bar-coding and electronic point-of-sale terminals to control their inventories. These systems are linked with those of their suppliers. Since it is mainly the larger retail chains that can afford such systems, this gives them a strong negotiating position in relation to their suppliers. Smaller companies or potential entrants are deterred by the relatively high cost of building these links.

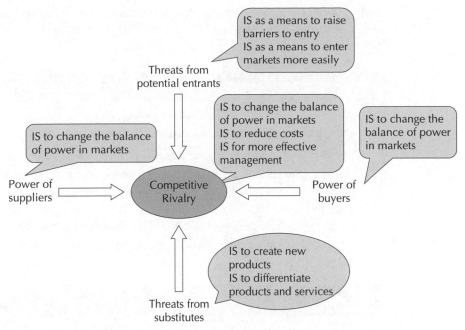

**Figure 4.7 IS can change the competition: Porter's model**
*Source*: Porter (2001). Reprinted with permission.

Many car manufacturers have information systems linked to importers and dealers. When a customer buys a car, the dealer can immediately enter the specifications into the system. This enables the dealer to access a great deal of information from the manufacturer, such as delivery time and available options, and pass it to the customer.

It is very hard for new entrants to overcome these entry barriers, leading to a 'winner takes all' situation in many sectors of the market.

## Using IS to enter new markets

IS enables companies to enter markets that were not previously accessible. By setting up Internet portals, relatively small companies can set up distribution channels that reach customers across the world, and so compete with local retailers. It is easy for businesses to use the Internet to enter a market. Fewer physical facilities are needed and all energy can be spent on web presence and other directly business-related activities. Some Internet-based businesses, such as search engines and electronic auctions, are creating completely new markets: Yahoo!, eBay and Facebook grew very rapidly as their founders were amongst the first to see the potential of the Internet as a way of putting their business idea into practice. Others enter established markets and challenge existing businesses – such as when broadcasters like the BBC offer online news services, which compete with print newspapers.

GoCargo (www.gocargo.com) is an exchange for the container shipping industry, which is expanding from a relatively small spot market to a far larger contract market and learning just how complex that is. Eyal Goldwerger, founder of GoCargo, quickly saw that old-style service contracts were not about to disappear. So he built a staff, based in New York, of 60 multilingual industry specialists and traders who could codify terms, certify shippers and carriers, and otherwise make this handshake business safe for Internet trading. As GoCargo got better at this, it started to turn into a real business. GoCargo is an example of an Internet-based newcomer that challenged the established 'handshake' business.

---

### Activity 4.2  Market change through information systems

Choose one of the markets mentioned above (music, news, books, information, finance, travel, cars, auctions, software and houses).

- Name one important traditional supplier of these services.
- Name one important online supplier of these services.
- How do you think that online suppliers have affected the market of the traditional supplier?
- How do you think that the traditional supplier responded to these changes?
- How do you expect this market to develop over (say) the next two years?

---

### MIS in Practice   Caterpillar Tractors

Caterpillar Tractors claims to use an IS to support its maintenance function and its market position.

A part on a Caterpillar machine operating at a copper mine in Chile begins to deteriorate. A district centre that continuously monitors the health of Caterpillar machines in its area by remotely reading the sensors on each machine spots the problem. It sends an electronic alert direct to the portable computer of the local dealer's field technician. The message specifies the identity and location of the machine, and includes the data that sparked the alert and its diagnosis. The technician validates the diagnosis and determines the service or repair required and which parts and tools are needed. Then the technician logs into Caterpillar's IS, which links dealers, parts distribution facilities, suppliers' factories and large customers' inventory systems, to determine the best sources of the parts and the time when each could deliver them.

The technician sends an electronic proposal to the customer, who responds with the best time to make the repair. The technician then orders the parts electronically from the most suitable source, where the message triggers the printing of an order ticket and sets in motion an automated crane to take the parts from storage and begin their journey to the dealer.

The repair completed, the technician closes the work order, prints out an invoice, collects by credit card and electronically updates the machine's history. That information is added to Caterpillar's databases, which helps the company spot any common problems that a particular model might have and thereby continually improve its machines' designs.

*Source*: Information supplied by the company.

---

### ● IS and the threat of substitutes

Companies can use IS to alter this force by differentiating their products or by creating new ones with which they can threaten competitors. An example is the market for news and information. Many people use the Internet as a primary or an additional source. In certain areas, such as for information about finance and sport, but also for advertisements for houses, job vacancies and second-hand cars, websites and Internet newspapers have become a substitute for television and paper-based newspapers.

Certain products or services are easier to substitute than others. When products or services are:

● digitisable (e.g. software, music, news, information, but not bricks, cars);

● standardisable (e.g. insurance, cars, commodity goods, but not works of art);

● portable (e.g. information, but not amusement parks); or

● low touch (e.g. books, music, but not shoes, vegetables);

they are often easy to substitute with Internet-based suppliers. Figure 4.8 shows that suitability can also be related to three dimensions: product, process and player. Each dimension can be physical or digital, which leads to different models for using electronic channels.

Figure 4.9 illustrates the model with examples of the digital options.

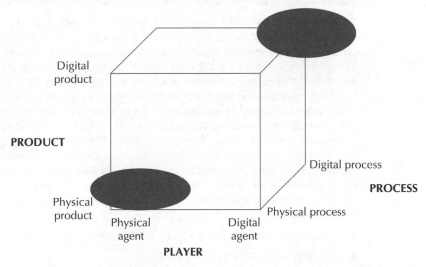

**Figure 4.8 Products, processes and players can be physical or digital or both**

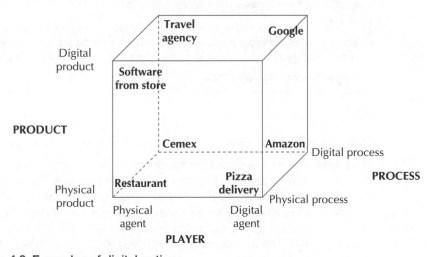

**Figure 4.9 Examples of digital options**

111

## Using IS to differentiate products and services

The Caterpillar case shows the company using the IS mainly to improve the speed and quality of customer service. When the system notes a deterioration the service starts immediately and the expensive machine will be repaired soon, saving the customer money. Other companies use the Internet to create and orchestrate active customer communities. Examples include Kraft (www.kraftfoods.com/kf), Intel (www.intel.com), Apple (www.apple.com) and Harley-Davidson (www.harley-davidson.com). Through these communities the companies hope to become close to their customers so that they can make product or service improvements that meet their needs. The Research Summary box below explains why it is essential for information providers to differentiate their products.

| Research Summary | Versioning information |
| --- | --- |

Shapiro and Varian (2004) suggest that selling information to a broad and diverse set of customers is one of the new products that information systems can provide. CD phone books and travel information are examples. What makes information goods tricky is their 'dangerous economics'. Producing the first copy of an information product is often very expensive, though subsequent copies are very cheap: the fixed costs are high and the marginal costs are low. Because competition tends to drive prices to the level of marginal costs, information goods can easily turn into low-priced commodities. This often makes it impossible for companies to recoup their investments, leading to failure.

To avoid that fate, the authors recommend that companies create different versions of the same information by tailoring it to the needs of different customers. Such a 'versioning' strategy can enable a company to distinguish its products from those of the competition and protect its prices. It is a form of mass customisation with higher value for customers and producers of information. They suggest that information can be differentiated by:

- restricting the time or place at which a customer can access information;
- offering more or less depth of detail;
- offering the ability to store, duplicate or print information; or
- offering more or less actual information.

The power of versioning is that it enables managers to apply established product management techniques in a way that takes into account both the unusual economics of information production and the endless malleability of digital data.

*Source*: Shapiro and Varian (2004).

## Using IS to create new products and services

Telephone and Internet banking are relatively new phenomena that have only become possible with new systems. The same is true of companies that use the power of database technology to offer new services in CRM and direct marketing. Wide Internet access has generated a huge increase in businesses offering new services. These include electronic auctions, search engines, electronic retailers, electronic hubs (Li, 2007; Martinelli and Gianluca, 2007; Son and Benbasat, 2007) and Internet providers. Caterpillar created new maintenance services.

## ● IS and the bargaining power of suppliers

### Increasing power of suppliers

Suppliers can increase their power by using IS to track more closely the costs of providing services to customers. They can set prices accordingly or decide that they do not want a particular piece of business. Airlines use yield management systems to track actual reservations against traffic forecasts for each flight, and then adjust prices for the remaining seats to maximise revenue. AKZO-Nobel, a large manufacturer of coatings, uses Internet-based systems in many of its B2B operations to manage orders from distributors. This allows it to manage internal processes more efficiently, and also to assess much more accurately the value of each order and the overall performance of its distributors. It can then be more selective about which distributors it supplies. CRM systems enable companies to track customers' requirements accurately, which may increase the suppliers' power (see Chapter 2 for more on CRM).

### Decreasing power of suppliers

Customers can also use IS to strengthen their power at the expense of their suppliers. Major motor manufacturers set up 'Covisint' (www.covisint.com) as an online marketplace. The objective was to offer these auto manufacturers a collaborative product development, procurement and supply chain tool that could substantially reduce costs and bring efficiencies to their business operations.

Suppliers to the industry are in one of three tiers. Level 3 suppliers make a simple component and pass it to a Level 2 supplier who combines it with others into a larger component. That goes to a Level 1 supplier who completes and delivers the full assembly. Traditionally the car makers dealt with the Level 1 supplier, who then passed the order down. These Level 1 suppliers were in a powerful position with respect to the car manufacturers as well as the Level 2 and Level 3 suppliers. Covinsint opened the component market to more suppliers and reduced the power of Level 1 suppliers.

Covisint has since developed into an organisation that serves more than 45,000 organisations by providing a common platform for exchanging information. It streamlines business processes in a wide range of industries including manufacturing, healthcare, the public sector and financial services. It also illustrates how inter-organisational systems can increase cooperation as well as competition between business partners, whether suppliers or customers.

## ● Increasing power of buyers

A good example of the increasing power of buyers is when retail chains use modern communication technologies to make electronic links with their suppliers. Such systems reduce inventory costs and warehouse expenses and improve fulfilment time and information flows. The retailer's computer continually monitors its suppliers' finished goods inventories, factory scheduling and commitments against its schedule. The purpose is to ensure the stores always have adequate stocks. A supplier who is unwilling to join the system is likely to lose business. The MIS in Practice box overleaf shows how Wal-Mart used this.

More generally, buyers can use the web to access more suppliers and to compare prices for standard commodities much more widely than was practical with earlier technologies.

## MIS in Practice     Wal-Mart

Wal-Mart use **radio-frequency identification (RFID)** technology to automate the process of tracking merchandise through the supply chain. RFID technology involves attaching tiny RFID chips to merchandise, which can then be scanned to find information about the product. Wal-Mart is rapidly extending the system to more stores, requiring that suppliers attach RFID tags to all crates. Crates are scanned as they leave the factory and tracked as they enter and leave trucks and warehouses. Each time they are scanned, this updates the record in Wal-Mart's database. Wal-Mart staff scan these to determine, for example, what it contains, how long it has been in transit and the expiry date.

Amongst the benefits Wal-Mart obtains is that items using RFID tags that are marked as out of stock are replenished three times faster than items from companies not using RFID tags. The amount of out of stock times that have to be manually filled has been cut by 10 per cent. The company is now experimenting with new applications of RFID, for instance in determining the order for unloading crates from trucks.

Tracking crates through the supply chain provides managers with valuable sales information. Wal-Mart can examine the sales of a given time, store by store, and determine whether a product did not sell well because it wasn't on the floor on the best day of the week or timed with an advertising campaign.

Senior management believes RFID technology is benefiting the company's supply chain operations, including a 30 per cent reduction in out-of-stock rates, and planned to extend the system to all their stores.

*Sources*: Heinrich (2005); Songini (2006); and Stair and Reynolds (2008).

## Activity 4.3  Research on IS strategy

Choose a major and important information system from a company you know and interview a manager about that system. Try to identify:

- the initial (strategic) objectives in acquiring and using that system;
- whether the system meets or exceeds the expectations in relation to those objectives;
- whether the system aligned with the strategy or also impacted and changed the strategy.

Use the Porter model and the value disciplines of Treacy and Wiersema to determine the degree of fit of the system with the strategy.

## ● IS and competitive rivalry

Two ways of using IS to strengthen competitive rivalry are by reducing costs and more effective management.

### Using IS to reduce costs

Online inventory systems and e-procurement enable radical changes in manufacturing supply systems. This greatly reduces inventory levels and the costs associated with them. Car manufacturers are only invoiced for components when the completed assembly leaves the factory. When the system knows that a specified number of headlamps have been used, it passes the information to the component supplier. The supplier sends an (electronic) invoice for the components used, and delivers replacements. These inter-organisational systems reduce the costs of inventory and working capital.

The Internet enables large companies to transfer their purchasing operations to the web. Secure websites connect suppliers, business partners and customers all over the world. This makes it easier for new suppliers to bid for a share of the available business, makes costs more transparent and improves the administrative efficiency of the supply process.

| MIS in Practice | Dell innovates with a new business model ww.dell.com |
|---|---|

Dell, which was the first PC manufacturer to use the Internet to take customer orders, is one example. Competitors have long imitated the practice, but Dell, first to gain the Internet audience, gained more experience than other PC manufacturers on the e-commerce vehicle and still sells more computers via the web than its competitors (Oz, 2006, p. 48). Figure 4.10 shows how Dell developed a new business model and integrated this in all its internal processes.

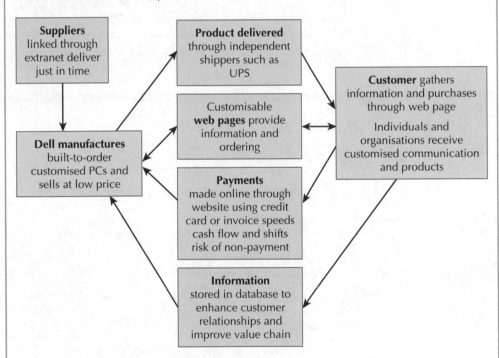

**Figure 4.10 Dell's business model**
*Source*: Bidgoli (2004). Reprinted with permission.

From the start, Dell used a direct sales business model that bypassed traditional sale channels. At the end of the 1990s it transformed its telephone direct sales business model to an e-commerce model. This model utilises various technologies to lower costs, increase efficiencies and enhance customer relationships. The inbound logistical system requires suppliers to use extranets to link to Dell. To speed delivery Dell demands that its suppliers locate inventory within 15 minutes of the Dell factory. Dell minimises its finished products inventory and is therefore able to use the latest products and take advantage of dropping inventory costs.

*Source*: Bidgoli (2004).

## Using IS to enable more effective management

A travel agent's branch accounting system provides detailed patterns of business to managers, enabling them to monitor trends more closely and to take better-informed pricing and promotional decisions. Ahold, a Dutch retailer, greatly improved performance in the supply chain by using IS to manage its customer database. Management information systems can expand the span of control of individual managers, which can support the flattening of organisations.

These examples show that IS may become opportunities for creating, supporting or changing generic strategies. On the other hand, competitors have similar opportunities, and there are costs and risks associated with using IS in this way.

### Activity 4.4  Online newspapers?

Many publishers of news and information papers use IS to collect, process and distribute information. Gather information about this trend, and then do the following.

● Use Porter's model (Figure 4.7) to analyse how this development influences the competitive environment for traditional publishers of newspapers.

● What opportunities and threats arise from this development?

# Intel's e-business deployment

## www.intel.com

Intel's initial e-business pilot consisted of 240 one-stop shopping sites for customers around the world. Using an iterative development approach to build the system, Intel's e-business website was serving more than 350 top customer accounts and thousands of individual users within the first year. Personalised data and applications were tailored to users' needs to provide an individualised experience.

The system enabled Intel's largest customers in almost 30 countries to place orders for Intel products, check product availability and inventory status, receive marketing and sales information, and obtain customer support at all times. Major successes included the following.

● Moving US$1billion in revenue online in the first 15 days, surpassing the goal of doing so in 3 months.

● Almost eliminating the use of faxes, which produced significant cost savings for Intel and its suppliers.

● After the first month of deployment, Intel continued to receive US$ 1 billion value of orders online each month.

Independent customer surveys rated Intel's e-business at a 94 per cent satisfaction level.

Intel employees who helped develop the system found it helped their promotion prospects. The most significant payoff from deploying the e-business system was what the company learned. Key success factors ranked by importance are as follows.

● *Building and continuing to strengthen their distinctive strategic position in the market*: the system complemented and enhanced the delivery of Intel's distinctive strategy, so that buyers continued to be willing to pay a high price for its products.

● *Support from top management*: the e-business development teams received necessary resources and cooperation to build the system.

● *Providing worldwide support and customer training*: to promote e-business cooperation across the supply chain, the company developed an online case study to educate customer staff, and developed online training to reduce the number of support calls. Intel engineers also provided basic training to customers in many parts of the world.

*Source*: Phan (2003).

## ● Summary

- From a strategic point of view IS brings important business opportunities, such as raising barriers to newcomers, ability to enter markets, changing the power balance in a beneficial way, developing new products or services in order to differentiate, reducing costs and implementing a more effective management style.

- IS can also be a threat for the same reasons as mentioned above – competitors can always do the same.

---

### CASE QUESTIONS 4.2

Use the frameworks proposed by Porter and by Treacy and Wiersma to analyse Intel's IS and e-business strategy.

- What kind of partners does Intel need to realise its strategy?
- How does Intel use e-business to create value for its customers?
- What project management lessons can be learned from this chapter case?

---

## 4.3 Aligning IS with corporate strategy

As information systems have become more central to strategic development, it becomes essential for managers to consider the **alignment**, or degree of fit, between IS and strategy. Questions to consider include why alignment is important, the value of the contingency approach to alignment and the contribution of the interaction approach.

### ● The case for alignment

Many writers have suggested that information systems need to 'fit' the organisation or unit in which they are used. Kearns and Sabherwal (2007) proposed that managers should aim for a good fit between current information systems and customers, IS strategy and the organisation. They advise managers to ensure that:

- strategy is driven by customer needs and expectations;
- processes selected for redesign by IS create value for the customer; and
- IS supports those processes in a way that supports the strategy.

These ideas are illustrated in the Chapter Case study of Intel, where customer-driven strategy, process orientation and information systems are aligned into an effective e-business strategy.

This is the central idea of 'strategic alignment': the search for the right fit between these variables. Figure 4.11 shows this. The business domain influences the IS domain and vice versa. The plan influences current practices and current practices influence the plan.

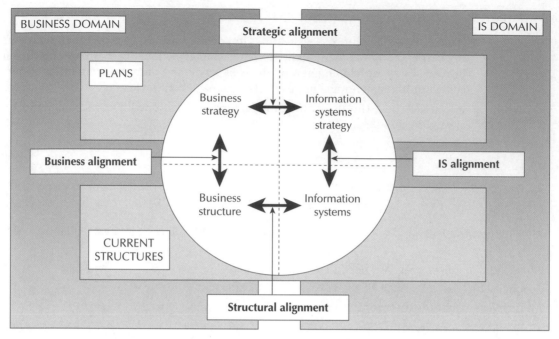

**Figure 4.11 Alignment between IS and organisation, in plans and in operations**
*Source*: Sabherwal et al. (2001). Reprinted with permission.

*We describe the alignment between business and IS strategies as 'strategic alignment', between business and information systems as 'structural alignment', between IS strategy and information systems as 'IS alignment' and between business strategy and business structure as 'business alignment'.*

*Much literature treats alignment as a static end-state, but in real life the search for alignment is a moving target and an emergent process. The business environment continues to change after alignment is achieved. If business strategy or structure is changed in response, the other elements should be altered in a synchronised fashion in order to maintain alignment.* (Sabherwal et al., 2001)

The concept of alignment allows management to establish whether (or not) business structures, IS strategy, and the IS themselves are aligned with business strategy. The Kwik-Fit example (see Research Summary, right) shows how the strategic alignment model can give such insight.

## The contingency approach to alignment

What factors should shape the nature of that alignment? One approach uses the idea, long popular in organisational theory, that the fit should reflect the situation in which the unit is operating. The theory, reflected in Figure 4.12, is that some characteristics of organisations influence how they use information systems within their core operations. The variables are:

● the primary tasks of the organisation: routine or non-routine;
● the degree of interdependency between those doing these tasks: high or low;
● the environment of the organisation: stable or unstable.

---

**Research Summary**   **Maintaining alignment over the long term**

Boddy and Paton (2005) studied how Kwik-Fit, a chain of roadside vehicle repair depots, used modern IS to gain, and retain, a competitive advantage. Every transaction generates administrative tasks, and in the early years the company kept these on paper – invoices, receipts, stock movements and so on. As the company grew, the paper system became increasingly burdensome and costly, and the company was one of the first to use an electronic payment system. This improved efficiency and enabled much tighter central control of the depots, as all information about their activities was now available at head office. It later decided to develop this system to introduce more decentralised operations, and later still to develop a new business – Kwik-Fit Insurance.

The research showed that throughout these moves the company continued to seek an alignment between its structures, strategies and information systems, doing so by a particularly successful approach to project management (see also Chapter 6).

*Source*: Boddy and Paton (2005).

---

Figure 4.12 expresses these variables on three dimensions, giving eight types of (pure) organisations. When the environment is relatively stable and there are many routine tasks (for example, an energy supplier, a water supplier or a tax administrator), companies will use IS mainly to support primary processes – they will focus on providing integrated and reliable systems to provide regular information to managers in a fixed way.

In an unstable environment of non-routine tasks (for example, consultancies, R&D departments, software houses), information systems have to be flexible and adaptive, and so are often unstructured and 'open'. Intranets, groupware systems and flexible decision support systems will be more helpful in such environments than structured and integrated data processing systems. The employees as well as the customers expect a flexible and supportive information environment they can easily adapt to changing circumstances.

Relatively independent units can develop an information environment to suit the needs and characteristics of that particular business unit. However, when units have to collaborate and exchange information regularly (interdependency), they will move towards more integrated systems.

The model suggests that there is no single best way to use IS, but that effectiveness depends on selecting the form of system best suited to the situation. This implies that

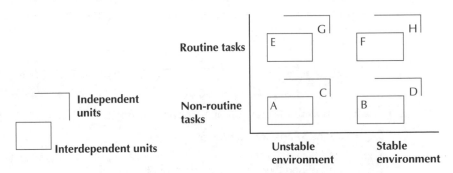

Figure 4.12 Strategic alignment approach, based on the contingency concept

managers should not follow fashion, but ensure that their systems match the present and evolving nature of their organisation. The contingency approach challenges approaches that seek a universal solution or pay most attention to current fashion.

### An interaction approach?

On the other hand, do not interpret the model too mechanically. As presented, it ignores other variables such as cultural, political and historical features. It also stresses only one aspect of the external conditions. The best solution probably depends on both internal and external conditions, and how managers see and interpret them. To use it in a mechanistic and deterministic way is an oversimplification. In addition, people can use information systems to influence these variables, as the example in the MIS in Practice box below shows.

---

**MIS in Practice    Changing alignment – from a D firm to an A**

A small consultancy firm, located in one building in a medium-sized city, had about ten management consultants and a small staff of four people. They had a good reputation in the region, based on personal relationships between the consultants and their clients. The consultants all had their own personal style. IT was only used for word-processing and the financial data processing. It resembled a 'D firm': non-routine, independent and stable. Its IT systems fitted that description.

However, when the owner and director retired, the consultancy firm was taken over by a big international consultancy. That firm imposed a common working style, based on its 'generally accepted standards'. Project management and groupware systems were implemented to share the knowledge and experience of the worldwide operating firm. Positions were more tightly regulated and consultants from other areas were brought in. The business expanded to more than 40 consultants. The environment became more unstable, interdependency became higher and tasks were still non-routine. It was now a typical 'A firm'.

This example shows that changing circumstances and conditions, but also IT applications like groupware and project management systems, can change the characteristics of companies.

---

People in the original company developed a way of working and used information systems to support that. A change in circumstances brought new people into the business, and they introduced new information systems. These required people to work in new ways. We see an interaction between people, how they see the environment and the kinds of systems they use.

---

**Activity 4.5  Evidence on the contingency approach**

Find an example of a company for each position in Figure 4.12 (A–H).

● Are these positions stable or changing?
● If they have changed, what were the drivers of this change (for example, technology, competition, customer expectations)?

---

## ● Summary

- There is no best way to organise and use information systems. Many alternatives are available and it depends on the business and its environment which combination fits best with the company.

- The challenge for managers is to align information systems in an optimal way with their business and to use them to support strategy and organisation.

- Important factors in alignment are: processes (routine or non-routine), interdependency between units (high versus low) and environment (stable or unstable).

- The form of information system will also reflect how people see other factors, such as the culture, politics and history of the organisation.

## 4.4 Positioning e-business models within the company

Established companies that decide their strategy should involve some form of online presence then have to decide how the Internet relates to their existing business (Figure 4.13). Will the Internet be the exclusive channel (e.g. to sell or to buy) or will it be complementary? The possibilities are as follows.

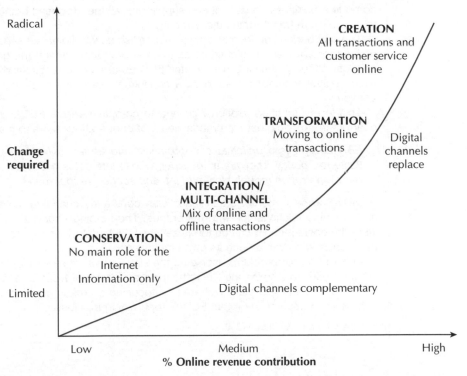

**Figure 4.13 Strategic options for a company in relation to the importance of the Internet as a channel**

*Source*: Adapted from Chaffey (2007) with permission.

121

| Conservation | Brick – continue to operate without Internet or information only |
| Integration/ multi-channel | Brick and click – Internet combined and integrated with existing firm |
| Transformation | From brick to click – from existing to new form |
| Creation | Clicks – setting up a business that only uses electronic channels |

---

### MIS in Practice   E-business at an automotive manufacturer

Chu and Smithson (2007) describe how Autocorp, a major American automotive manufacturer, became a global company by acquiring European (and also Japanese) brands. Since the 1960s, it had operated under an autonomous regional structure, with Europe hosting its own assembly plants and national headquarters. In the late 1990s the CEO retired and was replaced by a successor at the height of the dot-com boom.

One of his first actions was to find out how the Internet could improve the company. He articulated a vision to transform the company from a traditional manufacturer to a consumer-led company. Web-based technologies would reshape the firm and transform its culture, enhancing supply chain efficiency and developing customer-centric strategies.

A European e-business department (EBD-Europe) was set up, headed by an externally recruited executive with a consultancy background. EBD-Europe was to be the autonomous e-business consultant and supplier for all the European brands, seeing itself as the 'catalyst in transforming the company'.

The unit began confidently, obtaining a stylish new building set separate from the rest of Autocorp. It was positioned as an internal profit centre with the goal of an eventual spin-off. Although the CEO had created EBD-Europe he never clarified its role, so people were unclear whether it was to be a consultant, an in-house service or something in between.

This led to strained relationships and to complaints from EBD-Europe to the headquarters in America that the brands were not cooperating. A brand manager:

*EBD-Europe is a unit that over-promises and under delivers, unprofessional, poor value for money. They are an outsider, whose interest is not in Autocorp. They forget our organisation model, blow budget, and scope-creep issues.*

EBD-Europe's internal organisation was constantly changing, lowering staff morale and straining relationships with the brands. The funding structure was also unclear, as were the costs it could charge for its services – which further reduced its credibility with the brands and even among its own employees.

Other strategic problems, including the slow launch of new models and poor quality, led the board to dismiss the CEO, the main supporter of EBD-Europe. His replacement announced a 'back to basics' strategy, refocusing on manufacturing, finance and products. It soon became clear that EBD-Europe would be closed.

*Source*: Chu and Smithson (2007).

## ● Integration: brick and click

If a company decides to integrate the Internet activities in the existing business, it can combine various facilities and offer multiple channels to customers. At many banks, customers can use the call centre, the Internet or the branch. Advantages of this approach are that traditional customers are not put off by a new medium and can become used to it gradually. The company can also attract new customers at the same time. Established retailers and newspapers often take this approach, using the Internet to complement conventional channels. They recognise that their existing strengths, such as a trusted brand name, established supplier networks, established customers and a distribution and payment infrastructure, can be essential supports to an Internet venture, while start-up companies need to create them from scratch. Chu and Smithson (2007) describe how a major American automotive manufacturer tried to make a radical change (see the MIS in Practice features, left).

## ● Transformation: from brick to click

This means a gradual move from non-use of the Internet to becoming a complete Internet company. Read the following example.

---

**MIS in Practice  KLM**

One example of a company in transformation is Royal Dutch Airlines, KLM (www.KLM.com), which is following a strategy of gradually moving its business on to the Internet. The firm aims to secure 40 per cent of sales from online sources to achieve three objectives.

- *Cost-reductions* from simplifying booking and payment processes and reducing human intervention – for example by sending e-tickets to customers.

- *Better services* by faster check-in and by enabling online customers to select their seats while booking their flight – cutting the time the customers have to spend at the airport.

- *Increased market share* by having better Internet performance than competitors. This involves using intelligent strategies and CRM tools to identify the preferences and patterns of purchasing decisions of online customers.

KLM's website has become increasingly important for the firm as a source of sales. This success led to larger volumes of online traffic and to demands from customers for new and advanced features, availability and reliability of the website. Consequently, KLM's online operations required a new assessment model to capture the many dimensions of online operations and what each can contribute to profits and customer growth.

*Source*: Boonstra and Harison (2008).

---

## ● Creation: clicks

This option describes new businesses based entirely on the Internet. Such entrepreneurial creations do not carry the burden of traditional structures and distribution channels, so they avoid the problems of transformation that face bricks-and-mortar rivals. They tend to have young, Internet-literate customers, and have clearly been able to attract substantial amounts of venture capital. Their disadvantages include lack of established reputation, brand name or order-fulfilment processes.

These issues related to the Internet show how information systems developments raise fundamental and strategic questions for companies. Established companies are sometimes slower in their reaction to such innovations than newcomers, but they are increasingly challenged to transform their business to electronic channels.

---

### Activity 4.6  Analysing an Internet strategy

Choose a firm that is currently using the Internet and analyse its Internet strategy.

- Which strategy did they follow – conservation, separation, integration, transformation or creation?
- Have competitors the same or other strategies?
- What are in this particular case advantages and disadvantages of these strategies?

---

## ● Summary

- The Internet gives completely new opportunities for businesses to reach new groups of customers and to develop new products and services.

- The Internet confronts existing businesses with fundamental strategic questions of how to deal with this new technology while giving entrepreneurs chances to set up new businesses using the Internet extensively.

- Strategic issues with respect to the Internet include: the organisation of the value chain, the approach of current and/or new customers, and the positioning of Internet activities within the company – as the exclusive channel or complementary to the old way of doing business.

---

# 4.5 Opportunities and problems of IS planning

Implementing a major system takes a great deal of management time – a cost that managers rarely include when evaluating investments. It requires managers to look inward at (important) operational problems of staff, system design and security. The danger is that they do not look at (even more important) issues of how to use the systems for strategic advantage. In other words, managers are often balancing between a 'problem orientation' and an 'opportunity orientation'. Senior management frequently underestimates the resources required to implement IS, especially of managing the organisational implications. Implementation often takes place in an uncertain competitive and technical environment, which makes it difficult to plan the change even though the stakes are high in terms of costs, people and other resources.

**Table 4.1** What happens when senior managers ignore their IT responsibilities

|  | IT decision | Senior management's role | Consequences of abdicating the decision |
|---|---|---|---|
| **Strategy** | How much should we spend on IT? | Define the strategic role that IT will play in the company and then determine the level of funding needed to achieve that objective. | The company fails to develop an IT platform that furthers its strategy, despite high IT spending. |
|  | Which business processes should receive our IT budget? | Make clear decisions about which IT initiatives will and will not be funded. | A lack of focus overwhelms the IT unit, which tries to deliver many projects that may have little value or cannot be implemented well simultaneously. |
|  | Which IT capabilities need to be company-wide? | Decide which IT capabilities should be provided centrally and which should be developed by individual businesses. | Excessive technical and process standardisation limits the flexibility of business units or frequent exceptions to the standards increase costs and limit business synergies. |
| **Execution** | How good do our IT services really need to be? | Decide which features – for example, enhanced reliability or response time – are needed on the basis of their costs and benefits. | The company may pay for service options that, given its priorities, are not worth the costs. |
|  | What security and privacy risks will we accept? | Lead the decision-making on the trade-offs between security and privacy on the one hand and convenience on the other. | Overemphasis on security and privacy may inconvenience customers, employees and suppliers; underemphasis may make data vulnerable. |
|  | Who do we blame if an IT initiative fails? | Assign a business executive to be accountable for every IT project; monitor business metrics. | The business value of systems is never realised. |

*Source*: Reprinted from Ross and Weill (2002) p. 87, with permission.

Ross and Weill (2002) provide guidelines to senior management regarding the IS decisions they should be making (summarised in Table 4.1) – emphasising especially that they need to define a clear IS policy and decide how to fund, organise and control its implementation.

All these arguments suggest a need for flexible and open methods for defining information strategies. Plans quickly date in uncertain business conditions, so plans should be seen as a road map indicating the:

- direction of system development;
- rationale;
- current situation;
- management strategy;
- new technological developments;
- implementation plan; and
- budget.

**Table 4.2 Complexities in forming an information systems strategy**

| Complicating factors | Description |
| --- | --- |
| Links to other functional areas | Enterprise resource planning (ERP) and similar systems link functions and have expectations of IS. It is hard to change just one part. |
| Potential IS developments | Infinite possibilities for changing the way the firm works, and for the strategy it follows. Strategy needs to remain fluid. |
| Interaction | Changes in IS and organisations affect each other, making it hard to see cause and effect. |
| Lack of expertise | Managers lack IS knowledge; IS experts lack business knowledge. |

Modern IS planning is integrated into the overall strategic plan, coming not from IS managers but from senior and business unit managers, and users. There are several prerequisites for IS planning (Oz, 2006). Senior management must:

- recognise IS as an indispensable resource;
- understand that IS is a complex resource that must be planned and controlled;
- regard IS as an essential resource for the whole company;
- regard IS as a source for strategic advantage and for control of processes.

Ideally, an IS plan is developed by focusing on the mission and a long-term vision of the company. Derived from this, goals and objectives are set and the strategic plan of necessary IS made. Strategic IS plans should not be rigid, since most strategic plans are dynamic and revised frequently – probably every year. Strategic IS plans have to be translated into tactical objectives and result in action. At this stage, projects are defined and assigned resources, including staff and funds.

Other complexities are shown in Table 4.2.

## ● Summary

Some guidelines for improving the effectiveness of IS strategy would include the following.

- Understand the complex impact of different kinds of IS. Develop iterative and adaptive modes of planning in situations where IS plans influence, and are influenced by, the broader strategy.

- Recognise the importance of IS to strategy by appointing to senior positions people with a broad experience of applying IS to business.

- Strive towards a balance between IS opportunities and problems of managing IS. Some top management teams spend more time managing current problems (e.g. troubles with systems, people, outsourcing) than on developing a clear direction for IS, which may in itself solve some of the problems.

- Educate employees in the potential opportunities and effects of modern IS. This may be especially important among middle and senior managers.

## Conclusions

The theme of this chapter appears quite straightforward: how IS can support an organisation's strategy. An observer who sees business organisations as rational, well-informed decision-making bodies blessed with foresight would have no problem in advising how managers should do the job. Yet, as the chapter has unfolded, we have shown how much more uncertain and provisional the link between IS and strategy is.

Right from the start we continued the theme of the interactive approach, in which IS affects strategy and strategy affects IS. We then examined the ways in which IS can be used to affect all aspects of the five forces driving competitive behaviour. This is made more difficult by the continuing developments in technology, where a decision that seems right today may well seem to have been a mistake in a few months' time. Rapid developments in Internet technology are opening up new opportunities and threats for many businesses – so much so that current prescriptions will date very quickly. The Internet is changing consumers' expectations, and is encouraging new entrants into many markets – as well as increasingly strong responses from established players. So technology is one of the driving forces of a volatile competitive landscape in many industries. This means that IS strategies have to be adaptive and flexible.

Above all, IS is not an isolated part of the organisation. It interacts not just with broad strategy, but also with most other functional areas of the business – which may have different expectations of IS. This suggests that developing an IS strategy can at best be a cautious, provisional approach, with an emphasis on learning and reflection, and a willingness to change course if business requirements change, as they inevitably will.

## Chapter questions

1. How can information systems play a role in the competitive position of a firm? Illustrate your answer by giving five examples.

2. Implementation of computer-based IS can be an opportunity but also a threat. Explain when and why it can be a threat and illustrate your answer with two examples.

3. How does the Internet play a role in changing the competitive landscape in many industries?

4. What is an Internet strategy and what choices have to be made when a firm formulates an Internet strategy?

5. Give examples of how information systems can hinder strategic objectives of organisations.

6. Products or services and characteristics of organisations play a role in the way they use information systems. Explain (a) how a product or service can be critical and (b) how the characteristics of a firm can play a critical role in using IS.

7. Many managers find it very difficult to formulate an information strategy. Give four possible reasons for this. Give suggestions or guidelines to deal with these difficulties in practice.

8. This chapter presented different (e)business models: conservation, separation, brick and click, from brick to click and clicks. Suggest possible advantages and disadvantages of each model.

## Further reading

Li, F. (2007) *What is e-Business?* Blackwell, Oxford. This provides a thorough and reflective introduction to business strategies for the networked world. Topics include the context of e-business, strategies and business models developed in response to the Internet and organisational innovations necessary to implement and manage e-business strategies.

Shapiro, C. and Varian, H. (2004) *The Economics of Information Technology: An Introduction.* Cambridge University Press, Cambridge. A book that gives an authoritative analysis of the effects of IT and the Internet, drawing on well-established economic principles to develop some fundamental and valuable lessons.

Four empirical studies of companies developing their strategies in relation to the Internet:

Chu, C. and Smithson, S. (2007) 'E-business and organizational change: a structurational approach', *Information Systems Journal*, **17**(4), 369–89. A description of how an automotive company struggled with the introduction and organisation of e-business. Tried first to set up a separate e-business unit but later integrated it within the business units.

Cooper, B. (2007) 'Business information strategy', *CIO*, **20**(17), 54–7. A study of how the CIO of Toyota Motor Sales USA combined focus groups, critical analysis and information integration to bridge Toyota silos, craft a long-term vision and cultivate a strategic orientation.

Naranjo-Gil, D. and Hartmann, F. (2007) 'How CEOs use management information systems for strategy implementation in hospitals', *Health Policy*, **81**(1), 29–41. A study in healthcare – shows how in this sector too IS and strategy are highly interrelated.

Ross, J.W. and Weill, P. (2002) 'Six IT decisions your IT people shouldn't make', *Harvard Business Review*, **80**(11), 84–91. A clear plea for general managers to take the lead in managing the strategic aspects of IS but to get out of the way of the routine aspects.

## Weblinks

Freely available articles by IBM researchers and others in different journals, including *IBM Systems Journal*: www.research.ibm.com/journal

Online newsletter on information management: www.managinginformation.com

Journal of McKinsey, a management consultancy. This link focuses on IT management, with a variety of recent articles: www.mckinseyquarterly.com/Information_Technology/Management

# CHAPTER 5

## Using IS to rethink business processes

### Learning objectives

By the end of your work on this topic you should be able to:

- Understand the role of IS in supporting changes to business processes

- Explain how IS enables people to rethink business processes within and between organisations

- Apply some approaches to process innovation

- Identify the human and organisational issues that arise in IS-enabled process change

- Contribute to sound decisions on such change by understanding the management dilemmas

CHAPTER CASE: PART 1

# Inditex-Zara

## www.zara.com

Inditex is one of the world's largest fashion distributors, including the Zara, Pull and Bear, Massimo Dutti, Berschka and Stradivarious formats. In 2008 it had over 3500 stores in 64 countries. Over 200 designers help meet the aim to be close to their customers and do away with seasons in fashions. They now introduce 20,000 new items a year – and to do this they need to have very responsive information systems.

Customers know that if they do not buy a product when it appears in the shops they might miss the opportunity altogether, since that same item may never appear again. This encourages customers to keep visiting the stores to catch the new ideas before someone beats them to it.

By 2008 Zara had become the flagship brand of the holding company Industria de Diseño Textil, SA, better known as Inditex. Growth is central to the Inditex vision: 'Zara is a growth company; this is what defines the group from the point of view of investors' (CEO, José María Castellano Ríos).

The Inditex philosophy can be summed up as:

*good design and good quality at good prices. Right from the start, Ortega's vision was totally customer focused and that's still a defining feature of Inditex. Every day, customers take a long, hard look at us; our challenge is to live up to their expectations.* (José María Castellano Ríos)

The Zara way involves total control of the fashion process, from design and manufacture to distribution and retail. The accent is on time-to-market rather than costs. Vertical integration provides maximum flexibility, speed-to-market, minimum inventory and fine-tuning to customers' needs. Zara stores renew almost half their stock every two weeks, taking out much of the risk inherent in the fashion industry. Tailoring is outsourced, mainly to local companies.

Product development at Zara begins with market research. This combines information from visiting university campuses, discos and other venues to observe what young people are wearing, and from daily feedback from stores. This means that trend information is immediately transmitted to people who are making product and business decisions. At the other end of the process, sales associates and store managers place orders in handheld computers over the Internet to Zara Headquarters based on what they see selling. They do not only place orders, but also add ideas for cuts, fabrics or complete new lines. They base this on customer comments or observations of what customers are wearing.

*Sources*: Dutta (2006); company website.

## Introduction

It will be clear from this short account that management at Zara (part of Inditex, a Spanish fashion group) takes a radical approach to the way it manages its retail business. As customers become wealthier and more fashion conscious, they expect retailers to provide a constant flow of new designs, yet these may be designed and made thousands of miles away, posing significant challenges for companies in this business. Zara depends on information from customers about emerging trends – but also needs information about its internal processes if it is to meet those needs at an acceptable price. The case will trace Zara's approach to processes within this industry, using IS to respond quickly and flexibly to changing demands.

Early IS supported separate business functions, which often worked well for the function concerned, but were usually incompatible with systems in other functions. This led to inconsistent management data, so the next step was to link the systems to a common database. This included (ideally) consistent data about all functional areas and often led to more efficient, reliable and accessible information systems – but management was still using the technology to support existing business processes. The way of doing business and organising work did not fundamentally change.

Developments in IS technology, and some prominent experiments, led others to think more radically. They saw that modern IS could enable business to work in a fundamentally different way. Management writers such as Hammer (1990) and Davenport (1993) advocated a new approach that they called 'business process re-engineering' or 'business process redesign'. Other terms representing similar ideas are enterprise resource planning (ERP) and customer relationship management (CRM). Lewis et al. (2007) and Harmon (2007) developed these ideas – the latter conducting a survey of some 230 organisations, which showed that 88 per cent of them were engaged in business process improvement. Of these, 67 per cent indicated that they were largely driven by the need to implement e-business systems using the Internet.

This chapter elaborates this perspective, showing how people can use IS to organise processes more effectively. This includes inter-organisational as well as internal processes, since the Internet and other networks make it easier to link all the processes within a value chain. This may blur the boundaries between organisations and change the value chain of a business. Figure 5.1 illustrates these stages.

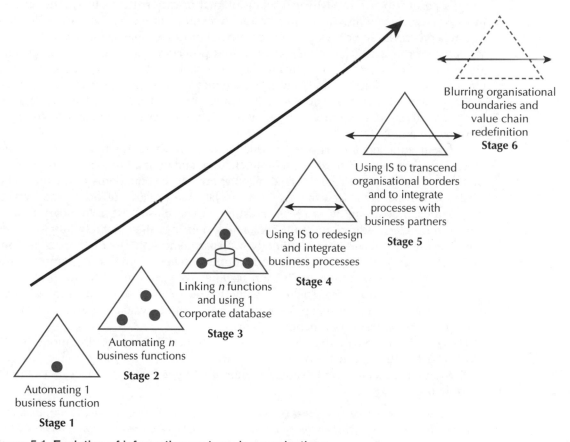

**Figure 5.1 Evolution of information systems in organisations**

The first section defines the topic more precisely, while the next section describes some approaches to innovating business processes. We then explain how IS can play an important role in process innovation. Next, we consider the managerial and organisational aspects, and conclude by discussing management dilemmas in process innovation. The overall aim is to understand the managerial issues when people use information systems to change business processes in and between organisations.

## 5.1 Rethinking and innovating business processes

Day-to-day pressure and the force of habit mean that established ways of doing things become taken for granted as the only possible way to work. People in an established department, say purchasing, see themselves as specialised, experienced and knowledgeable. Purchasing is their job. If someone suggests that production operators could, with the assistance of modern IS, order materials, purchasing staff are likely to resist the suggestion instinctively, whatever the possible merits. This illustrates a central challenge of rethinking and innovating business processes – an independent position, an open mind and a critical attitude to things that people take for granted are all needed.

What is a business process? For Lewis et al. (2007) 'A **business process** is a collection of interrelated tasks, performed to achieve a business outcome' (a business outcome being a product or service delivered to an internal or external customer). The business process is the chain of tasks from purchasing to manufacturing to selling and delivering. Business processes can be divided into operational processes, management processes and supporting processes (Ettlie, 2006). **Operational processes** constitute the core business and create the primary value stream. Typical operational processes are purchasing, manufacturing, marketing and sales. **Management processes** are those that govern the operation of a system and typically include corporate governance and strategic management. **Supporting processes** support the core processes and include accounting, recruitment and IS.

Different functional departments usually perform these interrelated tasks. They specialise in one step, such as design or purchasing, and design internal systems to make that part of the process efficient. The difficulties arise at the boundaries as the product or service moves between departments. This can become a source of trouble and wasted time, which Goldratt and Cox (2004) illustrate in an amusing way. Boundary troubles lead to misunderstandings and time-consuming meetings since nobody fully owns the complete process or takes responsibility for it. Departments optimise their partial responsibility. Purchasing tries to buy goods under optimal delivery conditions. Manufacturing focuses on an optimal use of production facilities. The sales unit tries to meet all the expectations of its customers. The result will often be a slow process, full of mistakes and with more attention to internal procedures than to customer value. It is also very difficult to connect the different information systems.

These problems led to the idea that people should manage organisations from a process, rather than a functional, view. This would lead to customer-directed processes that would raise quality and lower costs, supported by IS. An early advocate (Hammer, 1990) wrote:

*we should re-'reengineer' our businesses: use the power of modern information technology to radically redesign our business processes in order to achieve dramatic improvements in their performance.*

This implies the critical analysis and radical redesign of business processes – especially by breaking away from the historical rules and assumptions that underlie current operations. Zara is an example of a company that has developed design and production processes using modern IS in conjunction with sales staff (observing fashion trends, for example). This illustrates that, while information technology is often important in process innovation, it is not the only place to start. Critical evaluation of business practice and creative thinking can also lead to process innovations, as the MIS in Practice feature, below, shows. However, computer-based systems such as enterprise resource planning (ERP) systems can strengthen the case for radical process change. They make possible what was previously impossible, and the Internet has also opened up possibilities for e-commerce and supply chain management systems.

| MIS in Practice | Self-planning in a university hospital |
|---|---|

In a university hospital in the Netherlands, planners and department heads were used to making schedules for nurses and others who had to work in departments with 24/7 opening hours. These schedulers always received many comments and complaints about unsatisfactory schedules. These complaints often led to updates, which often caused new complaints, now from others.

Then the hospital started a 'self-scheduling' project. In this project they experimented with a scheduling process where employees had to place themselves in the plan, within certain constraints (e.g. a minimum number of hours had to be worked during less popular working hours). This led to fewer conflicting demands and, when these arose, they could be solved more easily. Now the hospital needs fewer planners and the employees are more satisfied with their working hours.

Managers usually make process innovations by combining separate processes and designing the remaining ones to be more efficient. They often find that most of the time in a process is taken up waiting for the next process to start – a sure sign that it involves too many departments.

| MIS in Practice | Port of Rotterdam |
|---|---|

The Port of Rotterdam (www.portofrotterdam.com) controls approximately 100 km of waterway. This process starts at sea as each ship reports its approach to the harbour. That information is used for traffic control, tariffs and special arrangements for dangerous cargoes. Not long ago the harbour had 126 departments, each with its own IT systems, and used more than 100 applications. 'That became unmanageable,' says Chris van de Weerd, IT manager at the Traffic Management department:

*At the start of this year we moved from a departmental structure to a process-based organisation. This move also led to an IT audit and a redesign of our information systems architecture. Now we only have a few information systems which support the arrival and departure of any ship. One of these systems is a knowledge system which helps to analyse all relevant data and to determine whether a ship needs a pilot to enter the harbour.*

While the principles are easy to understand, the practice is more difficult, since process innovation involves changes in responsibilities and a more explicit orientation towards the customer. The changes also need to be aligned with broader strategy. They might involve closer cooperation with suppliers and customers as there are further benefits in innovating processes between, as well as within, organisations. Finally, new information systems will support the new processes. They are challenging projects to manage, and the failure rate is high.

## ● Summary

- Changing environments and new IT generates ideas for process innovation.
- IT enables a process orientation (as opposed to functional ways of organising).
- Process changes potentially affect all aspects of the organisation, including IS.

## 5.2 Approaches to innovating processes

**Process innovation** involves implementing a new or significantly changed production or delivery method. However, it is important to understand that, in an organisational context, there are different types of innovation and process innovation is one of these. Other possible ways to innovate are:

- **product** or **service innovation** – introducing a new good or service;
- **business model innovation** – changing the way a business adds value to resources (such as identifying new sources of revenue);
- **supply chain innovation** – changes in sourcing inputs from suppliers and delivering outputs to customers.

## ● Organising process innovation

Process innovation usually takes place as a project within an established organisation, with staff seconded from several units to work with external consultants. Figure 5.2 shows a common sequence of activities.

Most authorities take the view that a company should start with a view of the organisation (or business unit) as a whole and clear strategic goals for the business and the environment.

Programs of process innovation are typically tightly linked to organisational goals such as:

- improved quality;
- faster processes;
- reduced labour costs;
- reduced materials, environmental damage and reduced energy consumption;
- conformance to regulations.

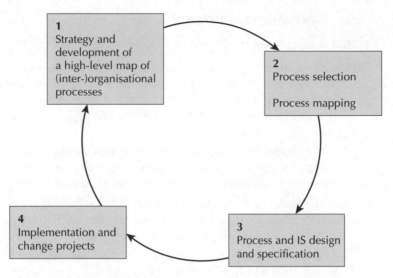

**Figure 5.2 Phases of process innovation**

Business processes should not be (re)designed in isolation, so the first step is to construct a high-level map of the (inter-)organisational processes. From that map, particular processes or sub-processes can be prioritised for innovation.

Common criteria are:

- the health of the process (unhealthy processes are dysfunctional and prone to error, with extensive information exchange, redundancy of work and iteration of tasks);

- the criticality of the process (processes can be ranked in order of importance relative to the competences and the performance of the organisation – which processes have the greatest potential for improvement?);

- the feasibility of innovation (it is more feasible to change some processes than others, either on technical grounds, e.g. a new software package, or organisational, e.g. readiness to change).

Then the process innovation can be designed, specified and implemented.

## ● Systematic design or clean sheet?

Within this view on the organisation of process innovation there are two methods (Harmon, 2007):

- **systematic redesign**: identify and analyse existing processes, evaluate them critically and plan major improvements;

- **clean sheet approach**: fundamentally rethink the way that the product or service is delivered and design new processes from scratch.

The first approach will probably get more support from staff who are actively involved in processes and may lead to certain improvements more quickly. The danger is that starting from the current situation may limit radical thinking. The second approach is more fundamental but can probably be carried out only with the help of external advisers because of the bias of staff inside a company.

## ● Systematic approach

If a company follows a systematic approach, Harmon (2007) suggests four questions.

1. Is it possible to eliminate process steps? Many processes contain unnecessary steps and consequently cause unnecessary waiting times. For example, insurance claims move between departments and have a waiting time in each one. Every stage of transport, and each activity, takes time and effort. Managing and monitoring each of these steps is also time-consuming.

2. Is it possible to simplify process steps? Often, unnecessary forms and too many procedures are used. Nowadays many firms use the Internet to enable the customer to key in necessary data to start a process. That is an example of simplification.

3. Is it possible to integrate process steps? Some tasks that are separated and executed by different people or different departments can easily by done by one. This often makes it easier to manage a process and divide responsibilities more clearly.

4. Is it possible to automate process steps? For example, can dangerous or boring work be eliminated, and is there scope for eliminating duplication in capturing and transferring data?

### Process mapping and modelling

There are various approaches to mapping and modelling processes (e.g. Sousa et al., 2002, and Schaap, 2007, see weblinks, p. 154). Such approaches can be used to describe, to analyse and to (re)design processes for organisations or for value chains. Harmon (2007) developed an approach that models a process and then uses this model to analyse and innovate the process. This approach distinguishes three constructs (see Figure 5.3):

1. Processes are represented by boxes and are labelled with titles like manufacturing or with names that begin with a verb, such as Pay for registration, Ship for product or leave.

2. Events are represented by circles and are perceived changes of status at one point in time that is of interest to the organisation.

3. Waits are represented by a W and are significant delays before the start of an event or a process. This method can be used for both the systematic design and clean sheet approaches.

The process diagram itself is divided into a series of horizontal rows, sometimes called 'swimlanes'. Movement generally goes from left to right and indicates the passage of time. So a process begins on the left-hand side of the diagram and proceeds to the right.

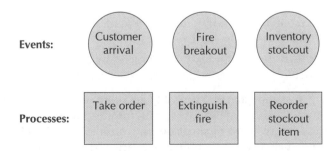

**Figure 5.3 Symbols in modelling process change**

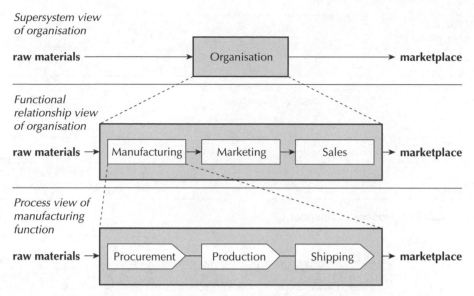

**Figure 5.4** An illustration of how successive process diagrams can provide more detail

The actors, often organisational departments or external parties, such as customers or suppliers, are the 'swimlane labels' on the left side of the process diagram. By mapping processes in this way, process diagrams are workflow diagrams with swimlanes.

A process can be the responsibility of an individual, the organisation or a chain of organisations, so the scope of process representation varies. High-level processes are generally analysed first, and then parts of these processes can be analysed in detail (Figure 5.4). This means that on the highest level a process can be named 'producing cars' and at successively lower levels this divides into the many sub-processes required. Possible levels are (Harmon, 2007) the following.

- Organisation in its environment. This is a supersystem view that includes the organisation in the context of the supply chain, including suppliers, customers and so on.
- Value chains, processes and sub-processes. This looks at functional relationships within the organisation, and at the core processes.
- Activities and performance. This level describes in more detail the processes within each function, such as manufacturing or marketing, which it analyses in terms of activities and roles. These are then divided into roles of employees, information systems and activities that combine both. At this level, performance indicators are often provided.

In the hospital example in the MIS in Practice feature overleaf, the approach will be explained by describing the old process and the design of a new one.

Figure 5.5 models this process in a diagram, which helps us to analyse the process flow. We can use the model to give an accurate picture of the present situation and to identify how it can be improved. We also need to consider whether those improvements should be made radically or incrementally.

Each process (boxes P1–P3) can be divided into sub-processes – Figure 5.5 only shows the broad picture. The challenge is to improve the process by cutting lead times and

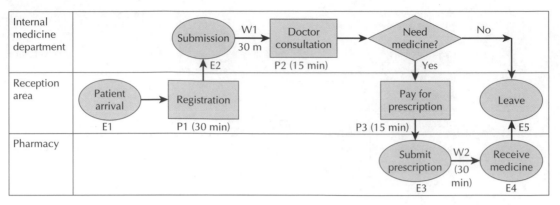

**Figure 5.5** Old process at hospital

---

**MIS in Practice | A hospital process**

John Smith arrives at a private hospital with stomach ache at 1.30 p.m. He has to go to the reception desk first to register. He has to fill in a form, wait his turn and pay the doctor's fee in advance (as required by this particular healthcare scheme). After receiving a consultation slip from the reception desk, he has to go to the internal medicine department on the second floor. It is now 2 p.m.

At the second floor reception, John gives his form to a nurse and waits for his turn. This is normally at least an hour even when he has an appointment. Consultation with the doctor lasts about 15 minutes. The doctor diagnoses food poisoning and prescribes some medicine. John takes the prescription to the cashier's desk in reception, pays the bill and goes down to the pharmacy in the basement. After waiting another half an hour, he receives his medicine.

By the time he leaves the hospital, it is already 4 p.m., too late to return to work. John wonders if anything can be done to speed up this slow process.

---

reducing the number of people involved without reducing quality. Here are some useful principles for designing processes.

1. Start with the most critical process.

2. Reduce the number of process steps by eliminating unnecessary ones.

3. Transform processes into events. In Figure 5.5 the registration process can turn into an event by issuing each patient with a smart card containing personal health and bank account information.

4. Minimise travel distance. When the chain moves up and down a 'red flag' is raised. The number of people involved should be as small as possible.

5. Make processes and events parallel. In Figure 5.5, processes P1 and P3 can be done simultaneously while event E3 can be done by the doctor during the consultation.

6. Reduce the waiting time before a process but eliminate it before an event. Events take hardly any time and it is irritating and often unnecessary to have to wait.

To illustrate what can be done, Figure 5.6 shows the improved process.

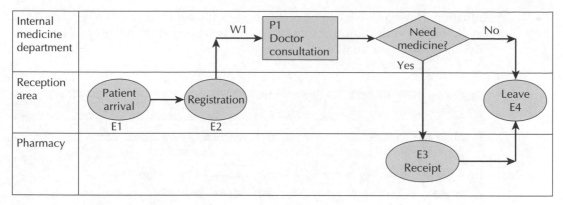

**Figure 5.6** New process at hospital

Harmon suggests that a process should be as short as possible (less time) and as narrow as possible (fewer people). Comparing the old and the new processes we can see that IS (card readers, smart cards, networks and databases) make it possible to:

● change the registration process (old P1) into an event (new E2);

● remove the wait (old W2), changing it into an event (new E3);

● remove the payment process (old P3) by integrating it with the receipt event (new E3).

This illustrates how computer-based information systems open many opportunities to rethink a process and bring significant reductions in process steps and waits.

## Activity 5.1 Analysing a process

Use a process mapping method to describe the process from a customer entering a restaurant to the payment of the invoice.
Then use the following questions to analyse this process.

● Is it possible to eliminate process steps?

● Is it possible to simplify process steps?

● Is it possible to integrate process steps?

● Is it possible to automate process steps?

This analysis can be characterised as a systematic approach. An alternative would have been the clean sheet approach to process design.
How can restaurants deliver meals in non-traditional ways and how can IS play a role?
Indicate the consequences for the information systems of each alternative. Discuss also consequences for other factors, including people.

This method can stimulate discussions about 'IS' and 'SHOULD' processes. A clear diagram of the 'IS' situation shows how things really are and how much time and how many steps they take. A danger is that it is close to 'systematic design': it improves the situation without designing a fundamentally new process, disconnected from the old situation. However, in designing processes, a clear diagram of proposed alternatives helps to choose between them. For that reason it can be helpful to create speculative alternative diagrams, so-called COULD diagrams.

---

### Activity 5.2 Zara

Read the Chapter Case on Zara, and collect some additional information about the company from the company website or other sources.

- What are the key elements of Zara's strategy? (Apply Figure 5.2.)
- How do Zara's processes differ from those of most of its competitors?
- What are the implications for Zara's information systems?

---

## ● Summary

- Process innovation can take place by analysing the old processes or by designing a new process from scratch; both have advantages and disadvantages.

- In doing a systematic design, asking 'can we eliminate, simplify, integrate or automate' can help to stimulate ideas.

- Modelling and analysing old and new processes can help in making new designs.

## 5.3 The role of IS in process change

Information systems and process change provide a further illustration of the interaction model. One perspective is that managers should first innovate their processes and then implement IS to support them – as in Figure 5.7(a).

The alternative view is that rapidly developing information technologies are themselves often driving business process change. There are many examples of information technologies that enable new processes. Such technologies are generally called 'disruptive', which means that the power of information technology sets new 'rules', which enable change in the way people and organisations work – as shown in Table 5.1.

The Internet is the driving force behind many of the electronic marketplaces that are changing purchasing processes so radically. As these markets develop, people need to update their processes – and they need more advanced systems to support these new processes. So process change and IS are becoming mutually reinforcing factors – as shown in Figure 5.7(b).

A further interaction, of great practical significance, is that, as people use IS to improve their processes, they learn what is possible. This helps them to become more confident in breaking out of the old mindset. They are more willing to abandon the traditional ways of thinking, which, as we remarked at the outset, can block attempts at process change. They can see new possibilities of process change – which will require further new systems. The additional interaction is shown as Figure 5.7(c).

Chesbrough (2003) suggests that there are many opportunities to use IS to support fundamental process changes. He distinguishes nine categories of impact, shown in

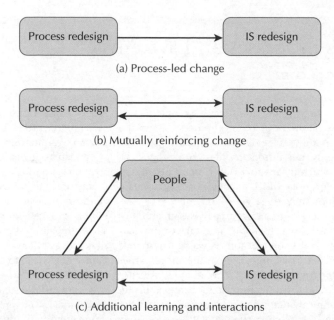

Figure 5.7 Interaction between processes, information systems and people

Table 5.1 How information systems can change the rules

| Old rule | Disruptive technology | New rule |
| --- | --- | --- |
| Information can appear in only one place at one time. | Shared databases. | Information can appear simultaneously in as many places as it is needed. |
| Only experts can perform complex work. | Expert systems. | A generalist can do the work of an expert. |
| Managers make all decisions. | Decision support tools. | Decision-making is part of everyone's job. |
| Field staff need offices where they can receive, store, retrieve and transmit information. | Wireless data communication and portable computers. | Field personnel can send and receive information wherever they are. |
| You have to find out where things are. | Automatic identification and tracking technology. | Things tell you where they are. |

*Source*: Adapted from Wisner and Stanley (2008) with permission.

Table 5.2. This shows that IS enables organisations to work on a wider geographic scale and in a more consistent, controlled and reliable manner. Customers can be anywhere (Internet), employees can be anywhere (groupware, Internet, portable systems) and processes can be controlled more effectively (workflow management systems, expert systems).

The case illustrates how IS enables process innovation and strategic change. It reduces the number of steps, the departments and people involved, and supports individuals by helping them to access data and make well-informed decisions quickly. The information

# Zara's processes and systems

**www.zara.com**

What sets Zara apart from many competitors is the flexible nature of its business processes, and the information it uses to guide them. Retailers often take 12 months to move from an idea to a product in the shop, which means that they depend heavily on long-term forecasts, which are notoriously inaccurate in the fashion industry (Figure 5.8).

Zara has developed a fast garment design and production process, which enables it to take to the market only what it knows customers want. It responds to actual needs based on calls from the shops, rather than on long-term forecasts. The designer sketches out the garment, details the specifications and prepares a technical brief. Approvals are quick, since the entire team is working in the same physical area. As soon as a new design is approved, instructions are issued to cut the appropriate fabric. This is done in Zara's highly automated cutting facilities.

The cut pieces are distributed for assembly to a network of small workshops mostly in Galicia and northern Portugal, none of which is owned by Zara. The workshops are provided with a set of easy-to-follow instructions, which enable them quickly to sew up the pieces and provide a constant stream to Zara's garment-finishing and packing facilities.

A high tech distribution system ensures that no style sits around long at the head office. The garments are quickly cleared through the distribution centre and arrive at the stores within 48 hours – each store receiving two deliveries a week. Figure 5.9 shows the business process at Zara. Through this business process, Zara produces in small batches, which almost never lead to excess stock and unmet demand. Production stops when the market saturates.

Information systems play an important part in the Zara model, and are a key element in the whole group's ability to innovate. The General Manager:

*Innovation is absolutely fundamental; our growth as a group is based entirely on our ability to innovate; that's how we've broken so many moulds in the fashion industry.*

*Source*: Based on information from the company website.

**Figure 5.8 Traditional fashion business process (8–12 months)**

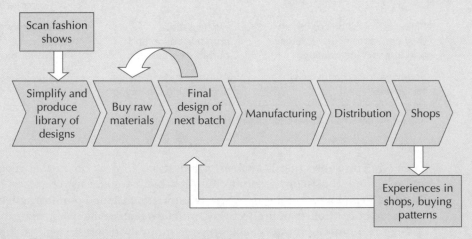

**Figure 5.9 Zara's business process (1–2 weeks)**

**Table 5.2** How information systems can support business process change

| Category | Description | Example |
|---|---|---|
| Integrative | Coordinating and integrating tasks and processes. | With all the relevant information easily available at one time and place, bank staff can help customers with different needs. |
| Geographical | Transferring information over long distances. | Using the Internet, businesses can perceive the whole (connected) world as their marketplace, rather than a limited region. |
| Automational | Eliminating or reducing human labour. | In the retail industry, many inventories are connected electronically with suppliers in order to automate the stock control completely. |
| Analytical | Support decision-making by better analysis of information. | Decision support systems help users to develop different scenarios and make better decisions. |
| Informational | Providing information in right amounts at the right time. | Information systems can be helpful in providing managers with information in the form of, e.g., exception reporting. |
| Sequential | Changing the process sequences or enabling parallelism. | Because information is available at many places at the same time, people can work simultaneously on the processing of an order. |
| Intellectual | Capturing and distributing intellectual assets. | Expert systems, for instance in financial services, can distribute corporate knowledge to financial advisers. |
| Tracking | Monitoring processes. | Point-of-sale systems to constantly monitor inventory levels. |
| Disintermediation | Eliminating intermediaries. | IT can replace the information previously supplied by the intermediary (e.g. wholesalers). |

*Source*: Adapted from Chesbrough (2003) with permission.

systems are built around points of contact with customers instead of around functions that are just a small part of a process. Information systems follow from the chosen organisational design and become increasingly cross-functional and inter-organisational. In this case, the IS has enabled new ways of organising. That does not always happen, and depends on management decisions.

Clearly, Table 5.2 identifies links between process innovation and broader strategy and choices for companies about whether to perform certain processes themselves or outsource them, supported by information systems. Whether or not companies can realise the potential in practice depends on how well managers deal with the elements in Figure 1.5 (p. 15).

At Zara, information systems are used for *integration* when store managers scan preferences and transmit this information to the design departments in Spain. In doing so they also transcend *geographical* barriers and automate a part of the environmental scanning process. The design process also makes the traditional fashion business process more parallel and less *sequential*. The Zara business model also *disintermediates* design and wholesaler functions.

### Activity 5.3 Zara

- Make a process flow diagram of Zara's business process.
- How do roles of store managers and designers of Zara change?
- How may competitors respond to the Zara business model?
- What are potential weaknesses of the Zara approach?

## ● Summary

- IS will often support or drive process change.
- IS can (among other things) be used to facilitate easy access to process information across functional boundaries.
- A management issue is to relate IS used to support process design to the overall IS strategy.

## 5.4 Examples of IS-enabled process change

### ● Enterprise resource planning

Many companies now use information systems for enterprise resource planning (ERP) (see also Chapter 2). An ERP system helps coordinate all facets of business, including planning, manufacturing, sales and finance (Schwarz, 2006), and can eliminate expensive links between isolated IS in different business functions. Within an ERP system, sales representatives can easily enter online orders from customers and verify inventory levels. Manufacturing and purchasing files are automatically updated. If the system has a link to the Internet, customers can check the progress of an order.

Implementing an ERP system implies changing processes. Vendors advise changing these radically before putting such a system in place. Information flows across functional borders and different units can access the same data. Enterprise systems are usually implemented in stages, with the most essential modules first (often finance, purchasing, manufacturing and marketing). Many organisations choose to extend their system to suppliers and customers (often using the Internet) so that it becomes an inter-organisational system. In this 'extended enterprise', borders become unclear and several partners use the same database and information systems.

Figure 5.10 shows business and technology drivers that lie behind the wide acceptance of ERP. They lead to an integrated business from an information flow point of view. Customers trigger a chain of activities (a business process) when they make a transaction. People in companies who share responsibility for a process have an overview and can make decisions more confidently. Technology, as mentioned in the figure, makes this possible. But, as Figure 1.4 (p. 14) shows, people and processes are also part of the system and their response will affect the outcomes of process innovation.

The MIS in Practice feature, right, illustrates the implementation of an ERP system at a dairy company and shows the strong relation between strategy, process change and IS.

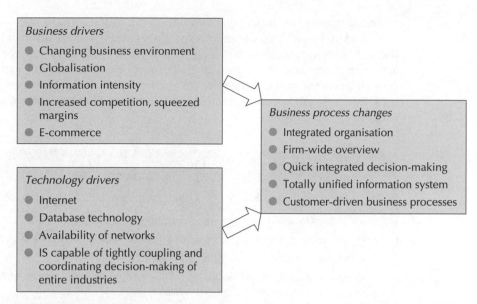

**Figure 5.10 Business and technology drivers behind process change through ERP systems**

While ERP has many advantages, there are also disadvantages. These include possible inflexibility and the difficulty of securing a fit between the system and the characteristics of the business. Many managers say that they have to adapt their business to the ERP system rather than vice versa to make the system work. The system forces the company to organise its processes in a prescribed way – which may lose a distinct advantage.

---

**MIS in Practice  ERP at FFC dairy food**

At the end of 2000 the board of management of FFC, a dairy food company, agreed that many of the transaction processing systems of the milk processing business units (Milk, Cheese and Special Products) were obsolete. The symptoms included:

- some transaction systems were not connected and used inconsistent data;
- there was little consistent management information;
- the systems were hard to maintain;
- the systems were not available for suppliers, which made e-procurement impossible.

Faced with these problems, the board started an ERP project, creating a project group, chaired by the IS manager, to acquire, adapt and implement an enterprise-wide information system. This system had to replace all the existing transaction processing systems at the three business units – Cheese, Milk, and Special Products. The system had to provide real-time management information and enable e-procurement with main suppliers.

The major benefits that managers expected were improved information flows within and between business units, better connections with staff departments and senior management, and the ability to make electronic connections with external parties.

*Source*: Boonstra (2006).

This brings us to a more general point: IS can also constrain real process innovation. Information systems that are expensive legacies of the past are difficult to adapt and limit the ability of organisations to change their processes radically. New systems, such as ERP, can urge organisations to arrange their processes in a specific way without leaving enough space for creativity and for doing things differently. Managers who are aware of these dangers can, however, ensure that they try to obtain the benefits of such systems, without the limitations.

### Activity 5.4  ERP implementation

Read the case history ERP at FFC Dairy Food (see MIS in Practice, previous page).

● What are the main reasons for this company to implement ERP?
● What is the possible impact of ERP implementation on business processes?
● What are potential pitfalls of ERP implementation?
● Research activity: read Boonstra (2006) for the implementation history and provide suggestions for new implementations.

## ● Using the Internet for e-commerce

Another example of IS-enabled process change is the use of the Internet (see also Chapter 2). This opens up enormous possibilities for the transformation of processes. Most organisations now have an Internet presence through their website, which has to reflect a strategic vision about how the business will use the Internet. If the site is going to manage transactions with customers, reliable methods for handling them need to be organised. This implies a new design of that core business process.

When organisations decide to use the Internet, they also have to decide between combining it with non-Internet activities or transferring all their operations to the Internet. The companies taking the former (multi-channel) route have to combine processes consistently and clearly for their customers (see Figure 5.11).

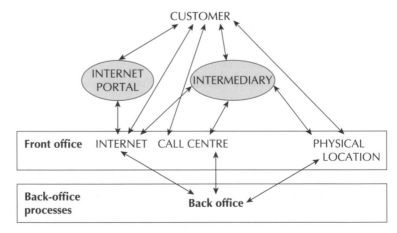

**Figure 5.11 Multi-channel approach: customers choose their own channel for every transaction**

Organising such complicated processes in order to have an efficient and reliable fulfilment is a major focal point for many project managers. An important concern for companies that move (a part of) their processes to the Internet has been to ensure they can handle the associated physical processes, such as handling orders, arranging shipment, receiving payment and dealing with after-sales service. This gives an advantage to traditional retailers who can support their websites with existing fulfilment processes. Effective B2B applications require that the business processes between customers and suppliers fit with each other. This has been a bigger task than many expected.

Mobile phones (so-called m-commerce) and other devices increase the number of channels that people may use to contact companies. This means that the forefront of customer contact increases in variety and options, while back-office systems need to collect all relevant information and make it available to all front-office contact points, such as call centres and branches.

---

## Zara Home moves products online
### www.zarahome.com

Zara Home has started selling products online in European countries, including the UK. As many as 2000 products, from its Zara Home and Zara Home Kids collections, are available online at the same prices as found in store. Zara Home will aim to dispatch the products purchased online within a maximum of ten days. Products bought through the website could also be exchanged or returned in the chain's stores, the company said. Zara Home was established in 2003 and now has 174 stores in 18 countries. Last year, sales reached £97m in 2006, and parent company Inditex said it was on course to add between 35 and 45 stores this calendar year. Visitors to www.zarahome.com will be able to subscribe to a weekly bulletin on sales and new products. A specialised customer service will also be available by e-mail as well as by telephone, and in six languages.

*Source*: *Financial Times*, 22 October 2007, p. 24.

**CHAPTER CASE: PART 3**

---

## ● Innovating procurement and invoicing processes

**Procurement** refers to all activities involved with obtaining items from a supplier; this not only includes purchasing, but also inbound logistics such as transportation, goods in and warehousing before the item is used (Chaffey, 2007). Since the advent of the Internet, procurement is increasingly perceived as a business process that can be used to achieve significant savings and other benefits. A traditional procurement process includes activities and process steps such as:

- search for goods;
- fill in paper request;
- send to buyer;
- into buyer's in-tray;
- buyer enters order number;
- buyer authorises order;

147

- buyer prints order;
- order copied to supplier and goods in;
- delivery from supplier;
- order copy to accounts;
- three-way invoice match;
- cheque payment.

This process can be characterised by a long cycle time and by many process steps that all lead to a slow, expensive flow of activities open to errors. Hammer (2001) says of traditional procurement processes:

> It's the mirror image of your supplier's order-fulfillment process, with many of the same tasks and information requirements. When your purchasing agent fills out a requisition form, for instance, she is performing essentially the same work that the supplier's order entry clerk performs when he takes the order. Yet there's probably little or no coordination between the two processes. (p. 84)

Information systems can be used to reduce the number of steps and to reduce the number of people involved (see Section 5.2) – e-procurement is the electronic integration and management of all procurement activities (Chaffey, 2007). An important driver for e-procurement is of course cost reduction; in many cases the costs of ordering exceed the value of the products purchased. Direct cost reductions are achieved through efficiencies in the process that may result in less staff time spent in searching and ordering but also in reduction of inventory costs by lower cycle times. Other advantages include: improved budget control, quality improvement and elimination of errors, increased buyer productivity (now they can concentrate on more strategic issues), lower prices through company-wide standardisation and control, and better management information (Turban and Volonino, 2008). The MIS in Practice example below of an e-procurement process by the Italian government illustrates this.

---

**MIS in Practice    E-Procurement in Italy**

Recently, the Italian government has developed an e-procurement system. On the one hand, a revision and centralisation of policy and procedures was involved, while on the other hand the budgetary autonomy of government agencies had to be respected. Laws were changed, as was the existing procurement approach, ICT applications were developed and processes redesigned. Three procurement channels were introduced: online catalogues, e-auctions and an e-marketplace. The new e-procurement website was implemented, based on the three platforms, enabling a fully trans-national and e-enabled capacity allowing for online bids and purchases. The result is a 30 per cent reduction in the overall costs involved in the entire goods and services procurement process.

*Source*: Bouwman et al. (2005).

---

A typical e-procurement process may include the following process steps:

- search for goods;
- order on the Internet;
- delivery from supplier;

- receive invoice;
- cheque payment.

Even these steps can be automated, however, if company systems are integrated with supplier systems. This is illustrated in the MIS in Practice example from Toyota below.

| MIS in Practice | Ordering seats at Toyota |
| --- | --- |

At the appropriate point in the assembly line, the IS sends an electronic message to a supplier for the precise seat configuration needed for the specific car. The supplier of seats sends these to the Toyota factory every four hours, in the exact sequence that they are needed on the assembly line. Such a precise system enables Toyota to operate without stored inventory, reduces errors, and satisfies customer demand for customised seat configuration.

*Source*: Laudon and Laudon (2007).

A related development that can be integrated with e-procurement is electronic invoicing and e-payment. Most business-to-business processes still involve paper invoices and checks. Electronic invoicing means that vendors send electronic bills to buyers and let buyers reconcile invoices with purchase orders and authorise payment through a financial services provider's online platform (Berez and Sheth, 2007).

There are risks with e-procurement and electronic invoicing. One issue is that the integration of company systems with those of suppliers demands trust and a long-term partnership with the supplier. Building up such a relationship may take years and will not always be perceived as desirable, since system integration with a supplier may lead to dependency.

Another internal issue is that e-procurement and e-invoicing has implications for the procurement staff. When the e-procurement process is operational, they have to focus on more strategic activities, such as contract management. An implication for other employees is that they may all be able to authorise procurement, leading to unclear responsibilities. Security issues may arise as more people become involved in the process.

## ● Summary

- Implementing an ERP system is an example of IS-based process change because it integrates information resources and innovate processes. Managers should think carefully about which modules of ERP will be implemented, given the strengths and limitations of such systems.

- Doing business over the Internet by electronic commerce is another example of (inter-organisational) process change. Implementing such a change has huge implications and demands a new process design.

- The Internet can also be used to enable electronic procurement and electronic invoicing. This may lead to ongoing improvements in the buying process. The organisational issues are associated with dependency on suppliers, the reorganisation of the procurement function and the involvement of other members of the organisation with the e-procurement process.

## 5.5 Managing process innovation

Many authors on process innovation emphasise the radical organisational change with information technology. They suggest a strong reduction of process steps and lead times by making fewer people responsible for the process. Critics argue that this approach is too narrow and fails to address important issues, particularly those concerning organisational change and politics. Process innovation projects usually have wide consequences (Lewis et al., 2007):

- work units change, from functional departments to process teams;
- jobs change, from simple tasks to multidimensional work;
- people's roles change, from controlled to empowered;
- focus of performance shifts, from activity to results;
- values change, from protective to productive.

If such changes are not managed carefully and consciously, problems may arise, going from indifference and passivity to stronger forms of resistance. A potential danger is that the focus of the project team is on the development or adaptation of the IS behind the

---

### MIS in Practice    The Toyota way    www.toyota.com

Toyota is well known for its consistent philosophy and leadership characterised by continuous improvement and learning-by-doing. The development of the Lexus (a premium brand of Toyota) and the Prius (a successful hybrid electric vehicle) demonstrates how these principles led to real products. The principles are divided into four Ps – Philosophy, Process, People and Partners, and Problem-solving and are described in *The Toyota Way Fieldbook* (Liker, 2006). Toyota's commitment is directed at eliminating steps that do not add value, being flexible, developing and valuing people, and focusing on quality.

The principles related to processes can be summarised as follows. Decisions should not be based on short-term objectives but on *long-term goals (1)*. The company believes that the right processes will lead to the right results. The principles of *continuous flow (2)*, '*pull*' *systems (3)* and *levelled (4)* production demonstrate the fact that production in Toyota is very *closely linked to the customer (5)* order. And it is achieving these seemingly contradictory principles that Toyota's success is all about. The sixth principle of the Toyota way is passion for *quality (6)*. The driving force behind this, according to the author, is the realisation on Toyota's part that it is cheapest to fix problems at the first instance rather than do it later. The quality initiative is not driven by complex statistics, but on observing the problem and using the 'five whys' technique to solve it.

The seventh principle is managing *standardisation (7)* as a foundation for continuous improvement and employee empowerment, while the eighth is about the *extensive use of visual controls (8)* so that no problems are hidden. The use of single A4 sheets of paper for most of the communication demonstrates the principle. The last principle is on technology adoption: Toyota is very *slow in adopting new technology (9)*, and believes that only tested technologies in sync with the people and existing processes should be adopted.

*Source*: Lander and Liker (2007).

**Table 5.3** Positive and negative starting points for process change

| Positive starting points for process innovation | Negative starting points for process innovation |
| --- | --- |
| Senior management support. | No sponsor or wrong sponsor. |
| Realistic expectations. | Technical focus. |
| Independent and cooperative staff. | Low-level support. |
| Project directed at growth and development rather than cost reduction and savings. | Too many changes at the same time. |
| Joint vision and mission. | Project leader without authority. |
| Continuing communications. | Poor financial conditions. |
| Full-time project team with competent members. | Fear and lack of optimism. |
| Resources. | Animosity towards IT. |

*Source*: Reprinted from Markus (1994) with permission.

process change and the design mechanics of the new process. Human issues can easily be ignored, which may lead to problems during implementation and operations (Davila et al., 2006).

Causes of failure in process innovation have been widely researched. Some are external to the organisation and beyond its control. Others are internal, arising from inadequate attention to the context or to the innovation process itself. Common context-based failures (O'Sullivan, 2002) are poor leadership, poor organisation, poor communication and poor empowerment. O'Sullivan finds that common causes of failure within the innovation process are poor goal definition, poor alignment of actions to goals, poor participation in teams and poor monitoring of results.

Markus (1994) researched the organisational issues that surround process innovation by interviewing more than 50 management consultants. The objective was to identify which process innovation projects have a good chance of succeeding. From the interviews various positive and negative starting points arose. These are summarised in Table 5.3.

Markus concluded that if there are more negative than positive starting points and it is better to improve these conditions rather than to start IT-enabled process innovation. The Chapter Case shows how the context of change influences the outcome.

## ● Summary

- Process design projects are broad projects where different dimensions demand explicit attention. These dimensions include: IS, politics, people and financial resources.

- The human side especially demands a lot of attention because of the implications it may have for people: their work units and their jobs may change.

- This implies that process design projects need to take account of the challenging task of managing not only the technical aspects but also the interactions between the many organisational elements.

# Information systems of Zara

At the heart of Zara's business are four information-related areas that give Zara its speed.

- Collecting information on consumer needs: trend information flows daily, and is fed into a database at head office. Designers check the database for these dispatches as well as daily sales numbers, using the information to create new lines and modify existing ones. Designers have access to real-time information when deciding with the commercial team on the fabric, cut, and price points of a new garment.

- Standardisation of product information: Zara warehouses work to common definitions, allowing the company to quickly and accurately prepare designs, with clear-cut manufacturing instructions.

- Product information and inventory management: being able to manage thousands of fabric, trim and design specifications, as well as their physical inventory, gives Zara's team the capability to design a garment with available stocks, rather than having to order and wait for the material to come in.

- Distribution management: its state-of-the-art distribution facility functions with minimal human intervention. Approximately 200 kilometres of underground tracks move merchandise from Zara's manufacturing plants to the 400+ chutes that ensure each order reaches its right destination. Optical reading devices sort out and distribute more than 60,000 items of clothing an hour.

## Activity 5.5  Approaches to process innovation

Process innovation can be done at departmental, organisational or inter-organisational levels.

- What would you advocate and what are the pros and cons of each?
- What are the approaches of Zara and Toyota, both described in this chapter?
- Relate your answer to the findings in Table 5.3.
- What are possible implications of Zara's business model when they move online, as described in Part 3?

## Conclusions

In this chapter we have outlined the idea of process innovation and how it is being enabled by developments in computer-based information systems. Some advocates of process redesign take a mechanistic approach: they perceive the design of a process as an engineering task rather than as a socio-technical problem. Such a focus on information technology and the mechanics of the process design, while important, can easily be overemphasised. The cases and other material presented in this chapter show that real organisational innovations involve people, jobs, skills and structures as well as the latest software.

The central theme of this chapter has been interaction. This was introduced at the start, showing the mutual interaction between IS and process innovation. We then extended it to include people's interaction with both of the other elements, and later brought in wider issues of strategy and culture. The evidence is clear: effective use of information systems to innovate processes depends on managing a range of interactions; it is not a narrow technical project. These issues are examined elsewhere in this book – Chapter 4 (strategy), Chapter 6 (organisation) and Chapter 8 (people).

Many process innovators believe that such projects must be conducted from the top down, but this opinion can be challenged. The detailed understanding of process design and customers often resides with the people who do the work. In many cases resistance to new work designs has occurred when people do not want their jobs defined by someone else. There is growing empirical support for the view that changes with more of a bottom-up character may be more successful, besides which such major changes will have a strong political element as vested interests try to shape the direction of the project.

A related issue is whether process change should be conducted as a radical one-off approach or a continuous and incremental activity. How managers resolve this dilemma will depend on factors such as the urgency of the problem and the readiness of the organisation for radical change. Some will stress the urgency of pressures from the market, while others will want to take time to ensure the commitment and support of influential stakeholders. Whichever approach is taken, those implementing it will confront some challenges – not dissimilar from those experienced by the managers in the tax administration. The ideas and techniques outlined in Chapter 9 may be of some help.

## Chapter questions

1. Why might IS drive process change? What other factors can also be drivers?
2. What phases of IS use in organisations can be distinguished, and what could be the next phase?
3. What are the main failure factors in IS-driven process change? How can managers deal more effectively with these factors?
4. To what extent is the use of the Internet for transactional purposes an example of process innovation? What management issues arise because of that?
5. What are the advantages and disadvantages of a diagramming method to analyse processes?
6. What are the advantages and disadvantages of using ERP systems to enable process change?
7. What has to be managed in an IS-enabled process change project?

## Further reading

Three up-to-date texts that extend the ideas included in the chapter:

Chaffey, D. (2007) *E-Business and E-Commerce Management*, Financial Times/Prentice Hall, Harlow.

Harmon, P. (2007) *Business Process Change*, Elsevier/Morgan Kaufmann, San Francisco, CA.

Lander, E. and Liker, J.K. (2007) 'The Toyota production system and art: making highly customized and creative products the Toyota way', *International Journal of Production Research*, **45**(16), 3681–98. A paper on Toyota's production philosophy and how it can be used in other industries and services.

Wisner, J.D. and Stanley, L.L. (2008), *Process Management: Creating Value along the Supply Chain*, South-Western College Publishing, Mason, OH.

# Weblinks

Schaap, D.J. (2007), an academic at the University of Groningen, developed a systemic method to describe and analyse business processes, called 'actor activity diagramming' (AAD). This method is extensively described on the following website: www.aadmodeling.eu

# PART 3

# Organisation

In a review of research into the relationship between IS and organisations, Eason (2001) noted that a common theme was the diversity of the effects observed:

> *For every study which found increases in job satisfaction there was a study which found increases in job dissatisfaction. In an international study of the effects on power we found every possible outcome . . . centralization, decentralization, lateral transfer across departments and no impact at all.* (p. 323)

He attributed this diversity to the fact that computers are flexible technologies that enable change, but do not determine its form. This depends on the specific application, the objectives that the promoters hope to achieve (such as lower costs or a more distinctive service), and how users respond. As Eason points out, the:

> *many stakeholders at the receiving end of a new system will be active in responding to the technical system to avoid negative consequences for themselves and if possible achieve benefits.* (p. 324)

Internal and external stakeholders try to shape the outcomes of IS investments, just as they do with other management activities. They aim to support their interests by invoking existing cultural, structural and political arrangements, and/or seek to adapt these in a favourable direction during the project. This implies that the organisation which evolves during an IS project may not be what those advocating the IS project expected. It also implies the need for alertness on the part of those responsible for the project to ensure that, as far as they can, they balance political interests with those of performance or return on investment.

A related theme in IS research is that people typically manage projects with a technical or (sometimes) a business focus, rather than an organisational one. This is despite the clear and accumulating evidence that applications accompanying technical innovation with suitable organisational innovation are more successful than those attending only to technical factors (Brynjolfsson and Hitt, 2000). Those promoting IS projects are more likely to benefit the organisation, its members and their own careers if they are able to combine organisational and technological changes in a way that enhances human satisfaction and performance.

This part illustrates the range of organisational options and the processes that shape their evolution. This will enable readers to take an informed and critical view of proposals.

Chapter 6 deals with three elements of the organisational context of IS: culture, structure and power. Chapter 7 deals with one aspect of structure, namely the place of the information system function itself within the organisation. It outlines options such as centralised, decentralised, federal or outsourced provision, and the benefits and costs of each. Chapter 8 examines the interaction between information systems and people – whether as staff, retail customers or members of the public.

# CHAPTER 6

## Cultures, structures and politics

### Learning objectives

By the end of your work on this topic you should be able to:

- Explain how the culture of an organisation or unit may affect staff reaction to IS

- Contrast examples in which organisations use IS to increase or decrease central control

- Use a model to decide whether to integrate or separate an online venture from a business

- Recognise how stakeholder power shapes an IS project

- Compare organisations in terms of the degree to which they have become virtual, using Venkatraman and Henderson's model

- Use the ideas to evaluate the interaction of culture, structure and power with an IS project

# The world's largest civil IS project – NPfIT

## www.connectingforhealth.nhs.uk

The UK government is undertaking the world's largest civil IS programme to improve patient care within the National Health Service (NHS). This strategically important work was expected to cost some £6 billion over ten years, and to affect almost all aspects of the provision of healthcare to the UK population.

The UK NHS is responsible for providing free healthcare to about 60 million people. While many aspects of policy are established centrally, service delivery is managed by regional health authorities and within them by local health boards. General practitioners, usually a patient's initial contact with the system, operate as independent businesses, paid by a local health board to provide defined services to people in the area.

In the late 1990s the government recognised the potential benefits of major investments in IS, and set out the broad vision for the complete automation of various patient databases (Department of Health (UK), 2000). This service would not be provided in-house, but by a selection of IT service providers. The challenge of implementing change on this scale is indicated by a government report that noted:

*there is a history of failure of major IT-enabled projects, characterized by delay, overspend, poor performance and abandonment.* (National Audit Office, 2004, p. 3)

The National Programme for Information Technology (NPfIT) is intended to improve patient care, ensuring that all staff and GPs work with accurate, up-to-date information. It plans to do this by implementing an IS infrastructure for the whole of the NHS in England, with the major components being:

- a Care Records Service to improve the sharing of consenting patients' records across the NHS;

- Choose and Book – a system to allow GPs and their staff to book hospital appointments for patients online;

- an electronic prescriptions transmission system;

- an IT infrastructure to support future needs;

- a Picture Archiving and Communications System (PACS) to capture, store, and distribute digital medical images.

The national programme is being provided in two ways: National Application Service Providers (BT Syntegra, Lockheed Martin and IBM) are responsible for purchasing and integrating systems that are common to all NHS users – for example BT is responsible for national aspects of the Care Records Service; and Local Service Providers work closely with local NHS IT professionals to deliver systems and services to units (hospitals, laboratories, etc.) within one of five regions, with the providers varying by region – Accenture is providing the Care Records Service in the North East. They ensure that local systems comply with national standards, and ensure that data is able to flow between local and national systems.

As with many large IS projects, the NPfIT had, by 2008, experienced delays and public criticism. For example, there had been delays to the Choose and Book system, with fewer GPs using the system than had been expected. On the other hand, the PACS system appeared to be a success, with many staff using the system and reporting significant improvements in the service.

*Source*: Department of Health website; Currie and Guah (2006); and other published sources.

## CASE QUESTIONS 6.1

Go to the website to see more information about NPfIT and the NHS. Use Figure 1.6 to identify three features of the context that are likely to make the programme challenging.

# Introduction

The Chapter Case traces the evolution of a large IS programme, intended to support other strategic changes in the delivery of healthcare. While the technology itself is complex (not least because of the high levels of security required when dealing with patients' medical data), so too is the context into which it is introduced. While the NHS appears to be a unified organisation, in practice it is highly fragmented, both vertically – from the centre to local units – and horizontally – between many powerful professional interests. These have developed working practices that are difficult to change, and do not necessarily help the implementation of IS. The healthcare professions also have distinct cultures that affect the implementation of the National Programme.

More broadly, Chapter 4 showed how managers in most organisations can use the power of computer-based IS to improve the strategic position of the enterprise. Tesco (Chapter 1) has clearly used IS to improve its competitive position, as have companies like the Royal Bank of Scotland, Virgin and many more. Like those managing the NPfIT, they also needed to consider if their present organisation was consistent with both their business strategy and their strategy for IS. Deciding, for example, to launch an online service requires a decision about the organisation that will deliver it. This is highly uncertain as there are conflicting views about the form of organisation that best suits particular circumstances. The existing organisation affects whether or not people see a technological opportunity, and if that develops into a new strategy. If it does, it in turn may lead to change in the organisation from which it grew.

Numerous studies (such as Voss, 1988; Symon and Clegg, 1991; Brynjolfsson and Hitt, 2000) have shown that, if managers want to benefit from their investment in IS, they need also to make complementary changes in organisation. Yet it is an equally common finding that few companies make the organisational changes which would support use of the technology. As Robey and Boudreau observe:

*While many speculations of widespread transformations have been made, the projected emergence of new organizational forms has not materialized and has not been documented in the research literature. Fulk and DeSanctis (1995) characterized the rates of progression by firms towards the new forms as 'gradual in most firms, dramatic in some, and nonexistent (or nearly so) in others' (p. 339).* (Robey and Boudreau, 1999, p. 170)

They suggest that (consistently with the interaction model presented in this book) this reluctance to make organisational changes may in part be explained by understanding the forces that promote or resist change – see the Research Summary overleaf.

The chapter first outlines how perceptions of the prevailing culture in a unit colour the way people view an information system. A second theme is that IS enables managers to alter the balance between central and local control – the dilemma is whether to use the technology to control staff more closely or to support local autonomy with better information. A third section considers the structure of online ventures: if managers decide to launch online services, do they integrate them within the existing business or create a separate operation? We then consider the increasingly fluid links between organisations as IS makes it possible to conduct some aspects of a business through 'virtual' forms. The chapter concludes by examining the relationship between IS and the exercise of power.

The aim of the chapter is to indicate the range of organisational choices available, to illustrate the interaction between information systems and their cultural, structural and political context, and to offer tools with which to analyse those links.

---

**Research Summary**   **Logics of opposition**

Robey and Boudreau (1999) suggest that apparently contradictory findings about the effects of IS on organisations may best be understood by using theories that identify forces promoting and resisting change. Here are four such theories.

- **Determinism:** a rational view – managers implement available technologies to remain competitive or to meet the standards of service people expect.
- **Culture:** organisations contain multiple cultures, members of which will tend to accept IS consistent with their culture, and resist those that challenge it.
- **Institutions:** established, authoritative rule-like procedures that people accept as familiar, taken-for-granted features of an organisation may limit acceptance of IS.
- **Politics:** organisations contain multiple political interests that use, or oppose, an IS proposal in the light of how they believe it will affect their power.

Being aware of these alternative theories may help to explain why the outcomes of IS projects sometimes differ from what promoters expected, especially if they were guided by a rational (determinist) perspective.

*Source*: Robey and Boudreau (1999).

---

# 6.1  Cultures and IS

**Culture** is often linked to examples of organisational success or failure, and there is growing evidence that it exerts an equally subtle yet powerful influence on the outcomes of information systems. At the national level, research such as that by Chau et al. (2002) shows how differences in culture affect consumer responses to the Internet, while at the organisational level Robey and Boudreau (1999) focus on culture as one of several possible explanations for the contradictory consequences of IS within organisations. There is also evidence (consistent with the interaction model) of IS influencing the culture within which it operates.

## ● National and organisational cultures

Schein (2004) believes that cultures are most usefully studied by focusing on differences in the values held by members of a group. Such **values** are a set of social norms that identify what is important to a group and how they interact with each other. They set the boundaries of acceptable behaviour, so studying culture:

> *may be particularly useful in explaining certain behaviours with respect to how social groups interact with and apply [information systems].* (Leidner and Kayworth, 2006, p. 359)

Differences in cultural values have been studied at national, organisational and sub-unit levels. Most national studies use Hofstede's (2001) work that distinguishes between cultures on five dimensions – power-distance, uncertainty avoidance, individualism–collectivism, masculinity–feminism, and long-term and short-term orientation (see Boddy, 2008, pp. 130–3 for a fuller account of Hofstede's approach). At the organisational level many use the competing values model developed by Quinn et al. (2003), which proposes

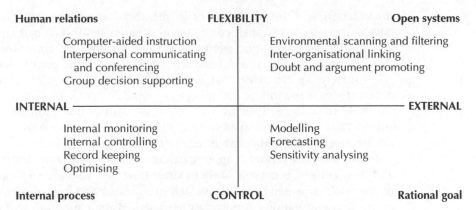

**Figure 6.1** Information systems associated with cultural types

*Source*: Based on Cooper (1994) and Quinn et al. (2003).

that organisations have inherent tensions along two dimensions – between flexibility and control on one axis, and between an internal and an external focus on the other. The resulting four cultural types (shown in Figure 6.1) express 'competing values' that influence how people work and interact.

## Open systems (external, flexibility)

In an **open systems culture** people focus on the external environment, seeing it as a vital source of ideas, energy and resources. They also see it as complex and turbulent, requiring entrepreneurial, visionary leadership and responsive behaviour. Key motivating factors are growth, stimulation, creativity and variety. Examples include start-up firms and business development units – organic, flexible operations.

## Rational goal (external, control)

In a **rational goal culture** members see the unit as being a rational, efficiency seeking operation. They define effectiveness in terms of production or economic goals that meet familiar and stable external requirements. Managers create structures to deal efficiently with this stable outside world. Leadership tends to be directive, goal-oriented and functional. Motivating factors include competition and achieving targets. Examples are large production or service activities in established organisations – mechanistic, rule-driven.

## Internal process (internal, control)

Members of an **internal process culture** pay little attention to the external world and focus instead on internal issues. Their goal is to make the unit efficient, stable and controlled. Goals are known, tasks repetitive and methods stress specialisation, rules, procedures. Leaders tend to be conservative and cautious, emphasising technical issues. Key motivating factors include security, stability and order. Examples include utilities and public authorities, and internal administrative departments such as payroll or tax – cautious, suspicious of change.

## Human relations (internal, flexibility)

People in a **human relations culture** emphasise the value of informal, interpersonal relations rather than formal structures. They place high value on maintaining the organisation and the well-being of its members, and define effectiveness in terms of developing people and their commitment. Leaders tend to be participative, considerate and supportive. Motivating factors tend to be attachment, cohesiveness and membership. Examples include professional service firms and some internal support functions.

Intuitively we can sense that people with these different cultural values will react differently to many things, including a proposed IS. People in an internal process culture are likely to welcome systems that give more control and promote order and predictability. They will be critical of systems that increase the flow of new ideas and external information, threatening established methods.

People associate certain IS applications more closely with one culture than with others and their cultural context is likely to affect how they respond to IS. One of the authors of this book presented the model to staff from a bank and invited them to identify which of the four cultural descriptions best represented their sub-unit, and then to react to a proposed Internet banking scheme. Two cultures were present – open systems (mainly people from the bank's business development unit, charged with building new markets) and internal process (mainly people from the IS department, running established computer systems). Those in the open systems culture welcomed online banking, as it would be consistent with, and support, their culture. Those in the internal process culture were uneasy, since online banking would disrupt their well-established and effective operation.

---

| Research Summary | Culture affects use of IS |
| --- | --- |

Boonstra et al. (2004) studied the low rate of acceptance by general practitioners (GPs) in the Netherlands of an electronic prescription system (EPS). Some GPs accepted the new system (which was intended to reduce the cost of prescriptions) quite readily, but many did not. A research team concluded that a major factor in this variability was the culture of the different practices.

Interviews using the competing values model enabled the researchers to assign each GP to one of the cultural types. Those who expressed the values of the rational goal culture – efficiency, standards, etc. – accepted the EPS as consistent with that culture. Those who expressed the values of the human relations culture – individuality, informality, an interpersonal relationship – rejected EPS, as they interpreted it as an attack on that culture. More broadly, they interpreted the motives of the ministry trying to promote EPS as an attempt to undermine the professional autonomy of GPs, which for many has been, and remains, an important feature of their position.

*Source*: Boonstra et al. (2004).

---

These examples support the idea that if people interpret a proposed IS as being consistent with their culture they are likely to accept it with enthusiasm and commitment. If there is a mismatch between the culture and the IS, they will resist it.

---

## CASE QUESTIONS 6.2

What may the results of the Boonstra et al. (2004) study mean for those managing NPfIT?

Go to the website (www.connectingforhealth.org.uk) and read about the choose and book system. Assuming that GPs in the UK have similar cultures to those in the Netherlands (see Research Summary above), how may these have affected their attitudes to the system?

Table 6.1 Three perspectives on organisational culture

| Cultural perspective | Focus | Metaphor |
| --- | --- | --- |
| Integration | Consistency between aspects of culture, consensus, clarity. | A monolith that most people see as being the same, from whatever angle. |
| Differentiation | Inconsistency between subcultures in different parts of the organisation. | Islands of clarity in a sea of ambiguity. |
| Fragmentation | Ambiguity – people interpret aspects of culture in an uncertain way, depending on the issue. | An audience in which each member responds to an issue uniquely, in a transient combination with others. |

*Source*: Adapted from Martin (2002) pp. 94–95 with permission.

## ● Organisational and sub-unit cultures

Early studies of culture focused on identifying the unified cultures of whole organisations, but now they emphasise the diversity of organisational sub-units (Ogbonna and Harris, 2006). Martin (2002) identifies three perspectives in cultural research – integration, differentiation and fragmentation – which Table 6.1 summarises.

Those who take an integration perspective look for consistency in how people respond to organisational issues, and for consensus around established policies. They will expect people to support management proposals for, say, an information system and may regard opposition to a project as due to misunderstanding or poor communication. Those who take the differentiation perspective acknowledge the likelihood of conflict between business units or functional groups, based on distinctive interests and views of the world. These may be expressed in conflicting views about the benefits or otherwise of an IS as people interpret its likely effects from the perspective of their subculture. A fragmentation perspective sees organisations as being in a state of flux, with people expressing different views in shifting alliances with others as they interpret and reinterpret events and policies around them. This ambiguous position may reflect, and perhaps exacerbate, confusion over the intentions of new policies, especially among people far from the centre who receive little information.

One way in which sub-units differ is in their view of information in general, and an information system in particular. Do they see information as:

● belonging to individuals or to the organisation;

● a means of control or a source of creativity;

● something you protect and hoard or something you share;

● more valuable if it is hard and quantitative or if it is soft and qualitative?

People in subcultures differ in the information they require and how they obtain and process it. This will affect how satisfied they are with an information system and how they view a new one. They will welcome a system that fits the culture and resist one that conflicts with it. A study by Pliskin et al. (1993) showed a wide gap between the actual culture in an organisation and the culture that an IS vendor presumed to exist. The company had a central headquarters group and several geographically separate plants – each of which had a relatively high degree of autonomy. In particular, the plants had a culture, the members of which believed that informal interpersonal relationships worked well, and valued that management approach. Senior management engaged a consulting firm to implement a computerised employee evaluation system, the design of which made several assumptions about the culture in the plants. It depended, for example, on instituting a formal and structured process of employee evaluation. This clashed with the culture of autonomy: several similar examples led the authors to conclude that the culture presumed by the consulting firm and the actual culture at the company clashed so dramatically it led to the failure of the project.

In their review of research on culture and IS, Leidner and Kayworth (2006) identified five prominent themes, summarised and illustrated in Table 6.2.

Their review led them to conclude that the available research provides:

*a rich narrative of how different types of [organisational] and national values have an impact on information systems development, [adoption, outcomes, and management].* (Leidner and Kayworth, 2006, p. 373)

The evidence is clear that this is an aspect of the context of IS that those managing such projects need to include in planning and implementing such systems.

**Table 6.2** Examples of research conclusions on culture and IS

| Themes | Example of research | Summary of research conclusions |
| --- | --- | --- |
| Culture and IS development | Dube (1998) | Fit between the values embedded in the software development process and the organisation's values leads to more successful implementation. |
| | Walsham (2002) | National cultural differences between team members led to (initial) conflict in software development process. |
| Culture and IS adoption and diffusion | Hasan and Ditsa (1999) | Organisations in risk-averse cultures (high uncertainty avoidance) less likely to adopt IS. |
| | Ruppel and Harrington (2001) | Intranets are more likely to be adopted in open systems cultures, which emphasise flexibility and innovation. |
| Culture and IS use and outcome | Chau et al. (2002) | Consumer attitudes towards the Internet differed significantly between Hong Kong (used mainly for social communication) and United States (used mainly for information search). |
| | Harper and Utley (2001) | People-centred cultures tend to experience greater levels of implementation success than those with more production-centred cultures. |
| Culture and IS management | Husted (2000) | Software piracy more prevalent in countries with individualistic cultures. |
| | Kettinger et al. (1995) | Dimensions of IS service quality varied significantly between certain Asian and North American cultures. |
| IS influence on culture | Doherty and Doig (2003) | Improvements in data management ability led to changes in customer service and flexibility values. |

*Source*: Reprinted from Leidner and Kayworth (2006) with permission.

## www.connectingforhealth.nhs.uk

In an article summarising their research on NPfIT Currie and Guah (2006) note:

> As a nationwide program with several thousand users, each of whom will require different levels of access, need to share different databases, and receive different levels of training, it is likely that media attention to any shortcomings of the project will continue for several years to come . . . Our research suggests that E-government projects should embrace these wider challenges rather than focus solely on technology imperatives. If this is not done before technologies are identified and installed, the people affected by them are likely to develop attitudes and behaviour patterns that will circumvent their implementation . . . Government IT strategists need to address the wider cultural imperatives and the extent to which . . . people are predisposed to adopting new IT-enabled working practices . . . A top-down approach is likely to engender feelings of resentment and frustration among health-care workers, rather than a willingness to adopt and adapt to these changes. (p. 15)

*Source*: Currie and Guah (2006).

## ● Summary

- People may interpret the culture of their organisation not as something unified and integrated, but as one in which there are several subcultures.
- One dimension or manifestation of a culture is how its members see information.
- If people interpret an IS application as supporting their current culture they are likely to accept it; if they believe it will threaten their culture they are likely to reject it.

### Activity 6.1 Research on culture

If you have the opportunity in an assignment or project, you could test the competing values model by interviewing people in several departments about their reaction to an IS. Try to find out the following.

- What the IS was, what it was intended to achieve and what the current status is?
- What people in (say) three different departments think of it – support, oppose, mixed?
- What is the culture in the respective departments? Investigate this by giving them a copy of the descriptions of the four cultural types and asking them which description best represents their department.
- Consider if their replies and comments have affected their attitudes to an IS project.

## 6.2 IS can support central or local decision-making

One aspect of an organisation's structure is the extent to which decisions are made by people at different levels in the hierarchy.

- **Centralisation** is when those at the top make most decisions, with those at middle and lower levels following the policies thus established.

● **Decentralisation** is when a relatively large number of decisions are made by those working at middle and lower levels.

Each has benefits and costs. Centralisation enables people to respond consistently and avoids duplicating resources, but may mean they take less account of local conditions. Decentralisation enables local responsiveness but at the cost of some inefficiencies, and the risk that customers observe, and complain about, different practices in different parts of the business.

Computer-based IS can support either approach. Some early writers on the topic predicted that IS would lead to centralisation (Leavitt and Whisler, 1958), while others predicted the opposite – that it would promote decentralisation (Burlinghame, 1961). Both believed that technology would affect context (in this example, the degree of centralisation). An alternative, but still determinist, view is to reverse the causal link to show that context affects IS: a perceived need (for example) to increase financial control leads to a decision to implement a centralised financial IS. Boddy and Paton (2005) traced the evolving balance between central and local control at Kwik-Fit. The company operates a national chain of roadside repair depots. As the business grew it became progressively more difficult for senior managers to check that depot managers were making the right decisions – with a paper system it was almost impossible to check on stock levels or discounts. The next two MIS in Practice features trace the evolving balance between central and local control at the company.

---

| MIS in Practice | More central control at Kwik-Fit |
|---|---|

The company was an early adopter of electronic point of sale (EPOS) systems whereby terminals in each depot capture details of every transaction, and pass this overnight to head office for processing. Staff there now had very detailed daily reports on each depot's activity the previous day, and could immediately question any unusual transactions. The system enabled much greater central control, which had always been the founder's ambition. For example, a sales manager could review the performance of any depot:

*The systems have ensured that we have information to monitor what we are about – every morning I have a daily update. It tells me for the company as a whole, through our major product categories, what we sold across the depots, their value and the margin we generated. And we could have an individual depot if we wanted to. It gives us prices, margins and all the necessary monitoring elements. All this information goes to the manager as well, because they need to know how they are doing.*

*Sources*: Boddy and Gunson (1996); Boddy and Paton (2005).

---

Depot managers and staff at Kwik-Fit accepted the tighter central controls, as they were consistent with what had always been a relatively centralised company. The IT system did not introduce the idea of centralisation, but made it easier to apply the well-understood management practices. The system brought tangible benefits to depot managers and staff, which encouraged acceptance.

In other situations people may interpret a similar move towards more central control as an interference with their authority and as insensitive to local conditions. They may try to counter the proposals and resist centralisation. The outcomes will depend on the power of the respective groups to argue their case and to adapt the way people use the system during and after implementation. Markus' (1983) study of resistance to a centralising system at Golden Triangle (see p. 178) is a classic example – the Chapter Case Part 2 is a current example.

Managers can also use the capacity of IS to decentralise, and the next MIS in Practice box describes a later development at Kwik-Fit.

---

### MIS in practice — More local control at Kwik-Fit

Management changed the emphasis of their control as they installed a new generation of more powerful equipment, with the aim of keeping management close to the changing needs of the business. The board gave the (five) geographical divisions greater autonomy, and the divisional directors now had full responsibility for the profitability of their division. A senior manager explained:

*There was a large degree of autonomy within divisions, but there were a number of things they had to refer to the centre for approval. We have now decided that we do not really want to have a central core of people servicing these divisions. We would rather have the divisions as autonomous units.*

To support this organisational change, the company adjusted the computer systems to make them operate semi-independently for each of the divisions. It partitioned the database so that each division could access its data, but senior management were able to see the totality of the business. One of the new divisional directors noted:

*We process the invoices for all the purchases our depots make. Head office would previously have dealt with that, but now the supplier invoices the division. Head office still makes the payment electronically – but we initiate it. We only depend on head office for two things – marketing and advertising, and central computer services.*

He pointed out that the information to enable close monitoring of the depots was already available – but that divisionalisation allowed them to make better use of it. The divisional managers could combine it with their local knowledge to manage the business in a relatively decentralised way.

*Source*: Based on Boddy and Paton (2005).

---

Powerful computer systems allow management to rethink how they balance central and local control. Malone (1997) believed that the falling cost of communication would alter this judgement. When communication costs are high, most decisions, for the lack of any alternative, are made by relatively independent local decision-makers. As communication costs fall, managers can choose (for operational or political reasons) to bring more of the information to the centre. As communication costs fall further, managers have the new option of passing more information to local staff and empowering them to make more decisions.

---

### Activity 6.2 Explaining the Kwik-Fit story

- Summarise how (and why) Kwik-Fit shifted the balance between central and local control.
- What role did IS play in helping or hindering those changes?
- Does this account support or contradict Malone's theory?

The MIS in Practice box below contains an example of another company, Oticon, that used IS to eliminate a conventional hierarchy.

---

### MIS in Practice  Oticon – using IS to eliminate hierarchy

Oticon, a high-tech Danish hearing-aid company, is an example of a company that took a radical approach to its design, with IS at the centre. In 1994 the company was one of the five largest producers of hearing aids, exporting 90 per cent of its production. Changes in customer demands threatened its position during the 1980s and, after a period of financial losses, the board appointed a new chief executive, Lars Kolind. Kolind took a radical approach to the problem and sought to replace an existing organisation with one that was innovative, flexible and learning. To do this he:

- eliminated traditional departments – people now worked on projects, moving between them as the flow of work changed;
- created a project organisation – senior management appoint project leaders, who then advertise electronically for staff from within the company to join them;
- increased staff mobility – people occupy several positions, on different projects;
- removed private desks – and replaced them with mobile trolleys, the core of which was a mobile PC – these gave staff access to databases and other tools, and they wheeled them to meetings;
- eliminated paper – all documents were scanned and stored electronically and anyone with the relevant authority could access the data (results of meetings were stored electronically and can be used by people on other related projects).

By using IT, with radical structural changes, 'Oticon is able to bring a full range of resources to bear on a problem much more quickly than can their competitors'.

*Source*: Based on Bjorn-Anderson and Turner (1994); Foss (2003).

---

Other studies find evidence of increasing central control. Finnegan and Longaigh (2002) studied the use of IS in 15 subsidiaries of pan-national organisations located in Ireland, concluding that redesigned and standardised business processes were increasing the power of headquarters.

> *IT has facilitated more direct monitoring of day-to-day operations, while communication technology has vastly improved responsiveness to queries. This has enabled headquarters to take responsibility for many operations that were previously left to subsidiaries.* (p. 159)

Enterprise resource planning (ERP) systems are notoriously inflexible once they are designed and implemented. Their integrated nature imposes more discipline on users as their work is more tightly coupled, so their introduction often leads to greater centralisation of control and power (Schwarz, 2006).

We conclude from this contrasting evidence that in some circumstances people believe a relatively centralised structure is appropriate and in others they believe the opposite. Managers in successful organisations will have tried to develop a structure and information system that is aligned with strategy (Boddy and Paton, 2005). If they see new IS applications becoming available that will further support their established approach (whether centralised or decentralised) they will promote them. If other players accept management's diagnosis of the conditions they will accept it.

However, if managers seek to impose a system that others see as unsuitable for the conditions, they may experience a different reaction – as shown in Part 3 of the Chapter Case below.

# NPfIT – standardisation and the locus of design
**www.connectingforhealth.nhs.uk**

The National Programme is an attempt to enable electronic exchange of information across England by standardising the electronic healthcare record systems in use in all the Trusts across the country. The suppliers that have been commissioned to deliver the NPfIT applications are, in the case of national applications, expected to deliver the same systems throughout the NHS in England. In the case of the five geographical clusters, the suppliers are expected to deliver a similar suite of electronic healthcare records systems to all the NHS Trusts in their sector.

Within each Trust there are many healthcare teams delivering patient care . . . They can be considered as existing socio-technical systems with their own social systems deploying existing technical resources to accomplish their primary task of patient care . . . They have different histories and operate in different local circumstances.

The NPfIT may experience difficulties in part because of the diversity of these Trusts and the match between what is offered and what is needed is often very wide. In some cases this leads to Trusts rejecting what is offered and in other cases, the healthcare teams limit or construe what is offered in a way that does least damage to their work.

One application which appears to be successful is the Picture Archiving and Communication System which is being widely accepted by staff in many Trusts.

*Source*: Eason (2007, pp. 258 and 263).

---

## CASE QUESTIONS 6.3

● What clues can you find in the case about the balance between central and local control?

● What forces are likely to be shaping the pattern that develops?

● How may that affect the benefits of the investments in IS which the NHS is making?

---

## ● Summary

● Managers can use computer-based IS to increase central control.

● They can also use it to increase the ability of local units to make operational and sometimes strategic decisions.

● If people believe the established balance of control is suitable they are likely to accept an IS that reinforces that balance and oppose one that weakens it.

● Managers can also use IS to change the established balance, but changing both IS and structure will be a more challenging task than changing either on its own.

● The balance reflects how people interpret perfomance demands on the organisation and the interests of powerful players.

## 6.3 Structures to support IS-enabled ventures

Information systems give people the opportunity to develop new lines of business – and the challenge of deciding how to organise them. Should the new operation be integrated with the current business or established as a separate unit? Some banks create online banking services with a separate name from the parent – Egg, for example, is (now) owned by Citibank. Others, such as The Royal Bank of Scotland, integrate the two services. In retailing, Tesco and John Lewis offer online services through the physical stores, while others, among them Sainsbury's and Ocado, have built separate distribution facilities for the online business.

---

### Research Summary     New York Times Digital

Govindarajan and Trimble (2005) followed the evolution of the Internet venture at *The New York Times* (NYT). In common with most newspapers, the company launched an Internet business, naming the unit New York Times Digital (NYTD). At first most staff were from the print paper, adapting NYT content for the online version. Soon the product was losing market share to competitors that were making fuller use of the Internet than NYTD: perhaps being part of the (print) NYT constrained staff from being sufficiently innovative.

Management responded by creating a structure that signalled a more distinct business. The head of NYTD now reported to the company president, not the head of the NYT, and created a policy team that in turn:

● hired many new staff with Internet experience;

● moved to a different building;

● used different measures to assess performance;

● began to develop distinctive cultures and values within the online business.

This encouraged staff creativity, as they began to see that they were serving non-traditional readers and advertisers, who had different needs and expectations from those of the print paper. They explored new sources of revenue, and added content that was not in the paper, including material from other sources; audio, video and interactive features; and material from the NYT archive.

However, there were inevitably tensions between the two business units, made worse by the fact that NYTD depended on NYT for content, and for the advertising base. NYT circulation department feared that NYTD (which made content available at no charge) was reducing sales of the print paper. Editorial staff were concerned about protecting the brand, and there were conflicts over the processes of selling advertising.

Senior management were able to overcome these tensions by actively managing them, and seeking to ensure that NYTD came to be seen as a business that was adding new value to the group, not diminishing the role of the traditional paper.

*Source*: Govindarajan and Trimble (2005, pp. 63–4).

---

Gulati and Garino (2000) offer a model that helps to evaluate the options. They studied three retail companies that had developed online ventures and observed the choices the companies had made about relating the new venture to the old.

● Spin-off?

● Strategic partnership?

● Joint venture?

● In-house division?

The authors concluded that the appropriate choice would depend on how managers interpreted the answers to questions about the brand, the management and operation of the new venture, and about whether or not staff sought a financial stake. To illustrate the approach, Table 6.3 shows the suggested questions under each theme.

The authors advised that, depending on the balance of answers to these and similar questions, managers would get an insight into the decision to integrate or separate the venture. Note that the answers depend on judgement and interpretation, and will often point in different directions – so while they provide a way of structuring the decision, they may still leave it ambiguous and uncertain. Note also that the decision does not have to be complete separation or integration: it may be suitable to integrate IS provision for all units, while allowing the separate business considerable autonomy over pricing and advertising.

**Table 6.3** Questions on separating or integrating an Internet venture

| Separation | Questions | Integration |
|---|---|---|
| | **Brand** | |
| | Does the brand extend naturally to the Internet? | Yes |
| Yes | Will we target a different customer segment or offer a different product mix? | |
| Yes | Will we need to price differently online? | |
| | **Management** | |
| | Do current executives have the skills and experience needed to pursue the Internet channel? | Yes |
| | Are they willing to judge the Internet initiatives by different performance criteria? | Yes |
| Yes | Will there be major channel conflict? | |
| Yes | Does the Internet fundamentally threaten the existing business model? | |
| | **Operations** | |
| | Do our distribution systems translate well to the Internet? | Yes |
| | Do our information systems provide a solid foundation on which to build? | Yes |
| | Does either system constitute a significant competitive advantage? | Yes |
| | **Equity** | |
| Yes | Are we having trouble attracting and retaining talented executives for the Internet division? | |
| Yes | Do we need outside capital to fund the venture? | |
| Yes | Is a certain supplier, distributor or other partner key to the venture's success? | |

*Source*: Adapted from Gulati and Garino (2000) with permission.

## ● Summary

- Using the power of computer-based information systems for new business ventures raises major structural questions for managers.

- They need to decide whether to run the Internet venture as a separate enterprise or to integrate it with the existing business.

- One empirically based model suggests managers analyse this decision by considering the dimensions of brand, management, operations and equity.

## 6.4 IS enables new structures

Products and services are the outcome of a chain of activities linking internal processes to those in customers and suppliers – a value-adding chain that may stretch across continents and oceans. IS developments make it possible (though not easy) to transform the organisational structure through which people manage successive steps in the supply chain. IS makes it much easier for firms to coordinate activities in physically separate locations. This means that companies have much greater freedom over:

- the way they deal with customers (face to face or remotely);

- whether they own the resources they use (it may be easier to contract with other organisations to provide what they need); and

- how they manage knowledge (perhaps using expertise in other organisations as well as their own).

Some writers use the term '**virtual organisation**' to express the idea that IS makes it possible for firms to deliver goods and services with very little in the way of a physical presence. The development of Linux, outlined in the box, right, is one example.

However, with a few rare exceptions, all organisations have both physical facilities and some degree of physical separation within their value chain. Venkatraman and Henderson (1998) propose that the virtual organisation is not so much a state as a process. Organisations differ in the degree to which they are 'virtual' rather than being entirely one or the other. The authors suggest that 'virtualness' is a characteristic of any organisation, based on its position along three vectors – customer interaction, asset configuration and knowledge leverage (see Figure 6.2). This idea allows us to consider how IS developments enable long-established organisations to separate some activities physically.

## ● Customer interaction

Here Venkatraman and Henderson consider how IS makes it easier for customers to experience products and services remotely and perhaps engage in some dynamic customisation. Fundamentally this is no more than an extension of mail-order catalogues, which enabled physical retail stores to give customers some 'feel' for the products available without being physically present. IS, especially when linked with television, clearly offers many more possibilities for customers to view alternatives, select their options and conduct the transaction electronically.

| Vectors and characteristics | Stage 1 | Stage 2 | Stage 3 |
|---|---|---|---|
| Customer interaction (Virtual encounter) | Remote experience of products and services | Dynamic customisation | Customer communities |
| Asset configuration (Virtual sourcing) | Sourcing modules | Process interdependence | Resource coalitions |
| Knowledge leverage (Virtual expertise) | Work-unit expertise | Corporate asset | Professional community expertise |
| Target locus | Task units | Organisation | Inter-organisation |
| Performance objectives | Improved operating efficiency | Enhanced economic value added | Sustained innovation and growth |

**Figure 6.2 Virtual organising: three vectors and three stages**
*Source*: Venkatraman and Henderson (1998).

---

**MIS in Practice    Developing Linux**

The familiar story of how the Linux software system developed illustrates a new approach to organisation structure. Linus Torvalds, who developed the initial version, made it available on the Internet and invited other software developers to download it freely to test and modify it. It gradually attracted enthusiastic software developers, until the Linux community involved thousands of developers around the world, all sharing their work. Within a few years this informal group, working through the Internet, created a highly successful piece of software used by many corporate IT departments.

The community (and other 'open source' communities) have evolved mechanisms and processes to ensure order, despite the potential for chaos. These include the following.

● High intrinsic motivation and self-management among developers, ensuring they deliver high-quality work and appropriate social behaviour. They receive payment for their contribution to a software project, and recognition from other developers.

● Membership is fluid, but managed. Development teams typically have a core community, with additional members brought in for particular tasks.

● Control is exercised through a few simple rules, designed to ensure appropriate conduct and fair play.

● Self-governance is achieved formally through discussion and voting among community members, and informally through social control by other members.

*Source*: Markus et al. (2000b).

---

● **Asset configuration**

Here the focus is on the extent to which a firm coordinates resources and activities within a network – it does not depend only on assets it physically controls. This extends established practice, as firms have always depended on suppliers for things they preferred not to make themselves: IS enables them to be more active here than is possible with manual systems. The Internet allows access to a wider range of possible suppliers and customers, and can also be used to manage the relationships much more closely. These developments also encourage managers to consider outsourcing business support processes such as IS or recruitment.

Sun Microsystems, for example, has a corporate arrangement with three transport companies to manage its logistics – including not only transportation but also warehousing, pre-assembly work and final delivery. In more extreme cases, Venkatraman and Henderson envisage companies not as collections of physical assets, but as coalitions of resources. The competitive advantage comes from managing the resources, physically present in other companies on the network, in the most imaginative and productive ways.

## ● Knowledge leverage

This means gaining access to wider sources of expertise, including that in other organisations. IS allows staff in a work unit to have access to information generated elsewhere – staff in a call centre can access data about customer histories and spending patterns so that they can discuss a transaction more confidently. Groupware tools enable teams to share information more widely. A second level of development is when the firm shares information across the organisation as a whole – again by groupware or similar systems. A third level is when an organisation actively draws on expertise beyond its boundaries – in professional communities or from customers and suppliers. Internet developments make the rapid sourcing of such expertise technically possible.

### Activity 6.3  Linking theory and practice

Use the Venkatraman and Henderson model to assess the position of an organisation (such as your college or university) as a virtual organisation. Gather evidence to show which stage it has reached now on each of the three vectors (customers, assets and knowledge) and what plans there are, if any, to move to a 'more virtual' position.

Andal-Ancion et al. (2003) also deal with this issue, although they do not express the issue in terms of progressing through the stages suggested by Venkatraman and Henderson. Instead they suggest that managers need to decide what kind of relationship they want to have with other organisations. They set out the options.

● **Disintermediation:** A company uses the capacity of information systems to eliminate intermediaries (such as distributors) between itself and its customers or suppliers. Example: easyJet only sells tickets over the Internet, eliminating the travel agent as an intermediary.

● **Remediation:** A company uses IS to enable it to work more closely with intermediaries in close, long-term relationships that add value to its service. Example: Sainsbury (a UK supermarket chain) sells electricity under its own brand by (invisibly) using the expertise of a power company (Scottish Power) to deliver energy to customers.

- **Network-based mediation:** Companies use IS to build a network of alliances and partnerships, which they use in fluid and variable ways in response to changing supplier offers and customer needs. Example: Nokia has developed an extensive network of partners with manufacturing and logistics expertise, allowing it to focus on software development – which it also does in collaboration with scientists in other organisations.

In all cases the new arrangements are supported by sophisticated IS – and the choice for managers is which kind of relationship will best suit their business. Andal-Ancion et al. offer a model helping managers analyse this choice based on ten 'business drivers'. These include factors such as the characteristics of the product (whether it can be delivered electronically or not), the scope for aggregation (whether products from the separate organisations can be combined to add value) and missing competences (which IS can enable them to draw from other organisations).

Andal-Ancion et al. recommend identifying which drivers are most relevant to businesses and using that interpretation to help evaluate possibilities for transforming the organisation. They also stress that, whatever that evaluation suggests, there will still be a substantial task of organisational change to manage within the company, and possibly with suppliers and customers as well.

---

### CASE QUESTIONS 6.4

Relate this discussion of alternative organisational forms to the evolving NPfIT. Part of the context is that demand for healthcare inevitably exceeds the resources available to provide it, so all governments seek ways to use resources more efficiently. Many elderly people require regular monitoring for non-critical conditions, and live considerable distances from physical healthcare facilities. Staff travelling to patients is an inefficient use of resources.

- Use the Venkatraman and Henderson or Andal-Ancion models to speculate about how the structures of healthcare organisations may change.
- Also consider what factors may constrain this.

---

### ● Summary

- Computer-based IS increasingly support the flow of data and information across company boundaries.
- This makes it easier to separate the physical aspects of a business and to perform them in geographically separate places.
- Managers therefore have more options over how they manage customers, assets and knowledge.
- They also have more options over their relations with other organisations as they can choose between disintermediation, remediation or network-based approaches.
- Implementing such systems is a major challenge, as other business partners may also need to make significant organisational changes.

## 6.5 The political aspects of information systems

The prevailing distribution of power within an organisation has considerable, if often hidden, influence on the direction of an IS project. Power is essential to get things done in organisations, including the achievement of personal goals and rewards. Those with power want to retain it, while those with less power may seek opportunities to increase it. People can use information systems to threaten or strengthen the existing distribution of power, so we need some tools to analyse the links between IS and power. People use power to get things done, and seek to protect or increase their capacity to do so.

● Power is the capacity of individuals to exert their will over others.
● That capacity comes from five bases of power: coercion, reward, administrative expertise, technical expertise and referent.

### ● Bases of power

Building on early work by French and Raven (1959), Hales (1993) showed that a person's power is not just a personal characteristic, but follows from their position in the organisation. The five sources of power (each of which can have both a personal and an organisational aspect) are outlined below.

● **Coercive:** This is the authority to give instructions with the threat of sanctions or punishment available to back them up. Managers with this power can use it to instruct development staff about priorities or to instruct users to use (or not use) a new system.
● **Reward:** This is the ability to use the financial and other resources of the organisation to bestow status or rewards on others in return for their support. Managers with large budgets and links into valuable networks of contacts have power. They can commit some of their resources to others in return for the support they need – for example to persuade a manager in another department to support their IS project or to commit staff to work on the design.
● **Administrative expertise:** This is the power that the holder of a position has to create organisation policies that bolster their influence. They may use their position to decide which IS projects go ahead, what their objectives are or who will be on the project team – which in itself will shape the direction of the project.
● **Technical expertise:** As well as an individual's personal expertise, power can also arise if a person holds a position that gives them access to information so that they are aware of what is happening and of emerging threats or opportunities. They can use their position, and the contacts that go with it, to build their image as a competent person and to influence the direction of an IS project.
● **Referent:** This refers to situations where managers can use their position to influence others by showing that what they propose is consistent with the accepted values and culture of the organisation. They invoke wider values in support of their proposal or of their opposition to a proposal.

### ● Power and IS

The relevance of this to information systems is that people compete for access to, or control over, information and the power that goes with it – as the 'flowering of feudalism' MIS in Practice feature, right, indicates.

| MIS in Practice | The flowering of feudalism |
|---|---|

'Knowledge is power' has become such a managerial cliché that many at the top of big companies tend to forget that the principle can work both ways. Those lower down the management hierarchy also have an interest in husbanding information – and the power that goes with it. According to a survey of large European companies by the management consulting arm of KPMG, an accounting firm, the vast majority have found it impossible to establish pan-European management information systems for the simple reason that middle-ranking managers in different countries do not want those at headquarters to know what they are up to.

By 1993, few companies had succeeded in taking the first step by collecting information on their own far-flung European operations in a uniform way. After interviewing the chief executives or financial officers of 153 large European companies, KPMG found that only 8 per cent of them had established common information systems across their European subsidiaries. And this was not because of glitches with computers. 'Technically, of course, anything is possible with information systems these days,' observed the boss of a Danish tobacco firm. 'It is not the technical aspect that we find daunting; it's the time and energy we have to spend explaining it to people and persuading them to accept it.'

When they try to introduce the computers and procedures to gather such information, reported Alistair Stewart, who conducted the survey, European firms meet 'Ghandi-like' resistance from their subsidiaries. European HQs may be sending mixed signals to subsidiary managers: preaching autonomy and responsibility while trying to computerise all aspects of their business so that staff at headquarters can monitor their every move. 'People are reluctant to share their information,' complained the head of one French company, which manufactures industrial equipment. 'Managers in particular seem to think it gives them extra power.' Clever chaps.

*Source*: Based on 'The flowering of feudalism', *The Economist*, 27 February 1993.

If people are concerned about their power within the organisation, one of the criteria they will use to evaluate an information system is its likely effect on their power. Will it increase it, reduce it or have no effect? They are likely to promote and favour IS applications that enhance their power, and resist those that threaten it – as Markus (1983) showed (see the Research Summary overleaf).

More recently, Knights and Murray (1994) showed how managers at Pensco, an insurance company, used their respective power to try to shape the services provided by an IS project. Dysfunctional conflicts between them appeared to result in a system that was more expensive and less useful than the promoters had expected. Power is also essential when implementing systems, a theme we explore in Chapter 9.

## Activity 6.4 Researching power and IS

Try to identify an example of an information project that has been implemented (or perhaps has been blocked), and discuss it with someone who works there.

● Has it affected the power of any groups or departments?
● Which sources of power has it affected?
● Did any groups attempt to block the project, and were they concerned about power or influence?

### Research Summary   Golden Triangle Corporation

Golden Triangle Corporation grew from a merger between a chemical company and two energy companies. The structure consisted of a headquarters staff group, including corporate accounting, and four operating divisions. The divisions had a relatively high degree of autonomy over marketing and investment decisions, reflecting the diverse businesses they conducted. Traditionally, the divisional accountants collected and stored transaction data however they saw fit, but reported summary data to corporate accountants in a standardised form.

The corporate accounting department proposed the creation of a financial information system. A task force from corporate accounting analysed the need for such a system, and recommended the purchase of a financial accounting package. This would enable a single corporate database to replace the divisional databases.

The system collected, summarised and distributed financial data. Divisional accountants entered their transactions into the system, and the IS automatically summarised the data into reports (e.g. monthly profit and loss statements) for corporate accountants and for the relevant division. The first division went into the system in January 1975.

In October 1975, an accountant from the division wrote that: 'Except for providing more detailed information, the IS has not been beneficial to us.' In October 1977, he wrote: 'After two years and seven months my opinion has not changed. Even worse, it seems to have become a system that is running people rather than people utilising the system.' Other divisional users shared his views. One division kept on using its old accounting methods after it started using the IS, even though this required time and effort. Some divisional accountants admitted to 'data juggling' to circumvent the system.

The corporate accountants welcomed the system enthusiastically. It automatically performed tedious tasks of calculation and reporting that they had formerly done by hand. Corporate accountants could not account for the resistance of divisional staff members. One said: 'I can't understand why the divisions don't like the IS. There are so many benefits.'

*Source*: Markus (1983).

## ● Summary

- People in organisations value the power that ensures their capacity to influence others.
- Power comes from both personal and positional sources of coercion, reward, administrative and technical expertise, and referent.
- Each of these sources can be strengthened or weakened by an information system.
- One factor in how people react to an information system is its likely effect on their power.
- If they see an IS as a means of enhancing their power they will use their existing power to support the project, and vice versa.

## Conclusions

We have examined the interaction between three aspects of organisation – culture, structure and power – and information systems. The Chapter Case shows the challenges of implementing a national system in diverse local settings, in which cultural and political considerations will influence events.

Information systems open up choices for managers over how they adapt the organisation – whether to adapt the culture or the information system, how much centralisation for which to aim, how closely to integrate an online with a traditional business. While managers can analyse these dilemmas using rational analyses such as those suggested here, they do so within their cultural contexts. This will affect how they and others interpret events, how receptive people are to change and whether the change supports or challenges the distribution of power.

At least as important as the choices in any one area is whether or not the sequence of changes complement each other, so building a coherent response to external events. That is also true of how they organise the IS function itself, which we examine in the next chapter.

## Chapter questions

1. What are the implications for management wishing to implement a company-wide IS if they find that major departments occupy different positions in Figure 6.1?

2. Evaluate Malone's theory about the evolution of centralised and decentralised organisations, in the light of your experience and/or other evidence.

3. Suppose your university is considering offering an online learning programme. Use the Gulati and Garino model to develop an appropriate set of questions that would help the university to decide whether to integrate the online venture with traditional courses or launch it as a separate venture.

4. What are likely to be the main difficulties facing a company that wants to create an extranet to link it to all of its suppliers?

5. Summarise in your words the main features of the Venkatraman and Henderson model.

6. Use the Andal-Ancion et al. model to gather and compare examples of organisations changing their relationships with other organisations or customers.

7. Have you any personal examples of political interests affecting how managers reacted to a proposed IS?

## Further reading

Eason, K. (2001) 'Changing perspectives on the organisational consequences of information technology', *Behaviour and Information Technology*, **20**(5), 323–8. An overview of the topic of this chapter from a leading scholar.

Jasperson, J., Carte, T.A., Saunders, C.S., Butler, B.S., Croes, H.J.P. and Zheng, W. (2002) 'Power and information technology research: a metatriangulation review', *MIS Quarterly*, **26**(4), 397–459. An extensive review of the literature on power in relation to IS.

Two articles on culture – the first a review, and the second an empirical study in a financial services firm:

Leidner, D.E. and Kayworth, T. (2006) 'A review of culture in information systems research: towards a theory of information technology culture conflict', *MIS Quarterly*, **30**(2), 357–99.

Ogbonna, E. and Harris, L.C. (2006) 'Organization culture in the age of the Internet: an exploratory study', *New Technology, Work and Employment*, **21**(2), 162–75.

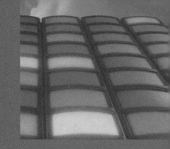

# CHAPTER 7

## Organising and positioning IS activities

### Learning objectives

By the end of your work on this topic you should be able to:

- Recognise and compare alternative ways of dealing with IS strategy, acquisition and operation

- Give examples of alternative IS structures:

    - user department

    - centralised

    - decentralised

    - federal

    - distributed

    - resource pool

    - outsourced

  and state their advantages and disadvantages.

- Evaluate proposals for and against outsourcing IS

- State some staff issues and activities relating to IS provision

- Compare different ways of controlling IS activities and relate these to wider strategy

- Compare approaches to IS governance

## Cemex – global growth through information capabilities

**www.cemex.com**

Cemex is a large supplier of cement and other building materials, with operations in many countries. It is also an example of an agile, efficient, e-business pioneer. The corporate philosophy involves whole-heartedly embracing new technology and imposing tightly controlled standards worldwide, for both its technology and in-house management techniques. The company, founded in 1906, grew domestically and diversified into mining, hotels and petrochemicals (see www.cemex.com). At the end of the 1980s, it set up a satellite network so that it could transmit all the internal data to its headquarters in Monterrey, Mexico. Cemex deployed this system, Cemexnet, to allow data and voice transmission between the 11 production facilities in Mexico. More valuable than cost savings was the data the system produced about all aspects of the business.

Computerisation spread throughout the group, though Cemex has never had a mainframe computer, relying instead on distributed, interconnected systems to share information across the company. These allow top managers to see what is going on, but they also give lower-level employees some access – enough to allow 'a healthy degree of competition between the different units', says Hector Medina, Chairman Zambrano's number two.

The Internet allowed transparency to spread outside the company, provoking some complaints that it was making too much information public. Cemex is now pushing the information culture even further, putting computers with Internet access into its employees' homes. Connectivity has also transformed many of the company's internal processes – most notably the delivery of ready-mixed concrete. Getting mixer trucks from the plants to the building sites at the right time, with cement needing to be poured within 90 minutes of mixing, is always a challenge. Cemex trucks now contain a computer and a global positioning system receiver – combining their positions with information about output at the plants and orders from customers helps smooth the process, and enables each truck to meet many more orders per day.

Cemex also developed systems to collect and process customer feedback. Truck drivers surveyed customers upon delivery and the information was entered into online customer files. Based on this information, the order-taker would be able to apologise when a dissatisfied customer called.

The goal of Cemex is to become fully web-based, with all its employees having access to their own files, the company's data and outside information through a single, personalised portal. Operations will be centralised through the Internet, even though the management teams themselves are spread around the globe. Corporate finance is already run in this way, and procurement, sales, distribution, and supplier and customer relations are managed over the Internet.

*Sources*: IMD (2005) 'The Cemex way: the right balance between local business flexibility and global standardization', Case number 1341, IMD Lausanne; company website.

## Introduction

Cemex has been innovative in the way it has used computer-based IS to support the business, continuously gathering information to support management decisions and operational improvements. It has seen IS as a valuable tool to integrate this highly dispersed company and in doing so has faced many decisions about how to organise the IS function – such as which aspects to manage centrally and which to leave to local business units. We can trace these decisions from the initial limited use of information technology to the current intensive use throughout the business. From the beginning IS governance has been a high priority.

As information systems grow in significance, so too does the question of how to provide them. Chapter 4 examined how IS can support competitiveness and how to align them with broader strategy. That depends on how managers position their IS function and who is responsible for delivering IS services. There is always competition for the IS budget. How should managers divide this between units? How can the company ensure that IS professionals understand business needs and customers? Equally, how can they ensure that non-IS professionals understand the business implications of information systems? Managers now debate how they should organise Internet and e-commerce activities. Questions related to decision-making on IT are often called **IT governance** (Weill and Ross, 2005).

The chapter first outlines alternative ways to position IS activities within the organisation. Outsourcing is a further option and we examine the dilemmas around this. Then we look at how managers can divide and control the IS budget for competing units. The next topic is the complexity of the culture gaps between three constituencies: IS management, user management and general management. The final topic presents an approach to governing IT management.

The aim of the chapter is to show alternative ways of providing computer-based information systems, and the dilemmas within these options.

## 7.1 Alternative ways to structure IS activities

If we enquire into how and why a company has organised its IS in that way, we are likely to find a range of historical and contemporary influences. Centralised organisations will tend to centralise information systems. Decentralised organisations will usually give responsibility for IS to the business units, to cope with the variety of systems required. Established IS managers in either type of business will try to maintain oversight of IS activities. They will resist attempts to decentralise or outsource the service. Managers of local units will try to increase their control over IS resources.

There is no right answer. We can only indicate the alternative information system architectures and some of the factors that influence the choice. By **information system architecture** we mean the way in which the IS assets (hardware, software, telecommunications) are deployed and connected and the ways they interact with each other (Oz, 2006). Positioning IS architectures in ways that do not fit the culture or structure will cause tensions.

We present the alternatives as pure forms, though organisations typically combine them to reflect local features and circumstances.

### ● Concentrating IS activities in one user department

In the early days of computing, IS functions were part of the department that made most use of them – often finance and accounting. Figure 7.1 represents this. This works well when most users are in that area, and they can build experience and expertise. Difficulties arise as other departments begin to use IS, and so depend on the resources, willingness and ability of the 'responsible' department.

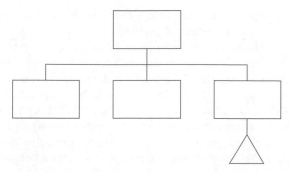

**Figure 7.1** IS positioned in one functional department: computers, software and data directed to one specific functional department

---

**MIS in Practice   TDC**

TDC installs complex technical installations in offices and factories and employs approximately 80 highly skilled technicians and about 20 managers and support staffers. It is deliberate company policy to keep overheads as low as possible in order to survive in a highly competitive market. The management consists of three directors and a CEO. The three directors have respectively main responsibility for: 1) Installations and technicians, 2) Finance and 3) Sales and Marketing. The Finance director is also responsible for information systems and IT. These systems are used for the overall information storage and provision, including management information.

---

## ● Centralising IS activities

In this arrangement, a central IS unit is responsible for most computing activities (Figure 7.2). When a user department requires a new or enhanced system, it applies for it through the IS department. The IS department prioritises requests, using guidelines agreed with senior management, and then delivers and supports the services.

The MIS in Practice example, right, shows that systems integration, accessibility and concentrated expertise are major advantages of centralised IS. It allows people to focus on corporate rather than local needs. A disadvantage is that the dominant, centralised department can be inflexible and remote from the business and may appear

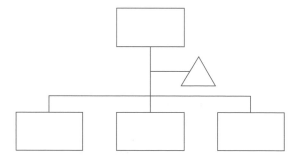

**Figure 7.2** Centralised IS architecture: centrally controlled computers, software and data

---

**MIS in Practice** | **Centralised IS organisation at Gasunie**

Gasunie is one of the largest gas transporters in Europe. It provides and develops gas transport activities. Its main tasks include management, maintenance, renovation and expansion of a national and international gas transport grid. It has a centralised IS department that develops and maintains a range of IS applications that are used to support its operational and management processes. The management at Gasunie thinks that it is crucial to use company-wide systems, such as enterprise resource planning (ERP) systems, to overview the interrelated range of business processes. The combined expertise of IS professionals in one central unit is also perceived by management as a major advantage.

---

technologically arrogant to users. Departments have different information needs; with centralised systems, all receive a common service so that few are fully satisfied. The centralised model fits best with organisations that make other decisions centrally, that work in a stable environment and where there is little communication between units.

## ● Decentralising IS activities

When IS is decentralised the organisational units become responsible for their systems – including development, acquisition, operations and maintenance. Figure 7.3 represents this. This is only possible when the units are independent, with little communication between them. Specialists from the (former) central IS department now work in the

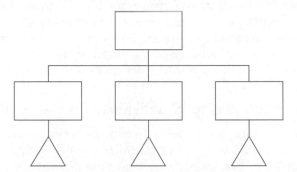

**Figure 7.3** Decentralised IS architecture: workers and departments at different sites use information resources directed to their work or department

---

**MIS in Practice** | **Examples of decentralised IS**

Unilever, a worldwide operating company in food and healthcare, has many different business units and a variety of brand names and products. It organises its IS activities at a business unit level. The business units only have to agree on harmonised reporting structures to the top level.

NDC, a publisher of newspapers and books, has various business units that are responsible for a range of products. Each business unit maintains its own IS organisation, including IS professionals, IS applications and IS infrastructures.

---

185

**Table 7.1** Characteristics of centralised and decentralised dominance

| Centralised – IT dominance | Decentralised – user dominance |
| --- | --- |
| Emphasis on database and system maintenance | Emphasis on user needs and problems |
| New systems must be compatible with existing ones | Growth of new systems |
| Requests for service require sound justification and tangible benefits | Multiple and frequently changed suppliers; little hard evidence of benefits |
| Standardisation dominates | Lack of standardisation and control over data and systems |
| Specialisation in technical frontiers, not user- or business-oriented benefits | Users building networks to meet local needs, not corporate |
| Focus on control | No coordination between users to learn from experience or transfer technology |
| Users dissatisfied | Duplication of technical staff |

*Source*: Reprinted from Corporate Information Systems Management: Text and Cases (Applegate, L.M., McFarlan, F.W. and Kennedy, J.L.) 2007, Irwin/McGraw-Hill, p. 420. Copyright © McGraw-Hill Companies, Inc.

business units. Kahay et al. (2003) discussed with more than 100 IS executives their plans to decentralise IS. The researchers concluded that, while most believed that IS should be decentralised in the interests of responsiveness, they also advocated that a central unit should be responsible for security, standards and IS governance.

Applegate et al. (2007) discuss the implications of centralised 'IT dominance' versus decentralised 'user dominance' and identify an extensive list of consequences. Table 7.1 summarises the consequences of the two approaches to organising IS.

In a decentralised setting, the business units and the users control IS and make their own decisions. If managers see the advantages of decentralisation but also the disadvantages of full independence, they may choose the federal model.

## ● Federalising IS activities and distributed information systems

Some companies choose to decentralise IS tasks such as specification and administration, while maintaining central control over others such as data standards and hardware compatibility. A centralised department can determine information strategy for the organisation and administer the corporate system and database. The decentralised departments can develop and manage local IS within those corporate guidelines. A **distributed IS**

| MIS in Practice | Federal IS organisation at Ahold |
| --- | --- |

Ahold, a retailer with headquarters in the Netherlands, operates with four retail formulas in several counties. At head office the IS unit maintains strict guidelines with regard to enterprise applications, system definition, data management and contracts. Within each retail formula and also within each country managers can develop unique applications within these corporate guidelines.

*Source*: Information provided by the company.

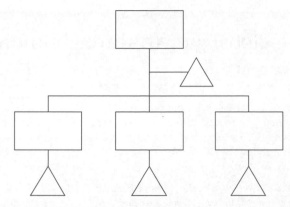

**Figure 7.4** Federalised or distributed model of IS architecture: resources are jointly owned and maintained, and are shared by using some degree of central control

**architecture** means that departments have some independence in developing and using IS without losing the benefits of centralised control over data and communications. Figure 7.4 shows this model.

In adopting the federal model, companies have to determine which IS activities to centralise, decentralise or outsource. This often leads to a dynamic situation where activities move from one level to another. Other terms for the federal model are 'distributed' and 'cooperative'. This model fits best in organisations with a high interdependence, a high need to share data, and a turbulent environment.

People who take a rational view of things believe that managers select from these alternatives a model that best suits their unique circumstances. They may aspire to this, but history and subjective factors also influence events.

- Using the Internet for e-commerce suggests a centralised or business unit approach to IS, to ensure that systems can connect with those of other organisations. Such a change is impossible in situations of anarchy or feudalism.

- Implementing an ERP system can lead to monarchy or technocratic utopianism – a more centralised, standardised and integrated management structure (Boonstra, 2006). That may not be right for the business at that time.

## Activity 7.1 Positioning IS activity

Identify, for an organisation you know, which of the models (Figures 7.1–7.4) best describes the positioning of its IS activities.

- What are the most important reasons for organising that way? Use the factors in the models to prepare your answer.

This chapter identifies a number of possible reasons for positioning IS activities in a certain way. These include the need to share data as well as a range of organisational factors.

- Try to assess which of these reasons best explain the pattern in that organisation.

# Cemex – global growth through information capabilities

**www.cemex.com**

Zamrano believed that there were opportunities for synergy if information processes could be replicated regardless of country. He also realised that people could be a stumbling block during integration. Iniguez, the CIO, explained:

> When you make a foreign acquisition you face biases and reluctance to give up current practices and corporate cultures . . . technology is not an end in itself. Management must figure out how its processes, functions and systems can accommodate the different needs of the employees.

Cemex included being people-oriented as a selection criterion for hiring IT managers. In the mid-1990s the company launched a business process re-engineering programme, including a three-year training course on human philosophy. The program helped shift the focus of global information system design from technological infrastructure to information processes and information use. Iniguez said:

> I don't like IT. The interpretation of IT is really poor. I have never focused on the technology part. During my stay in Cemex, the centre of IT was human beings. We could leverage human beings and business processes with technology.

*Sources*: IMD (2005) 'The Cemex way: the right balance between local business flexibility and global standardization', Case number 1341, IMD Lausanne; company website.

## CASE QUESTIONS 7.1

- How does Cemex organise its information services? Use the model in Figure 7.5 and/or the Weill and Ross model, below, to help arrange your answer.
- What would be some alternative ways to organise these services? What would be their advantages and disadvantages?
- Identify another organisation and find out how managers there have organised these services. Compare that with the Cemex approach, and explain possible reasons for similarities and differences.

There is no single best way to organise and position IS activities. Arrangements vary from centralised to decentralised, with hybrid forms and federal arrangements in between. Weill and Ross (2005) present their business performance matrix as a model to help companies assess their IT governance (see the Research Summary). They identify five IT decision domains (IT principles, IT architecture, IT infrastructure strategies, business application needs, and IT investments) along the horizontal axis, and on the vertical set out five ways of organising IT (business monarchy, IT monarchy, federal, feudal and anarchy). The resulting matrix can help companies to consider their current and future way of organising and governing IT.

## ● Summary

- Management can use different models in positioning IS activities in their organisations; these include centralised, decentralised and federalised models.
- Each model has its own features, advantages and disadvantages. The pattern depends on factors such as the stage in using IS, and the structure and culture of the organisation.

## Research Summary   Information management policy

Weill and Ross (2005) see the positioning of IS activities and IS decision-making from a political point of view. They suggest that all these types of positioning are actually power battles between various parties with specific interests. They distinguish five approaches to managing information politics, which vary from all power at the top to anarchy (see Figure 7.5).

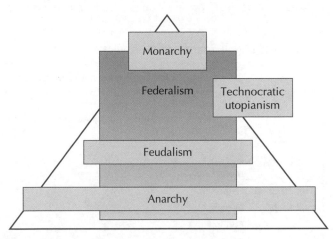

**Figure 7.5** Five approaches to information management and their centre of control

- **Technocratic utopianism:** A heavily technical approach to information management, stressing categorisation and modelling of an organisation's full information assets, with heavy reliance on emerging technologies. This approach will often lead to centralised IT activities, where IT experts are most powerful.

- **Monarchy:** The firm's leaders define information categories and reporting structures by the firm's leaders, and they may or may not share the information willingly after collecting it. Close to the centralised model, where senior management is in charge rather than IT experts.

- **Feudalism:** The management of information by individual business units or functions, which define their own information needs and report only limited information to the rest of the corporation. This is quite close to the federal model, with an emphasis on decentralisation.

- **Federalism:** An approach to information management based on consensus and negotiation on the organisation's key information elements and reporting structures.

- **Anarchy:** The absence of any overall information management policy, leaving individuals and user departments to obtain and manage their own information. This will often lead to the decentralised model.

| MIS in Practice | Applying the Weill and Ross model www.ingdirect.com |
| --- | --- |

ING Direct, an international direct banking unit of Dutch financial service conglomerate ING, takes a hybrid approach to IT governance. National units operate autonomously, but share a common business model. The bank uses standardised business solutions and standardised technical and infrastructural components, through which it offers a wider range of products, including savings, personal loans, mortgages, retirement plans and mutual funds. Its IT governance can be summarised as shown in Table 7.2.

**Table 7.2  IT governance at ING Direct**

| | | IT governance decision domains | | | | |
| --- | --- | --- | --- | --- | --- | --- |
| | | IT principles | IT architecture | IT infrastructure strategies | Business application needs | IT investments |
| | Business monarchy | X | | | | X |
| Governance archetype | IT monarchy | | X | X | | |
| | Federal | | | | X | |
| | Feudal | | | | | |
| | Anarchy | | | | | |

## 7.2  Outsourcing or in-house?

To try to overcome the centralisation–decentralisation problem, some organisations have concentrated part of their IS expertise in a resource pool. Business units or departments can hire this as required. Figure 7.6 illustrates this 'resource pool' approach.

| MIS in Practice | Example of a resource pool   www.achmea.nl |
| --- | --- |

Achmea is a Dutch insurance company that has many business units and brand names, following and acquisitions. The business units concentrate on certain groups of insurance and related products, such as social insurance, life insurance, banking activities and health insurance. Every unit has its own IS department. The company recently began an integration policy to concentrate resources and know-how. It will also promote data-sharing about customers. Management created a company-wide IS organisation – 'Achmea Active' – that every business unit can hire. This operates as a resource pool. It works with service-level agreements and charges market prices for its services. Business units are also free to buy services from other providers.

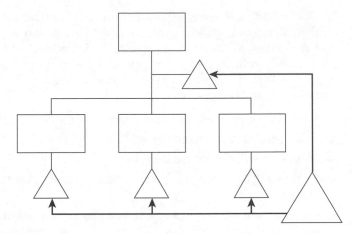

**Figure 7.6** Information service supply as a resource pool

Resource pools concentrate expertise, while business units decide whether or not to use them. The approach raises questions such as the following.

- Can other organisations hire the resource pool?
- Can business units hire expertise from other providers?

Such arrangements are often an introduction to the (partial) **outsourcing of IS**; this is the transfer of the management and/or day-to-day execution of an entire business function to an external service provider. The client organisation and the supplier enter into a contractual agreement that defines the transferred services. Under the agreement the supplier acquires the means of production by transferring people, assets and other resources from the client. The client agrees to procure services from the supplier for the term of the contract. **Offshoring** is the transfer of IS to another country, regardless of whether the work is outsourced or stays within the same corporation. **Multisourcing** refers to large outsourcing agreements in which different parts of the client IS will be sourced from different suppliers. This requires an IS governance model that communicates strategy and specifies the rights and responsibilities of those involved in the provision and use of IS.

The idea behind outsourcing is that it allows management to concentrate on the core activities of the business. It also allows companies with fluctuating IS needs to pay only for what they use. Other reasons are to keep up with technological changes and to overcome the problems of hiring good IS staff. Figure 7.7 represents an organisation that outsources IS.

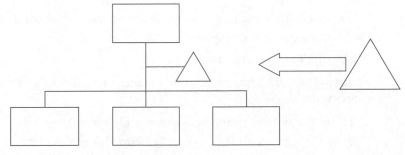

**Figure 7.7** Outsourcing IS activities

Outsourcing can mean either a short-term contractual relationship with a service firm to develop a specific application or a long-term relationship in which the service firm takes over all of an organisation's IS functions. We focus on the latter, in which outsourcing includes application development, software, hardware and telecommunications purchasing and maintenance. Common reasons for and potential advantages of outsourcing are (Gonzalez et al., 2006):

- access to highly qualified know-how and consulting;
- lower personnel and fixed costs;
- greater attention to core business;
- services will be provided to a legally binding contract with financial penalties and legal redress;
- use of an outsourcing agreement as a catalyst for major step change that cannot be achieved alone;
- acceleration of the development or production of a product through the additional capability brought by the supplier;
- standardising business processes, IT services and application services, enabling businesses to buy intelligently at the right price.

---

### MIS in Practice    IT outsourcing at General Motors

General Motors, the world's largest automobile company, is also the largest consumer of IT products and services. All of GM's IT operations are fully outsourced. In April 2004, GM invited many IT vendors to its plants to begin the bidding process for a new outsourcing contract. The company's earlier contract with EDS was to expire in June 2006. The consolidated value of the new contracts was estimated to be about $15 billion.

GM had concluded that its existing outsourcing contract with EDS was not satisfactory, since it became too dependent on one supplier that knew the company's business very well. GM now wanted to use several vendors so that their collective expertise could bring more cost-effective results. They would do this through the use of Service Level Agreements (SLAs). The IT division of GM would become mainly responsible for managing the IT outsourcing programme. They have developed policies and frameworks to enable multiple vendors to work on common IT projects.

*Source*: Chaturvedi (2005).

---

Equally, outsourcing carries major risks:

- loss of control and greater dependency on the service company;
- loss of experienced employees;
- paying too much for the service.

Lacity (2001) therefore suggests that managers considering outsourcing should ask these questions.

1. Are the systems (being outsourced) truly not strategic?
2. Are we certain that our IS requirements will not change?
3. Even if a system is a commodity, can it be broken off?

4. Could the IT department provide this more efficiently than an outside provider?

5. Do we have the knowledge to outsource an unfamiliar or emerging technology?

6. What pitfalls should we expect when negotiating the contract?

7. Can we design a contract that minimises risks and maximises control and flexibility?

8. What in-house staff do we need to negotiate strong contracts?

9. What in-house staff do we need to ensure we get the most out of our contracts?

10. What in-house staff do we need to enable us to exploit change?

Outsourcing of information systems management will be encouraged by the advent of companies known as **application service providers** (ASPs) (Hirschheim and Bandula, 2003). An application service provider (ASP) is a business that provides IS applications to customers over the Internet. The applications are installed at the ASPs' locations, along with the databases and other files that the application processes for the client. Employees access these over the Internet. Software offered using an ASP model is also sometimes called **on-demand software**. One example of a provider of such services is Covisint (see MIS in Practice below). The most limited sense of this business is that of providing access to a particular application program (such as medical billing) using a standard protocol. The need for ASPs has evolved from the increasing costs of specialised software that have far exceeded the price range of small to medium-sized businesses. As well, the growing complexities of software have led to huge costs in distributing the software to end-users.

| MIS in Practice | Covisint – a provider of IS facilities www.covisint.com |
|---|---|

Covisint is a global company that provides computer applications and access to information to many organisations through one common technology infrastructure. Companies of all sizes, locations and technical capacities make use of Covisint's services for the secure sharing of business information, applications and business processes across their internal processes and with their suppliers and customers.

Covisint's identity management products allow companies and governments to share information and applications with their suppliers, partners and in joint ventures, as well as with citizens or end-consumers.

Covisint's hub-based identity management model is delivered as software as a service (SaaS), meaning that the majority of the technology components are hosted, operated and managed in Covisint facilities. Covisint uses its own hardware, application servers, web servers, database software, networking devices and monitoring tools so that customers of Covisint do not have to install and configure such tools themselves.

*Source*: Company website.

Through ASPs, the complexities and costs of such software can be reduced. In addition, the issues of upgrading have been eliminated for the customer, as the ASP provides continuous technical support and security for their systems. For example, a bank can process loans in the traditional way or by web services architecture. In the former the process is usually supported by a very complicated application maintained by an individual bank. With web services architecture, the bank connects with the most appropriate institution for such transactions. Different suppliers offer various bank modules and the bank can shift between providers, using one service for (say) risk analysis of loans to restaurants and another for loans to hospitals (Hagel and Brown, 2001).

As the Internet gets faster, more reliable and more secure, many people expect that more companies will outsource their computer operations to more ASPs. This may lead to so-called **web-services architecture**, which means that companies rent the functions they need – data storage, processing power or applications – from service providers.

---

**MIS in Practice       ASP at Talbert Medical    www.talbertmedical.com**

It was a techie version of a heart transplant. When the doctors of Talbert Medical Group spun their practice out from a bankrupt physician management company last year, CIO Al Herak faced a daunting task: to build the computer underpinnings for the new company in just three months. It would normally take at least a year. If he couldn't pull it off by the time the bankrupt outfit closed its doors on 1 August, Talbert's 110 doctors would be helpless – unable to schedule appointments or track records, potentially forcing their patients to look elsewhere for care. If botched, this manoeuvre might have wrecked the partnership. Instead, Talbert is in the pink of health – on track to do $80 million in business this year. And Herak is a hero. He got the job done cheaper, faster and better than he had ever thought possible. How?

He turned to TriZetto Group Inc. in Newport Beach, California, a new breed of tech company that houses computing gear at its own facilities and dishes out software to customers such as Talbert over the Internet: no fuss, no muss – and fast. Herak doesn't have to spend upwards of $1 million on computer systems and then more every year to keep them running. Instead, he pays a monthly fee of some $100,000 – the same way he pays a utility bill. 'We're just saving money, and if it goes down, I just make a phone call and say, "It's your stuff, you work it out",' says Herak. 'I love it.'

*Source*: 'Technology on tap', *Business Week*, 19 June 2000.

---

However, IS outsourcing is not an isolated decision, as other activities (such as manufacturing, R&D, finance) can also be outsourced. There are two extreme positions.

● All activities are carried out in-house. The company even tries to buy suppliers and customers in order to control the value chain completely. This can lead to powerful conglomerates and hierarchically managed and controlled bureaucracies.

● All non-managerial activities are performed by others. The company buys services from specialised companies for almost all its activities – purchasing, manufacturing, marketing and so on. This is close to the concept of the networked organisation. The organisation becomes lean, flexible – and dependent on its partners.

Most companies are positioned somewhere between these two extremes. This raises the question of which activities are performed by the company and which by other companies (Applegate et al., 2007). The Internet raises new strategic considerations on this issue (Gilley and Rasheed, 2000). Applegate (2007) suggests that the impact of IS on core strategy and on core operations determine the suitability of IS outsourcing. For companies with a low impact of IT on strategy and operations, the outsourcing presumption is 'yes'. When the importance for operations is 'high', the outsourcing presumption is 'yes', unless the company is huge and well managed. High impact on strategy and low

| Research Summary | Unbundling production from delivery |
| --- | --- |

Technology helps companies to utilise fixed assets more efficiently by disaggregating monolithic systems into reusable components, measuring and metering the use of each, and billing for that use in ever-smaller increments cost-effectively. Information and communications technologies handle the tracking and metering critical to the new models and make it possible to have effective allocation and capacity-planning systems.

Amazon.com, for example, has expanded its business model to let other retailers use its logistics and distribution services. It also gives independent software developers opportunities to buy processing power on its IT infrastructure so that they don't have to buy their own. Mobile virtual network operators, another example of this trend, provide wireless services without investing in a network infrastructure. At the most basic level of unbundled production, 80 per cent of all companies responding to a recent survey on web trends say they are investing in web services and related technologies. Although the applications vary, many are using these technologies to offer other companies – suppliers, customers, and other ecosystem participants – access to parts of their IT architectures through standard protocols.

Companies that make their assets available for internal and external use will need to manage conflicts if demand exceeds supply. A competitive advantage through scale may be hard to maintain when many players, large and small, have equal access to resources at low marginal costs.

*Source*: Manyika et al. (2008).

impact on operations implies a mixed view on outsourcing. The same for high impact on strategy and operations – as shown in Table 7.3.

If a company decides to oursource IS, they also need to establish a governance programme to manage the various obligations of the parties involved and to realise that the interests of the firms are aligned as much as possible. For most firms this means investing a portion of the total contract value in governance people, structures and processes as well as in acquiring the skills needed to design and build them. Depending on the complexity of the outsourcing deal, comprehensive IS outsourcing governance includes:

- quality measurement and management;
- preparation and management of change;
- policies and practices management;
- contract and financial management;
- communication and stakeholder alignment;
- functional organisation;
- roles and responsibilities;
- redesign of the retained organisation (for the outsourced business process);
- assessment and management of inter-company relationship alignment.

Knowledge of each of the above areas does not typically reside within the skill set of the outsourcing client. Also, outsourcing provider firms implement the above functions only from the requirements of the provider, not to satisfy the fiduciary responsibilities of the client.

The continuation of the Cemex case shows how the company has moved through these phases of organising IS, and how organisational and technical changes affect the IS

**Table 7.3** Strategic view on IT outsourcing

| | | IT impact on core strategy | |
| --- | --- | --- | --- |
| | | Low | High |
| IT impact on core operations | High | Uninterupted service-oriented information resource management. Oursourcing presumption: yes. **Reasons to consider outsourcing:** Possible economies of scale for small and medium-sized firms. Higher-quality service and backup. Management focus facilitated. | Strategic information resource management. Outsourcing presumption: mixed. **Reasons to consider outsourcing:** Rescue an out-of-control IT unit. Tap source of cash. Facilitate cost flexibility. Facilitate management of divestiture. Access to technology and skills otherwise not available. |
| | Low | Support-oriented information resource management. Oursourcing presumption: yes. **Reasons to consider outsourcing:** Access to higher IT professionalism. Access to current technologies. Risk of inappropriate IT architecture reduced. | Turnaround information resource management. Outsourcing presumption: mixed. **Reasons to consider outsourcing:** Internal IT unit not capable in required. technologies and/or project management skills. Access to technology and skills otherwise not available. |

*Source*: Applegate et al. (2007).

department. IS staff become relationship managers, maintaining relations between senior management, users and service providers.

---

## Activity 7.2  Research on the IS function

Take a familiar company and describe how it has organised the IS function.

- What advantages and disadvantages do people in the organisation see in that structure?
- What alternative forms might be realistic for the company?
- Has it considered using ASPs or outsourcing its IS requirements?

---

## ● Summary

- Outsourcing IS services can range from small services to the complete function.
- The advantages will vary between organisations and with circumstances.
- Lacity (2001) suggests some questions for those considering outsourcing.
- IS outsourcing may be considered as part of an overall strategy of the organisation towards outsourcing of processes or services.
- Application service providers are a further possible way of securing IS services.

# Global growth through information capabilities

## www.cemex.com

The company spun off its internal IT arm, Cemtec, and joined it with four other Spanish and Latin American firms to create Neoris, an IT consultancy. Neoris has 3000 professionals (compared with Cemtec's 600) and offers services to Cemex customers and suppliers as well as other companies such as American Express and Coca-Cola. Also part of Cemex is Construmix, a construction industry online marketplace, including an e-procurement site.

With regard to Construmix, the construction industry portal, Mr Iniguez, CIO of Cemex, thinks that its future lies not simply in buying and selling online, but in providing other services for customers who already buy Cemex cement. For instance, it could create an online meeting place for everybody involved in a particular construction project. The blueprints could be put on the Internet and updated online. The contractors and suppliers would then be able to consult an up-to-date version at all times. Construmix might also become a place to sell insurance, financing and other ancillary services.

Neoris expanded further by acquisitions and remained profitable and competitive. It planned to reduce its reliance on Cemex from 95 to 30 per cent. With the contribution of these new ventures, Cemex has numerous options for growth: international acquisitions, e-business consulting, horizontal B2B e-procurement portals, distribution logistics and expansion in the construction industry.

*Source*: Company website.

---

### Activity 7.3 Cemex

Analyse the Cemex example by describing the successive ways of using and structuring information systems. Use the models in Figures 7.2–7.7 to illustrate the changes.

- How does Cemex deal with outsourcing?
- How does this change the characteristics and core competences of the firm?

## 7.3 Charging for IS activities

Another organisational issue is how to divide the costs of information systems. This relates to how management responds to questions such as these.

- Should IS be a business within a business or managed as a service centre?
- Should IS be an expense or an investment, and what are the consequences of each?
- Should IS be charged at cost prices or at market prices?
- Should business units be able to use external IS providers?

In response to such questions, companies have devised four ways to control and charge for IS activities.

- **Service centre:** Users do not pay for IS resources. The service is 'free'. Non-financial goals are more important than financial ones and IS does not have to earn revenue or recover costs.

- **Cost centre:** Here the costs of services are allocated to users through charge-out. Users are as responsible for cost consciousness and financial accountability as the specialists. IS investments are intended to reflect cost–benefit analysis, but are not necessarily funded by cost recovery.
- **Profit centre:** IS services are charged at 'cost-plus' or market prices. The IS department operates as a business unit. Managers expect it to earn a return on the investment made.
- **Hybrid centre:** Users pay for some services and some receive a central subsidy. Innovative and turnaround activities are managed loosely, while routine core activities are managed tightly. The IS function has clear financial and non-financial goals.

The way organisations deal with these questions depends on factors such as:

- stage of use of IS: many organisations will grow from a service centre to a profit centre and from a profit centre to a hybrid centre;
- structure of the organisation: decentralised organisations tend to profit/cost centre structures and centralised organisations tend to cost/hybrid centre structures;
- culture, power and people issues: charging for IT services is a more formal approach, while offering them free is better suited to small and informal organisations;
- financial resources: charging for IT services is often a reaction to growing IT expenses;
- technology choices: company-wide technologies such as corporate databases and corporate networks will often be seen as overhead costs that should be divided in an arbitrary way between user departments. Technologies used by specific departments are charged more easily. See Figure 7.8.

Table 7.4 sets out the advantages and disadvantages of each approach and summarises these.

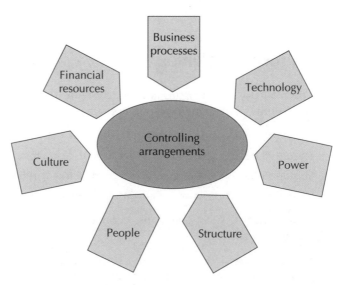

**Figure 7.8** Interacting factors, influencing the charging arrangements

**Table 7.4** Advantages and disadvantages of four ways of managing the cost of IS

| Advantages | Disadvantages |
| --- | --- |
| *Service centre* | |
| Stimulates usage and experimentation. | Can create uneconomic requests. |
| Suited to first stages of assimilation. | Can protect IS from accountability. |
| Avoids accounting complexities. | Requires good funding decisions. |
| Avoids organisational conflicts. | May dilute organisational learning. |
| Fits turnaround and support activities. | Inappropriate for strategic and factory activities. |
| Can fit centralised IS unit. | Rarely fits decentralised IS organisation. |
| *Cost centre* | |
| Encourages reasoned use requests. | Can be a deterrent to IS use. |
| Creates control of IS. | Can focus on costs, not on benefits. |
| Suits later stages of assimilation. | Can cause arguments. |
| Satisfies desires for charge-out. | Many accounting choices. |
| Fits cost centre organisations. | Often unsatisfactory in practice. |
| Relatively simple accounting. | Disliked in profit centre organisations. |
| *Profit centre* | |
| IS function has to control costs. | IS function can cut costs and service. |
| IS function has to market itself. | IS function may go external. |
| IS–user partnership can be forged. | Users may act as short-term traders. |
| IS activities may become innovative. | IS function may become too entrepreneurial. |
| *Hybrid centre* | |
| Can manage IS loosely or tightly. | Can be confusing. |
| Suits later stages of assimilation. | May be misfit with host management controls. |
| Suits different assimilation stages for different technologies. | Can cause internal conflicts. |
| Fits turnaround and strategic activities. | Needs strong direction. |
| Facilitates central push in decentralised context. | Can be complex accounting. |

● **Summary**

● Management has to decide which part of the IS resource should support existing operations and to acquire and maintain operational systems.

● Depending on the organisational properties mentioned, this may lead to the provision of IS activities as a service centre, a cost centre, a profit centre or a hybrid centre.

# 7.4 Managing IS as a partnership of three interest groups

Much of the complexity of information systems management stems from managing the conflicting cultures of three groups – general management, users and IS staff (see Figure 7.9). Many observers have recognised that a cultural gap, which can severely damage relations, develops between these players.

These groups have different expectations, tasks and responsibilities in relation to IS. The IS staff have to respond to the needs and requirements of users within management

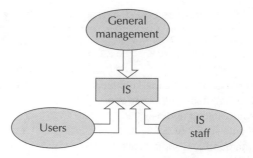

**Figure 7.9** Three (internal) interest groups in relation to IS

**Table 7.5** Perceived failings from other parties' perspectives

| General managers' failings | Users' failings | IS staff's failings |
|---|---|---|
| No clear business plan available. | No clear expression of needs and expectations of IS. | Inability to match information systems to business needs. |
| Inability to spot strategic uses of IS. | Focus only on operational support, no strategic vision. | Preoccupation with the technicalities of IS. |
| Failure to communicate requirements to systems staff. | Lack of appreciation of technical complexities. | Lack of understanding of business environment. |
| Insistence on cost justifying all investments. | No contribution to planning and policy of IS. | Failure to market business successes of information systems. |

guidelines and limited resources. Users expect a high level of IS support to do what management expects of them. Management has to decide about IS strategy in coordination with the other parties. This all takes place in a dynamic environment, causing tensions and problems:

● IS staff do not understand what users and managers do and need;

● users and managers do not understand what IS staff do and need.

It is not surprising that relations between these groups are tense, and Table 7.5 lists how each group perceives the others. The challenge for management is to deal with these potential problems and to develop a more productive organisational arrangement. Some possible measures are shown in the following sections.

## ● To improve good communications between the parties

Here are some examples.

● An IS manager on the board (CIO – chief information officer) can help to place IS challenges and problems on the agenda at the highest level.

● A steering group including representatives from the three groups mentioned can improve communications and understanding between these groups.

## ● To improve understanding in IS matters

Let us take some examples.

● Education programmes, information meetings and distribution of internal or external publications on IS can improve understanding between the three parties. Line managers need to know enough about IS to view it as a crucial factor in strategic and operational business planning. They must be in a position to manage IS as a normal part of their business management responsibilities.

● Systems staff must be educated in such a way that they become committed supporters of line management IS initiatives. Many of them still have to make a determined effort to shake off their traditional image, which is often perceived by line managers as alien and obstructive. Education in this field is most successful when it is organisation specific and action related, and it should be a continuous process, not a one-off 'awareness' course.

## ● To position the IS function at an appropriate place in the organisation

As suggested earlier, a structural solution may also help – such as positioning IS in such a way that business units are themselves responsible for IS. The federal model may improve communications and put responsibilities at the right level of the organisation.

---

### Activity 7.4 Interest groups

This section suggests that IS should be managed as a partnership of three interest groups that should balance each other. Discuss and describe what will go wrong when:

● IS staff are in charge and make the main decisions on systems without considering the management's or the users' points of view;

● users and user departments are in charge and make the main decisions with respect to IS without considering the IS and the managerial perspective;

● managers make the main IS decisions without consultation or the participation of IS staff and users.

---

A solution proposed by Markus (2004) is the development of technochange managers. She distinguishes between IT projects, organisational change programmes and technochange – each type has a different target outcome and needs a certain approach, as shown in Table 7.6.

**Technochange managers** need to combine technical (IT) skills and business literacy. The idea is that managers with this (extremely rare) combination of skills will be able to guide senior managers towards uses of information systems that are appropriate for the business. Table 7.7 summarises the ideal knowledge and skills that are necessary for technochange managers (Harison and Boonstra, 2008).

**Table 7.6 Technochange vs. IT projects and organisational change programmes**

|  | IT projects | Technochange | Organisational change programmes |
|---|---|---|---|
| Target outcomes | Technology performance within time and budget. | Improvement in organisational performance, enabled and facilitated by new IT. | Improved organisational performance. |
| Solution | New IT. | New IT in conjunction with complementary organisational change. | Intervention focuses on people, structure and culture. |
| Approach | Project manager who is expected to produce a working system that meets stated specifications on time and within budget. | A programme of change, including new IT but in combination with coherent changes in processes, job redesign, structures, etc. | Changes in processes, structures, job redesign, etc. |

*Source*: Based on Markus (2004), pp. 94–5.

**Table 7.7 Taxonomy of competences and knowledge related to technochange processes**

| Competence |  | Description and source |
|---|---|---|
| Knowledge | IT | Insight into new IT applications and system development processes. |
|  | Organisational change | Insight into general nature of change. Effective individual response to change. Insight into human aspects of project management. |
|  | Technochange | Ability to oversee IT applications in conjunction with complementary organisational change. |
|  | Risks and success factors | Understand the crucial success factors of change: completeness, implementability, appropriateness of benefits. |
| Skills | Communication | Interviewing, speaking, listening, writing. Organisational communications. |
|  | Process management | Managing the organisational and people sides of change. |
|  | Leadership | Planning and evaluating change. Project manager as a planning agent. Project manager as a facilitator and a team builder. Directing, delegating and controlling. Managing, patience, leadership, sensitivity. Diplomacy, empathy, politics. Cooperation, leading teams. |
|  | Consequences of change | Ability to oversee and to anticipate on the consequences of change. |

## ● Summary

- It is a management challenge to create optimal working conditions between business units, users and IS experts in order to make the best use of information systems.
- Some writers have encouraged people to develop the skills of hybrid managers, able to bridge the cultural gaps between the three communities.

## 7.5 IS staff

A typical IS department employs programmers, system analysts, operators and so on. In a federal or decentralised situation, they may also work in other departments or areas to support a particular unit. IS staff need, of course, technical skills to do those jobs, but also skills in written and verbal communications and a deep understanding of the business operations of the organisations they are serving. Since IS staff often work in teams, together with other IS staff members or employees from business departments, they also need teamworking skills. When a part of the IS operations is outsourced, internal IS staff members have to work closely together with the outside service providers, which can be located overseas (see Section 7.2).

Typically, an internal IS department has four responsibilities: IS strategy, operations, acquisition and development, and support; see Figure 7.10.

The **chief information officer (CIO)** is primarily responsible for the overall effectiveness of information systems in the organisation and the management of information resources. A CIO is member of the board of directors. In some organisations, this is one of the tasks of a board member. IS operations staff run and maintain the information systems, and ensure they are available and reliable. They also deal with maintenance of the computer facilities. IS **acquisition and development** staff are responsible for the development or acquisition of systems. Software packages are often adapted to the specific demands of firms. This will often demand some programming and adaptation. The same goes for the firm's websites. The acquisition/development department has to work closely together with the operations department in order to reach a seamless transition from development and maintenance to availability and use. The IS **support unit** is responsible for assisting users by advising and training them when new systems are implemented. They also operate help desks to receive calls for help or service, which they sometimes pass to staff in operations or development.

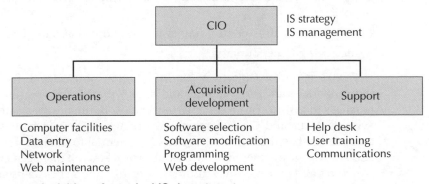

**Figure 7.10 Activities of a typical IS department**

---

**Activity 7.5 Research project**

Select a company that you know and identify major tasks with regard to information systems.

- How are these tasks structured?
- Was this structure recently changed?
- What were the reasons of this change?

---

## ● Summary

- IS personnel work in centralised, decentralised, federalised or outsourced departments.
- Such departments employ different IS professionals, including programmers, system analysts, operators and so on.
- IS departments have four responsibilities: IS strategy, IS operations, IS acquisition and development, and IS support.
- The CIO is primarily responsible for the overall effectiveness of the information systems in the organisation.

## 7.6 IT governance

There are narrower and broader definitions of **IT governance**. Weill and Ross (2005) focus on 'specifying the decision rights and accountability framework to encourage desirable behaviour in the use of IT'. In contrast, the IT Governance Institute (2007) expands the definition to include underpinning mechanisms: 'the leadership and organisational structures and processes that ensure that the organisation's IT sustains and extends the organisation's strategies and objectives'. Following ITGI's definition, IT governance is directed to an understanding and management of the challenges and risks associated with implementing new technologies. Among these are:

- aligning IT strategy with the business strategy;
- cascading strategy and goals down the enterprise;
- providing organisational structures that facilitate the implementation of strategy and goals;
- insisting that an IT control framework be adopted and implemented;
- measuring IT performance.

COBIT (Control OBjectives for Information and related Technology) is a system that provides managers, auditors and users with a set of measures, indicators and best practices to assist them in using IT in the most optimal way, created by the Information Systems Audit and Control Association (ISACA). These measures, indicators and best practices are based on the notion that IT is essential to manage transactions, information and knowledge in order to be successful. It provides top management with organisational structures and processes that ensure the organisation's IT sustains and extends the organisation's strategies and objectives.

BUSINESS OBJECTIVES

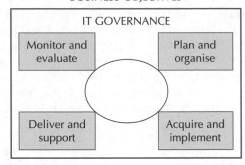

Figure 7.11 Domains of IT governance according to COBIT (2007)

As Figure 7.11 shows, COBIT covers four domains:

● plan and organise;
● acquire and implement;
● deliver and support;
● monitor and evaluate.

Each domain includes a number of activities.

## ● Plan and organise

The Plan and organise domain covers the use of information and technology and how best it can be used in a company to help achieve the company's goals and objectives. It also highlights the organisational and infrastructural form IT is to take in order to achieve the optimal results and to generate the most benefits from the use of IT.

## ● Acquire and implement

The Acquire and implement domain covers identifying IT requirements, acquiring the technology, and implementing it within the company's current business processes. This domain also addresses the development of a maintenance plan that a company should adopt in order to prolong the life of an IT system and its components.

## ● Deliver and support

The Deliver and support domain focuses on the delivery aspects of the information technology. It covers areas such as the execution of the applications within the IT system and its results, as well as the support processes that enable the effective and efficient execution of these IT systems. These support processes include security issues and training.

## ● Monitor and evaluate

The Monitor and evaluation domain deals with a company's strategy in assessing the needs of the company and whether or not the current IT system still meets the objectives for which it was designed and the controls necessary to comply with regulatory requirements. Monitoring also covers the issue of an independent assessment of the effectiveness of the IT system in its ability to meet business objectives and the company's control processes by internal and external auditors.

The COBIT standards, as described above, can be used by managers responsible for IT governance to compare their activities with standards in order to assess IT operations. However, the relevance of each standard depends on the specific context of the company, such as size, relative importance of IT and complexity of IT systems. A potential pitfall of such extensive IT governance standards is that they can promote inflexibility and bureaucracy.

## ● Summary

- IT governance includes the specification of decision rights and accountability of desirable behaviour in the use of IT.
- IT governance concerns are: aligning IT with business, cascading strategy down the organisation, appropriate IT structures, IT control and measurement of IT performance.
- COBIT provides a set of measures, indicators and best practices of IT governance.
- The relevance and usefulness of such measures depends on the specific context and characteristics of the organisation.

## Conclusions

In this chapter we have examined the issues companies face in organising and positioning their increasingly influential information systems activities. We outlined a range of structural choices, covering functional, centralised, decentralised and federal arrangements. There is also the more radical option of outsourcing. Whichever is chosen, there is the question of how to share the costs.

The Chapter Case illustrates how a company develops its IT function and IT use through various stages. This is caused by technological change as well as organisational development and growth. The company moves from a small function providing IT support towards centralisation and outsourcing. The corporate culture also plays a significant role in the way IT is organised and structured.

That change can occur even in very traditional organisations and is demonstrated by many other examples throughout this book. The skill appears to lie in managing the partnership between the various parties with an interest in the system, and in building their support during implementation. These are topics to which we turn in Chapter 9.

## Chapter questions

1. List some IS activities and decide who should do them (e.g. managers, users, IS staff, customers, suppliers, ASP, outsourcing companies). Explain your opinion.

2. Give examples of (a) an integrated and secure system and (b) an open and accessible IS. Explain when integration and security are the top priority, and when openness and accessibility are the top priority.

3. Many organisations implement ERP systems. Can you relate ERP to:

   ● the centralisation versus decentralisation issue;

   ● the in-house versus outsourcing issue;

   ● the rational versus participative issue.

4. Under what circumstances would you advise a company not to outsource IS?

5. An organisation wants to promote the use of the Internet for internal and external transactions and for sharing of information. At the moment, few staff use this kind of service. Would you advise the service centre approach, the cost centre approach, the profit centre approach or the hybrid centre approach? Explain your choice.

6. An organisation uses a groupware system. Managers want to evaluate this system and ask three groups (management, users and IS staff) to define evaluation questions. Provide six questions (two from each group) to illustrate the perspective of each group.

7. When would you assess if you were responsible for the audit of the IT organisation of a company?

# Further reading

Applegate, L.M., McFarlan, F.W. and McKenney, J.L. (1997) *Corporate Information System Management: Text and Cases*, Irwin McGraw-Hill, Chicago. Extensive text on strategic and managerial issues of IS management, including the decentralisation–centralisation dilemma and various aspects of outsourcing.

Two papers on aspects of IS provision – the first a review of outsourcing literature, and the second on the idea of shared services, application service provision and web services architectures:

Gonzalez, R., Gasco, J. and Llopis, J. (2006) 'Information systems outsourcing: a literature analysis', *Information & Management*, **43**(7), 821–34.

Hagel, J. and Brown, J.S. (2001) 'Your next IT strategy', *Harvard Business Review*, **79**(10), 105–13.

Two papers on aspects of IS governance:

Nolan, R. and McFarlan, F.W. (2005) 'Information technology and the board of directors', *Harvard Business Review*, **83**(10), 96–106.

Ross, J. and Weill, P. (2005) 'A matrixed approach to designing IT governance', *MIT Sloan Management Review*, **46**(2), 26–34.

# Weblinks

The IT Governance Institute (ITGI) exists to assist managers in their responsibility to ensure that IT is aligned with the business and delivers value, its performance is measured, its resources properly allocated and its risks mitigated. They provide an interesting website with free documents, report, articles, best practices and case studies: www.itgi.org

# CHAPTER 8

## People and information systems

### Learning objectives

By the end of your work on this topic you should be able to:

- Explain the nature and significance of an interpretive approach to IS
- Describe the discipline and contribution of human–computer interaction
- Summarise the variables in the TAM/UTAUT model and some empirical results
- Use the work design model to analyse the actual or possible effects on motivation of an IS
- Explain the contextual factors that support the use of IS in distributed working
- Outline the idea behind the socio-technical approach to system design
- Evaluate proposed IS projects from these perspectives and plan accordingly

# Nokia

## www.nokia.com

Nokia is the world's leading manufacturer of mobile phones. With an estimated market share of 35 per cent, it sells about twice as many handsets as its nearest rival Motorola and many times the number of others such as Samsung and Ericsson. A Finnish company, founded in 1895 as a paper manufacturer, Nokia grew into a conglomerate with wide interests, but in the early 1990s senior managers decided to focus on the mobile phone industry, then in its infancy.

Two factors favoured this move. First, the Finnish government had taken a lead in telecoms deregulation and Nokia was already competing vigorously with other manufacturers supplying equipment to the national phone company. Second, the European Union (EU) adopted a single standard – the Global System for Mobile Telephony (GSM) – for Europe's second generation (digital) phones. This became the standard used by two-thirds of the world's mobile phone subscribers. Finland's links with its Nordic neighbours also helped, as people in these sparsely populated countries adopted mobile phones enthusiastically.

Nokia has strong design skills, but above all managers were quick to recognise that mobile phones are not a commodity but a fashion accessory. By offering smart designs, different ring tones and coloured covers Nokia became the 'cool' mobile brand for fashion-conscious people. And as phones become less about making calls and more an extension of people's connected lives, Nokia is transforming itself: 'We're not a cell phone company, we're a software and services company as well' (Anssi Vanjoki, Nokia Vice President, quoted on BBC News, 27 February 2008).

It is also a formidable logistics company, having mastered the challenge of delivering millions of phones to customers around the world. Every *day* it builds over one million phones in over 100 designs, which it distributes in 70 languages to 150 countries. It has been especially successful in the large and rapidly growing markets of China and India.

One factor in the company's sustained success appears to have been a culture that encourages cooperation within teams, and across internal and external boundaries. Jorma Ollila, CEO until 2006, believed that Nokia's innovative capacity springs from multifunctional teams working together to bring new insights to products and services. Staff work in teams, which may remain constant for many years. However, from time to time they join with other teams to work on a common task.

The company also encourages a culture of communication by creating small groups from around the company to work on a strategic issue for four months. This helps them to build ties with many parts of the company – some of which continue to flourish in their later careers. The induction process for new employees also encourages team-building and cooperation: the newcomer's manager must introduce them to at least 15 people within and outside the team.

*Source*: *The Economist*, 19 June 2004; *Financial Times*, 20 June 2006; Grattan (2005).

## Introduction

Computer-based information systems touch people in many roles. As users, customers, individuals, technical specialists, managers or project sponsors, information systems are a taken-for-granted element of our context. Nokia is a prominent example of the many technology companies that are bringing about that change, and is itself constantly changing. It no longer sees mobile phones as a convenient means of voice communication, but as platforms for a widening range of mobile software. Its expertise is computer software providing useful services – which it sells on mobile devices.

It is therefore intently focused on people as consumers and producers. It recognises that the company which understands the end-user experience is going to have an edge – and at the same time recognises that it must manage its employees in such a way they deliver software and devices that give consumers an experience they value.

All companies using IS face a similar challenge, though often in less dramatic ways. To the extent that they are using IS to improve products or services, they need to understand the benefits that people value and how IS can enhance those benefits by, amongst other things, offering better-quality or more timely information. Auction sites like eBay, search engines like Google or online newspapers like FT.com continuously develop their sites to add to customers' experience and to generate more business.

They also need to ensure that staff are motivated to work with the technology in a way that meets those expectations: Google and Nokia are renowned for their imaginative approaches to employee benefits to support creativity and innovation of software engineers. Siemens' ShareNet (Chapter 2 Case) works because its designers took the trouble to find out what users require, and managers then created incentives to use the system. The ambulance service command and control system reported on p. 226 worked because managers ensured staff would welcome the design – as was the case with the Kwik-Fit EPOS system (Chapter 6, pp. 166 and 167). These are success stories, of which there are many more. Equally there are examples of companies using IS in ways that ignored the skills and knowledge of staff. Boddy and Gunson (1996), Lloyd and Newell (1998) and Wright and Lund (2006) all report cases in which employees have experienced less satisfying and motivating work after their employer introduced a new IS. Managers either ignored the human aspects of the system or used the new technology to impose inappropriate controls. These proved self-defeating and almost certainly ensured that the companies received a poor return on their investment.

Managing IS therefore means being alert to the interactions between the system and the people who engage with it. In this chapter we focus on people as individuals, in contrast to Chapter 6 which focused on the organisation. We present ideas about human capabilities, needs and motivation – ideas that help us understand how people, whatever their roles, interact with IS.

The chapter begins by tracing how people interpret their context, and how this shapes the meanings they attach to a system. It then presents three approaches to understanding and managing people in relation to information systems: human–computer interaction, the technology acceptance model and theories of human needs. This leads to a comparison of underlying management policies (control or commitment?) and of distributed working arrangements. The chapter concludes with ideas about socio-technical design and user-centred design methods.

## 8.1 People and context interact

IS projects develop when people with sufficient influence come to believe that the potential benefits (however measured) of an enhanced system will exceed the costs (however measured). Even with technically sophisticated technology, people remain essential to most value-adding processes. Organisations do nothing: people do things. Figure 1.4 showed that an IS includes people and processes as well as hardware and software, while Figure 1.6 (repeated here as Figure 8.1) shows that it is also located within its internal and external contexts. A delivery system that needs to respond quickly and imaginatively

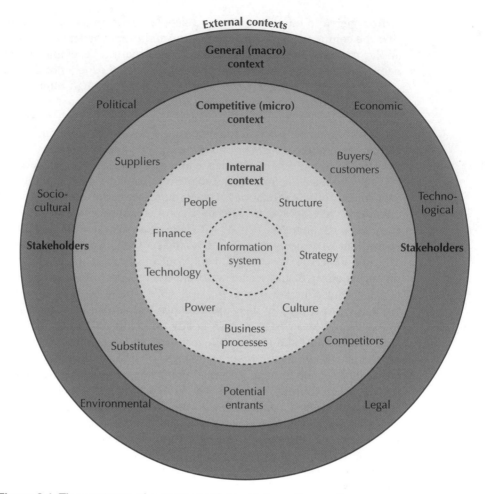

**Figure 8.1** The contexts of a computer-based information system

to customer preferences needs well-informed, motivated people: they have knowledge and skills that an IS can support and complement, but rarely replace. Of course, technology eliminates people from routine operations and many processes now operate without human intervention. But automated processes are usually only part of the customer-service process, and the complete experience is made or marred by interactions with people – whose commitment (or otherwise) makes the difference between a good and a bad experience. Otim and Grover (2006) show that the most significant factor influencing customer loyalty to a website is the quality of post-purchase support, including order tracking, on-time delivery and customer support – the last two of which clearly depend on people.

People are not usually passive recipients of information systems, but active players who shape their use. As they sponsor, design, adapt or use an IS they observe and interpret their context and try to shape it to their needs. People promote, or react to, a project in the light of how they see the historical and present context. They act to change that context – by proposing a new system or process – that others then interpret in the light of *their* objectives. The players use their power (also part of the context) to influence decisions and how to implement them. If they believe a system will enhance their power, or support their cultural values, they will support it. If not, they will find ways of opposing it. The outcomes of this interaction between people and context may or may not support the intentions of those promoting the change.

An interaction perspective means paying particular attention 'to the context of the information system, and to the process whereby the information system influences, and is influenced by, this context' (Walsham, 1993, pp. 4–5).

Studying context means identifying elements, such as those in Figure 8.1, and recognising that people will interpret these from different perspectives. Walsham (1993) also observed that:

> *a more subtle set of contexts for an information system are the various social structures which are present in the minds of the human participants involved with the system, including designers, users and any of those involved with the system.* (p. 5)

This implies that people not only observe the physical aspects of the system and its relation to (say) organisational strategy, but also the likely effects on social structures – such as relations between departments, between centre and local, and on personal networks. They will consider how best to influence events in a way that meets their interests, using the sources of power and influence available to them.

As they do so, they interpret elements of the context to give meaning to events, perhaps through questions such as 'why are they proposing that system rather than another one?' or 'what may that do to the position of our department?' As they attempt to develop or adapt the system they try to create or reinforce meaning – 'if we use this system it will show that we are a modern, efficient business' or 'that will undermine the way patients expect us to work'.

The interaction perspective also draws attention to the shifting nature of the context. People draw on aspects of the context (such as new technology becoming available) and their perceived authority (an aspect of power) to propose and develop an IS. Some players may make similar interpretations and support and develop the project; others may see things differently and propose changes or abandonment. Both will use apparently rational and objective arguments to back their case. The evolving system will reflect the relative ability of each party to influence the actions of other players – it will reflect the multiple realities that exist in the minds of those involved. Being willing to recognise multiple realities affects how people develop IS. It affects, for example, whether promoters recognise critics as having equally legitimate views of the world that they need to take into account or they dismiss them as symptoms of a communication problem.

## ● Summary

- How people respond to an IS system reflects their interpretation of the system and its context – including the social system of which they are part.
- They favour applications that support their interests, and vice versa.
- They interpret a system and its context as a source of meaning – a way of understanding what the change implies for them and the organisation.

## 8.2 Human–computer interaction

The discipline of human–computer interaction (HCI) or **ergonomics** tries to understand both the human user and the computer system, and to make the interaction between the two more satisfying and productive. In this it is dealing with two complex systems: the computer and the human. Analysts aim to understand how users function, the tasks they perform and how best to create a computer-based system that supports them.

*The aim is to create computer applications that will make users more efficient than if they performed their tasks with an equivalent manual system.* (Faulkner, 1998, p. 2)

This involves users, their tasks and the environment in which they work.

People interpret the world through five senses – vision, hearing, taste, smell and touch. The most important of these (for those without serious eye defects) is vision – which depends on the brightness and colour of the light entering the eye. This influences the layout of screens, as the combination of brightness and colour will influence whether people find the display (of an internal system or a customer-centred website) visually pleasing or not. Too many colours confuse people, who prefer them sparse and uncluttered, with menu choices arranged in a way that makes sense. Touch is also important, especially in the design of keyboards.

IS designers inevitably make assumptions about human memory – the design represents what they expect users to remember when working with the system. Experiments on memory provide many relevant pointers: Miller (1956) found that the typical capacity of short-term memory is 7 plus or minus 2 chunks of information. Chunking means grouping information in a way that makes sense to the individual – a nine-figure number is hard to remember, but becomes easier if divided into three chunks, each with three digits. Most people would find a password with 15 digits (combining letters and numbers) unacceptable.

Another HCI issue is to understand the task that an IS will support. This is done by analysing the whole into its component parts, by asking questions such as these.

● What does the performer of the task do?
● What information do they use for each task?
● What affects task performance?
● What are the good features of the present system (to retain if possible)?
● What are the bad features (to eliminate if possible)?

A **task analysis** should produce a clear picture of what the activity's purpose is, which must then be converted into a new, or more likely enhanced, computer-based form. That leads to a consideration of the interface between the human and the technology.

That interface affects how users react to an IS. It shapes the mental model people form and enables them to predict what the system will do. Faulkner (1998) proposes five principles of interface design.

● **Naturalness:** it should seem to be the natural way to perform the task and reflect the natural language for the task involved.
● **Consistency:** it should be consistent in its requirements for input and should have consistent mechanisms for the user to make demands on the system. The language and position of messages should as far as possible be the same throughout.
● **Relevance:** the interface should not ask for redundant material; on-screen information should be short and relevant (a problem for users of online banking systems is the

volume of 'small print' that industry regulators require the banks to post on their sites).

- **Supportiveness**: the interface should provide adequate information to allow the user to perform the task.
- **Flexibility**: users have different requirements, skills and preferences. While meeting these is an ideal, doing so may run counter to the ideal of consistency. Too much personal flexibility will also make it harder for people within an organisation to share information.

HCI draws on many other disciplines, including ergonomics, which takes account of the physical aspects of work. Practitioners study how systems can best be designed to suit the physical and mental processes of users. Examples include:

- how the layout and brightness of screens affects eye-strain;
- comparing the physical workload required by different input devices;
- the effect of the height of visual display units on fatigue of users; or
- the effects on productivity of different work–rest schedules.

As managers respond to competitive pressures by increasing performance expectations, they risk endangering employees' physical and psychological health. Ergonomic studies help to identify the risks involved, and encourage designers to produce systems that are compatible with the physical attributes of people using them.

The scope of HCI work is expanding as rapidly as the scope of IS – especially as local and national governments use IS to deliver services and benefits. As computers have moved from being pieces of scientific equipment to tools for increasing productivity and then to support many aspects of social life, so the scope of HCI has widened. In a communication-intensive society users:

*are not only the computer-literate, skilled, able-bodied workers driven by performance-oriented motives . . . but could include the young and the elderly, residential users, as well as those with disability.* (Stephanides, 2001, p. 6)

### ● Summary

- Practitioners of human–computer interaction aim to make the interaction between people and computers more satisfying and productive.
- They observe the physical and mental capabilities of users, and encourage system designers to take account of them.
- They can be expressed in the design of the interface, which should be natural, consistent, relevant, supportive and flexible.
- HCI concerns are extending as people widen IS to new applications (especially in providing public services) as this broadens, and varies, the constituency of users.

## 8.3 The technology acceptance model (TAM) and UTAUT

Davis (1989) developed the technology acceptance model (TAM), which predicts that whether or not people accept and use an IS depends on two variables: **perceived usefulness (PU)** and **perceived ease of use (PEU)**. He defined PU as 'the degree to which a person believes that using a particular system would enhance his or her job performance' (p. 320).

Since people usually receive rewards that reflect in some way their job performance, it is plausible to assume that the more they think a system will help them achieve valued rewards, the more likely they are to use it. PEU is 'the degree to which a person believes that using a system would be free of effort' (p. 320).

Users have to allocate effort to alternative demands, so are more likely to accept a system that they believe will be easy to use.

Davis' studies showed that the relationship between PU and usage was stronger than that between PEU and usage – people welcome a useful system more than one that is easy to use. They are likely to cope with a system that is difficult if it provides them with valuable information, but unlikely to use one the only virtue of which is that it is easy to use.

Many researchers have validated and sometimes extended TAM, such as Igbaria (1993) and Straub et al. (1997), adding and refining the variables to improve its predictive value. Horton et al. (2001) used the model to explain the extent to which people in two organisations used their respective Intranets. The model has also been used to predict the behaviour of customers – Lin (2007) analysed the factors that influence customers' use of online bookshops, finding that perceived usefulness and ease of use were (perhaps not surprisingly) significant predictors of attitudes to online shopping. Shih (2004) came to similar conclusions, but also noted that customers varied in one significant dimension: those who valued information quality highly prefer to shop online, but those who value service quality highly were less willing to do so.

Venkatesh et al. (2003) reviewed many such studies, enabling them to develop and test the Unified Theory of Acceptance and Use of Technology (UTAUT), shown in Figure 8.2. The main variables were defined as:

- **performance expectancy:** the degree to which individuals believe using the system will help attain gains in job performance;

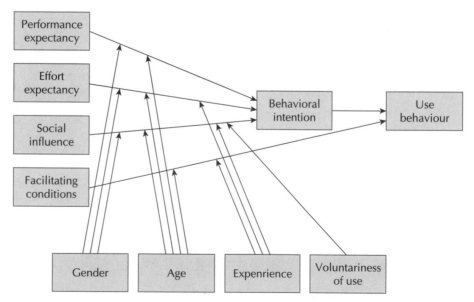

**Figure 8.2 Unified Theory of Acceptance and Use of Technology (UTAUT)**
*Source*: Venkatesh et al. (2003).

| Research Summary | UTAUT scale items |
| --- | --- |

Venkatesh et al. (2003) provide valuable detail on the way they developed and tested the scales used in the research. For example, performance expectancy and effort expectancy were each measured by four items, which respondents were asked to rate on this seven-point scale:

|            | Likely  |          |         | Unlikely |       |           |
|------------|---------|----------|---------|----------|-------|-----------|
| Extremely  | Quite   | Slightly | Neither | Slightly | Quite | Extremely |

**Performance expectancy**
I would find the system useful in my job.
Using the system enables me to accomplish tasks more quickly.
Using the system increases my productivity.
If I use the system, I will increase my chances of getting (a pay rise).

**Effort expectancy**
My interaction with the system would be clear and understandable.
It would be easy for me to become skilful at using (the system).
I would find the system easy to use.
Learning to operate the system is easy for me.

**Social influence**
People who influence my behaviour think I should use the system.
People who are important to me think I should use the system.
In general, the organisation has supported the use of the system.

**Facilitating conditions**
I have the resources necessary to use the system.
I have the knowledge necessary to use the system.
The system is not compatible with other systems I use.
A specific person (or group) is available for assistance (with system difficulties) to do what I want it to do.

*Source*: Venkatesh et al. (2003), p. 460.

- **effort expectancy:** the degree of ease associated with use of the system;
- **social influence:** the degree to which individuals perceive that important others believe he or she should use the system;
- **facilitating conditions:** the extent to which an organisation has put in place arrangements (for example training) to support those using a system.

The first three variables have a positive influence on:

- **behavioural intentions:** an individual's positive or negative attitude towards using the system.

Behavioural intentions do not in themselves ensure that people use the system – that also depends on the quality of the facilitating conditions.

Figure 8.2 shows that all these variables are mediated to some degree by gender, age, experience and the voluntariness of use.

Venktatesh et al. (2003) conclude that the Technology Acceptance Model, and its successor the Unified Theory of the Acceptance and Use of Technology, will help those

# Meeting customer needs

## www.nokia.com

While Nokia, like all mobile phone companies, regularly introduces more technically sophisticated devices, these account for a small proportion of the units that the industry sells each year. The most rapidly growing demand is for basic models that often handle just voice and text messaging. Market penetration exceeds 50 per cent in developed countries. Observers expected that, as prices for phones and services continue to drop, many millions of customers will sign up in places like China, India, Brazil and Russia.

Nokia has been particularly successful in meeting this demand, making great efforts to secure first-time buyers and then build lifelong loyalty to the brand. The scale of its global production allows it to offer basic units very cheaply: even low-cost suppliers in China do not produce enough units to match the efficiency of Nokia, and so cannot match their prices. Moreover, status-conscious buyers in the developing

world have disdain for unknown brands: 'Brazilians want brand names and are willing to pay a bit more for Nokia or Motorola' (quoted in *Business Week*, 7 November 2005, p. 21).

More than any other handset maker, the Finnish company has connected with consumers in China and India. Greater China (the mainland, Hong Kong and Taiwan) is the company's biggest market: it supplies about 33 per cent of all sets sold there, well ahead of the 10 per cent from second-place Motorola. It has about 60 per cent of the market in India, which it expects will be the company's biggest market by 2010. It owes its strong position in both countries in part to a decentralised organisation that can spot local sales trends very quickly, and an ability to produce sets tailored to local tastes and languages.

*Sources*: *Business Week*, 27 March 2006; *Financial Times*, 19 October 2007, p. 25.

---

## CASE QUESTIONS 8.1

Review the first two parts of the Nokia case.

● What do customers expect of a Nokia handset – what needs will it satisfy?
● What evidence is there that the company is meeting these expectations?
● Use the UTAUT model to compose questions that, if used in a research project, might explain this.
● Test these questions with actual or potential users of a Nokia device.

---

wishing to assess the likely success of an IS project. They indicate the factors that encourage acceptance and use, which managers can take into account when designing a system and its context. However, the Research Summary feature, right, shows that usefulness and ease of use are not the only considerations that affect acceptance of IS: other contextual factors also play a part.

## ● Summary

● The technology acceptance model attempts to predict whether or not people will accept an information system, and empirical studies indicate that perceived usefulness has more effect than perceived ease of use.

| Research Summary | An electronic prescription system |
| --- | --- |

To control the cost of drugs prescribed by general practitioners, the Netherlands' Ministry of Health decided to implement an electronic prescription system (EPS). The Ministry had found that, for similar cases, prescription costs varied by up to 40 per cent and calculated that if all GPs used the most cost-efficient prescriptions, drug costs would fall by 20 per cent. They therefore invested funds to develop and promote the EPS.

The doctor types in the patient number and a code representing the diagnosis. The EPS uses a list of available drugs and the patient's medical record to prescribe the required drugs, which it can print or e-mail directly to the pharmacist if the patient wishes. GPs are autonomous, self-employed professionals and they reacted to the system in different ways – some used it fully, some partially and some not at all. Only 12 per cent of all GPs used the system as intended, so the cost of prescription drugs did not fall as expected.

To gain insight into GPs' attitudes to the system, researchers interviewed designers and managers at the Ministry and 36 GPs. They identified five influential factors:

● the system itself – usefulness and ease of use;

● finance – the costs associated with using the system;

● the system as part of the consultation process – did it help, or interrupt, this;

● culture – GPs' values, and how they saw their role in relation to patients;

● policy environment – perceived government plans to control healthcare more closely.

The research concluded that, while the factors in the Technology Acceptance Model (PU and PEU) were relevant to some GPs, they did not affect the majority. Their decisions to accept or reject the system were more influenced by culture and the policy environment. Those with a traditional, personal culture rejected the system as being inconsistent with their culture, while those who saw themselves as running professional and efficient practices accepted it, as they perceived EPS as supporting that culture.

The system had different meanings for people, which affected their decision to accept or reject it.

*Source*: Boonstra et al. (2004).

● The model has also been used to predict customer attitudes to online shopping and other Internet ventures.

● UTAUT builds on TAM to improve its predictive ability.

● Other contextual factors also affect acceptance and use in addition to the UTAUT variables.

## 8.4 Theories of human needs

The HCI and TAM/UTAUT approaches attempt to understand attitudes to IS by analysing factors such as perceived usefulness and ease of use. Other theories have identified additional factors.

People involved with an IS assess (however informally) whether or not the effort they put into it matches the rewards. It is up to project sponsors or managers to create conditions

**Figure 8.3 The Porter-Lawler model of work motivation**
*Source*: Huczynski and Buchanan (2007). Reproduced with permission.

in which that calculation produces a positive response, so people are willing to make the effort. People willingly do things if they feel they are acting in their best interests and achieving their personal goals. Those designing and implementing IS increase the chances of acceptance if they understand something of human motivation.

Motivation is a decision process through which an individual chooses desired outcomes, and sets in motion behaviour that will help achieve those outcomes. Figure 8.3 shows this.

Human needs are complex and changing, yet people managing a project need some practical guidelines – a theory of motivation that is understandable even if it lacks sophistication. Many readers will be aware of the range of motivational theories and the factors that affect commitment (for a review see Boddy, 2008).

Part of Frederick Taylor's method of scientific management was the careful design of the 'one best way' of doing a piece of manual work, which usually involved breaking the whole task into small parts that people could learn quickly. Jobs of this sort are boring to many people, and often lead to dissatisfaction, absenteeism and carelessness. As the limitations of work designed on these principles became clear, researchers began to seek other approaches, including one that distinguished between extrinsic and intrinsic rewards. **Extrinsic rewards** are those that are outside the job and separate from the performance of the task – pay, security and promotion possibilities. **Intrinsic rewards** are those that people receive from performing the task itself – such as using skills or achieving something useful. Research by Frederick Herzberg and Douglas McGregor supported the view that people would be more motivated if their work offered intrinsic rewards – a line of thought that led to the work design model.

## ● The work design model

This proposes that managers (or staff) can change identifiable elements of a job so that it meets human needs more closely – especially the intrinsic rewards inherent in the work itself. Advocates believe this will motivate employees and promote job satisfaction. Managers have choices – they can consider how the design of the proposed system could affect working practices and how to shape these choices to enhance user needs and motivations. Richard Hackman and Greg Oldham (1980) developed a widely quoted model (see Boddy, 2008 or Huczynski and Buchanan, 2007).

The model identifies five core job dimensions that contribute to a job's motivational potential.

- **Skill variety:** The extent to which a job makes use of a range of skills and experience.
- **Task identity:** Whether a job involves a relatively complete and whole operation.
- **Task significance:** How much the job matters to others or to the wider society.
- **Autonomy:** How much freedom a person has in deciding how to do their work.
- **Feedback:** The extent to which a person receives feedback on performance.

It also shows how these implementing concepts can affect motivation.

- *Combine tasks*, so that people use more skills and complete more of the whole task.
- *Form natural workgroups* that perform a complete operation.
- *Establish customer relations* so that staff know what customers expect.
- *Vertical loading*, which enables workers to take on some responsibilities of supervisors.
- *Open feedback channels* to ensure people receive feedback on performance.

Figure 8.4 summarises the model. This model was developed in the context of work on established, regular tasks but the principles are likely to apply to IS projects. These are creating something new, and offer opportunities to arrange tasks to enhance motivation by asking, for example, how best to design the system to enhance the skills people use or the feedback they get. Conversely, people can be alert to the danger of unintentionally limiting (say) task significance or autonomy. Alongside appropriate extrinsic rewards, the intrinsic aspects of the job will affect staff motivation.

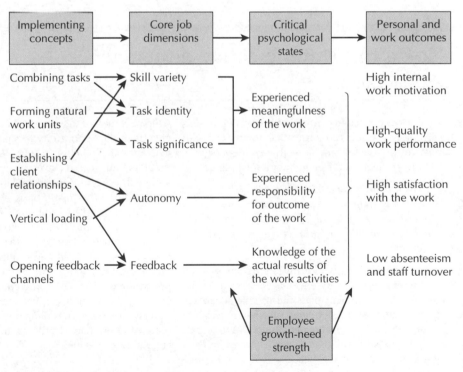

**Figure 8.4** The work design model

*Source*: Adapted from Hackman and Oldham (1980) with permission.

221

**Table 8.1** The work design model and IS design

| Implementing concept | Possible use in designing IS |
| --- | --- |
| Combining tasks | Use the information system to combine several processes into a single task so that staff use more skills and complete more of the whole task. See Chapter 5 on process redesign. |
| Form natural work groups | Give team responsibility for a significant part of the task, and ensure the information system provides information to the team. |
| Establish customer relations | Use technology to provide staff with more or better information about the customer they are dealing with. Link staff to specific customers, with awareness of customer needs. |
| Vertical loading | As the system takes over routine tasks, give staff more responsibility, supported by the information system, for scheduling, planning, budgeting, client liaison, etc. |
| Opening feedback channels | Use the power of the system to pass on information from customers. Ensure positive as well as negative messages. Encourage more internal review and evaluation of performance. |

The theory can guide practice by using the implementing concepts in the design process. Those managing an IS project may not be able to influence extrinsic rewards, but will usually be able to influence the intrinsic – by using some of the options in Table 8.1.

# Nokia motivates creative designers

**www.nokia.com**

Nokia is committed to continuous innovation in software design – and recognises that to succeed staff must continuously come up with new ideas beyond existing products, services and ways of working.

*Only with truly innovative ideas will we be able to define the future development of our industry, and profoundly shape the way in which people understand and use mobility in their everyday lives.* (Nokia website)

To encourage this innovative spirit amongst all employees the company encourages them to create their own development plan and to take advantage of the many off-the-job and on-the-job learning opportunities. They also see coaching as a vital part of continuous learning, and experienced employees are encouraged to share their experience and knowledge. Employees also participate in different teams, which is expected to enhance their development and give them the opportunity to share ideas with other talented staff. To help stay at the forefront of software development it has invested in research centres around the world, building relationships with universities and other institutions – for example it has a partnership with Cambridge University on the application of nanoscience to mobile phones.

The company claims to provide employees with market competitive rewards, made up of a basic salary and both short-term and long-term incentive programmes. The latter includes awarding 'stock options', which allow employees to share in the continued success of the company by taking up the option to buy shares in the company at below their current market value.

*Sources*: Nokia website; BBC News, 27 February 2008.

**CASE QUESTIONS 8.2**

- What do employees expect of Nokia?
- To what extent does it seem to be meeting those expectations?
- Use the implementing concepts of the work design model to suggest how these could be used to further enhance motivation.

---

### Activity 8.1 Using the work design model

Review an IS with which you are familiar and consider how it will have affected the work of those involved. Use the 'implementing concepts' within the work design model to suggest opportunities for redesigning their work.

---

### ● Summary

- Theories of human needs identify intrinsic as well as extrinsic motivational factors.
- The work design model provides a tool for analysing the intrinsic motivation of jobs.
- The theory can be used to assess motivational effects as people design the human aspects of information systems.

## 8.5 Using IS for commitment or control?

As managers promote and develop IS they have a choice about how they relate them to staff. They can either use the systems to increase control over staff by monitoring performance more closely or they can use them to give staff the information that will support more self-control and autonomous working – the commitment approach. This section gives examples of both.

Examples of the changes that computer-based information systems bring to individuals' work are all around us. When customers make a purchase through a website, the roles of staff change. They spend less time discussing options and handling the routine aspects of the transaction, such as payment and delivery requirements. They can then spend more time on tasks that develop the business.

Google expects high levels of commitment from its staff, and seeks to attain this with low levels of control. Candidates for jobs at the company are judged not just on their technical ability, but on their 'Googliness', a quality denoting a willingness to work collaboratively, a non-hierarchical attitude and friendliness, among other traits. While Google takes care of many aspects of daily life, providing free meals, transport and an unconventional working environment, these are not the main attraction for leading software engineers. For them the attraction is the whole management approach. Thomas Hoffman, Director of Google's Engineering Centre in Zurich, said:

*I value the non-hierarchical culture where people feel relaxed. I like the free atmosphere of universities, but I want the challenge of doing something in the real world. (Financial Times, 27 September 2007, p. 16)*

### MIS in Practice · Changing work in a call centre project

Reviewing his experience of call centres, a leading UK call centre consultant provided an example of the benefits from changing working arrangements:

*It's also a time to think about the work people do. A couple of companies had a field sales force and, before we started the call centre, I thought it would be useful to collect some benchmark data. When they put the call centre in place, they found the call centre agents were selling far more than any of the salesmen. So they did some very basic things. They still wanted salesmen, but wanted to direct them to the things they should be doing, like building strategic partnerships and moving the business on. They could leave the selling to the call centre to maintain the relationship and exploit the database.*

*The call centre people were looking ahead, and starting to use cross-selling and up-selling. That again is relationship selling; because you have all the information about the customer in front of you, it tells the customers that you know about them. The technology re-establishes and supports the personal link, and it is the people that transmit that relationship position, the human link.*

*Source*: Personal communication.

### Activity 8.2 Call centre work

Review the above account of the views of an experienced call centre consultant.

● Which of the implementing concepts from Table 8.1 does it mention?

There is a difference between systems that replace and those that complement human skills. Most people welcome the delegation to the machine of boring, repetitive, error-prone tasks. Where people see that an IT system can perform these more effectively than they could themselves, they usually react positively (Clegg et al., 1997). This is most likely to happen when people interpret the situation as being one in which they will still have a job and that they will be able to do more interesting work.

What people do not welcome is the delegation to the machine of significant or valued skills and experience. Nor do they welcome losing their employment if they are replaced by the machine. If they remain in the job performing only residual tasks, they become psychologically distant from the task. They are likely to lose interest and commitment, and so add little value.

In contrast, **complementarity** refers to a situation in which the technology supports or enhances the value of an existing skill. Staff receive better or faster information that allows them to apply their skills productively, helping performance and commitment. Giving staff information about the inner workings of the process they are managing enables them to act more confidently, as they can see the effects of what they do and gain a deeper understanding of the process. They know how things work and can use their

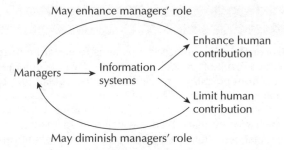

**Figure 8.5** Information systems, human contribution and management role

knowledge to suggest improvements, do higher-value work and use their initiative to respond to change. That in turn enables managers to spend more time on external or higher-level contacts that will enhance their role. Figure 8.5 shows the possibilities.

Shalk and Rijckevorsel (2007) note that, even if the primary tasks of those working in a call centre are highly automated and so offer little discretion, this does not necessarily lead to dissatisfaction. Studying the attitudes of staff in an insurance company call centre (using amongst other instruments the work design model), they concluded that the low autonomy, discretion and variety were offset by the way management dealt with these drawbacks:

● employees were involved in training and coaching newcomers;

● employees could participate in special projects;

● management ensured employees received respect and recognition for their work; and

● success was acknowledged. (Shalk and Rijckevorsel, 2007, p. 270)

A similar conclusion can be drawn from Wright and Lund (2006), who compared three retail distribution companies. All had installed highly automated systems such as for warehouse management, stock ordering and integrated data handling across the supply chain, yet the effects on employees were very different for the three companies, reflecting the beliefs of their managers about how they should treat their employees.

## Activity 8.3 Using models to analyse the ambulance case

● How may the design of the computer-based system have affected the variables in the UTAUT model?

● How may it have affected each of the implementing concepts in the Work Design Model?

● How is that likely to have affected users' attitudes to the system?

Two messages come from this example. The first is that there is choice in the way people design work around IS. In the ambulance case these choices included:

● designing the command and control system to recommend rather than prescribe the vehicle to go to an incident – people had the final say;

> ## MIS in Practice   The ambulance service: complementing skills
>
> The organisation transports patients to and from hospitals – either for routine treatment or as a result of an accident or other medical emergency. Traditionally the task of taking calls from hospitals or members of the public, and of despatching ambulances, was a routine manual task. Though flexible, it was also costly, and provided no management information. As part of wider changes the service introduced computer-based systems, which closely resembled the established manual systems, to support staff allocating ambulances. Staff readily accepted these systems, and a control manager speaking two years after they went live commented:
>
> > *The basic system we introduced has not changed but we have made some changes in how we use it. We used to tell the crews in the Patient Transport Service how to action the run: now we put all the patients in a geographic area onto a log sheet, with their appointment times. We have devolved responsibility to the crew members to decide how best they should schedule that journey to meet the patients' appointments. How they pick them up is up to them – they also take breaks to suit the overall schedule: we do not schedule them. We hand out the work in the morning, and we only want to hear if the crews are having operational problems.*
> >
> > *The command and control system identifies the patient by urgency, and recommends the most suitable resource. I stress 'recommends' – the essential point is that the controller makes the decision as to who goes. The system only recommends the deployment – we do not want the computer deciding. We will keep in the human element. It is user-friendly because we insisted that the software writers made it so. It mirrored very closely the old paper system, and it has been very successful. It is now extremely quick to deploy ambulances.*
>
> *Source*: Based on a case in Boddy and Gunson (1996); and discussion with a control manager.

- designing the command and control system so that it closely matched the existing paper system – this had worked effectively, staff were familiar with it and transition to the new system was correspondingly easy;
- in the Patient Transport Service, devolving responsibility to the crew to decide the route to follow in collecting their patients, rather than the original method of having the system prescribe the route;
- using the machine and control assistants for routine work, and the control officer to improve links with hospitals and community – adding value to the service.

The second message is that these choices reflected a clear view of the nature of the work and an acknowledgement of the skills of those doing it. Using the technology to remove routine tasks enhanced work. Retaining human control of decisions that staff themselves could make enhanced it further.

A good IS design lets staff see the links between processes and the wider picture – they can then act intelligently according to the latest situation. Providing timely and accurate information complements their skill and supports responsible action. Lloyd and Newell (1998) reported an example of a database system that failed to complement the knowledge of the 70 sales representatives, who were nevertheless required to use the system: see the Research Summary, right.

| Research Summary | A database that ignored experience |
|---|---|

The representatives visited doctors, nurses and pharmacists and encouraged them to prescribe Pharma products. They were relatively well educated, and 40 per cent had been with the company for more than seven years. They covered a defined territory and had developed their own target lists, based on their knowledge of doctors and their prescribing practices.

Management installed on the reps' laptop computers a marketing database of the most fruitful sales prospects in each rep's area. They expected staff to call on these prospects at a specified frequency and to ignore doctors not on the list.

Staff were keen to use new technology to support their work, but they complained about the poor quality of the database, as management themselves later acknowledged. A market research company had compiled the database and staff believed it was inaccurate. They could change no more than 10 per cent of the entries in any year. Moreover:

*The computer system linked to the database meant that the reps' performance was being assessed on the basis of calls which could not be made because the targets were no longer in the territory, were not interested in [the product] or never saw reps. The system would only accept data about recognised target customers.* (p. 112)

The reps claimed the database information did not reflect their knowledge and experience. Staff turnover rose sharply, staff did not meet sales targets and the number of calls declined.

*Source*: Based on Lloyd and Newell (1998).

---

The MIS in Practice feature overleaf provides a direct contrast to the Pharma case. The company has several plants, including some in the United States, and makes high-quality chemicals for the semiconductor industry. The parent company decided to introduce an ERP system, mainly to improve financial control of the group. The manufacturing manager of the UK plant saw that the system had much greater potential and has enthusiastically adopted the system to help manage the whole of the manufacturing process. Of particular interest here, he has used the opportunity to change the role of production operators. The MIS in Practice feature records part of an interview.

Managers can use IS to reduce the human contribution (as in Pharma). Activities previously done by people are embodied in the system or become highly structured. Staff do the task by following highly specified on-screen scripts or prompts. While this enables a business to handle routine transactions quickly, consistently and cheaply, it also carries the danger that staff will see it as an attempt to impose tighter control.

IS make it possible to monitor staff and operational performance very closely. The issues arise much more widely. Wherever staff use an IT system for their operational work, or where they need to record specified stages through the computer, it is possible to monitor, track and compare performance. The management issue is how to use this technical capacity. Some managers will choose to use it to monitor tightly, in the belief that this will enable them to control and then enhance performance. Others will be more wary, conscious that staff may resent this and see it as intrusive and showing a lack of trust. It also reduces the autonomy that people experience in the job. As Watad and DiSanzo (2000) observed in relation to telecommuting: 'business managers need to change their focus of control from attendance monitoring to managing for results' (p. 96).

| MIS in Practice | ERP changes staff roles at Chem-Tec |
| --- | --- |

Most of the operators have never travelled – now they are travelling. A culture change has happened that says the power and the information are no longer in the management team. The people who are driving the business process and producing the management reports are the people on the machines. They have not generally been looked on as the people who have that knowledge. The whole ERP process is pushing that. They can see the information directly on the screen by their machine. The system generates information for each process rather than in a global form. That means the people down there running the process have more information than management has got. I have asked them to structure the reports and tell me every week what's happening. They order materials directly – they know what they've used, and what is in the production plan.

If we then bolster that by having them travel to other plants to see how they work, you are driving a whole improvement process on the spine of ERP. Then you see the things that are possible. That whole bar-coding team, of which three are manufacturing operatives, will be going to [Company X] to see their barcoding system. They would never have had that opportunity before, and probably no one else other than myself will see it. They will come back and probably spend £100k on implementing a barcoding system. A whole change of management style.

*Source*: Interview with Chem-Tec manufacturing manager.

## ● Summary

- There is some scope for choice in the way work is designed as IS are introduced.
- Companies have benefited from using IS to eliminate routine work, thus cutting duplication, errors and costs.
- They have also benefited from using IS to complement the skills of their staff, and obtain more value from the tasks performed.
- Managers also use IS to monitor and control staff more closely – which may be counter to staff needs for greater autonomy and self-control.

# 8.6 Managing distributed work

Developments in technology make it possible to change where and when work is done. Practice takes many forms but a broad division is between 'individualised' and 'collective' forms. The former (often called **telecommuting** or **teleworking**) refers to practices in which companies provide the technical facilities that enable people to work with more independence of time and place than conventional workspaces allow – sometimes called **remote working**. The latter occurs when a company uses the power of technology to redistribute tasks between locations, within which people work in conventional ways.

## ● Individual remote working

Technical developments have made it increasingly possible for people to work away from the conventional central office space, and to do so at times and intervals that

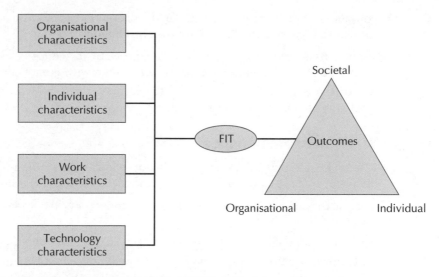

**Figure 8.6 A framework for studying distributed work arrangements**
*Source*: Belanger and Collins (1998). Reproduced with permission.

vary individually. A review of 46 studies of telecommuting by Gajendran and Harrison (2007) examined the positive and negative effects. They found that telecommuting had small and mainly beneficial effects on outcomes such as perceived autonomy and lower work–family conflict. At low levels (working away from the office for a day a week) it had no detrimental effects on the quality of workplace relationships. It also had positive effects on job satisfaction, performance, turnover and role-related stress. However, high-intensity telecommuting (more than 2.5 days a week) had conflicting results – it further reduced work–family conflict, but harmed relationships with co-workers.

Evidence such as this suggests that, to ensure the potential benefits without the human costs, managers implementing such schemes need to consider carefully what practices best support telecommuting. A review by Belanger and Collins (1998) of 58 studies provides a useful indication of useful practices that help to achieve positive outcomes. They defined three forms of distributed working, in which people:

- do not have a permanent work location on company premises – they work in a building regularly but do not have a designated personal space or use 'hotelling', where staff book space when they need it;

- work at sites intentionally located near their home – sometimes called 'satellite' or 'neighbourhood' work centres, they are mainly in response to employee demands to avoid long journeys to work;

- work at least part of the time at home – supported by computers and telecommunications equipment, this is known as 'telecommuting' or 'teleworking'.

Figure 8.6 illustrates the model, and we explain each factor briefly.

## ● Individual characteristics

If managers decide to implement teleworking, they need to establish who will move to this system, since it will not suit those, for example, who require the stimulation of colleagues or the control of a structured work environment. The authors identified two individual characteristics important for distributed work.

1. **Objectives:** it is attractive to people who want to reduce costs (mainly travel) and increase control over their work schedule (often with family commitments).
2. **Skills:** it is most suited to people with computer skills and who are self-sufficient, self-disciplined and good communicators.

## ● Work characteristics

Whether work can be done remotely or not follows from its interdependence with other people or units. A common typology of interdependence is as follows.

1. **Pooled:** each worker contributes to the product, but has little communication with others.
2. **Sequential:** one-way flow between workers, like an assembly line.
3. **Reciprocal:** information flows to and from all those involved in the task.
4. **Team:** similar to reciprocal, but with the flow taking place more quickly.

Tasks with reciprocal or team interdependence imply intense and rapid communications, which would be hard to provide in a distributed environment, even with good information systems. Tasks with pooled or sequential interdependence may be more suited to remote working patterns.

## ● Organisational characteristics

The authors identified three organisational aspects affecting distributed work.

1. **Goals:** companies hope to save money through lower building costs and perhaps through lower staff costs – though they incur substantial set-up costs.
2. **Culture:** staff working at a distance may not develop the beliefs and values held by those in close, daily, informal contact – organisations cannot transmit their values through a computer terminal.
3. **Control:** managers exert control through outcomes (rewards for what is produced), behaviour (rewards for specified behaviour), social (members of the group ensure appropriate behaviour) and personal control (self-control). Outcome and personal controls should raise few new issues in a distributed work environment, but behavioural and social controls will be more problematic.

## ● Technology characteristics

This refers to the quality of the distributed working environment itself, such as physical facilities, IS and security.

While distributed work arrangements are still comparatively rare, the Belanger and Collins (1998) review provides a framework with which experience can be compared and related, and the factors that those considering distributed work arrangements could consider.

## ● Collective remote working

The spread of global organisations means that staff from different units often need to work together, even though they are physically separate. Several technologies will help this process, such as group decision support systems, video-conferencing and computer-based scenario planning. They can, collectively, make it easier for members at widely separated locations to share ideas, draw on a wider knowledge base to meet customer or project requirements and ensure that all are working from the same information or database.

While technologies make collective remote working easier, managers need to ensure that the context supports their use – such as by ensuring that cultures and incentive systems encourage collaboration. Another issue is whether it affects the kind of knowledge that they exchange. Belanger and Allport (2008), for example, found that an improved collaborative technology for a group of highly skilled teleworkers led to an adjustment in their communication patterns. The new system included a centralised and regularly updated database, with the unexpected result that communication became more centralised around their district manager. There were fewer exchanges of tacit knowledge amongst group members, and more exchanges of explicit information with their manager.

## ● Creating a context to support remote working

The main message from this and other evidence is that management needs to create a supportive context for the technology. Kotlarsky and Oshri (2005) studied the evolution of two system development teams working respectively at SAP (a software company) and LeCroy (an instrumentation business). Both have development teams working on projects around the world, and the research sought to identify how social ties and knowledge sharing developed between members of these distributed teams. They identified mechanisms and activities that helped them to build the social ties necessary for successful remote working – see the Research Summary below.

---

| Research Summary | Support for distributed teams |
| --- | --- |

Observations, e-mail analyses and interviews with team members and managers identified tools that these teams had applied to build social ties and knowledge sharing. The teams occasionally met face to face, but for most of the time worked in physically distant places. The research identified these organisational mechanisms the teams used.

*Before face-to-face (F2F)*

- Promote initial (non-F2F) introduction (e.g. virtual F2F by video-conferencing, e-mail exchanges and short visit to remote location).
- Reduce communication barriers (e.g. English courses, set up contact person, distribute newsletters and communication protocol).

*After F2F*

- Routinise communications (e.g. regular reflection sessions, short visit to remote location).
- Open communication channels (e.g. direct (non-hierarchical) communication channel between developers, centralised source of shared information).
- Ensure message quality (e.g. detailed e-mail, use phone, ensure understanding of message received, use graphics).

*Source*: Kotlarsky and Oshri (2005).

---

---

### Activity 8.4  Remote working

Have you or your organisation experienced remote working? If not, try to find someone who has, and ask for their views on these questions.

- Which of the several forms of remote working did it resemble?
- What advantages did people expect, and what did they find, from remote working?
- How many of the recommendations above were put into effect?
- What other factors helped or hindered the change?

---

## ● Summary

- Distributed working arrangements can be either individual or collective in form.
- Individual forms (teleworking) are more likely to work if the individuals and tasks are suitable.
- Some forms of organisational control will be harder to use.
- Collective forms of distributed working depend not only on technology but also on creating an appropriate context of incentives and roles.

## 8.7 Implications for design – the socio-technical approach

The theme that emerges from the cases and research throughout this chapter is that IS projects need to take account of human and contextual factors as well as technical ones. This is the basis of the **socio-technical approach** to system design, the advocates of which see organisations as interdependent systems. The approach developed from the work of Eric Trist and Ken Bamforth at the Tavistock Institute in London during the 1950s. Their most prominent study was of an attempt by the coal industry to mechanise the mining system. Introducing what were in essence assembly-line technologies and methods at the coal face had severe consequences for the social system encouraged by the older pattern of working. The technological system destroyed the fabric of the social system, and the solution lay in reconciling the needs of both technical and social systems – as indicated in Figure 8.7.

Studies in many different countries showed the benefits of seeing a work system as a combination of a material technology (tools, machinery, techniques, physical location) and a social organisation (people with capabilities, needs, relationships, communication patterns, authority structures and so on). Each affects the other, so people need to manage them together so that they work in harmony rather than aiming to optimise one without regard to the other. A design that completely satisfied the social system while ignoring technological requirements would not survive. Similarly, a design that perfected the technological system but ignored the needs of users or customers would soon be rejected. So the aim is joint optimisation of both.

Clegg (2000) has also noted that the use of the socio-technical approach in designing new systems is rare, with most IS projects being technology-led:

> *Many organizations lack an integrated approach to organizational and technical change and, in most cases, users do not have substantial influence on system development . . . Interventions often take technology as given, and the task becomes that of designing the social system around the technology.* (p. 464)

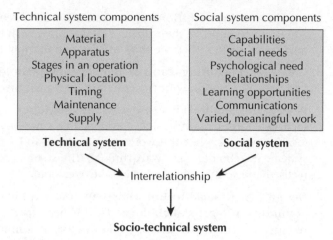

Figure 8.7 The organisation as a socio-technical system

---

**Research Summary    IS and user satisfaction**

Clegg et al. (1997) studied two companies that had introduced IS. They found that user attitudes (satisfaction, sense of ownership, commitment) were most affected by functionality, usability, skill utilisation and expectations about the impact on the company. The results led the authors to recommend that:

> *if you are managing the development and introduction of a new system, these results imply that functionality, usability, skill utilization and job demands are of critical importance; without active consideration of these, the new system may fail . . . New technologies are often used to reduce skill use and to increase job demands. The implication for practice is that managers implementing new technologies should explicitly consider the impacts on the job designs and work organization of the users. The evidence . . . is that this is undertaken only rarely and [is a major reason why new systems fail]. Managers introducing new technology . . . should spend time and effort discussing with users what they need to undertake their work, and ensuring that they understand what the new system will do and what impact it will have on them.*

*Source*: Clegg et al. (1997), p. 25.

---

Doherty and King (2005) agree, noting that, despite its many advocates:

> *progress in producing socio-technical approaches that explicitly address the human and organizational aspects of systems development projects, has been painfully slow.* (p. 2).

Eason (2005, 2007) has used the socio-technical approach in IS projects in healthcare, and has developed an approach based on six principles.

1. **Study the primary work process as a socio-technical system:** The focus of work should be on the current socio-technical system that is geared to local healthcare. Finding effective new inputs (such as an IS) depends on understanding how the work is done in each context, not on generalised prescriptions of how it should be done.

2. **Understand the ambitions of local stakeholders:** People delivering healthcare have ambitions to improve their practice. Stakeholders will be receptive to the adoption of new systems when they see they will serve local aspirations.

3. **Create local planning teams of all relevant stakeholders:** Commitment comes from involvement, especially in the design of their own practice in relation to IS.

4. **Review the implications of externally developed systems for the current socio-technical system:** Any system developed at a national level needs to be adapted to local contexts – what the work flows will be, and who will be doing what on the system. Stakeholders can 'walk through' the system and identify how benefits can be realised and what problems have to be overcome.

5. **Design a new socio-technical system that exploits IS resources and meets the ambitions of local stakeholders:** IS staff need to tailor and integrate the technical resources to meet user needs, while the user community needs to rethink working practices, plan training, etc.

6. **Adopt an action research approach:** Implement systems in phases, using pilots where possible, and gather systematic evidence of newly emergent work practices. This information can be reviewed by the local design team and used to adjust the local system and guide its broader dissemination.

Although developed in the context of healthcare, Eason's principles could be used in IS projects in other settings. Those advocating the approach acknowledge that it will enable people to articulate different objectives for a system if it is to satisfy social as well as technical criteria. They recommended open discussion to resolve these conflicts, in the belief that this process is not creating the conflict but merely bringing it out into the open. Resolving it early in the process will be more productive than ignoring it.

## ● Summary

- Organisations combine technical and social systems.

- Those advocating a socio-technical approach maintain that IS designers should deal with both, rather than give primacy to either.

- Explicit use of this approach is rare, though Eason has developed guidelines from using the approach in healthcare IS projects.

## Conclusions

The evidence of this chapter is that information systems have widely varying effects on how people experience work. We have suggested that established and accessible theories of human motivation can guide the questions we ask about the motivational effects of IS. Some systems have clearly been implemented in a way that reduced the motivational effects. In others the effects have been the reverse – they have enhanced motivation.

We have introduced three theoretical approaches to analysing systems from a human perspective: human–computer interaction, the technology acceptance model and UTAUT models, and theories of human needs. The work design model in particular illustrates the range of choices available to those designing new information systems. They will probably be guided by fundamental beliefs about whether they (or their senior managers) aim for a culture of control or one of commitment. We then indicated some models relevant to the increasingly common practice of distributed working arrangements, and concluded with a review of socio-technical approaches to IS design.

The chapter has also shown the importance of the interaction between IS and the wider context. The effectiveness of distributed working arrangements (like the knowledge management systems in Chapter 2) depend on whether the prevailing culture and structure support the change. People will not use a system to share information or work cooperatively at a distance if the culture has encouraged individual competition. The outcomes of an IS depend on the interactions between the system, the people affected by it and their context.

## Chapter questions

1. Evaluate a system or website that you use in terms of the quality of the interface, using the criteria that this should be natural, consistent, relevant, supportive and flexible.
2. What do the TAM/UTAUT models suggest are the main factors affecting users' willingness to use a system? List each with a short example.
3. What examples are there in the chapter of the factors identified in these theories having affected staff and/or customers?
4. List, with examples, the core job dimensions of the work design model.
5. Show how any two of the items you listed in answer to question 4 could be supported by using one or more of the implementing concepts.
6. What factors does the Belanger and Collins research suggest will affect the outcome of individual or collective distributed working?
7. Explain briefly the general principles of socio-technical design, and list the six factors that Eason has developed in using the approach in healthcare IS design projects.
8. What forces in the wider environment may encourage managers to use IS as a means of control?

## Further reading

Three studies on TAM/UTAUT models – the first being the full story of the development of UTAUT, the second an application to customer choices, and the third showing that it acceptance and use also depends on other factors:

Venkatesh, V., Morris, M.G., Davis, G.B. and Davis, F.D. (2003) 'A unified theory of acceptance and use of technology', *MIS Quarterly*, **27**(3), 425–78.

Otim, S. and Grover, V. (2006) 'An empirical study on Web-based services and customer loyalty', *European Journal of Information Systems*, **15**(6), 527–41.

Boonstra, A., Boddy, D. and Fischbacher, M. (2004) 'The limited acceptance by general practitioners of an electronic prescription system: reasons and practical implications', *New Technology, Work and Employment*, **19**(2), 128–44.

Three articles on distributed work arrangements. The third of these is a useful case study that complements material in that section:

Belanger, F. and Collins, R.W. (1998) 'Distributed work arrangements: a research framework', *Information Society*, **14**(2), 137–52.

Belanger, F. and Allport, C.D. (2008), 'Collaborative technologies in knowledge telework: an exploratory study', *Information Systems Journal*, **18**(1), 101–21.

Maruca, R.F. (1998) 'How do you manage an off-site team?', *Harvard Business Review*, **76**(4), 22–35.

Two articles on socio-technical methods:

Doherty, N.F. and King, M. (2005) 'From technical to socio-technical change: tackling the human and organizational aspects of systems development projects' *European Journal of Information Systems*, **14**(1), 1–5.

Eason, K. (2005) 'Exploiting the potential of the NPfIT: a local design approach', *British Journal of Healthcare Computing and Information Management*, **22**(7), 14–16.

# PART 4

# Implementation

The first chapter in this part focuses on process – how managers implement an information system in a way that achieves, or exceeds, its objectives. It outlines four complementary models of change, each of which can guide management action in a project, and then considers ways of monitoring and controlling what is happening. The chapter then moves from considering projects to the additional techniques required to manage programmes, groups of related projects, such as that undertaken by The Royal Bank of Scotland to integrate its acquisition, ABN Amro Bank.

Chapter 10 considers how to evaluate the costs and benefits of investing in information systems. The dilemma that all managers face is, while they can usually predict the costs of an information system, they are much less certain about the benefits: a dilemma facing the BBC as it decides how much to invest in digital networks alongside its conventional broadcasting channels. The chapter outlines briefly the principles, and the weaknesses, of conventional investment appraisal methods. It then introduces some alternative methods that give more weight to non-financial criteria.

# CHAPTER 9

## Managing implementation

### Learning objectives

By the end of your work on this topic you should be able to:

- Distinguish four models of project management, and indicate when each is appropriate

- Understand why project managers seek to identify stakeholders who can affect the project

- Summarise techniques that help to monitor and control progress

- Distinguish programmes from projects, and understand the differences in management techniques

- List some tools and techniques for managing projects and programmes, describing their benefits and limitations

- Explain the concept of quick wins and describe why these are important to the long-term success of a project or programme

# RBS and the integration of ABN Amro

**www.rbs.com**

In mid-2007 The Royal Bank of Scotland (RBS) was regarded by many observers as one of the most innovative and best-performing banks in the United Kingdom. It was by then (on market capitalisation) the UK's seventh largest company, and the fifth largest bank in the world. In the UK alone RBS has more than 15 million customers and 2200 branches. It had 130,000 staff worldwide and a (low) cost:income ratio of 42 per cent.

In October 2007 RBS, along with partners Fortis and Santander, pulled off the biggest bank deal in history – and arguably the worst timed. Following a long battle with Barclays (RBS's UK-based banking rival), the partnership secured ownership of the Dutch ABN Amro banking group for £49bn.

The takeover came in the midst of turbulent times for the banking industry. The UK financial services market was experiencing a severe shortage of credit, as banks did not trust the quality of the assets held by other banks, and so were unwilling to lend to each other. July 2007 saw the first run on a major UK bank in over a century when customers lost confidence in the Northern Rock and queued in the streets to withdraw over £2bn of their deposits. Banks around the world announced major bad debt allowances, with RBS itself declaring around £1.5bn of losses in November 2007.

Nonetheless, RBS remained confident, announcing that the takeover of the Dutch bank ABN Amro represented a major step in its global strategy. The acquisition had raised RBS significantly in world rankings of financial services institutions – to number five in the world for transactional banking and number one in Europe for corporate banking. It also gained footholds in some particularly tough-to-enter markets in Asia.

The challenge was to make the acquisition add value for shareholders, who would expect to see benefits in the share price and dividends. A senior team from RBS moved into the Amsterdam offices and began to plan:

● how best to divide the ABN Amro Group businesses between Fortis and Santander;

● how to integrate the newly acquired businesses; and

● how to deliver the £1.2bn of cost savings that RBS had promised to the markets during the takeover battle.

This was not a new challenge for RBS, since between 1999 and 2007 it acquired and integrated 26 businesses with a combined market value of £33.7bn, and developed a strong reputation for buying and integrating other banks (Kennedy et al., 2006). However, as the ABN Amro integration programme began, few doubted the scale of the task that lay ahead. The programme would combine the operations of an organisation with facilities in 55 countries, bringing 99,000 new staff together with the existing 130,000 to deliver services more efficiently. To succeed this time, RBS would require every bit of its project management expertise to be applied to the integration.

From an IS perspective, the challenge deepened further. Where the NatWest integration had focused on migrating all processing onto the single RBS platform, this was never going to be possible with the ABN Amro integration, owing to the diverse range of international and multi-currency systems operated by the Dutch bank.

*Sources*: Kennedy et al. (2006); internal company literature.

## Introduction

The Royal Bank of Scotland is clearly implementing a major change programme to integrate its acquisition as quickly as possible, so that shareholders will benefit. Equally it needs to take account of the interests of customers and staff, who will be seeking to protect their interests during the change. Particular challenges face the bank in the IS area:

merging these systems was a major source of savings when it integrated NatWest, but these will be much harder to realise in this takeover. Major IS change is hazardous in one organisation, and disproportionately more difficult in two.

Information systems cannot be implemented, changed or withdrawn without starting ripples that go far beyond the systems themselves (McDonagh, 2003). This challenge grows as IS extend from background, internal tasks to those that involve customers, suppliers or other organisations. There are likely to be structural changes, changes to business processes, new work patterns and perhaps electronic links to other organisations. This complexity was shown in an earlier programme at The Royal Bank of Scotland to integrate NatWest Bank's IS with those of RBS. This required the alignment of operating procedures, staff roles and the outsourcing of a major activity to a third-party supplier. To integrate ABN Amro with RBS would require a strong project and programme management discipline between many coherently linked projects. The issues raised throughout this book imply that those leading such projects are unlikely to have an exclusively technical background.

While many IS projects transform business operations, enhance customer satisfaction and improve performance, others fall far short of expectations. Examples of successful projects are all around – the spectacular growth of Google, Nokia and more recently the social networking sites are clearly based on successful IS development projects. We have also given examples of traditional companies that have implemented successful projects, including Kwik-Fit, Ahold and Siemens. Equally there are public examples of spectacular failure – such as the Taurus project at the London Stock Exchange (Drummond, 1996) and the slow uptake of many projects in healthcare. An example of IS failure that is often cited is the London Ambulance Service's first computer-aided command and control system. When this went live in 1992 it quickly collapsed, leading to senior resignations, a public inquiry and several academic analyses (see, for example, Beynon-Davies, 1995). Yet a few years later Fitzgerald and Russo (2005) showed that a new command and control system was working well – the technology was robust, staff had accepted it and the public were satisfied. They attributed this almost entirely to the way the service managed implementation. The common lesson from both successes and failures (Sauer, 1993) is that whether an IS project succeeds or fails depends on how people manage it: most so-called IS failures are better described as management failures.

This chapter presents some ideas relevant to implementing IS projects, especially when these are part of a larger programme of change. It begins by presenting four complementary models of change, each of which can contribute to a successful outcome. It then outlines the steps to take at the very earliest stages of a project, and follows this with ideas on project control. The final section considers the tasks required in managing a large programme of related projects. The aim is to provide ideas and methods that will help people implement major IS projects and programmes.

## 9.1 Models of change – planning, emergent, participation and politics

There are four alternative, but complementary, perspectives on the management of projects in general, which also apply to IS projects. Each has different implications for those implementing the change.

## ● Planning

Much of the advice given to those responsible for managing projects uses a **planning model**. Projects go through successive stages, and results depend on conducting the project through these stages in an orderly and controlled way. The labels vary, but major themes are:

- define objectives clearly;
- allocate responsibilities;
- fix deadlines; and
- set budgets.

The approach reflects the assumption that planned change in organisations unfolds in a logical sequence, that people work to the plan and that they notice and correct deviations from the plan. In relation to IS projects, advocates of tools such as the system development lifecycle make similar assumptions. Designers created this model to bring some order to the task of developing computer-based information systems and advocate following steps such as those shown in Figure 9.1.

There are evident benefits in using an easy-to-understand sequence like this to keep track of the many activities in a large project, and the method is widely used. The method implies keeping a project on track, with minor adjustments, towards a fixed goal. For some projects, and for some parts of other projects, the emphasis on planning embodied in the lifecycle model is useful.

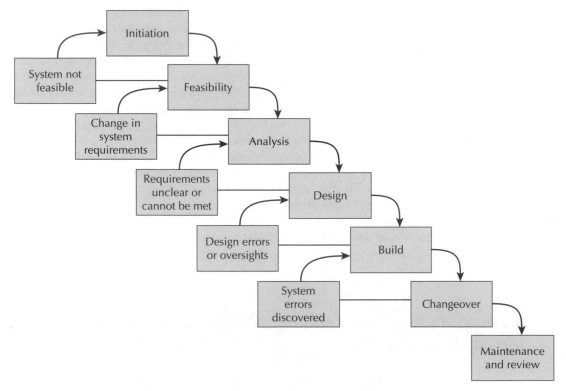

**Figure 9.1 The waterfall model of systems development**
*Source*: Reprinted from Chaffey, D. (2003) with permission.

The model is less useful where requirements are ambiguous and where the work is being done in a constantly changing environment. In these circumstances, managers who rely too much on a linear approach will run into difficulty. If circumstances (such as customer requirements, competitor actions or available technologies) change during a project, then working to meet the original specification will deliver a result that is obsolete by the time it is implemented. They may draw on a different perspective, one that gives more emphasis to the emergent rather than the planned nature of change.

## ● Emergent or incremental approaches

An influential group of writers (Quinn, 1980; Mintzberg, 1994) propose that if projects take place in uncertain conditions – because customer demands are changing or because of rapid technical development, an **emergent** (or incremental) **model** will work better. People taking this approach make plans, but see them as temporary and provisional, being ready and able to adapt them as circumstances change and people learn more about the task. Some departure from a plan is inevitable due to unforeseeable changes or new opportunities. Managers working in this way are likely to seek out new information actively, from frequent interactions between a wide range of participants (Fletcher and Harris, 2002).

These ideas apply to IS projects as much as they do to any other forms of change. They too take place in a volatile, uncertain environment in which people with different interests and priorities try to shape both the ends and the means of projects. At the system development level the emergent approach implies dividing development work into subtasks that IS staff can complete quickly and test with users. 'If you don't know what you are doing, keep it small' summarises this approach. Developers who use this approach often use prototyping, whereby they offer the user a prototype, or working model, of the end product. This will include how it interfaces with users – such as through the screen layout or paper reports. A related approach is known as **Joint Application Development (JAD)** – a method in which users and designers discuss requirements in workshops and use this information iteratively to design and test successive systems. Figure 9.2 shows the **prototyping** technique of systems development.

Developing a working system as soon as possible allows users to gain experience, thereby enabling them to make informed comments about the system and how it fits into their work. Developers can take account of these comments as they adapt the system. Working this way depends on close cooperation between users and designers, resulting in an incrementally designed system. It reflects the idea that IS projects need to be able to evolve to meet changing needs and circumstances, rather than follow a fixed plan.

## ● Participative models

Those viewing projects from this perspective emphasise the benefits of establishing a sense of ownership of the change by those whose support it will need or who will have to live with the change when it is implemented. Typically this includes involving those affected in the design of solutions; consulting widely about possible options; ensuring that information is fully communicated; providing training and support; and ensuring that conflicts or disagreements are openly and skilfully dealt with. **Participative models** (Ketokivi and Castañer, 2004) are an established aspect of the management literature and few openly argue that it is not an effective way to implement change. People expect such an approach to overcome resistance and to win commitment to new

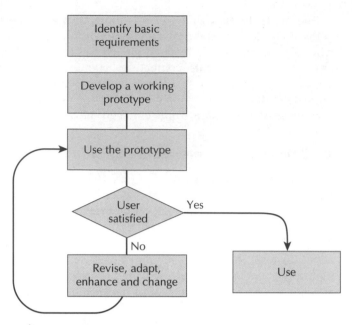

**Figure 9.2** System development by prototyping

ideas. The underlying and reasonable assumption is that, if people can say 'I helped to build this', they will be more willing to live and work with it, whatever it is.

In the IS field, Enid Mumford developed the ETHICS system design methodology (Mumford and Weir, 1979). This includes involving users in system development, recognising the social issues in implementation and using socio-technical principles to redesign work. More recently, Clegg (1996) developed five tools that those involved in system development could use to give explicit consideration to human issues. The tools support:

● **organisational scenarios:** to identify and evaluate the choices facing an organisation;

● **task analysis:** to record information about the tasks undertaken in a work system;

● **task allocation:** to help allocate tasks to people and technology;

● **job design:** to help design jobs that meet organisational and individual needs;

● **usability:** to evaluate the usability of a planned or actual computer system.

However, people rarely use participative methods in a formal way or they do so at a relatively late stage in the system development cycle.

*The focus of interest and expertise [of system developers] is predominantly technical; psychological and organisational knowledge and expertise are largely excluded from these processes.* (Clegg, 1996, p. 485)

For all the potential advantages, there are sometimes valid arguments for not encouraging users to participate in development – lack of knowledge or time, and users who are widely dispersed. In other cases management is powerful enough to force changes through without the need to ask for opinions or there is deep disagreement between those involved that the opportunity to participate would not in itself resolve.

## ● Political models

Those who see change projects from a political perspective (such as Markus, 1983; Knights and Murray, 1994, Buchanan and Badham, 1999) start from the assumption that IS projects inevitably affect people with different interests. They will pull in different directions, and pursue personal and local as well as organisational goals – as the example in the MIS in Practice feature below shows.

| MIS in Practice | Eastern Electronics |
|---|---|

The company has 150 staff who design, manufacture and sell various kinds of electronic equipment. At the time of these events it was part of the Asia Industrial Group (AIG), a major holding company on the subcontinent. AIG had had increasing problems in gathering financial data from units within the group as each company had adopted its own methods. Head office wanted to control the financial system more closely so that it would reduce its workload and give more insight into group performance. It decided to introduce a computer-aided production management (CAPM) system.

Head office decided to establish the CAPM system without consulting the group companies. The implementation experienced four major problems.

● CAPM is an integrated system that cannot simply replace the existing manual system. Other organisational changes are needed. These included changes in the way Eastern staff handled and processed information and how departments cooperated.

● Eastern felt no ownership of the system because the investment and selection decision had been imposed by AIG.

● Eastern managers believed that their company was too small to require such a sophisticated system.

● Eastern had an organic management structure, with little definition of responsibilities, unclear tasks and a belief that change occurs at its own pace.

However, a manager in the company noted that departments within Eastern were divided in their view of CAPM. The purchasing department disagreed strongly with the system. The purchasing manager had created the current manual system and believed that CAPM was created for group needs, rather than to benefit the companies. The engineering department did not at first see the value of the system. But when it saw some of the functions it could provide, it supported the change. The production department was strongly in favour. Both the director and manager had previously worked in a computerised environment and could see the advantages. After two years of work the system was still not implemented, though considerable work had been done.

*Source*: Personal communication from a manager in the company.

In the same vein, Pfeffer (1992) argues that power is essential to get things done. Decisions in themselves change nothing – it is only when they are implemented that anyone notices a difference. He proposes that change, including IS projects, requires more than an ability to solve technical problems. An IS system frequently threatens the status quo and people who benefit from the present arrangements are likely to resist it. Innovation depends on promoters being aware of **political models** of change, and developing political will and expertise – to ensure that it is on the agenda, and senior managers support and resource the change. Promoters need to build and use their power.

From a political perspective, two approaches are necessary to implement large-scale IS changes. Those promoting the change have to produce a public, front-stage performance of logical and rationally planned change – using established techniques associated with the lifecycle approach. This may help to convince senior management and expert staff that the change is technically rational, logical and fits with the strategic direction of the organisation. They may also undertake some work to consult with users, using methods associated with participative models. Together these public activities may sustain the image of project managers by reassuring senior management that they are following established practice.

Project managers also have to pursue back-stage activity. They have to exercise power skills: influencing, negotiating, selling, searching out and neutralising resistance. Keen (1981) highlighted how stakeholders who oppose a project can try to put it off course. Since overt resistance to change is risky, those wanting to block a change may use covert tactics – even while appearing to support the change. The MIS in Practice feature below summarises these 'tactics of counter-implementation'.

---

### MIS in Practice     Peter Keen on counter-implementation

- **Divert resources:** Split the budget across other projects; have key staff given other priorities and allocate them to other assignments; arrange for equipment to be moved or shared.

- **Exploit inertia:** Suggest that everyone wait until a key player has taken action or read the report or made an appropriate response; suggest that the results from some other project should be monitored and assessed first.

- **Keep goals vague and complex:** It is harder to initiate appropriate action in pursuit of aims that are multidimensional and specified in generalised, grandiose or abstract terms.

- **Encourage and exploit lack of organisational awareness:** Insist that 'we can deal with the people issues later', knowing that these will delay or kill the project.

- **'Great idea – let's do it properly':** And let's bring in representatives from this function and that section, until we have so many different views and conflicting interests that it will take for ever to sort them out.

- **Dissipate energies:** Have people conduct surveys, collect data, prepare analyses, write reports, make overseas trips, hold special meetings . . .

- **Reduce the champion's influence and credibility:** Spread damaging rumours, particularly among the champion's friends and supporters.

- **Keep a low profile:** It is not effective openly to declare resistance to change because that gives those driving change a clear target to aim for.

These inertial forces may make the implementation of the structural and organisational issues identified earlier that much more difficult to implement.

*Source*: Keen (1981).

---

Keen recommends a 'counter-counter-implementation' strategy that establishes who can damage the project, co-opts opposition, provides clear incentives and benefits from the new system, and tries to create a 'bandwagon' effect. This is a back-stage political strategy and depends heavily on the presence of a 'fixer' with prestige, visibility and legitimacy.

**Table 9.1** Content and process skills for managing IS projects

| Approach to project | Situation in which most likely to be appropriate | Influencing tactics |
| --- | --- | --- |
| Planning | Uncontroversial projects with limited scope in stable conditions. | Setting objectives; allocating tasks; setting milestones; monitoring progress and exercising control. |
| Emergent | Projects where conditions are changing rapidly and there is high uncertainty about the future of the business. | Observing changing conditions and being able to adapt; identifying changing user needs and interests; adapting projects to meet changing circumstances. |
| Participative | Where users are knowledgeable about the project, do not feel threatened by it and have ideas to contribute. | Identifying stakeholders, their interests, commitment and power; exchanging ideas, encouraging contributions; presentation and communication; consulting and negotiating; resolving differences and reaching agreement. |
| Political | Where the project threatens established interests of players who have the power to defend their position. | Identifying stakeholders, their interests, commitment and power; building coalitions; manipulating information; identifying and blocking opposition; negotiating. |

These four views (planning, emergent, participative and political) are not necessarily competing. They are complementary in the sense that a large IS project is likely to require elements of each. Table 9.1 summarises the conditions in which each approach to managing an IS project is likely to be suitable, and the tactics a project manager may use to influence others. It is important that those driving the project are able to assess the situation reasonably accurately and choose the right combination of tactics.

## ● Managing stakeholders

Whatever the project's nature, the project manager will focus on managing stakeholders. These are the people and groups with an interest in the project and who can affect the outcome. They may be active promoters or supporters of the change, keen to have it succeed. Equally, they may oppose the project and try to delay or stop it (Howard et al. 2003).

Stakeholders have an interest in the outcomes of change, and in how the change is managed. They can make a difference to the situation, and project managers need to gain and keep their support. Stakeholders can be within the organisation – functional or departmental groups, users, the IS department and so on. External stakeholders will also have an influence – customers, suppliers, hardware and software vendors or consultants (Howard et al., 2003). In major changes shareholders will have an interest, and will put strong pressure on managers to deliver results. As an example, Figure 9.3 shows the movement of the RBS share price relative to other bank shares since the bank announced its intention to bid for ABN Amro. They will be watching the integration closely and questioning RBS management about progress towards achieving the expected financial benefits.

More generally, stakeholders have different interests and will interpret an IS project from its likely effects on those interests. Their power to influence the direction of the

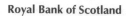

**Royal Bank of Scotland**
Share price and FTSE index rebased
since offer for ABN Amro proposed

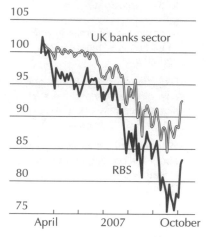

**Figure 9.3** RBS share price relative to UK banks since offer proposed

project will also vary. An early task for the project manager is to identify stakeholders, and to assess their likely interest in, and power to affect, the project.

The role of the change agent in major projects is inherently manipulative and political. While the front-stage activities of technical and strategic logic and user participation provide credibility, back-stage political activity is key to success or failure. A change agent who lacks insight into organisational politics will fail.

---

## CASE QUESTIONS 9.1

● Which models of change can you envisage being used to manage the RBS ABN Amro integration project?

● Give examples of the kinds of issues for which you think each would be most suitable.

● Identify the main stakeholders in the integration project, and note their likely interests in the outcome. Which of them will have most power to affect the outcome?

---

## ● Summary

● We have identified four complementary perspectives on IS projects, each of which can be useful within a project.

● Each has different implications for managing the project, and requires the project manager to exercise a different set of skills.

● These skills include the ability to decide when each perspective is appropriate.

● Stakeholders can be internal or external to the organisation, and can have a significant impact on an IS project, either positive or negative.

- Successful project delivery depends on both the 'front-stage' technical skills and the 'back-stage' political skills of the change agent.

## 9.2 Establishing the project

Once management decides to start a major IS project it needs to identify and allocate those who will do the work to make it happen. Some organisations have defined and well-understood processes for this, with departments dedicated to change management using standardised methods and tools. For others, this initial stage is a step into the unknown, using staff from operational or administrative functions to take on the role of project managers, developing methods as they go.

### ● The early days – things to do *before* the project starts

Initial discussions need to focus on understanding what powerful stakeholders expect the project to achieve, and documenting and confirming this. Producing a Terms of Reference document is a critical early step as it should clearly describe:

- *what* is to be done: the intended activities and the desired outcome, including the **critical success factors** (CSFs, the main things that must happen as a result of the project in order for it to be considered successful);
- *who* is to be involved: the names, roles and responsibilities of all the main project team and any others whose support will be required;
- *how* it will be done: the approach to be taken, resources to be used, costs to be incurred, anticipated risks and issues to be managed;
- *when* it will be done: a high-level plan of the main schedule of activities,

During these initial discussions the project team can also consider what could go wrong during the project and make plans to reduce the chance of them happening. Klien (2007) describes the project pre-mortem technique. This involves the team imagining a scenario in which the project has failed, and identifying the possible reasons for this. By listing these and discussing how to avoid them, the team stands a better chance of managing its way around the most likely and foreseeable problems.

It is important to define and agree with senior stakeholders in advance the critical success factors (CSFs) for the project – what will a successful outcome look like, what must the project achieve to be considered a success? These will guide and motivate the team towards the results that stakeholders expect them to achieve, and which they are likely to reward. Lu et al. (2006) describe the definition of seven CSFs for an IS to manage information flows between Cisco and Xiao Tong, a distributor in China. These are likely to be relevant to many IOS projects:

- strong internal and external commitment;
- shared motivation and vision;
- cross-organisational implementation team;
- high integration with internal information systems;
- inter-organisational business process re-engineering;

- advanced legacy information system and infrastructure;
- shared industry standards.

## Establishing and managing the project team

In many walks of life, from sports to community to business, much is made of the import-ance of assembling the 'Dream Team' – that supposedly perfect blend of skills, knowledge and behaviours which brings outstanding results. How do IS project managers build this Dream Team, and how often do they even get the chance to pick and choose their team? Belbin (2004) identified nine types of behaviour that people displayed in teams – their preferred team roles. He also showed that the composition of a team affects performance – some combinations of these roles produce successful teams, while others lead to failure. Unfortunately, most project managers have little choice about who is on their team, and need to manage with who is available.

A high-quality team is essential to a successful project, as the most talented individuals can seldom perform as well as an effective team on complex projects. Boddy et al. (2000) studied the evolution of major change projects and in particular how (unplanned) teams emerged during the projects because of the benefits which they brought. These included the following.

- **Providing a structure** to deal with complex problems. They provide a mechanism or a forum in which issues or problems can be raised, put on the table and dealt with – rather than being left unattended.

- **Increasing the perspectives** available. While an individual may find a solution on their own, no one can be familiar with all sides of an issue. So, by bringing in more people, ideas can be tried on other members and encouraged or discarded in the light of their reactions and other sources of knowledge.

- **Encouraging acceptance and understanding** of the problem and the solution pro-posed. If those closely affected by a decision have been able to express their views they are more likely to accept the result than if it were imposed. They will know more of the constraints and limitations, and probably be more committed to implementing the result. Taking part in a group effort usually builds a sense of ownership in over-coming difficulties and achieving a result.

- **Promoting learning**. As people work together to solve problems, they not only deal with the present task, but may also reflect on what they can learn from the experience, and perhaps see how they could do the job differently next time. People often use tacit, taken-for-granted knowledge to reach solutions; working in a team is more likely to lead to those assumptions being challenged and tested against reality, rather than continuing to be applied in an established way.

Project teams also have disadvantages, and are a source of failure if not managed well. Members have varied technical skills, and those less familiar with the technical aspects, perhaps from a user department, may be reluctant to raise questions in public. Most members have other jobs to do, as they continue with their regular work while also contributing to the project. They will also have political and possibly personal agendas, being there as representatives of a department rather than as individuals. These problems do not negate the argument for teams where these will add value, but merely make the point that teams need to be managed (see Boddy, 2002, for a fuller discussion of teams).

# Maximising potential at RBS

**www.rbs.com**

Faced with an ever-growing list of urgent projects, a set of managers from Group Business Improvement (the main change management department for RBS) were tasked with finding ways of doing more work with the same staff. Rather than 'working harder', the team was asked to consider ways of 'working smarter'. Under the heading of Maximising Potential, the team reviewed current project activity, and identified 'best practice' techniques within and beyond RBS. The result was a series of 'smarter working principles' to be followed by all change management staff. These focused on building closer working relationships between departments and included:

● less duplication of governance activities (such as project reporting and change control);

● locating project teams from functional departments such as business, technology and HR in the same area;

● combining roles (such as test manager and implementation manager) wherever possible.

By applying these principles to pilot projects, the team calculated that it could use about 25 per cent less resources, without any loss of output. While obvious and apparently simple, the team was surprised that project teams had rarely followed these practices. In the rush to get things done in individual projects, people overlooked simple ways of working more efficiently.

# 9.3 Controlling the project

IS projects, like any other management activity, require control if they are to deliver worthwhile results: circumstances change, unexpected events disrupt plans, activities take longer than expected – unless these are identified and dealt with they delay or destroy a project. Control processes help to ensure that all aspects of the project, and changes to it, are well understood by the stakeholders. Available techniques include a project control committee, project plans, a change control procedure, an escalation procedure, managing dependencies, and rollout planning.

## ● Project control committee

Adequate consultation with stakeholders depends on a specific mechanism – some institution at which stakeholder representatives can meet to hear of progress and contribute ideas to the project. This can be called, for example, the project control committee (PCC). Opinion varies on whether the PCC should meet regularly or by exception (i.e. when required to take a particular decision), and practice will reflect local circumstances. The important thing is that those involved are aware of, and committed to, the institution.

The project manager needs to consider membership of the PCC with care. Getting the right people involved reflects the participative model of change by establishing a sense of ownership amongst those who will be most required to support implementation. From a political perspective, the PCC can also engage those with differing views who might, if left outside, undermine the project (Keen, 1981).

## ● Plans

Some question the benefits of planning – it takes time that could be spent getting the job done, and the emergent view of change implies that the plan will change anyway. Nevertheless, Table 9.2 outlines the benefits that can follow from a suitable form of planning in IS projects.

Figure 1.6 on p. 18 (especially the area representing the internal context) provides a useful checklist of the items that project managers may consider when drawing up their plan. As shown throughout this book, successful IS project managers take account of the contexts in which the system will work. A preliminary list of project tasks could therefore include any changes that may be required in people, processes, structures and so on. On the other axis, the plan would set out who was responsible for these items, checkpoints, and possibly project meeting dates.

A further benefit of a plan is that this single view of the project can be shared with all relevant people, probably across multiple locations. Many applications provide online shared access to plans and other project documentation. These support communication and encourage active participation by project staff and stakeholders. No plan retains its value for long and will change as events unfold. Constant review and updating is required if the plan is to provide continuing benefits.

**Table 9.2 Benefits of a plan**

| Requirement | With a plan | Without a plan |
|---|---|---|
| Communication | Confirming and sharing with all stakeholders what needs to be done, when, and by whom. The plan is a communication tool, telling anyone who needs to know what the project will do, and has already done. | Different understandings of what has been agreed and what will be done. Confusion and misunderstanding. |
| Confidence in the project | Plans demonstrate how the desired outcomes can be achieved, and enable debate to take place on how, or even if, this should be done. | Strong challenges from budget-holders and sponsors. Possible favouring of other projects that are better communicated. |
| Reporting | Once set up and agreed, plans provide a quick and accurate way of reporting on progress. As dates in the plan are reached, it is easy to see if the project is on track. | Project teams have to prepare and challenge separate reports on progress. |
| Resource allocation | Tasks can be allocated to the right people for the right time. All project participants can then be sure about what their role is and when they are required to do it. | Resources applied inefficiently – alternately waiting around for things to happen or running around to complete things at short notice. |
| Financial planning | The plan clarifies for how long people and facilities are needed, allowing budgets to be agreed. It also tells people when to expect the benefits. | Uncertainty over the cost of a project, or what benefits it will provide, is unlikely to be tolerated by many organisations. |

## ● Managing change within the project – change control

In dynamic environments a project to bring about change will itself be subject to change. Common sources include:

- the emergence of new information and knowledge as the project develops;
- improved understanding of the activities or the environment;
- key people becoming available, or leaving, unexpectedly;
- lessons from prototyping exercises being fed back into the design;
- the evolution of organisational priorities;
- developments by competitors;
- market fluctuations.

The project team needs to manage change within the project by making sure that the impacts of changes are fully understood and agreed to by all affected areas. This involves working systematically through several stages.

- **Identification:** Initial awareness that change has occurred and requires action.
- **Definition:** Quantification and analysis of the scope and nature of the change.
- **Impact assessment:** Likely project effects in terms of cost, time and quality.
- **Documentation:** Recording how activities, schedule, cost or outputs will be altered, and distributing this information to relevant stakeholders.
- **Agreement:** Recognition of, and agreement to, the changes by the stakeholders.
- **Re-setting the plan:** Changing the baseline plan to reflect the agreed change.
- **Re-distributing and reporting** on the new plan.

While change to a project plan may at first sight seem a sign of failure, it is more likely to be a sign that project managers have been alert to changing circumstances, and have wisely adapted the project to take account of these. A critical factor in successfully managing change is for it to be an open and transparent process, driven by constant vigilance and awareness of the project environment. Continuing to work to a plan that has effectively been broken by the impact of changes will never produce a good result.

## ● Escalating problems (risks and Issues)

Major projects rarely go according to plan – this is inevitable since they are by definition dealing with novel, unique situations. A hazard in IS projects is that of **escalating commitment** to a failing course of action (Drummond, 1996; Pan et al., 2004). This occurs when those in charge of a project continue to commit resources to a project, despite clear warning signs that this will make a bad situation worse. The skilled project manager is one who deals with unexpected problems effectively – or, even better, anticipates them and acts to ensure that they do not occur. To manage problems effectively, it is useful to distinguish two categories:

- **Risks:** These are *potential* problems. Things that could, or will, go wrong, if no action is taken to avoid them.
- **Issues:** These are problems that have *already occurred* and require corrective action immediately to reduce the impact on the project outcome.

**Figure 9.4 The risk and issue management process**

Figure 9.4 illustrates a process for dealing with both categories.

The risk or issue must first be *identified*, and this requires a vigilant monitoring of the project and the environment in which it is operating. Risks, in particular, require careful consideration since their effects are not yet being felt. Workshops with the project staff to discuss progress and encourage the identification of problems are helpful, as are discussions with stakeholders. The project pre-mortem exercise described earlier can help to identify risks.

Having identified a risk or issue, the project team needs to carry out an *assessment* of what the impact on the project may be – cost, delay or reduced quality of deliverables. Then there must be an *allocation* of responsibility to someone to deal with the problem: clear ownership of problems is important in the busy project environment, as otherwise incorrect assumptions are often made about who is responsible for sorting it out. The problem owner is responsible for arranging the necessary *actions* to avoid, minimise or control the impact on the project. These could include changes to the plan, allocation of new tasks or agreeing changes to the project's scope or outputs. Finally the agreed actions are documented in a risks and issues log, agreed with the PCC and followed up until *resolution* of the risk or issue is confirmed.

Online, tracking tools help to make sure that all interested parties can gain access to the latest versions of the risks and issues log, and update this where changes occur or actions are undertaken.

## ● Dependencies – managing links with other projects

IS projects are normally part of a range of organisational changes taking place at the same time, and these may depend on each other to deliver value for the organisation. Once dependencies have been identified between projects, the relevant project managers must agree the definition and timing of each dependency. They must also agree to monitor them in case changes in one project affect the others. Where this occurs, advising the dependent project manager enables them to make any required adjustments to their project.

## ● Rollout planning and implementation control

All the work of designing, developing and testing an IS can be lost if it is not introduced into the operational environment with care and sensitivity. The rollout is where theory meets practice, and it is here that any hidden failures in the earlier stages appear. Rollout is where actual end-users operate the new system in a real working environment with real customers and real data for the first time, and this can be when political forces become most visible. Users who were reluctant about or felt threatened by the changes now have their opportunity. They can demonstrate how badly the new system works ('I told them at Head Office that this wouldn't work and now look – I've been proved right!') It is one of the most stressful areas of project management.

The project will aim to roll out completed projects in an orderly way, but is likely to be foiled since the task involves integrating many factors. In technical terms alone the list is daunting:

- hardware purchase and installation;
- software installation;
- property surveys and modifications, including cabling, furniture, security;
- staff training, and cover for staff absent on training;
- asset control procedures;
- health and safety measures;
- financial control;
- installation contractor selection and management;
- communications with staff, contractors, customers;
- activity planning and progress tracking;
- contingency planning, including fallback on previous systems in cases of failure.

There are also the many organisational, cultural and structural ripples that we have examined throughout this book. The project is rolling out a change in organisation, not a change in technology.

The central dilemma is between the Big Bang approach (installing at all your operational sites at once) and a phased introduction. One consideration is whether the operational areas can cope with large change in a short period or small changes over a long period would be more acceptable. Where reliability is critical, a slower pace lowers the risk of large-scale failure. Where speed to market is critical, the Big Bang approach may be essential.

Active communication is vital during rollout. Staff need to know what is happening to their area, when it will happen and how it will affect them personally. Local management must also understand and approve the process or it will not promote the project to staff. Surveys of completed areas will provide the rollout team with vital information on how to improve by learning from the experiences of end-users and their managers.

---

## CASE QUESTIONS 9.2

- Which aspects of this section do you think will be especially relevant in the RBS ABN Amro integration programme?
- Select any ONE of these control techniques, and envisage how members of a team working on one of the projects might use the method.
- To gather ideas, you could visit the RBS website and look for recent news about the integration programme (probably under 'Media Centre' or 'Investor Relations').

---

### ● Post-implementation reviews

Throughout the life of the project, lessons can be learned. These may confirm a successful idea or approach or may be unpleasant surprises that caused additional work and worry. Whether good or bad, these lessons are important parts of the learning process for all concerned, and are vital to capture and share if the organisation is to learn and continuously improve. It is therefore important to spend some time at the end of the project to capture these lessons and share them with other teams. This can be done at a post-implementation review session where all the project team get together to share their thoughts on what went well in the project and what could have been done better. It is important to emphasise that the objective is not to allocate blame, but to learn and improve.

# Establishing the integration programme

## www.rbs.com

In setting the programme to integrate ABN Amro, the RBS team had many complicated and dynamic factors to manage. Before starting the integration RBS and its partners had first to split ABN Amro into separate businesses – a process many executives believed was fraught with complexity and potential for conflict. RBS took ABN Amro's corporate finance business together with most of the Asian and European operations. The challenges then included the following.

- **Cultural, organisational and geographic diversity**: 55 countries across 5 continents, each with a unique blend of banking regulations, currencies, legal frameworks, social and work ethics, customs, practices and traditions.

- **Many incompatible IT systems** to carry out similar functions across the newly joined businesses.

- **Difficult market conditions**: The integration work began at a time when the banking markets were unusually disturbed, with low asset valuations due to continuing concerns about exposures to bad debts from the USA.

Using experiences from the NatWest and other integration work, they focused on a small number of tasks.

- Establishing the project teams to carry out the early analysis and planning work.

- Quickly mobilising project staff in the early stages meant cancelling or delaying existing initiatives. This undoubtedly caused some internal frustration, and some tough decisions were required.

- Understanding the new business areas. Carrying out detailed analysis of each business area to gain a full picture of the acquired functions and how these could be most effectively integrated with RBS.

- Identifying the most promising integration opportunities. Seeking out opportunities for integrating work, delivering services in new and improved ways, and reducing costs.

- Establishing the control procedures. Setting up the organisational structure and defining the processes by which the integration programme must operate. For example, setting up PCCs, building plans, reporting formats and timing, change controls, etc.

- Communications as, when the ownership of a company changes hands, it can quite naturally create uncertainty amongst the employees. To help in the days and weeks following the initial confirmation, a series of walkabouts and roadshows were held around the world.

*Sources: Financial Times*, 5 and 22 October 2007; company documents.

## ● Summary

- The record of implementing major IS projects is mixed, with cases of success being matched by those of failure. Promoters cannot take the intended outcome for granted, but need to act in ways that increase the chance of success.

- These actions can be focused on project control committees, planning, change control, risk and issue management, and dependency management.
- High-quality rollout management is critical to gaining the support of end-users; the pace and extent of rollout should be matched to the ability and willingness of the end-users to cope with change.
- Post-implementation reviews help to capture lessons that people can use in other projects.

---

**CASE QUESTIONS 9.3**

1. Imagine you are in the team establishing the integration programme. What negative outcomes might you pessimistically envision, and what steps might you take to lessen the probability of these occurring?
2. If you were a senior stakeholder in the integration, what critical success factors would you define? In particular, think about the things you would really like to see happening as a result of the project, and what would disappoint you if it did not occur.

---

# 9.4 Programmes – managing a series of projects

IS projects are usually one of several related projects taking place. Organisations can try to ensure they align with each other by managing them collectively as a programme. Programme management takes many of the principles of project management and applies them to achieving the longer-term, strategic or even visionary outcomes for the business as a whole. Table 9.3 compares features of projects and programmes.

The project manager is concerned with the detail of individual activities and tasks – who will do what by when. The programme manager aims to understand the high-level timetable and deliverables of that project, and how they fit with other projects. The programme manager focuses on the interdependencies between the individual projects. This role can also include responsibility for 'de-escalation' (Keil and Robey, 1999) to prevent failing projects taking ever more resources.

**Table 9.3** Differences in the outputs of projects and programmes

| Function | Project | Programme |
|---|---|---|
| Customer sales and service | Deliver a new Internet channel for purchasing products. | Make the organisation more accessible to customers through improved channel delivery. |
| Staff | Introduce a new performance management and reward process. | Enable the organisation to attract and retain the best-quality staff. |
| Property | Refurbish the Dublin office building. | Enhance and standardise the European property portfolio. |

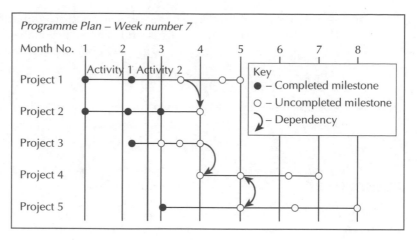

**Figure 9.5** The programme overview chart

## ● The programme overview chart

Project plans define and display every task and activity, and project reports provide updates on the detailed progress with all current activities. A programme manager would soon become swamped with such detail and focuses instead on the planning and reporting of just the major milestones and delivery points of each project in the programme.

The programme manager needs to maintain a quick-to-understand snapshot of the programme. This should show progress to date, the main events being planned, interdependencies, issues and expected completion dates. This also helps the programme manager to communicate with senior management and project managers.

One way to do this is to create a single chart with a simplified view of each project on an indicative timeline. Figure 9.5 illustrates this.

Details vary but the main features are usually:

● an indicative timeline, along which the individual projects are plotted;

● a simplified representation of the major milestones in each project or change area;

● descriptions of actual progress against expected progress for each project;

● indications of interdependencies between projects.

## ● Programme reporting

Most programmes only survive if the sponsors remain confident that progress is being made towards their critical success factors, which means they need regular reports. Apart from keeping sponsors on side, these bring other benefits:

● earlier recognition of problems;

● improved learning from past activities;

● more justification for continued or increased resources;

● greater support from senior executives (maintaining their confidence);

● more motivated staff (from recognising their achievement).

The most useful reports will include nothing more complicated than:

- progress made against plans;
- time expended by project staff;
- actual costs incurred against budgets;
- issues being encountered.

Trying to produce more sophisticated information than this will probably become a distraction from the project. Accuracy, presentation and timeliness are more important than detail in programme reporting.

| MBI in Practice | Web-based reporting at a semi-conductor company |
|---|---|

A multinational firm in the electronics industry reorganised its worldwide facilities. This involved rearranging capacity between the sites and implementing various information systems to support manufacturing. The IS department designed a web-based reporting system, in which each sub-project manager completed a standard report showing progress against actions. The site also contained standard programme documents that would previously have been paper files.

The information entered by each project manager was visible to everyone with access to the site (most staff). In addition, the programme manager called a weekly meeting of all project managers. Each brought up their report on a large screen in the conference room and talked the programme manager through the report, together with any issues on which they needed support.

The system worked so well that it has now been adopted as standard programme management practice throughout the company.

*Source*: Personal communication from a project manager.

## ● The programme office

The programme manager's job involves a great deal of information handling and processing. Information on the status of the projects is continually flowing to the programme manager, who must be able to distil this into a meaningful picture. A separate programme office function is a good way to achieve this. This can typically take the form of an individual or small team separate from the project teams and dedicated to establishing and maintaining plans, tracking and recording progress and reporting to senior management.

### Activity 9.1 Project and programme managers

Make two lists of the skills that you would look for in a project manager and a programme manager. Highlight the common skills and consider the ways in which the roles differ and are similar.

- In what ways might conflicts arise between the roles?

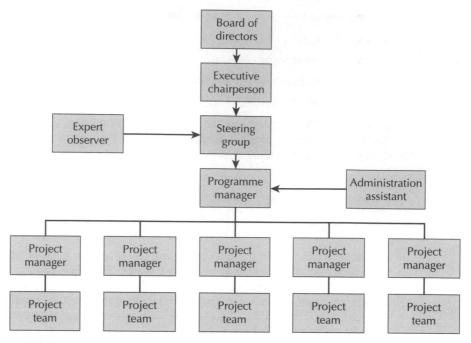

**Figure 9.6** Example of a programme management structure

## ● The programme management structure

To control a series of projects successfully the programme manager requires a supportive organisation structure. Figure 9.6 shows the typical components of this structure.

The programme management structure usually consists of senior managers representing each of the main operational and business departments affected by the programme. It meets regularly to receive reports on progress from the programme manager, and give guidance on outstanding issues.

### The executive chairperson

This is usually a board director or other member of executive management. Their status signals that the project is being taken seriously. It is essential that the programme manager maintains their confidence and support – the chair will be receiving any bad news through their own networks.

### Board of directors

The executive chairperson will report directly to the board. The board provides the direct link to the strategy and operations of the organisation. The quality of this link determines how well the programme contributes to broader strategy.

### Expert observer

An informed outsider can give valuable impartial observations on difficult dilemmas facing a programme or project within it. They can help the group avoid believing its own publicity, and take a critical view of reported achievements. This is especially important when a programme is beginning to escalate and is seeking more resources than can be justified by progress. They can more easily advise termination than an insider. The best expert observers contribute only when asked for an opinion or when the group has reached an impasse. They can then state the relative merit of each option to help the steering group take a more informed decision.

### The programme administrator

Someone needs to keep the books – meticulously maintaining the minutes of meetings and background notes with clear and accurate filing. An experienced administrator to manage information in support of the programme manager is essential. They will prompt others for progress reports before meetings and handle all the usual support work.

## ● Summary

- Programmes contain a set of projects with a common aim.
- Programme managers need to understand how individual projects contribute to the overall programme.
- Programme overview charts help to illustrate progress at a high level.
- Progress reporting is key to maintaining support and confidence in the programme; reports need to be accurate, well presented, and timely.
- The programme office provides a single source for information and a focus for managing day-to-day issues.

## 9.5 Building the energised environment

Throughout the life of a project, it is important to develop and maintain an environment that encourages its members to continually improve their capabilities and those of their colleagues. Staff should feel that they are being given the opportunity to increase their value to the organisation, while being valued for the contributions they are already making.

When the project manager has developed an energised environment of this type, in which staff want to surprise and delight their colleagues and are willing to work hard to do so, then he or she will have gone a long way to ensuring the successful outcome of the overall initiative. Some of the vital components of the energised environment are discussed below.

## ● Clearly understood strategy and vision

For project staff to be able to work cohesively towards the overall aims of the initiative, they must understand what those aims are and how they can contribute towards them. Defining and communicating the project strategy and how it will support the organisation is essential.

## ● Clear personal objectives, regularly reviewed

Closely aligned to the strategy for the project with an energised environment will be a set of clearly defined personal objectives for each member of staff. These will carefully describe the behaviours and results that are expected from that individual, and how these will be measured and rewarded.

Achievement of these individual objectives will demonstrably contribute to the achievement of the overall strategy for the project. Ideally, a Balanced Scorecard of objectives for the project will be prepared from which the individual objectives are derived (Kaplan and Norton, 1996). Personal objectives can be set at the start of a review period and reviewed regularly throughout that period by the individual's line manager. High-quality feedback recognising the value of the individual's contribution, and pointing out areas for development, will be backed up with practical examples from recent project work. Ideally, feedback will also be received from the individual's peer group and reportees, providing a 360-degree perspective on performance.

---

### Activity 9.2 Personal objectives

- List the personal objectives that you would expect to be set for you if you were a project manager working as part of a large programme.
- How would you ensure that these were both motivational to you and brought benefit to the organisation? (Refer to Chapter 8 for some models to structure your answer.)

---

## ● Reward and recognition

Having taken the time to clearly define and review the work of the individual project members, it is necessary to ensure they receive a reward for their performance that fits with their contribution to the project aims. This reward will most commonly take the form of money and recognition by peers, and it is critical that this is provided in a fair and transparent way to everyone. Performance-related pay is a powerful motivational tool and can form a significant amount of the project members' remuneration package.

## ● A learning culture

No project of any meaningful content or duration will exist without mistakes being made. These should be viewed positively as learning opportunities from which competitive advantage will be derived. To realise this competitive advantage, it is necessary to recognise and understand these mistakes as they occur and apply the lessons that accrue from them immediately into subsequent project activities.

Regular interaction between members of the project staff, frequent review sessions and, in particular, post-implementation reviews (see earlier discussion in this chapter) are all sources of fascinating and invaluable knowledge on how to improve performance.

Having reviewed and refined project performance and behaviours, an organisation with a learning culture will record and store a set of ideal methodologies in a knowledge database. This can take a very simple form, such as a set of hints and tips for future work, or can be a large and sophisticated set of instructions for detailed project activity planning. Whatever method is chosen, the determination to learn from ongoing activities can only enhance the performance of the organisation.

## ● Quick wins – the fuel for long-term development

Some larger IS projects and programmes can last for several years, and staff can face the risk of project fatigue. This damages a project in several different ways.

- Staff and managers become demotivated.
- Executive sponsors lose interest.
- End-users become resistant to the outcomes.
- The project loses credibility, and becomes a target for criticism.

Project fatigue occurs when the enthusiasm of working on a particular project wears off. The pressures of day-to-day problems and new issues take precedence over the long-term benefits. People have done the work but see no benefits. Their belief in the value of the project fails.

The risks of this happening reduce if the project manager can produce short-term deliverables that have clear benefits. People respond to such 'quick wins', and the wise project manager will build several into the overall plans. They can take many forms – for example a new process that will generate new income, cut costs or improve conditions for a visible unit. This has a number of benefits.

- Staff gain a sense of achievement.
- Management can claim a success for the project.
- Board members see a return on their investment.
- End-users gain an improvement to their working processes.
- Customers get an improved service.

If they can build enough quick wins of real value into the project, management can claim that the project is self-funding. This sends a powerful message to the stakeholders about the overall value of the project, and severely weakens objectors. One danger of quick wins is potential to distract staff from the longer-term issues of the project. Project management is balancing short-term and long-term objectives.

## ● Summary

- The chances of the successful delivery of a project will be greatly enhanced if the people working there are given a positive, or energised, working environment.
- Elements of an energised environment will include a shared vision, rewards and recognition linked to performance, and positive support for personal development and a learning culture.
- Quick wins – short-term, tangible deliverables – can be an excellent way to maintain support for a long-term project.

## Creating an energised environment

**www.rbs.com**

As the integration programme began, a crucial factor for success was for the RBS management team to build an energised environment for the programme team. For such a wide-reaching, complex and lengthy set of activities to maintain focus and deliver consistently high-quality results, attracting and retaining the best-quality change managers was essential. Some of the methods that RBS used to achieve this in the early stages were as follows.

- **Defining a clear strategy and vision:** Specific targets for both the short (quick wins) and longer-term outcomes, with clearly stated and measurable outcomes for the programme. These included clear cost-reduction targets by specified dates, the definition of major projects and the outcomes they will achieve.

- **Recognising the project team:** The positioning of the integration team to be the place where all ambitious and motivated project staff wanted to be. This would be achieved by promoting the team's activities in staff communications, and highlighting the glamorous international locations where they could work.

- **Developing a learning culture:** RBS took care to build on the successful integration of the NatWest bank (which delivered a similar set of target cost savings in the early 2000s) and other integration programmes, while being mindful of the need to continuously develop their thinking.

Sir Fred Goodwin, Group Chief Executive, said:

> *I think you learn something every time you do an integration. Every integration is different – we've got to use the same planning tenets but we've got to go into it with our minds open.*

Utilising their experience and the tools and techniques developed in the recent past, the RBS team was hoping to further develop its reputation as a world-class integrator of new businesses.

*Source*: Company documents.

## Conclusions

In this chapter we have emphasised the importance of careful management of IS projects and programmes, highlighting the fact that many such initiatives fail. Managers need to be aware of the strategic implications of what they are undertaking, and how their work will interact with issues of structure, culture and human motivation.

We have introduced four distinct models of change, and described a range of tools and techniques to assist the IS project and programme manager. These tried and tested methods should help to identify and address the most commonly quoted reasons for project failure.

Finally, we have considered the importance of creating an energised environment for project teams to work in, building on our assertion that it is people, not technology, that will make IS projects a success.

## Chapter questions

1. Summarise the four models of project management (about two lines each). How would a project manager be able to assess which approach was likely to be most help in dealing with issues during a project?

2. List three reasons why it is important to analyse stakeholders of a project. What factors should a project manager take into account when considering how to deal with stakeholders?

3. How is the time spent in preparing a project plan justified to a busy project team? List three ways in which a good plan could save time and effort in a project.

4. Why is it often important for individual IS projects being carried out in an organisation to be considered together under the heading of a programme?

5. You are the programme manager for a large set of projects taking place across your organisation. What will you do to encourage a shared set of values, and why might individual project managers actively resist your well-intentioned actions?

# Further reading

Brooks, F.P. (1995) *The Mythical Man-Month*, Addison-Wesley, Reading, MA. A widely read introduction to project management, this is a collection of essays by a distinguished member of the IS community. Draws on vast experience to provide thought-provoking insights for anyone involved with IS projects.

Four empirical studies of project success and failure, showing the value of an effective implementation process:

Sauer, C. (1993) *Why Information Systems Fail: A Case Study Approach*, Alfred Waller, Henley-on-Thames.

Beynon-Davies, P. (1995) 'Information system failure: the case of the London Ambulance Service's computer-aided despatch system', *European Journal of Information Systems*, **4**, 171–84.

Fitzgerald, G. and Russo, N.L. (2005) 'The turnaround of the London Ambulance Service's Computer-Aided Despatch System (LASCAD)', *European Journal of Information Systems*, **14**(3), 244–57.

Kennedy, G., Boddy, D. and Paton, R. (2006) 'Managing the aftermath: lessons from The Royal Bank of Scotland's acquisition of NatWest', *European Management Journal*, **24**(4), 368–79. A study that gives more detail on an earlier RBS project, and so provides some historical context for the RBS-ABN Amro case.

Two empirical studies of the escalation phenomenon, and of how to avoid the dangers:

Drummond, H. (1996) *Escalation in Decision-making: The Tragedy of Taurus*, Oxford University Press, Oxford.

Pan, G.S.C., Pan, S.L. and Flynn, D. (2004) 'De-escalation of commitment to information systems projects: a process perspective', *Journal of Strategic information Systems*, **13**(3), 247–70.

# Weblinks

Follow the progress of RBS as it seeks to integrate ABN Amro by visiting the RBS website (www.rbs.com) and also those of major business newspapers: *Financial Times* (www.ft.com) and *The Economist* (www.economist.com).

# CHAPTER 10

## The costs and benefits of IS

### Learning objectives

By the end of your work on this topic you should be able to:

- List the main direct and indirect costs of an information system
- List the main tangible and intangible benefits of an information system
- Give the primary reasons for inaccurate IS project evaluation
- Describe alternative methods of evaluating IS take organisational factors into account
- Explain how organisational structure can influence the process of evaluation

# BBC faces tricky investment decisions

**www.bbc.co.uk**

Mark Thompson, Director-General of the BBC, said in 2006:

*There's a big shock coming. The second wave of digital will be far more disruptive than the first and the foundations of traditional media will be swept away, taking us beyond broadcasting. The BBC needs a creative response to the amazing, bewildering, exciting and inspiring changes in both technology and expectations.*

The British Broadcasting Corporation (BBC) was formed in 1922 to address the opportunities being presented by radio transmission, which was by then available across most of the UK. Over the following decades, the organisation gradually extended its coverage, first to Europe and then worldwide. The BBC television service began in 1936.

By 2007, the BBC was one of the world's most recognised brands. It operated 8 digital TV networks in the UK, along with 10 national and 40 local radio stations. The BBC also produced some 30,000 hours of TV broadcasts per year and managed the world's largest media archive. Employing 25,000 staff, it had a global reach of more than 260 million viewers through the international TV news channel BBC World and more than 150 million listeners via the BBC World Service.

Having grown through radio and then television, the BBC had further proved its flexibility by developing a successful online service during the 1990s that attracted 80 million users each month and was widely admired for the quality and integrity of its content as well as its overall user-appeal. The success of this channel was a critical strength for the BBC as it faced an expanding range of channel types and a new generation of tech-savvy, mobile and international consumers.

Mark Thompson realised that the BBC had to react to the new market. Consumers were increasingly using the web as their medium of choice for broadcasts, and the BBC was aware that many of its programmes were being watched on computers via broadband Internet, and on many kinds of mobile devices. The corporation was acutely aware that it needed to connect with younger audiences. Mark Thompson wanted a radical approach: 'We should aim to deliver public service content to our audiences in whatever media and on whatever device makes sense for them, whether they are at home or on the move.'

The changing marketplace saw many new forms of media options emerging.

- **Mobile phones:** Web-enabled mobile phones made it possible to supply content to users who wished to obtain news at a time and place that suited them.

- **Web 2.0:** This describes the growing interactivity amongst web users. The popularity of blogging and social networking sites create new forms of web-based communities and hosted services.

- **Increased bandwidth:** Wide adoption of broadband capacity in fixed and mobile networks created more potential for video- and audio-streaming and other high-capacity content downloads.

As Mark Thompson and his team pondered these emerging challenges and opportunities, the key question was: how should the BBC invest in this new market, and would it generate a worthwhile return?

*Source*: Saravanan and Bhaskaran (2007).

## Introduction

Staff are rarely short of ideas and proposals that promise to enhance their information systems. Suppliers of hardware, software and communications systems vie with each other in promising that their systems will dramatically enhance performance. From business process re-engineering (BPR) to enterprise resource planning (ERP) to customer relationship management (CRM), the conveyor belt of three-letter acronyms presents managers with the challenge of deciding between competing IS investment proposals. They will probably base this choice on estimates of what the project is likely to cost and potential benefits to the organisation. This is simple to say, but difficult to put into practice.

The costs and benefits of IS projects are notoriously difficult to determine.

- The cost of the Libra project to provide a national system for 385 courts in the UK soared from £146m to £390m. Despite spending more than twice what they expected, the court service still did not have a working system (*Computer Weekly*, 11 November 2003).

- In June 2003 the London Borough of Haringey Council commenced their 'Tech Refresh' project to 'meet a need to establish new effective working methods' through a series of IT investments with a budget of £9m. In June 2005, the Executive Committee reported that Tech Refresh was facing a 'number of difficulties' that were 'due to the scope and complex nature of the programme'. It was not until the Audit Commission's report of January 2006 that details on the causes of the overspending and its full extent emerged. By then the costs of the project had risen to £24.6m (*Computer Weekly*, 21 February 2006).

What went wrong with these projects? Why are the costs and benefits of information system projects so difficult to predict and control? This chapter reviews the commonest reasons. The Chapter Case considers the strategic response of the BBC to major changes in the technology available to the consumers of broadcasting services, and the way they live their lives. It raises questions, as yet unanswered, regarding the ability of such a not-for-profit organisation to justify its expenditure on developing new channels to provide its services.

---

## CASE QUESTIONS 10.1

Make some notes on your immediate responses to these broad questions.

- Why is it important for an organisation such as the BBC to be able to measure the return on investments it makes?
- What measures could it consider using to measure the success of its digital strategy?
- Assuming it is able to quantify these returns, how should it compare the return with other possible IS investments?

Refer back to your notes as you work through the chapter.

---

The chapter begins by outlining the elements of the formal–rational evaluation techniques. This appears simple – until we describe the problems with the approach. The following section details the wider considerations required when estimating the costs and benefits of information systems. Several alternative evaluation methods are described that take a more holistic approach to evaluation by incorporating human and organisational perspectives. Finally, we consider some organisation design issues that influence the effectiveness of IS projects. The aim is to identify the factors that influence the evaluation of information systems and what that means for those managing such projects.

# 10.1 Formal–rational methods for evaluating IS proposals

Traditional methods of project evaluation express the idea that the costs of an investment need to be related to the benefits the investment brings. The costs are (mainly) incurred now, while the benefits (hopefully) come later. So the calculation needs to take account of the timing as well as the amounts of costs and benefits. The longer the delay in receiving the benefits, the greater the risk: so that needs to be part of the calculation. Having done that for the projects under consideration, managers then have an apparently rational basis upon which to decide between them. The more the estimated payback from the investment in a project, the more likely managers are to approve it. To illustrate the principles, some widely used techniques are outlined below; Laudon and Laudon (2007) includes a fuller discussion.

### ● Payback period

This method calculates the number of years required before the cumulative financial returns equal the initial investment. If a company invests £10m, and expects to receive returns of £2m each year, the payback period is 5 years. A shorter payback period is more attractive as it means the investment is at risk for less time. The difficulty is that this ignores the fact that some investments will produce returns for longer periods than others.

### ● Return on investment

This method calculates the return on the investment (ROI) by estimating the annual benefits to be achieved over the life of the project, and dividing that number by the amount invested. The annual benefit is calculated as the expected cost savings, additional revenue or whatever other benefits people expect. In the example above, the annual benefit of £2m would give an ROI of 20 per cent.

### ● Discounted cash flow

Payback and ROI are simple and easy to understand. The difficulty is that neither takes account of the timing of the costs and benefits. A project that brings immediate benefits is worth more than one in which the benefits occur much later – but ROI calculations would not show this. Similarly, a project with a short payback period would be preferred to one in which the benefits took longer to repay the investment. This ignores the fact that the second project, while slow to deliver, may produce benefits for a much longer period.

To overcome these problems, accountants have developed more sophisticated appraisal methods that take account of the fact money itself has a value. In the discounted cash flow (DCF) method, costs and returns are calculated over the expected whole life of the project, but then adjusted for the fact that distant returns are worth less than those that are received soon.

All methods depend on identifying and estimating the costs and benefits of the project, and the major elements of these are outlined in the next section.

# 10.2 The costs of information systems

People make different interpretations of the cost of IS. Those in the finance function tend to consider the purchase invoice. Those in the IS department will think more about support and maintenance costs. Users will look at training and business process costs. Organisations have great difficulty establishing the true cost of their information systems. Viewing IS as a product that can be purchased, plugged in and forgotten fails to capture the cost impact of all but the most simple standalone applications. The complex and costly systems being implemented today – many of which transcend organisational boundaries – require a rigorous approach to cost estimation.

One method is to calculate the total cost of ownership (TCO) of an information system, rather than the more obvious purchase price. TCO refers to the activity of taking a holistic view of costs over the lifetime of an investment, rather than viewing the purchase price in isolation. This is difficult but essential. Knowing exactly what a system costs to buy and run is the first step on the road to reducing those costs.

The manager preparing a project proposal needs a checklist of the likely costs. This needs to include both the costs of initial purchase and the longer-term costs of implementation, ownership and change. The following pages indicate costs that people may overlook, but which add to TCO.

## ● Cost of purchase

For most IS projects the acquisition cost is mainly hardware and software. These costs dominate formal–rational evaluation techniques but become a smaller part of the true cost as systems become more integrated into organisational processes.

## ● Hardware costs

- The front end – user interfaces and peripherals (monitors, keyboards, control equipment, printers, scanners, etc.).
- The middleware – networking equipment (cabling, routers, switching devices, encryption devices and other communication linkages).
- The back end – processing equipment (servers, mainframes, desktop PC units, etc.).

When considering the total cost of a large project, it may also be worth separately considering any elements of the new system that could be described as infrastructure. These are elements that can be used by more than one system. For example, a national cable network for a bank's automated teller machines (ATMs) might also be used for a future communications system such as intranet or video-conferencing links. Desktop computers used for word-processing are also used for e-mail. Logically the infrastructure costs would be shared across such other projects, and so affect relative costs and benefits.

## ● Software costs

- Developments costs if built in-house, package and licence costs if bought-in;
- operating system software;
- application development tools;
- security and encryption packages;

271

- networking and communication software;
- systems management software;
- database and database management software;
- front-end software packages.

## ● Implementation, ownership and change

Information systems inevitably interact with other parts of the organisation. This brings further implementation costs that, while significant, are hard to measure:

- re-engineering current business processes;
- decommissioning and disposing of existing systems;
- staff communication and training;
- customer communication and training;
- costs of parallel running during the rollout period;
- error correction and compensation for quality 'dip' during initial use of the new system.

Those proposing and approving projects frequently ignore or underestimate these costs. This puts an extra burden on staff during implementation – which adds yet further cost elements.

Having purchased and implemented a new system, managers must understand the cost of maintaining and supporting it throughout its life. Costs of ownership will include the following.

- **Support**: help desk functions, user manuals, retraining of staff.
- **Disaster recovery**: duplication of facilities at alternative sites to ensure continuity of operation in the event of major problems at the main site.
- **Staff**: recruiting development staff, training developers, maintainers and users.
- **Maintenance**: Hardware and software incur costs of minor enhancements, bug-fixes and requests for change. Is the product high-quality/low-maintenance or low-quality/high-maintenance? Availability and cost of spare parts? For how long? Availability and cost of suitably skilled technicians and help desk staff?
- **Obsolescence**: Does the product comply with an industry standard with an established history and a foreseeable life? If not, the product may soon be impossible to maintain or upgrade.
- **Upgrade**: Both hardware and software are likely to need upgrading – to meet new communication standards, regulatory changes, new market requirements, expanded applications or new processes. Having bought a particular software package, it is hard to avoid paying for successive upgrades. This in turn may require additional hardware capacity.

In times when markets, technologies and regulatory requirements change rapidly, change itself becomes a major cost category. How rapidly will the IS department be able to adapt the system to changed conditions? Some points to consider.

- **Interoperability of hardware:** Can the proposed hardware platform operate with other platforms, operating systems, networks, peripheral equipment? Flexibility in this area allows future merging of systems and changes to operating platforms and software.

● **Openness of software:** Can the software be easily and cheaply modified or linked to other systems? Open, modular software is normally preferable to specialised one-use architecture.

## ● Summary

● The true costs of a new IT system extend well beyond the purchase costs of the hardware and software, covering the costs of implementation, ownership, change and infrastructure.

● Costs associated with the impact of the new system on staff, customers, suppliers and other stakeholders must be considered.

● Long-term costs are difficult to foresee, but choices in the design of the system influence their scale.

## 10.3 The benefits of information systems

No useful business case can be based on cost alone. Often the more important issue is not what is spent, but what is received in return and when it will appear. When working out the benefits of an investment, the project manager needs first to consider what business benefits senior managers or the project sponsor are expecting to achieve. Ideally these will contribute to the wider strategy (Chapter 4). Managers with high growth targets will be most interested in systems that increase sales capability, while those fighting for survival will prefer one that cuts costs.

Having established the benefits that managers expect, they need to be quantified if the policy requires a formal–rational assessment of the proposal. While staff can estimate immediate costs reasonably accurately, benefits are a different matter. These are in the future and depend on factors beyond the control of the project team. Even more than with costs, people make subjective judgements about benefits. Supporters will be most optimistic about the potential benefits both tangible (directly quantifiable) and intangible (difficult to quantify).

## ● Tangible benefits

### Direct cost savings

The most obvious benefit of an IS may be that it will cut costs by automating processes and so replace people. More accurate and timely distribution of work (e.g. using document imaging or telephone call routing systems) can decrease operator waiting time and lead to efficiency-based cost reductions. Fewer staff can mean lower property costs. In practice these are usually less than expected owing to:

● agreements with trade unions preventing job losses;

● staff time savings may be spread over several locations, limiting the ability to reduce staffing at any one location;

● time saved only counts as a benefit once people have moved to other profitable work.

| MIS in Practice | RBS Manufacturing – using IS to reduce costs |

The Royal Bank of Scotland (RBS) Group Manufacturing Division is responsible for the operational areas of the Bank that support the income-generating businesses. It has three functional areas: Technology (IT operations and development), Operations (account management, lending, telephony, payments) and Services (purchasing, property, other support units). As the primary back-office 'engine room' for the world's fifth largest bank, Manufacturing provides operational services to over 40 million customers across a variety of delivery channels (branches, Internet, ATMs, telephone, etc.).

Since 1999, RBS income has increased by an average of 14 per cent per year. During this period the costs of Manufacturing have remained static or even decreased when transfers from other divisions are taken into account.

### How has Manufacturing maintained stable costs at a time of significant growth?

One way has been by basing its IS strategy on the idea of 'build once, use many times'. This means developing a single IT platform to support the many different financial brands and delivery channels across RBS. By building newly acquired business areas, and the growing needs of existing businesses, into the same IT platform, Manufacturing has established a very large system with big economies of scale. By developing common processes for the different brands, this large platform operates very efficiently while meeting the different demands of the businesses.

Manufacturing's scale has allowed it to develop large information processing centres specialising in account management, lending, telephony, payments or credit cards and handling large volumes of transactions from low-cost buildings. Using integrated information systems to drive efficient processes, Manufacturing staff are dramatically increasing their productivity.

Initiatives include introducing image and workflow technology (see Chapter 5), improved customer query management systems, improved fraud detection, simplified account-opening processes and further consolidation of the IT platform.

*Source*: Information from managers and staff in manufacturing.

### Quality improvements

A major benefit is the ability of a computer-based system to reduce errors when it replaces a manual system. While people can provide a personal and flexible service, they can also make mistakes and be inconsistent. Customers become annoyed if they are treated differently each time they use a service or see others receiving better treatment. Errors are expensive since they take time to find and correct, and may lead to compensation or lost business. Other possible benefits include assessing the following.

● Which customers see benefits from consistent, standardised processing?

● What reduction in reworking and compensation costs will we achieve?

● What revenue may accrue if we reduce the number of customers lost?

● How much less money will we spend in servicing warranty agreements?

### Avoiding cost increases

A modern IS can avoid future costs. Like a car, an old system incurs high maintenance costs, and breakdowns disrupt operations and annoy customers. Most organisations replace their PCs after about five years, as maintenance costs then rise sharply. If a new system will avoid these costs, this should be in the evaluation.

### Revenue increases

Those advocating a new system will emphasise the prospects of increased sales through new services, delivery channels or market penetration. These can be real benefits – but are likely to be optimistic. They are also notoriously difficult to validate, since any change in sales is usually the result of a variety of factors, not necessarily connected to the new system.

### Staying in business

Sometimes introducing a new system is simply essential if the organisation is to continue. In a highly regulated environment, it may be necessary to be able to operate in a certain manner just to be allowed to continue to provide the service. Suppliers to Wal-Mart (Chapter 4) and many other retail chains have had to implement IS to manage their relationship with the customer or lose the business. Major engineering companies require suppliers to be able to receive drawings and specifications electronically. Those unable to do so have to merge with those that can.

As the MIS in Practice feature below shows, companies can also gain the intangible benefits of 'first-mover' advantage, if this gives them a lead in using a new process or system that others find hard to follow. The risks of being a first mover are considerable, however, and can more often lead to losses than profits (Markides and Geroski, 2005).

---

**MIS in Practice**  **Wachovia's gamble pays off**

In early 2004 the corporate and investment division of Wachovia Bank (based in North Carolina) took a gamble in implementing a new technology known as service-oriented architecture (SOA). The purpose of this very expensive risk was to catch up with, and overtake, the competition in this fast-growing sector of financial services. The division's new chief information officer could see the inefficiencies in the current operation, as each part of the business developed its own system that were then hard to link.

She therefore persuaded the board to invest in a complete overhaul of the IS development process, based on using a core of common reusable components that could be adapted by any of the business units. Three years on, the gamble seems to be paying off, as measured by:

- the speed of development of new applications – 90 days for a desktop application that traditionally could have taken a year;
- new business won; and
- growth of the data processing budget.

The bank has also benefited from being amongst the first to use the SOA approach, which meant that it had developed expertise it would be harder for others to follow.

*Source: Financial Times, 3 October 2007, p. 3.*

---

### ● Intangible benefits

The tangible benefits can be quantified to some degree, but still with a wide margin for interpretation. Other benefits, the intangible ones, are those that people cannot usually quantify. Table 10.1 lists some of these.

**Table 10.1** Some intangible benefits of information systems

| Possible improvements | Description |
| --- | --- |
| Communications | Between staff and suppliers, customers or investors. |
| Staff morale | Staff may see improvements in their role or working environment. |
| Customer satisfaction | Brings repeat business and reduces the cost of sales. |
| Reputation | New systems may send positive signals to the market about commitment to innovation. |
| Customer management | Using customer data in advanced information systems may improve reaction to customers' needs. |
| Value chain management | Building direct system links between partners in the value chain can improve responsiveness and reduce costs. |
| Flexibility | IS often enable an organisation to react more quickly and easily to changes in the marketplace. |
| Organisational learning | IS enable lessons from current practices to spread more widely; staff can also learn about external events, and be better placed to take advantage of new developments. |
| Differentiation | As discussed in Chapter 4, an important strategic use of IS is differentiation; it is hard to quantify the benefits, as we cannot know how soon competitors will match it. |

Brynjolfsson and Hitt (2000) propose that a large part of the benefits of IS investments come from intangible benefits such as variety, convenience and service – which are hard to measure quantitatively. Nevertheless, these lead ultimately to an economic contribution substantially greater than the initial investment costs.

## Activity 10.1  Identifying and assessing benefits

Choose an organisation with which you interact regularly – e.g. a bank or a supermarket.

- What benefits could it gain from using IS to improve quality of service that you would value?
- How easily could it quantify these benefits in monetary terms?
- What three intangible benefits (see Table 10.1) could it achieve with the help of IS?

## ● Summary

- Information systems can bring many tangible and intangible benefits, the monetary value of which is hard to predict with any accuracy.
- Overemphasis on costs (which tend to be immediate and certain) and underemphasis on benefits (which tend to be in the future and uncertain) leads to a reluctance to invest in IS.

# 10.4 Creating a balanced portfolio of project types

Large organisations typically undertake several related projects at once so they need to evaluate individual projects as part of a wider programme (see Chapter 9). The programme will contain projects representing different types of activity, such as:

● upgrading a network connecting different locations to a more modern platform that will provide capacity for new applications across all business areas;

● building a new web-based system for presenting product features to customers, collecting order and payment details and passing them to the operational area to complete the transaction.

While both projects provide vital functions, they have different types of costs and benefits. Building a new network will have specific costs, but the benefits are intangible as they are not related directly to customer sales.

Organisations typically support a portfolio of projects like this – some of them help to build the infrastructure. They develop the ability of the organisation to perform effectively and efficiently, but viewed in isolation deliver no tangible benefits. Nonetheless, shareholders will need reassurance that the investment is sound.

A simple approach is to categorise certain types of projects as 'enablers', making no attempt to determine benefits as they are hard to quantify in isolation. Instead managers justify them on the grounds that they cannot implement other specified projects until

CHAPTER CASE: PART 2

## How best to realise the competitive strengths?
**www.bbc.co.uk**

In considering its response to the changes in its market, the BBC recognised that it had a major competitive strength: its huge catalogue of recorded material that was ideally suited to delivery through the new high-capacity Internet and mobile channels. Ashley Highfield, Director for New Media, reflected in August 2006 that the power base of the BBC was to:

*put Britain at the forefront of internet-based technology and to transform all our lives by giving us access to the entire video archive of the BBC, a treasure trove of 1.2 million hours of film, where and how we want, and for free.*

This was seen as the unique proposition for the BBC to offer and one that, carefully applied, could place the BBC in a strong position in the second wave of the digital revolution. There was, however, a major obstacle to realising this potential. Setting up and managing such a vast database of content and offering this to consumers in a usable and accessible format would require a very high investment in technical expertise. Highfield admitted that it would demand a standard of navigation that would be in advance of those achieved by sites such as Google Video:

*It will require awesome metadata, great social software and recommendation engines, and clever cross promotion from our linear channels if we are to really unlock the hidden gems.*

Mark Thompson realised that the BBC was not able to meet this investment on its own, and decided on a strategic alliance with a suitable technical provider. After discussions with technology leaders, including Apple, Google and IBM, he chose Microsoft as the partner for this venture. An agreement was drawn up between the two organisations, setting out how they would collaborate in areas of search and navigation, distribution and content enablement.

*Source*: Saravanan and Bhaskaran (2007).

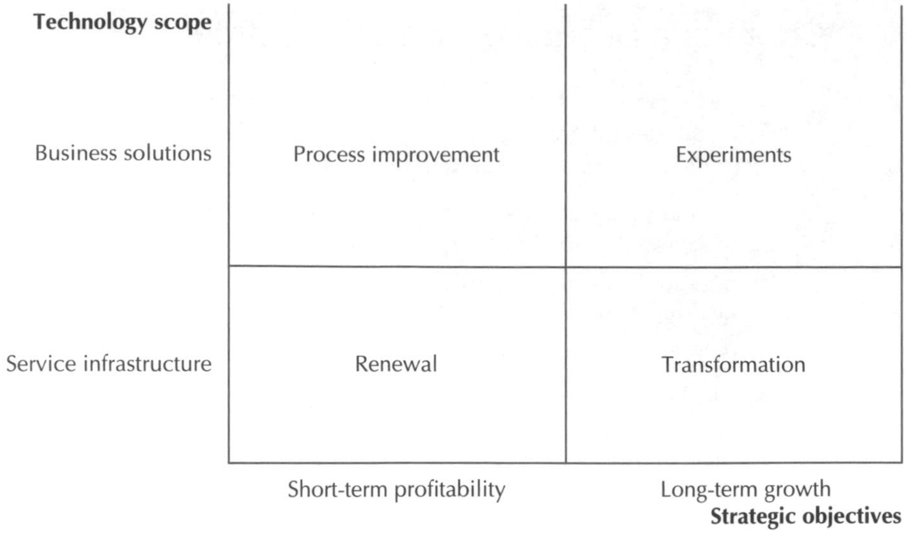

**Technology scope**

| | Short-term profitability | Long-term growth |
|---|---|---|
| Business solutions | Process improvement | Experiments |
| Service infrastructure | Renewal | Transformation |

**Strategic objectives**

**Figure 10.1 A framework for IT investment**
*Source*: Ross and Beath (2002).

they have implemented the enabler project. It makes sense to accept the proposal if its costs, added to those of the projects it enables, are covered by the benefits of the latter. The portfolio, or programme, of projects has a positive business case, being a balance of enabler and enabled projects.

Ross and Beath (2002) describe a more detailed approach to viewing IS investments across the organisation and suggest four categories of IS investment that make up the 'framework for IT investment' shown in Figure 10.1.

By balancing short- and long-term projects on the strategy scale, and infrastructural and business solutions on the scope scale, organisations can achieve an effective mix of IS investments.

### ● Summary

- Often, IS projects cannot be justified on a formal–rational basis in isolation, but must be viewed in the context of the other IS investments taking place at that time.

- Some IS projects must be justified on the basis of the benefits received from other projects that they 'enable'.

- Organisations often must achieve an effective mix of different IS investments – short- and long-term, infrastructural and business-specific.

## 10.5 Problems of formal–rational evaluation

Formal–rational techniques depend on the assumption that the costs incurred in purchasing the system, and the benefits obtained from it, can be identified and accurately estimated. This applies to both the values and their timing. This assumption is rarely met in the fast-changing world of IS. Technology changes during the course of the

**Table 10.2** Reasons often given for information system projects failing to meet investment appraisal targets

| Reason | Description |
| --- | --- |
| Overemphasis on purchase costs | When planning an IT investment, the most obvious costs are those related directly to the purchase of the necessary equipment and software. However, studies of existing systems show that these initial purchase costs are only a part, and often the lesser part, of the overall system costs. |
| Over-ambitious rates of return | In setting rates of return in DCF calculations, figures of 12 per cent and even 15 per cent are not uncommon. However, studies of the real cost of capital upon which these return rates should be based (e.g. Kaplan, 1996) indicate that a figure of 8.5 per cent per annum is a much more realistic target. |
| Underestimation of implementation time and costs | The project is not finished when the system is purchased or built. It then has to be rolled out to the operational areas of the organisation and start delivering the anticipated benefits. The time and costs incurred in this implementation stage are frequently misunderstood. |
| Poor communication with users and customers | Misunderstandings over the functions and uses of a new system add to costs. Alienating staff can make them reluctant to use the system. Both of these problems are caused by a lack of effective communication with staff. Further problems can be incurred when customers have not been kept informed and experience problems when they use the new system for the first time. |
| Unrealistic benefit predictions | Enthusiastic project managers overestimate the expected benefits. Careful analysis of the likelihood of achieving them can reveal significant overstatements. |
| Unexpected demand levels | When introducing a new system that customers access directly, such as a call centre or a website, it is difficult to anticipate early demand. Providing too much capacity is as costly as providing too little and losing business. |
| Not learning from past experiences | Most organisations fail to learn from their experiences with previous projects and so repeat mistakes. Formal post-implementation reviews are not popular with busy project teams, but can bring huge learning benefits. |

project – and will continue to do so during the expected life of the system. This plays havoc with the approach (Mahmood and Mann, 2000; Wu and Chen, 2006).

Table 10.2 lists the commonly quoted reasons for IS projects failing to meet their investment appraisal targets. These testify to the complexities surrounding such projects and limiting the ability of the formal–rational techniques to predict adequately the value of a project.

A common error in formal–rational investment appraisal is to overemphasise the costs, which tend to be easier to quantify, and underemphasise the benefits, which are less certain and harder to justify. This reduces the attractiveness of the project. It is also common for decisions to be biased towards those IS projects where the benefits are easy to identify, such as cost reduction through automation. This limits the success chances of revenue-generating projects and can lead to the late adoption of critical infrastructure investments. Research by Bensaou and Earl (1998) shows this to be a cultural factor, not a force of nature – see the Research Summary overleaf.

| Research Summary | Western and Japanese approaches to investment |
|---|---|

A study by Bensaou and Earl (1998) of the differences between Western and Japanese IS investment decision-making revealed an important difference in approach:

*In Japanese corporations, IT [sic] projects are not assessed primarily by financial metrics; audits and formal approval for investments are rare. Instead, because operational performance goals drive most investments, the traditional metric is performance improvement, not value for money.* (p. 123)

This was not an excuse for poorly defined benefit values. The Japanese companies in the study had very firm views on the performance improvements that were expected from a new system, and accurately tracked these before and after implementation.

*Source*: Bensaou and Earl (1998).

Many of the benefits of IS are qualitative and do not lend themselves easily to the quantitative approach of the formal–rational techniques. There is nothing new about this. In her study of 20 companies implementing CAD/CAM systems, Currie (1989) found that managers were routinely fabricating cost–benefit cases to pass formal–rational appraisal hurdles in order to gain the qualitative benefits that they knew were essential for the success of their departments. She later found that 85 per cent of managers believe qualitative benefits are as important as the financial ones, but only 53 per cent attempt to quantify them because of their vague nature.

## Activity 10.2  Evaluating a personal IS

Think of a computer-based information system you use regularly, e.g. the computer you use at work or your Internet connection at home.

● List all of the items of cost incurred in operating this system.
● List the benefits you gain from using it.
● How easy would it be to quantify these costs and benefits?
● If you had to justify keeping the system on a purely monetary basis, would you find it easy to do so?

Any evaluation process requires us to consider the size and timing of costs and benefits. Formal–rational techniques do this, but the depth to which information systems integrate themselves within organisations, and the impact of human factors, require a holistic, organisation-wide view of the costs and benefits. Information systems affect not just the processes to which they are applied, but a wide range of processes and stakeholders. They are central to strategic direction, cross divisional, brand and geographic boundaries, and alter the distribution of power. The organisation changes with the IS, and this too should be reflected in the appraisal. Section 10.6 presents some ideas on how to handle this problem.

## Summary

- The quantitative approach of traditional formal–rational evaluation techniques does not fit well with the complexity of information system projects.

- Information systems integrate themselves deeply into organisations. Their value therefore requires consideration of a wide range of factors beyond the system itself.

## 10.6 Wider criteria for evaluating IS

Given the difficulties with formal–rational methods, it is no surprise that people have attempted to develop other evaluation methods that take account of wider factors. For example, Doherty et al. (2003) list a set of measures for information systems success as shown in Table 10.3, only one of which covers the costs and benefits.

---

**MIS in Practice  MySpace and News Corp's investment**

Social networking sites are growing rapidly, with the market leaders MySpace and Facebook being joined by many new sites catering for different audiences and segments of the social networking markets. All face the challenge of turning the popular sites into a reliable revenue stream. Rupert Murdoch's News Corp clearly sees potential in the sector, as it invested $580 million in acquiring MySpace in 2005. Pressure is building on MySpace to show that it can deliver a return on that investment – but the business model (Chapter 4) with which to do this is not yet clear.

*Social networking advertising is still a work in progress.* (A senior analyst at a market research firm)

The challenge for News Corp is to transform the web phenomenon into a source of advertising revenue, without driving off the very users who make it popular. The race to wring money out of MySpace's huge audience became all the more urgent in late 2007 as Facebook was about to unveil its advertising strategy. One approach for MySpace was to speed up its international growth by launching locally targeted sites in Brazil, India, Poland and Russia – which is a further costly investment.

*Sources*: *Financial Times*, 15 October 2007, p. 25; *Business Week*, 1 November 2007, pp. 23–6.

---

Saarinen (1996) describes a four-dimensional model of IS success measurement, illustrated in Figure 10.2. The first dimension, development process, considers the success of the development of the system. This incorporates adherence to the allocated budget (costs) and time schedule, and the efficient use of development resources. The second dimension, use process, covers the effectiveness and efficiency of service delivery to the users of the system. Together, these define the process success of the system and relate to the costs of both build and ownership.

The third dimension described by Saarinen, quality of the IS product, relates to system factors such as reliability, accuracy, robustness, usability and flexibility to change. The fourth dimension, impact of the IS on the organisation, covers the extent to which the system contributes to cost savings, productivity improvements, increased market share,

**Table 10.3 Measures for system success**

| Measure | Description |
| --- | --- |
| Systems quality | Reliability, features and functions, response time. |
| Information quality | Clarity, completeness, usefulness and accuracy of information provided. |
| Information use | Regularity of use, number of enquiries, duration of use, frequency of report requests. |
| User satisfaction | Overall satisfaction, enjoyment, no difference between information needed and received, software satisfaction. |
| Individual impact | Problem identification, correctness of decision, decision effectiveness, time taken to make decision, improved individual productivity. |
| Organisational impact | Contribution to achieving goals, cost–benefit ratio, return on investment, service effectiveness. |

*Source*: Doherty et al. (2003).

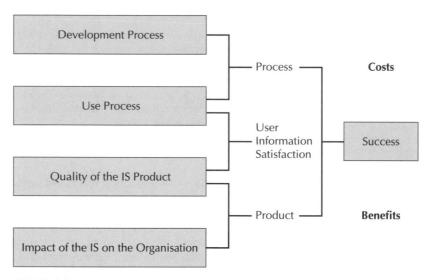

**Figure 10.2 Main dimensions of IS success**
*Source*: Saarinen (1996).

competitive advantage, etc. (i.e. the benefits). Together, these latter two dimensions define the success of the system as a product.

Strassman (1999) goes further by saying that there is no relation between a company's investment in IT and its profitability. The benefits of an effective system come from improvements in competitive advantage, strategic positioning and management style and quality – which merely investing in IT does not deliver. The benefits come from reshaping the organisational factors, not from spending on IT. A company that spends wisely – even if sparsely – on IT and makes the appropriate organisational changes will see its performance enhanced. A company that spends indiscriminately on IT will see its performance diminished, because IT will merely amplify its poor business practices.

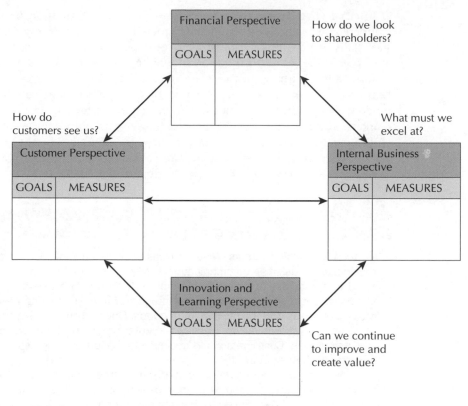

**Figure 10.3** Components of the Balanced Scorecard
*Source*: Reprinted from Kaplan and Norton (1992) with permission.

Many companies have used the Balanced Scorecard technique (Kaplan and Norton, 1992) to measure performance against strategic objectives. This technique seeks to develop an organisation-wide view of performance based on an appropriate balance of four measures: financial, internal effectiveness, customers and innovation/learning.

Kaplan and Norton developed the technique to offer an alternative to the formal–rational techniques, for much the same reasons as we have discussed above. They wanted to offer a way of viewing information systems from a broader organisational and human perspective. Figure 10.3 shows the four elements of the scorecard.

Financial measures will obviously still be important, and a favourable impact of the new system on these measures will be critical. This is the area that has traditionally been given most attention in organisations and is most supported by the traditional formal–rational approach, so requires least explanation here. The important lesson from the Balanced Scorecard technique is that concentrating solely on financial measures can lead to a dangerously short-term perspective.

Customer measures will drive the organisation towards the way it wishes to be perceived by its customers. They can include such specific goals as time taken to fulfil orders, customer satisfaction levels and market share. Information systems can do all of these things, but their benefits are hard to quantify. The formal–rational method would therefore be biased against such projects, to the detriment of the company.

283

Internal effectiveness measures define what the organisation must do internally to compete effectively. They can include productivity levels, error rates, safety records and staff skills. A new information system could be expected to impact on all these factors and so its value to the organisation should be assessed from all these perspectives.

Innovation/learning measures are intended to drive the organisation towards continuous improvement and the creation of ever greater value to customers and shareholders. These refer to such measures as percentage of revenue from new products and/or markets, research and development achievements, and improvements in operating efficiencies. Many of these measures are strongly influenced by the ways in which information systems improve performance and expand opportunities in organisations.

The MIS in Practice feature below illustrates the method.

## MIS in Practice    The Balanced Scorecard at WHC

Wayton Haulage Contractors (WHC) Ltd was considering implementing an Internet-based tracking and customer communication system. This system would create a website linked to a database of orders, items in transit, drivers, vehicles and customers. Head-office staff could access the database through a browser, entering new information and tracking progress with the movement of goods. Drivers could access the system through truck-mounted mobile network devices to enter progress with deliveries and to pick up new instructions. Customers could access information on progress with their deliveries through a secure extranet link.

To evaluate the system, WHC senior management applied the costs and benefits of the system to the measures in their existing Balanced Scorecard to ensure that a holistic view was taken, linked to their overall strategy.

Financial measures were considered first. Formal–rational techniques were applied to measure the rate of return on investment that could be achieved. This required some estimation of future costs and benefits that WHC knew could change due to the unpredictable nature of such initiatives. Nonetheless, the measures suggested adequate financial performance.

Next, the WHC management thought about their customers. Theirs is a cutthroat market, with tight margins and low customer loyalty. Providing leading-edge, convenient service based on reliability and timeliness was a key strategic goal. The new system would provide customers with a convenient means of tracking the progress of their deliveries, leading to higher satisfaction and retention rates.

From an internal effectiveness perspective, the new system would have several advantages. Responding to customer enquiries traditionally took up a great deal of staff time, and giving customers access to their own information seemed like an ideal way of reducing back-office processing costs and lead times. Further efficiencies could be expected from improved utilisation of drivers and vehicles through coordinated job allocation processes.

Finally, WHC management recognised that the system would provide them with opportunities to understand their work patterns and customer requirements better by providing a means of tracking trends and outcomes. Their ability to innovate and learn from the system was therefore assured.

Using the four elements of the Balanced Scorecard, WHC was able to take a holistic and strategic view of the new system. This went much further than financial measures, which required an element of guesswork, and ensured that the value of the system was considered from a relevant set of organisational perspectives.

● **Summary**

● To overcome the limitations of formal–rational evaluation, several alternative methodologies for measuring the value of information systems have been developed.

● The Balanced Scorecard technique in particular relates IS to strategy by considering the effects on customers, internal processes and learning, as well as on financial performance.

## 10.7  Organising for IS evaluation

Having reviewed some of the methods for evaluating IS proposals, this final section considers the place of evaluation within the organisational structure. This links closely to the discussion of IS governance in Chapter 7.

● **Central project evaluation teams – a structural solution?**

Project sponsors and owners are poor judges of the value of their projects. They naturally have a biased preference and are often familiar with only a single area of the business. These factors can lead to sub-optimal investment decisions if the individual project teams are left to fight it out for board funding.

One way of addressing these problems is to establish a central project evaluation team (CPET). Ideally, such a team will be made up of a selection of experienced project managers from different areas of the organisation, with a variety of skills, including marketing, economics, finance and IT. Their role would be to take an objective view of projects and assess their value using a standard approach based on the Balanced Scorecard or something similar. By putting every proposal requiring significant funding through the same assessment, but one more broadly based than the formal–rational approach, boards can be presented with a better set of options.

Another role for the CPET would be to carry out post-implementation reviews of the projects that have been previously approved. This is done very rarely, yet the omission prevents valuable learning. By measuring the actual costs and benefits (broadly defined) of a new system the team can learn useful lessons for future assessments.

However, the CPET approach will have disadvantages for the analysis of IS projects:

● the lack of local awareness and knowledge will detract from the team's ability to understand the less tangible aspects of a project's value;

● the systemic approach to evaluation could be viewed as 'bureaucratic' – slow and inflexible;

● a central team is less likely to react quickly to changes in the marketplace.

In many organisations the IS department owns the budget for system developments. Business divisions lobby IS to win part of the budget for their projects. The weakness of this approach is that IS departments are not responsible for the revenues of the organisation. This responsibility lies with the business divisions that own the value chains from which revenues flow. For IT budgets to be applied effectively, business areas need to be able to purchase requirements from whichever source, and at whatever price, supports their business.

The CPET may work best where:

- projects are related to a well-established system;
- organisations are more formal and risk-averse;
- environments are stable.

Localised business budget control may work best where:

- projects are related to new types of opportunity;
- organisations are flatter with more decentralised autonomy;
- environments are dynamic and uncertain.

## ● Summary

- To manage the costs and benefits of IS effectively, the organisation structure must be aligned to support the needs of the business areas in a technically aware manner.
- Central project evaluation teams have some advantages, but many disadvantages, for the evaluation of IS initiatives.
- Business areas will always claim budget ownership and view the technology departments as suppliers, potentially competing with outside suppliers.

# The hopes for the joint venture
**www.bbc.co.uk**

Bill Gates, Chairman of Microsoft, endorsed the agreement with the BBC in September 2006:

> *Microsoft's strength is in driving digital innovation and our vision is to open up rich new consumer experiences that allow people to enjoy digital content anytime, anywhere and on any device. This vision fits squarely with the BBC's charter to lead the industry in delivering content that is compelling and accessible.*

Using Microsoft's technical know-how as the key to unlocking their potential in providing recorded content to users of computers and mobile devices, the BBC began to plan the way forward. A UK government white paper on the future of the BBC spelled out the key developments that were envisaged, including:

- re-launching the bbc.co.uk website to include more personalisation, richer audio-visual and user-generated content, including a new teen-brand;

- easy access points for audiences via broadband portals around key content areas such as sport, music, health and science;
- a shift of energy towards continuous news on TV, radio, broadband and mobile;
- addressing the device-rich, time-poor audience with the introduction of a new interactive media player – iPlayer – to provide content wherever and whenever suited the consumer, whether by hand-held computer, iPod, PlayStation Portable, or even television!

By early 2008 examples of these plans were emerging, but the overall effectiveness of the BBC's new strategy and the alliance with Microsoft was yet to be proven.

*Source*: Saravanan and Bhaskaran (2007).

## CASE QUESTIONS 10.2

1. Many of the BBC's new developments to address emerging broadcasting IS functionality are offered free to users. In what ways might the BBC recover the costs of its investment in these new technologies?

2. In what ways can the BBC develop new income streams in the new marketplace?

3. The BBC's iPlayer media player was subject to some criticism when initially launched as it was only usable on Windows platforms. Has the BBC's choice of Microsoft as a strategic partner enabled or constrained its objective to 'deliver public service content to our audiences in whatever media and on whatever device makes sense for them'?

# Conclusions

This chapter has discussed the problems of using the traditional formal–rational techniques (rate of return on investment, payback period and so on) for evaluating information systems. The extent to which such systems integrate themselves in organisations, and the complex human interactions involved, require a more holistic approach that goes beyond simple financial measures.

The costs and benefits of information systems are in themselves complex in nature and require skilled judgement of many indirect and intangible factors. The common approach of ignoring factors that do not easily translate into definite quantities has led to the rejection of many valuable projects, and the acceptance of many poor ones.

In many cases, the costs and benefits of IS projects cannot be viewed in isolation, and an organisation-wide view of short- and long-term benefits accruing from all IS investments is needed.

Ideally, a company will evaluate its information systems taking account of organisational factors impacted by each system. Some methods of doing this have been presented, such as the Balanced Scorecard, which is a way of encouraging consideration of the broader range of organisational, human and strategic factors that information systems will inevitably influence. Finally, the importance of ensuring that the organisation structure is aligned to support quality IS decision-making has been discussed.

# Chapter questions

1. What are the attractions of using formal–rational evaluation techniques for information system project proposals?

2. What political influences might there be within an organisation that sustain the use of formal–rational evaluation techniques?

3. Discuss the difficulties that a department manager might have in justifying expenditure on a new computer system to senior management. What might they do to overcome these difficulties?

4. As senior IT manager in a large organisation, you know that you have to invest in the basic IT platform and supporting infrastructure to keep supplying businesses with the systems they need. However, there are significant costs and no direct benefits from this investment. How will you justify it to the senior management?

5. What aspects of an organisation structure hinder the quality of information system decisions?

## Further reading

Kaplan, R.S. and Norton, D.P. (1996) *The Balanced Scorecard: Translating Strategy into Action*, Harvard Business School Press, Boston, MA. The Balanced Scorecard approach has only been touched upon in this chapter. There are many good practical examples of its application in this book that will help you to make use of it in evaluating IS projects.

Strassman, P.A. (1999) *Information Productivity*, The Information Economics Press, New Canaan, CT. A book by an author who is acknowledged throughout the industry for his highly sceptical view about the way that companies invest in technology, concluding that 'there is no relationship between expenses for computers and business profitability' (having read this book you will of course understand why there is no such relationship).

Two articles that go more deeply into the problems of assessing the returns of IT investments:

Mahmood, M. and Mann, G. (2000) 'Special Issue: Impacts of IT investment on organizational performance', *Journal of Management Information Systems*, **16**(4), 3–10.

Wu, I.-L. and Chen, J.-L. (2006) 'A hybrid performance measure system for e-business investment in high-tech manufacturing: An empirical study', *Information and Management*, **43**(3), 364–77.

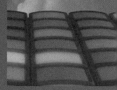

**Acquisition and development** A department or function that is responsible for the development or acquisition of information systems.

**Alignment** The fit between variables such as strategy, information systems, structure and culture.

**Anarchy** The absence of any overall information management policy, leaving individuals and user departments to obtain and manage their own information.

**Application service provider (ASP)** A business that provides IS applications to customers over the Internet.

**Autonomy** The amount of freedom a person has in deciding how to do their work.

**Back-office systems** Those that support functions not seen by customers, such as manufacturing or administrative processes.

**Behavioural intentions** An individual's positive or negative attitude towards using the system.

**Blogging** Contributing to an online diary prepared by an individual or group.

**Business model innovation** A change of the way the business is done to add value.

**Business monarchy** A centralised approach to IS, in which information categories and reporting structures are defined by the firm's leaders.

**Business process** A collection of interrelated tasks, performed to achieve a business outcome.

**Business-to-business (B2B)** When companies connect electronically all the links in their supply chain, so creating an integrated process to meet customer needs.

**Business-to-consumer (B2C)** When companies sell products and services over the Internet to individual retail customers.

**Centralisation** This occurs when a relatively large number of decisions arc taken by management at the top of the organisation.

**Centralised IS activities** When a central unit is responsible for most computing activities.

**Chief information officer (CIO)** Primarily responsible for the overall effectiveness of information systems and for the management of information resources.

**Clean sheet approach** When a firm fundamentally rethinks the way that the product or service is delivered and designs new processes from scratch.

**Co-creation** Product or service development that makes intensive use of the contributions of customers.

**Code of Fair Information Practices (FIP)** A set of principles setting out how organisations should handle customer information responsibly.

**Communication systems** Help people to communicate with each other and to overcome barriers of space and time.

**Community systems** Social network sites that people use to exchange information, ideas or videos, independently of an organisation.

**Company-wide systems** Those that integrate departments and people throughout the organisation.

**Competitive context (or environment)** The industry-specific environment comprising customers, suppliers and competitors.

**Complementarity** A situation in which the technology supports or enhances the value of an existing skill.

**Computer-based information system** An information system in which a computer performs many of the activities needed to transform data into information.

**Computer hardware** Physical components of a computer system, consisting of devices for input, memory, central processing, output, communication and storage.

**Computer software** The instructions that control the operation of a computer system.

**Configuration** Tailoring the software using parameters provided by the vendor.

**Cookies** Small files stored on an end-user's computer to enable websites to identify them.

**Copyright** A legally enforceable grant that aims to protect the creators of intellectual property from having their work copied, distributed, performed or lent without the consent of the owner.

**Cost centre** The costs of IS services are allocated to users and charged to them.

**Cost leadership** Using information systems to support a low-cost strategy.

**Critical success factor (CSF)** An activity that must go well to ensure success for a manager, a unit of the organisation, or a project.

**Culture** The pattern of beliefs developed by a group about effective task performance and the values they share about themselves and others.

**Customer-facing systems** Those that support processes seen by customers, such as sales and marketing.

**Customer intimacy** When a company seeks competitive advantage by providing a unique 'customised' service for every customer.

**Customer relationship management (CRM) systems** Information systems that track and analyse the interactions a company has with customers, to optimise revenues, profitability, customer satisfaction and customer retention.

**Customisation** Adding non-standard features to software by adding or changing code.

**Data** Facts, figures and events that have not been analysed.

**Database** A group of data files that are related to each other.

**Data controller** A defined person responsible for protecting data held by a company from misuse.

**Data mining** Using software to look for unexpected patterns and relationships in large sets of data.

**Data protection legislation** Laws intended to protect the privacy of consumers' data through defining how organisations can gather, store, process and disclose personal information.

**Data warehouse** A database that stores current and historical data which can be consolidated for management reporting and analysis.

**Decentralisation** When a relatively large number of decisions are taken lower down the organisation and in operating units.

**Decentralised IS** Business units are responsible for their information systems.

**Decision support systems (DSS)** These help people to calculate the consequences of different alternatives before they decide what to do.

**Differentiation** Using information systems to offer products or services that are unique or distinctive on a basis other than price.

**Disintermediation** Removing intermediaries such as distributors that formerly linked a company to its customers.

**Distributed IS architecture** Departments have some independence in developing and using IS without losing the benefits of centralised control over data and communications.

**E-business** The integration, through the Internet, of all an organisation's processes, from its suppliers through to its customers.

**E-business model** An abstract description of how an Internet-based enterprise delivers a product or service, showing how it adds value to resources.

**E-commerce** Selling a product or service to the customer (whether a retail consumer or another business) over the Internet.

**Effort expectancy** The degree of ease associated with use of the system.

**Emergent IS strategy** When information systems are developed gradually to take account of unanticipated events and conditions, rather than through a fixed plan.

**Emergent model (of change)** Recognises that some departure from a plan is inevitable, and that outcomes cannot be accurately predicted.

**Enterprise systems** Fully integrated enterprise-wide IS that coordinate key internal processes (also known as enterprise resource planning (ERP)).

**EPOS systems** Electronic point of sale systems that instantly record each sale, using a scanner that reads the barcode on the product.

**Ergonomics** The study of how people interact with machines, including the design of jobs, health issues and the end-user interface for information systems.

**Escalating commitment** The tendency to continue committing more resources to a failing project.

**Ethical decision-making models** These examine the influence of individual characteristics and organisational policies on ethical decisions.

**Explicit knowledge** Knowledge that people have codified, structured and probably written down as formulae or instructions.

**External context (or environment)** Elements in an organisation's competitive and general environments.

**Extrinsic rewards** Valued outcomes or benefits that come from others, such as a promotion or pay increase.

**Facilitating conditions** Arrangements (such as training) put in place to support those using a system.

**Federal IS activities** When companies decentralise IS tasks such as specification and administration, while maintaining central control over other tasks like data standards and hardware compatibility.

**Federalism** An approach to information management based on consensus and negotiation about the organisation's information elements and reporting structures.

**Feedback** The extent to which a person receives feedback on performance.

**Feudalism** The management of information by individual business units or functions, which define their own information needs and report only limited information to the centre.

**Focus strategy** When a company competes by targeting very specific segments of the market.

**Functional systems** These include technologies that perform standalone tasks and make separate business functions more efficient.

**Groupware** Software that provides functions and services to support the collaborative activities of physically separated work groups.

**General context (or environment)** (sometimes known as the macro-environment) Includes political, economic, socio-technological, (natural) environmental and legal factors that affect all organisations.

**Hacking** The process of gaining unauthorised access to computer systems, typically across a network.

**High context cultures** Those in which information is implicit and can only be fully understood by those with shared experiences in the culture.

**Human information systems** People in their function of collecting and interpreting data to make decisions.

**Human relations culture** Where people emphasise informal, interpersonal relations and place a high value on maintaining the well-being of the members, including developing their skills.

**Hybrid centre** Users pay for some services and receive a central subsidy for others.

**Implementation and learning processes** Activities that are intended to turn an idea or product into working form within an organisation. These offer opportunities for learning that may or may not occur.

**Individual systems** Systems that are used by individuals to support their tasks.

**Infomediaries** Internet-based collectors and providers of information, such as Google.

**Information** Useful knowledge derived from data.

**Information system** A set of people, procedures and resources that collects and transforms data into information and disseminates it.

**Information system architecture** The way IS assets (hardware, software, telecommunications) are deployed and connected, and how they interact with each other.

**Information systems management** The planning, acquisition, development and use of information systems.

**Information system project** A distinct task that aims to change an existing, or implement a new, information system.

**Intellectual property rights (IPR)** Protect the intangible property created by corporations or individuals under patent, copyright or trademark laws.

**Inter-organisational system (IOS)** A system that links organisations electronically by using networks that cross company boundaries.

**Internal context (or environment)** Elements within the organisation such as its technology, structure or business processes.

**Internal process culture** Where people focus on making the unit efficient, stable and controlled, through repetitive tasks towards known goals, and an emphasis on specialisation, rules and procedures.

**Internet** A self-regulated network of computer networks connecting millions of business, individuals, government agencies, schools and other organisations across the world.

**Intrinsic rewards** Valued outcomes that come from the work itself such as interest or a sense of achievement.

**IT governance** Specification of decision rights and accountability to encourage desirable behaviour in the use of IT.

**IT monarchy** A technical approach to information management, stressing categorisation and modelling of an organisation's full information assets, with heavy reliance on emerging technologies

**Joint Application Development (JAD)** A method in which users and designers discuss requirements in workshops and use this information iteratively to design and test successive systems.

**Knowledge** Derived from a person's experience and learning, and as such encourages them to act in a particular way.

**Knowledge management (KM)** Attemps to improve the way organisations create and integrate new knowledge.

**Local systems** Used by separate units or departments at a certain location.

**Low context cultures** People are psychologically distant so that information needs to be explicit if members are to understand it.

**Management processes** Govern the operation of the system and typically include corporate governance and strategic management.

**Market-centred applications** Systems that are used to improve customer benefits.

**Metcalfe's law** The value of a network increases with the square of the number of users connected to the network.

**Mobile CRM** Customer relationship management that uses customers' wireless devices, such as mobile phones or other handheld digital appliances.

**Monitoring systems** These check the performance of activities, functions or people at regular intervals.

**Multisourcing** When different parts of an IS are provided by different suppliers.

**Network-based mediation** When companies use IS to build a network of alliances and partnerships.

**Network systems** These help people to communicate with other enterprise systems and to overcome barriers of space and time.

**Offshoring** Transfer of IS to another country, regardless of whether the work is outsourced or stays within the same corporation.

**On-demand software** A concept that provides IS applications to customers over the Internet.

**Open source software** Software that is developed collaboratively, independent of a vendor, by a community of software developers and users.

**Open systems culture** One in which people focus on the external environment, seeing it as a vital source of ideas, energy and resources that requires people to act in an entrepreneurial and responsive way.

**Operational excellence** When a company seeks competitive advantage by the reliable and fluent organisation of operational processes.

**Operational information systems** These are designed to process operational (and often routine) transactions.

**Operational processes** Constitute the core business activities that add value to the resources.

**Outcomes** The results of an activity, as perceived by stakeholders.

**Outsourcing of IS** The transfer of the management and/or day-to-day work of the IS function to an external service provider.

**PageRank** A scale of 0 to 10 used by Google to assess the importance of websites according to the number of inbound links to the page (link popularity).

**Paper-based information systems** When paper is used as the main way of storing and retrieving data.

**Participative models** Recommend change managers to consult widely and deeply with those affected and to secure their willing consent to the changes proposed.

**Patents** A set of rights that the state grants to a person for a fixed period in exchange for the regulated, public disclosure of certain details of an invention.

**Perceived ease of use (PEU)** The degree to which a person believes that using a system would be free of effort.

**Perceived usefulness (PU)** The degree to which a person believes that using a particular system would enhance his or her job performance.

**Performance expectancy** The degree to which individuals believe using the system will enhance job performance.

**Personal digital assistant (PDA)** Handheld computers with built-in wireless communication facility.

**Planned IS strategy** Consciously developed strategy of IS development and use.

**Planning model of change** The belief that projects go through successive stages, and that results depend on conducting the project through these in an orderly and controlled way.

**Political models of change** Emphasise that change is likely to affect the interests of stakeholders unevenly and change agents need to use political skills to influence behaviour.

**Process innovation** Implementing a new or improved production or delivery method.

**Process mapping** Techniques for diagramming business processes to design new ones.

**Procurement** All activities involved with obtaining items from a supplier, including purchasing, transportation and warehousing.

**Product innovation** The introduction of a new product.

**Product leadership** When competitive advantage lies in focusing on product improvement and product innovation.

**Profit centre** IS services are charged at 'cost-plus' or market prices.

**Prototyping** Dividing development work into sub-tasks that IS staff can complete quickly and test with users.

**Radio-frequency identification (RFID)** An automatic identification method, relying on storing and remotely retrieving data using devices called RFID tags or transponders.

**Rational goal culture** One in which members see the unit as a rational, efficiency-seeking operation, for which they prefer familiar and stable ways of working.

**Reintermediation** Creating new intermediaries between customers and suppliers by providing (new) services such as supplier search and product evaluation.

**Remediation** When a company uses IS to enable closer, long-term working relationships with intermediaries.

**Remote working** See telecommuting.

**RFM model** Each customer is assigned an RFM score based on the recency, frequency and monetary value of their transactions.

**Service centre** Users do not pay for IS resources.

**Service innovation** The introduction of a new service.

**Skill variety** The extent to which a job makes use of a range of skills and experience.

**Social influence** The degree to which individuals perceive that important others believe he or she should use the system.

**Social networking site** A site facilitating exchange of text, audio or video content between individuals.

**Socio-technical approach** A systems development strategy that attempts to improve the performance of the organisation and the quality of working life.

**Spam** Unrequested e-mail, usually sent out in very large quantities.

**Stakeholders** Individuals, groups or other organisations with an interest in, or who are affected by, what an organisation does.

**Supply chain innovation** A change in the sourcing of inputs from suppliers and the delivery of outputs to customers.

**Support unit** Responsible for assisting IT users.

**Supporting processes** These include accounting, recruitment and IT services that support core processes.

**Systematic redesign** When people identify and analyse existing processes, evaluate them critically and plan major improvements.

**Tacit knowledge** This is inherent in individuals or groups, and is not written down – it is a sense about the way to do things, how to relate to each other and to situations.

**Task analysis** (in ergonomics) The work of identifying the elements in a task, and the sequence in which they are performed.

**Task identity** The extent to which a job involves a relatively complete and whole operation.

**Task significance** How much the job matters to others or to the wider society.

**Technochange managers** These combine technical (IT) skills and business literacy.

**Telecommuting or teleworking** Practices in which companies provide the technical facilities that enable people to work with more independence of time and place than is possible in conventional workplaces.

**Trademark** A badge of origin that distinguishes goods or services – it can be a word, name, logo, colour, shape or sound.

**User-generated content** (UCG) Electronic platforms that are created, maintained and developed by users.

**Values** A set of social norms that identify what is important to a group and how they interact with each other – they set the boundaries of acceptable behaviour.

**Versioning information** When people create different versions of the same information by tailoring it to the needs of different customers.

**Virtual organisations** These deliver goods and services but have few, if any, of the physical features of conventional businesses.

**Web services architecture** Companies rent the functions they need – data storage, processing power or applications – from service providers.

**Wikinomics** A term to describe a business culture in which customers are no longer only consumers but also co-creators and co-producers of the service.

# REFERENCES

Alavi, M. and Leidner, D.E. (2002) 'Knowledge management and knowledge management system: conceptual foundations and research issues', *MIS Quarterly*, **25**(1), 107–36.

Andal-Ancion, A., Cartwright, P.A. and Yip, G.S. (2003) 'The digital transformation of traditional business', *MIT Sloan Management Review*, **44**(4), 34–41.

Applegate, L.M., Austin, R.D. and McFarlan, F.W. (2007) *Corporate Information Strategy and Management: Text and Cases*, McGraw-Hill/Irwin, Boston, MA.

Applegate, L.M., McFarlan, F.W. and McKenney, J.L. (1997) *Corporate Information System Management: Text and Cases*, Irwin, Chicago.

Argyris, C. (1999) *On Organizational Learning* (2nd edition), Blackwell, Oxford.

Artail, H.A. (2006) 'Application of KM measures to the impact of a specialized groupware system on corporate productivity and operations', *Information & Management*, **43**(4), 551–64.

Bains, J.W. (2001) *Survey on Management Tools*, KPMG, London.

Balachandra, R. (2000) 'An expert system for new product development', *Industrial Management and Data Systems*, **100**(7), 317–28.

Balch, R., Schrader, S. and Ruan, T. (2007) 'Collection, storage and application of human knowledge in expert system development', *Expert Systems*, **24**(5), 346–62.

Balogun, J., Gleadle, P., Hailey, V.H. and Willmott, H. (2005) 'Managing change across boundaries: boundary-shaking practices', *British Journal of Management*, **16**(4), 261–78.

Baumer, D.L., Earp, J.B. and Poindexter, J.C. (2004) 'Internet privacy law: a comparison between the United States and the European Union', *Computers and Security*, **23**(5), 400–10.

Belanger, F. and Allport, C.D. (2008) 'Collaborative technologies in knowledge telework: an exploratory study', *Information Systems Journal*, **18**(1), 101–21.

Belanger, F. and Collins, R.W. (1998) 'Distributed work arrangements: a research framework', *Information Society*, **14**(2), 137–52.

Belbin, R.M. (2004) *Management Teams: Why they Succeed or Fail*, Elsevier Butterworth-Heinemann, Oxford.

Bensaou, M. and Earl, M. (1998) 'The right mind set for managing information technology', *Harvard Business Review*, **78**(5), 119–28.

Berez, S. and Sheth, A. (2007) 'Break the paper jam in B2B payments', *Harvard Business Review*, **85**(11), 28.

Beynon-Davies, P. (1995) 'Information system failure: the case of the London Ambulance Service's computer-aided despatch system', *European Journal of Information Systems*, **4**, 171–84.

Bidgoli, H. (2004) *The Internet Encyclopedia*, John Wiley & Sons Ltd., Chichester.

Bjorn-Anderson, N. and Turner, J.A. (1994) 'Creating the twenty-first century organization: the metamorphosis of Oticon', in R. Baskerville, S. Smithson, O. Ngwenyama and J. DeGross (eds), *Transforming Organizations with Information Technology*: *Proceedings of the Ifip Wg8.2 Conference on Information Technology and New Emergent Forms of Organizations*, North-Holland Publishing Co., Amsterdam.

Boddy, D. (2000) 'Implementing inter-organisational IT systems: lessons from a call centre project', *Journal of Information Technology*, **15**(1), 29–37.

Boddy, D. (2002) *Managing Projects: Building and Leading the Team*, Financial Times/Prentice Hall, Harlow.

Boddy, D. (2008) *Management: An Introduction* (4th edition), Financial Times/Prentice Hall, Harlow.

Boddy, D. and Gunson, N. (1996) *Organizations in the Network Age*, Routledge, London.

Boddy, D., Macbeth, D.K. and Wagner, B. (2000) 'Implementing collaboration between organisations: an empirical study of supply chain partnering', *Journal of Management Studies*, **37**(7), 1003–17.

Boddy, D. and Paton, R.A. (2005) 'Maintaining alignment over the long-term: lessons from the evolution of an electronic point of sale system', *Journal of Information Technology*, **20**(3), 141–51.

Boisot, M.H. (1998) *Knowledge Assets: Securing Competitive Advantage in the Information Economy*, Oxford University Press, Oxford.

Boonstra, A. (2003) 'Structure and analysis of IS decision-making processes', *European Journal of Information Systems*, **12**(3), 195–209.

Boonstra, A. (2006) 'Interpreting an ERP implementation from a stakeholder perspective', *International Journal of Project Management*, **24**(1), 38–52.

Boonstra, A., Boddy, D. and Bell, S. (2008) 'Stakeholder management in 105 projects: analysis of an attempt to implement and electronic patient file', *European Journal of Information Management*, **17**(2), 100–11.

Boonstra, A., Boddy, D. and Fischbacher, M. (2004) 'The limited acceptance by general practitioners of an electronic prescription system: reasons and practical implications', *New Technology, Work and Employment*, **19**(2), 128–44.

Boonstra, A. and Dantzig, T. van (2005) 'Bringing e-business to the world's largest flower auction: the case of Aalsmeer Flower Auction', *International Journal of Cases on Electronic Commerce*, **1**(1), 19–38.

Boonstra, A. and de Vries, J. (2005) 'Analyzing inter-organizational information systems from a power and interest perspective', *International Journal of Information Management*, **25**(6), 485–501.

Boonstra, A. and Harison, E. (2008) 'Reaching new altitudes in e-commerce: evaluating business performance of major airline websites', *Journal of Air Transport Management*, **14**(1), 92–8.

Bouwman, H., Hooff, B. van den, Wijngaert, L. van de and Dijk, J. van (2005) *Information & Communication Technology in Organizations*, Sage, London.

Brooks, F.P. (1995) *The Mythical Man-Month*, Addison-Wesley, Reading, MA.

Brynjolfsson, E. and Hitt, L.M. (2000) 'Beyond computation: information technology, organizational transformation and business performance', *Journal of Economic Perspectives*, **19**(4), 23–48.

Bryson, J.M. (2004) 'What to do when Stakeholders matter', *Public Management Review*, **6**(1), 21–53.

Buchanan, D. and Badham, R. (1999) *Power, Politics and Organizational Change: Winning the Turf Game*, Sage, London.

Burlinghame, J.F. (1961) 'Information technology and decentralization', *Harvard Business Review*, **39**(6), 121–6.

Cairncross, F. (2001) *The Death of Distance 2.0: How the Communications Revolution Will Change Our Lives*, Orion, London.

Chaffey, D. (2007) *E-Business and E-Commerce Management*, Financial Times/Prentice Hall, Harlow.

Chaturvedi, R.N. (2005) *IT Outsourcing, the GM Way*, European Case Clearing House Case No. 905-032-1, ECCH, Cranfield University, UK.

Chau, P.K., Cole, M., Massey, A.P., Montoya-Weiss, M. and O'Keefe, R.M. (2002) 'Cultural differences in the online behavior of consumers', *Communications of the ACM*, **45**(10), 138–43.

Chesbrough, H.R. (2003) *Open Innovation: The New Imperative for Creating and Profiting from Technology*, Harvard Business School Press, Boston, MA.

Chu, C. and Smithson, S. (2007) 'E-business and organizational change: a structurational approach', *Information Systems Journal*, **17**(4), 369–89.

Clegg, C., Carey, N., Dean, G., Hornby, P. and Bolden, R. (1997) 'User reactions to information technology: some multivariate models and their implications', *Journal of Information Technology*, **12**, 15–32.

Clegg, C.W. (1996) 'Tools to incorporate some psychological and organizational issues during the development of computer-based systems', *Ergonomics*, **39**(3), 482–511.

Clegg, C.W. (2000) 'Socio-technical principles for system design', *Applied Ergonomics*, **31**(5), 463–77.

Cooper, B. (2007) 'Business information strategy', *C10*, **20**(17), 54–7.

Cooper, R. (1994) 'The inertial impact of culture on IT implementation', *Information and Management*, **27**(1), 17–31.

Cormican, K. and O'Sullivan, D. (2007) 'A groupware system for virtual product innovation management', *Human Factors and Ergonomics in Manufacturing*, **17**(6), 449–510.

Currie, W. (1989) 'The art of justifying new technology to top management', *Omega*, **17**(5), 409–18.

Currie, W.L. and Guah, M.W. (2006) 'IT-enabled healthcare delivery: the UK national health service', *Information Systems Management*, **23**(2), 7–22.

Davila, T., Epstein, M.J. and Shelton, R. (2006) *Making Innovation Work: How to Manage It, Measure It, and Profit from It*, Wharton School Publishing, Upper Saddle River, NJ.

Davenport, T.H. (1993) *Process Innovation: Reengineering Work through Information Technology*, Harvard Business School Press, Boston, MA.

Davis, F.D. (1989) 'Perceived usefulness, perceived ease of use, and user acceptance of information technology', *MIS Quarterly*, **13**(3), 319–40.

Department of Health (UK) (2000) *NHS Plan: An Information Strategy for the Modern NHS*, DoH, London.

Doherty, N.F. and Doig, G. (2003) 'An analysis of the anticipated cultural impacts of the implementation of data warehouses', *IEEE Transactions on Engineering Management*, **50**(1), 78–88.

Doherty, N.F. and King, M. (2005) 'From technical to socio-technical change: tackling the human and organizational aspects of systems development projects', *European Journal of Information Systems*, **14**(1), 1–5.

Doherty, N.F., King, M. and Al-Mushayt, O. (2003) 'The impact of inadequacies in the treatment of organisational issues on information systems development projects', *Information & Management*, **41**, 49–62.

Drummond, H. (1996) *Escalation in Decision-making: The Tragedy of Taurus*, Oxford University Press, Oxford.

Dube, L. (1998) 'Teams in packaged software development: the Software Corp. experience', *Information Technology and People*, **11**(1), 36–61.

Eason, K. (2001) 'Changing perspectives on the organisational consequences of information technology', *Behaviour and Information Technology*, **20**(5), 323–8.

Eason, K. (2005) 'Exploiting the potential of the NPfIT: a local design approach', *British Journal of Healthcare Computing and Information Management*, **22**(7), 14–16.

Eason (2007) 'Local socio-technical system development in the NHS National Programme for Information Technology', *Journal of Information Technology*, **22**(3), 257–64.

Echikson, W. (2001) 'When oil gets connected', *Business Week e-biz*, 19–22.

Ettlie, J. (2006) *Managing Innovation New Technology, New Products, and New Services in a Global Economy*, Butterworth-Heinemann, Burlington, MA.

Faulkner, C. (1998) *The Essence of Human–Computer Interaction*, Prentice Hall, Hemel Hempstead.

Fearon C. and Philip, G. (2005) 'Managing expectations and benefits: a model for electronic trading and EDI in the insurance industry', *Journal of Information Technology*, **20**(3), 177–86.

Feeny, D. (2001) 'Making business sense of the e-opportunity', *Sloan Management Review*, **43**(1), 41–51.

Feng, K.C., Chen, E.T. and Liou, W.C. (2004) 'Implementation of knowledge management systems and firm performance: an empirical investigation', *Journal of Computer Information Systems*, **45**(2), 92–104.

Finnegan, P. and Longaigh, S.N. (2002) 'Examining the effects of information technology on control and coordination relationships: an exploratory study in subsidiaries of pan-national corporations', *Journal of Information Technology*, **17**(3), 149–63.

Fishman, K.D. (1982) *The Computer Establishment*, McGraw-Hill Osborne Media, San Francisco, CA.

Fitzgerald, G. and Russo, N. (2005) 'The turnaround of the London Ambulance Service's Computer-Aided Despatch System (LASCAD)', *European Journal of Information Systems*, **14**(3), 244–57.

Fletcher, M. and Harris, S. (2002) 'Seven aspects of strategy formulation', *International Small Business Journal*, **20**(3), 297–314.

Foss, N.J. (2003) 'Selective intervention and internal hybrids: interpreting and learning from the rise and decline of the Oticon spaghetti organization', *Organization Science*, **14**(3), 331–49.

Freeman, R.E. (1984) *Strategic Management: A Stakeholder Approach*, Pitman, Boston, MA.

French, J. and Raven, B. (1959) 'The bases of social power', in D. Cartwright (ed.) *Studies in Social Power*, Institute for Social Research, Ann Arbor, MI.

Fulk, J. and DeSanctis, G. (1995) 'Electronic communication and changing organizational forms', *Organization Science*, **6**(4), 337–49.

Gajendran, R.S. and Harrison, D.A. (2007) 'The good, the bad, and the unknown about telecommuting: meta-analysis of psychological mediators and individual consequences', *Journal of Applied Psychology*, **92**(6), 1524–41.

Gilley, K.M. and Rasheed, A. (2000) 'Making more by doing less: an analysis of outsourcing and its effects on firm performance', *Journal of Management*, **26**(4), 763–90.

Goldratt, E.M. and Cox, J. (2004) *The Goal: A Process of Ongoing Improvement*, Gower, Aldershot.

Gonzalez, R., Gasco, J. and Llopis, J. (2006) 'Information systems outsourcing: a literature analysis', *Information & Management*, **43**(7), 821–34.

Govindarajan, V. and Trimble, C. (2005) 'Building breakthrough businesses within established organizations', *Harvard Business Review*, **83**(5), 58–68.

Gowers, A. (2006) *Gowers Review of Intellectual Property*, Her Majesty's Stationery Office, London.

Grant, D., Hall, R., Wailes, N. and Wright, C. (2006) 'The false promise of technological determinism: the case of enterprise resource planning systems', *New Technology, Work and Employment*, **21**(1), 2–15.

Gulati, R. and Garino, J. (2000) 'Get the right mix for bricks and clicks', *Harvard Business Review*, **78**(3), 107–14.

Gupta, A.K. and Govindarajan, V. (2000) 'Knowledge management's social dimension: lessons from Nucor Steel', *Sloan Management Review*, **42**(1), 71–80.

Hackbarth, G. and Kettinger, W. (2000) 'Building an e-business strategy', *Information Systems Management*, **17**(3), 78–93.

Hackman, J.R. and Oldham, G.R. (1980) *Work Redesign*, Addison-Wesley, Reading, MA.

Hagel, J. and Brown, J.S. (2001) 'Your next IT strategy', *Harvard Business Review*, **79**(10), 105–13.

Hales, C. (1993) *Managing Through Organization*, Routledge, London.

Hammer, M. (1990) 'Reengineering work: don't automate, obliterate', *Harvard Business Review*, **68**(4), 104–28.

Hammer, M. (2001) 'The super-efficient company', *Harvard Business Review*, **79**(9), 82–91.

Harison, E. and Boonstra, A. (2008) 'Essential competences for technochange management: towards an assessment model', *International Journal of Information Management*, forthcoming.

Harmon, P. (2007) *Business Process Change*, Elsevier/Morgan Kauffmann, San Francisco, CA.

Harper, G.R. and Utley, D.R. (2001) 'Organizational culture and successful information technology implementation', *Engineering Management Journal*, **13**(2), 11–15.

Hasan, H. and Ditsa, G. (1999) 'The impact of culture on the adoption of IT: an interpretive study', *Journal of Global Information Management*, **7**(1), 5–15.

Heinrich, C. (2005) *RFID and Beyond: Growing Your Business with Real World Awareness*, John Wiley & Sons Ltd., Indianapolis, IN.

Hinds, P.J. and Pfeffer, J. (2003) 'Why organizations don't "know what they know": cognitive and motivational factors affecting the transfer of expertise', in M.S. Ackerman, P. Volkmar and V. Wulf (eds), *Sharing Expertise: Beyond Knowledge Management*, MIT Press, Cambridge, MA.

Hirschheim, R. and Bandula, J. (2003) 'Determinants of ASP choice: an integrated perspective', *European Journal of Information Systems*, **12**(3), 210–24.

Hofstede, G. (2001) *Culture's Consequences, Comparing Values, Behaviors, Institutions and Organizations Across Nations*, Sage, London.

Hofstede, G. and Hofstede, G.J. (2005) *Cultures and Organizations: Software of the Mind* (2nd edition), McGraw-Hill, New York.

Horton, R.P., Buck, T., Waterson, P.E. and Clegg, C.W. (2001) 'Explaining intranet use with the technology acceptance model', *Journal of Information Technology*, **16**(4), 237–49.

Howard, M., Vidgen, R. and Powell, P. (2003) 'Overcoming stakeholder barriers in the automotive industry: building to order with extra-organisational systems', *Journal of Information Technology*, **18**(1), 27–43.

Huczynski, A.A. and Buchanan, D. (2007) *Organizational Behaviour* (6th edition), Financial Times/Prentice Hall, Harlow.

Husted, B.W. (2000) 'The impact of national culture on software piracy', *Journal of Business Ethics*, **26**(3), 197–211.

Igbaria, M. (1993) 'User acceptance of microcomputer technology: an empirical test', *OMEGA International Journal of Management Science*, **21**, 73–90.

IT Governance Institute (2007) *COBIT control practices*, ISACA, Rolling Meadows, IL.

Jasperson, J., Carte, T.A., Saunders, C.S., Butler, B.S., Croes, H.J.P. and Zheng, W. (2002) 'Power and information technology research: a metatriangulation review', *MIS Quarterly*, **26**(4), 397–459.

Jeanneney, J.-N. (2007) *Google and the Myth of Universal Knowledge*, University of Chicago Press, Chicago.

Jenkins, H. (2006) *Convergence Culture: Where Old and New Media Collide*, New York University Press, New York.

Jones, R.A., Jimmieson, N.L. and Griffiths, A. (2005) 'The impact of organizational culture and reshaping capabilities on change implementation success: the mediating role of readiness for change', *Journal of Management Studies*, **42**(2), 361–86.

Kahay, P.S., Carr, H.H. and Snyder, C.A. (2003) 'Evaluating e-business opportunities: technology and the decentralization of information systems', *Information Systems Management*, **20**(3), 51–60.

Kanter, R.M. (2001) 'The ten deadly mistakes of wanna dots', *Harvard Business Review*, **79**(1), 91–100.

Kaplan, R.S. and Norton, D.P. (1992) 'The Balanced Scorecard: measures that drive performance', *Harvard Business Review*, **70**(1), 71–9.

Kaplan, R.S. and Norton, D.P. (1996) *The Balanced Scorecard: Translating Strategy into Action*, Harvard Business School Press, Boston, MA.

Kearns, G. and Sabherwal, R. (2007) 'Strategic alignment between business and information technology: a knowledge-based view of behaviors, outcome and consequences', *Journal of Management Information Systems*, **23**(3), 129–62.

Keen, P. (1981) 'Information systems and organization change', in Rhodes, E. and Weild, D. (eds), *Implementing New Technologies*, Blackwell/Open University Press, Oxford.

Keil, M. and Robey, D. (1999) 'Turning around troubled software projects: an exploratory study of the de-escalation of commitment to failing courses of action', *Journal of Management Information Systems*, **15**(4), 63–87.

Kennedy, G., Boddy, D. and Paton, R. (2006) 'Managing the aftermath: lessons from The Royal Bank of Scotland's acquisition of NatWest', *European Management Journal*, **24**(4), 368–79.

Ketokivi, M. and Castañer, X. (2004) 'Strategic planning as an integrative device', *Administrative Science Quarterly*, **49**(3), 337–65.

Kettinger, W.J., Lee, C.C. and Lee, S. (1995) 'Global measures of information service quality: a cross-national study', *Decision Sciences*, **26**(5), 569–88.

Kimble, C. and McLoughlin, K. (1995) 'Computer-based information systems and managers' work', *New Technology, Work and Employment*, **10**(1), 56–67.

Klien, G. (2007) 'Performing a project pre-mortem', *Harvard Business Review*, **85**(9), 18–19.

Knights, D. and Murray, F. (1994) *Managers Divided: Organizational Politics and Information Technology Management*, John Wiley & Sons Ltd., Chichester.

Kotlarsky, J. and Oshri, I. (2005) 'Social ties, knowledge sharing and successful collaboration in globally distributed system development projects', *European Journal of Information Systems*, **14**(1), 37–48.

Lacity, M.C. (2001) *Global Information Technology Outsourcing: In Search of Business Advantage*, John Wiley & Sons Ltd., Chichester.

Lander, E. and Liker, J.K. (2007) 'The Toyota production system and art: making highly customized and creative products the Toyota way', *International Journal of Production Research*, **45**(16), 3681–98.

Laudon, K.C. and Laudon, J.P. (2007a) *Management Information Systems: Managing the Digital Firm* (10th edition), Prentice Hall, Upper Saddle River, NJ.

Laudon, K.C. and Laudon, J.P. (2007b) *Essentials of Business Information Systems* (7th edition), Prentice Hall, Englewood Cliffs, NJ.

Laudon, K.C. and Laudon, J.P. (2007c) *Essentials of Management Information Systems* (8th edition), Prentice Hall, Upper Saddle River, NJ.

Leavitt, H.J. and Whisler, T.L. (1958) 'Management in the 1980s', *Harvard Business Review*, **36**(6), 41–8.

Leidner, D.E. and Kayworth, T. (2006) 'A review of culture in information systems research: towards a theory of information technology culture conflict', *MIS Quarterly*, **30**(2), 357–99.

Lewis, M., Young, B., Mathiassen, L., Rai, A. and Welke, R. (2007) 'Business process innovation based on stakeholder perceptions', *Information, Knowledge, Systems Management*, **6**(1/2), 7–27.

Li, F. (2007) *What is e-Business?* Blackwell, Oxford.

Liker, J.K. (2006) *The Toyota Way Fieldbook: A Practical Guide for Implementing Toyota's 4Ps*, McGraw-Hill, Maidenhead.

Lin, H.-F. (2007) 'Predicting consumer intentions to shop online: an empirical test of competing theories', *Electronic Commerce Research and Applications*, **6**(4), 433–42.

Lloyd, C. and Newell, H. (1998) 'Computerising the sales force: the introduction of technical change in a non-union workforce', *New Technology, Work and Employment*, **13**(2), 104–15.

Lu, X.-H., Huang, L.-H. and Heng, M.S.H. (2006) 'Critical success factors of inter-organizational information systems: a case study of Cisco and Xiao Tong in China', *Information & Management*, **43**(3), 395–408.

Lucas, H.C. (1975) *Why Information Systems Fail*, Columbia University Press, New York.

Lyytinen, K. and Hirschheim, J.R. (1987) 'Information systems failures: a survey and classification of the empirical literature', *Oxford Surveys in Information Systems*, **4**, 257–309.

Mahieu, Y. (2002), *Note on Customer Relationship Management*, Ivey Management Services, London, Ontario.

Mahmood, M. and Mann, G. (2000) 'Special Issue Impacts of IT investment on organizational performance', *Journal of Management Information Systems*, **16**(4), 3–10.

Malone, T.W. (1997) 'Is empowerment just a fad?: Control, decision making and IT', *Sloan Management Review*, **38**(2), 23–35.

Manyika, M., Roberts, R.P. and Sprague, K.L. (2008) 'Eight business technology trends to watch', *McKinsey Quarterly*, 7 January, online edition.

Markides, C. and Geroski, P. (2005) *Fast Second: How Smart Companies Bypass Radical Innovation to Enter and Dominate New Markets*, Jossey-Bass, San Francisco, CA.

Markus, M.L. (1983) 'Power, politics and MIS implementation', *Communications of the ACM*, **26**(6), 430–44.

Markus, M.L. (1994) 'Preconditions for BPR success', *Information Systems Management*, **11**(2), 7–14.

Markus, M.L. (2004) 'Technochange management: using IT to drive organizational change', *Journal of Information Technology*, **20**(1), 4–20.

Markus, M.L., Axline, S., Petrie, D. and Tanis, C. (2000a) 'Learning from adopters' experiences with ERP: problems encountered and success achieved', *Journal of Information Technology*, **15**(4), 245–66.

Markus, M.L., Manville, B. and Agres, C.E. (2000b) 'What makes a virtual organization work?', *MIT Sloan Management Review*, **42**(1), 13–26.

Markus, M.L. and Robey, D. (1983) 'The organisational validity of management information systems', *Human Relations*, **36**(3), 203–36.

Martin, J. (2002) *Organizational Culture: Mapping the Terrain*, Sage, London.

Martinelli, E. and Gianluca, M. (2007) 'Enabling and inhibiting factors in adoption of electronic-reverse auctions: a longitudinal case study in grocery retailing', *International Review of Retail, Distribution and Consumer Research*, **17**(3), 203–18.

Maruca, R.F. (1998) 'How do you manage an off-site team?', *Harvard Business Review*, **76**(4), 22–35.

May, C. (2006) 'A rational model for assessing and evaluating complex interventions in health care', *BMC Health Services Research*, **6**, 86.

McAfee, A. (2006) 'Mastering the three worlds of information technology', *Harvard Business Review*, **84**(11), 141–9.

McDonagh, J. (2003) 'Not for the faint hearted: social and organizational challenges in IT-enabled change', *Organization Development Journal*, **19**(1), 11–19.

McGinnis, T.C. and Huang, Z. (2007) 'Rethinking ERP success: a new perspective from knowledge management and continuous improvement', *Information & Management*, **44**(7), 626–34.

McGowan, M.K., Stephens, P. and Gruber, D. (2007) 'An exploration of the ideologies of software intellectual property: the impact on ethical decision making', *Journal of Business Ethics*, **73**(4), 409–24.

McKeen, J.D. and Smith, H.A. (2003) *Making IT Happen: Critical Issues in IT Management*, John Wiley & Sons Ltd., Chichester.

McLoughlin, I. (1999) *Creative Technological Change*, Routledge, London.

Miller, G. (1956) 'The magical number seven plus or minus two: some limits on our capacity for processing information', *Psychological Review*, **63**, 81–97.

Mintzberg, H. (1994) *The Rise and Fall of Strategic Planning*, Prentice Hall, Hemel Hempstead.

Mintzberg, H., Quinn, J.B. and Ghoshal, S. (2003) *The Strategy Process: Concepts, Contexts, Cases*, Financial Times/Prentice Hall, Harlow.

Mitroff, I.I. (1983), *Stakeholders of the Organizational Mind*, Jossey-Bass, San Francisco, CA.

Mumford, E. and Weir, M. (1979) *Computer Systems in Work Design: The Ethics Method*, Associated Business Press, London.

Narango-Gil, D. and Hartmann, F. (2007) 'How CEOs use management information systems for strategy implementation in hospitals', *Health Policy*, **81**(1), 29–41.

National Audit Office (2004) *Improving IT Procurement*, Her Majesty's Stationery Office, London.

Nolan, R. and McFarlan, F.W. (2005) 'Information technology and the board of directors', *Harvard Business Review*, **83**(10), 96–106.

Nonaka, I. and Takeuchi, H. (1995), *The Knowledge-creating Company*, Oxford University Press, New York.

OECD (1980) *Guidelines on the Protection of Privacy and Transborder Flows of Personal Data*, OECD, Paris.

Ogbonna, E. and Harris, L.C. (2006) 'Organization culture in the age of the Internet: an exploratory study', *New Technology, Work and Employment*, **21**(2), 162–75.

Orlikowski, W.J. (2002) 'Knowing in practice: enacting a collective capability in distributed organizing', *Organization Science*, **13**(3), 249–73.

O'Sullivan, David (2002) 'Framework for managing development in the networked organisations', *Computers in Industry*, **47**(1), 77–88.

Otim, S. and Grover, V. (2006) 'An empirical study on Web-based services and customer loyalty', *European Journal of Information Systems*, **15**(6), 527–41.

Oz, E. (2006), *Management Information Systems*, Thomson, Boston, MA.

Paik, Y. and Choi, D.Y. (2005) 'Cultural counterpoints: the shortcomings of a standardized knowledge management system: the case study of Accenture', *Academy of Management Executive*, **19**(2), 81–4.

Pan, G.S.C., Pan, S.L. and Flynn, D. (2004) 'De-escalation of commitment to information systems projects: a process perspective', *Journal of Strategic information Systems*, **13**(3), 247–70.

Peloza, J. (2006) 'Using corporate social responsibility as insurance for financial performance', *California Management Review*, **48**(2), 52–72.

Pettigrew, A.M. (1987) 'Context and action in the transformation of the firm', *Journal of Management Studies*, **24**(6), 649–70.

Pettigrew, A.M., Ferlie, E. and McKee, L. (1992) *Shaping Strategic Change*, Sage, London.

Pfeffer, J. (1992) *Managing with Power*, Harvard Business School Press, Boston, MA.

Phan, D.D. (2003) 'E-business development for competitive advantages: a case study', *Information & Management*, **40**(6), 581–90.

Pliskin, N., Romm, T., Lee, A.S. and Weber, Y. (1993) 'Presumed versus actual organisational culture: managerial implications for implementation of information systems', *The Computer Journal*, **36**(2), 143–52.

Porter, M.E. (1985) *Competitive Advantage: Creating and Sustaining Superior Performance*, Free Press, New York.

Porter, M.E. (2001) 'Strategy and the Internet', *Harvard Business Review*, **79**(2), 63–78.

Porter, M.E. and Millar, V.E. (1985) 'How information gives you competitive advantage', *Harvard Business Review*, **63**(4), 149–62.

Poynter, R. (2008) 'Facebook: the future of networking with customers', *International Journal of Market Research*, **50**(1), 11–12.

Quinn, J.B. (1980), *Strategies for Change: Logical Incrementalism*, Irwin, Homewood, IL.

Quinn, R.E., Faerman, S.R., Thompson, M.P. and McGrath, M.R. (2003) *Becoming a Master Manager* (3rd edition), John Wiley & Sons Ltd., Chichester.

Ricadela, A. (2000) 'Microsoft takes stake in application service provider', *Information Week*, **778**, 145.

Rigby, D.K., Reichheld, F.F. and Schefter, P. (2002) 'Avoid the four perils of CRM', *Harvard Business Review*, **80**(2), 101–9.

Roberts, P. and Dowling, G. (2002) 'Corporate reputation and sustained superior financial performance', *Strategic Management Journal*, **23**(12), 1077–93.

Robey, D. and Boudreau, M. (1999), 'Accounting for the contradictory consequences of information technology: theoretical directions and methodological implications', *Information Systems Research*, **10**(2), 167–85.

Roman, S. (2007) 'The ethics of online retailing: a scale development and validation from the consumer's perspective', *Journal of Business Ethics*, **72**(2), 131–48.

Ross, J.W. and Beath, C.M. (2002) 'New approaches to IT investment', *MIT Sloan Management Review*, **43**(2), 51–9.

Ross, J.W. and Weill, P. (2002) 'Six IT decisions your IT people shouldn't make', *Harvard Business Review*, **80**(11), 84–91.

Ross, J. and Weill, P. (2005) 'A matrixed approach to designing IT governance', *MIT Sloan Management Review*, **46**(2), 26–34.

Ross, J.W., Weill, P. and Robertson, D.C. (2006) *Enterprise Architecture as Strategy: Creating a Foundation for Business Execution*, Harvard Business School Press, Boston, MA.

Ruppel, C.P. and Harrington, S.J. (2001), 'Sharing knowledge through intranets: a study of organizational culture and intranet implementation', *IEEE Transactions on Professional Communication*, **44**(1), 37–52.

Saarinen, T. (1996) 'An expanded instrument for evaluating information system success', *Information and Management*, **31**, 103–18.

Sabherwal, R., Hirschheim, R. and Goles, T. (2001) 'The dynamics of alignment: insights from a punctuated equilibrium', *Organization Science*, **12**(2), 179–97.

Saravanan, I.B. and Bhaskaran, S. (2007) *BBC-Microsoft Tie-Up: Strategy for Next Generation Digital Presentation*, European Case Clearing House Case No. 307-035-1, ECCH, Cranfield University, UK.

Sauer, C. (1993) *Why Information Systems Fail: A Case Study Approach*, Alfred Waller, Henley-on-Thames.

Scarbrough, H. and Swan, J. (eds) (1999) *Case Studies in Knowledge Management*, IPD, London.

Schein, E. (2004), *Organization Culture and Leadership*, 3rd edition, Jossey-Bass, San Francisco, CA.

Schwaig, K.S., Kane, G.C. and Storey, V.C. (2006) 'Compliance to the fair information practices: how are the Fortune 500 handling online privacy disclosures?', *Information and Management*, **43**(7), 805–20.

Schwarz, G. (2006) 'Positioning hierarchy in enterprise system change', *New Technology, Work & Employment*, **21**(3), 252–65.

Shalk, R. and van Rijckevorsel, A. (2007) 'Factors influencing absenteeism and intention to leave in a call centre', *New Technology, Work and Employment*, **22**(3), 260–74.

Shapiro, C. and Varian, H. (2004) *The Economics of Information Technology: An Introduction*, Cambridge University Press, Cambridge.

Shih, H.-P. (2004) 'An empirical study on predicting user acceptance of e-shopping on the Web', *Information & Management*, **41**, 351–68.

Son, J.Y. and Benbasat, I. (2007) 'Organizational buyers' adoption and use of B2B electronic marketplaces: efficiency- and legitimacy-oriented perspectives', *Journal of Management Information Systems*, **24**(1), 55–100.

Songini, M. (2006) 'Wal-Mart details its RFID journey', *Computer-world*, March 2.

Sousa, G.W.L., Van Aken, E.M. and Groesbeck, R.L. (2002) 'Applying an enterprise engineering approach to engineering work: a focus on business process modelling', *Engineering Management Journal*, **14**(3), 15–24.

Spil, S. (2003) 'Dynamic and emergent information systems strategy formulation and implementation', *IT Management*, **9**(3), 22–37.

Stair, R. and Reynolds, G. (2008) *Principles of Information Systems*, Thomson, Boston, MA.

Stephanides, C. (2001) 'User interfaces for all: new perspectives into human–computer interaction', in C. Stephanides (ed.), *User Interfaces for All: Concepts, Methods and Tools*, Lawrence Erlbaum Associates, Mahwah, NJ.

Straub, D., Keil, M. and Brenner, W. (1997) 'Testing the technology acceptance model across cultures: a three country study', *Information & Management*, **33**, 1–11.

Strassman, P.A. (1999) *Information Productivity*, The Information Economics Press, New Canaan, CT.

Symon, G. and Clegg, C.W. (1991) 'A study of the implementation of CADCAM', *Journal of Occupational Psychology*, **64**(4), 273–90.

Tapscott, E. and Williams, A.D. (2006) *Wikinomics: How Mass Collaboration Changes Everything*, Viking Penguin, New York.

Tayeb, M.H. (1996) *The Management of a Multicultural Workforce*, John Wiley & Sons Ltd., Chichester.

Thomas, D., Ranganathan, C. and Desouza, K.C. (2005) 'Race to dot.com and back: lessons on e-business spin-offs and reintegration', *Information Systems Management*, **22**(3), 23–30.

Toffler, A. (1980), *The Third Wave*, Collins, London.

Treacy, M. and Wiersema, F. (1998) *The Discipline of Market Leaders*, Harper Collins, New York.

Trevino, L.K. (1986) 'Ethical decision-making in organisations: a person–situation interactionist model', *Academy of Management Review*, **11**(3), 601–17.

Turban, E. and Volonino, L. (2008) *Electronic Commerce: A Managerial Perspective*, Prentice Hall, Upper Saddle River, NJ.

Venkatesh, V., Morris, M.G., Davis, G.B. and Davis, F.D. (2003) 'A unified theory of acceptance and use of technology', *MIS Quarterly*, **27**(3), 425–78.

Venkatraman, N. and Henderson, J.C. (1998) 'Real strategies for virtual organizing', *MIT Sloan Management Review*, **40**(1), 33–48.

Vise, D.A. (2005) *The Google Story*, Macmillan, New York.

Voelpel, S.C., Dous, M. and Davenport, T.H. (2005) 'Five steps to creating a global knowledge-sharing system: Siemens' Sharenet', *Academy of Management Review*, **19**(2), 9–23.

Vogel, D. (2005) *The Market for Virtue: The Potential and Limits of Corporate Social Responsibility*, Brookings Institution Press, Washington, DC.

Voss, C.A. (1988) 'Success and failure in advanced manufacturing technology', *International Journal of Technology Management*, **3**(1), 285–97.

Walsham, G. (1993) *Interpreting Information Systems in Organizations*, John Wiley & Sons Ltd., Chichester.

Walsham, G. (2001) 'Knowledge management: the benefits and limitations of computer systems', *European Management Journal*, **19**(6), 599–608.

Walsham, G. (2002), 'Cross-cultural software production and use: a structurational analysis', *MIS Quarterly*, **26**(4), 359–80.

Watad, M.M. and DiSanzo, F.J. (2000) 'Case study: the synergism of telecommuting and office automation', *MIT Sloan Management Review*, **41**(2), 85–96.

Weill, P. and Ross, J. (2005) 'A matrixed approach to IT governance', *MIT Sloan Management Review* **46**(2), 26–34.

Wright, C. and Lund, J. (2006) 'Variations on a lean theme: work restructuring in retail distribution', *New Technology, Work and Employment*, **21**(1), 59–74.

Wisner, J.D. and Stanley, L.L. (2008), *Process Management: Creating Value along the Supply Chain*, South-Western College Publishing, Mason, OH.

Wu, I.-L. and Chen, J.-L. (2006) 'A hybrid performance measure system for e-business investment in high-tech manufacturing: an empirical study', *Information & Management*, **43**(3), 364–77.

Zentner, A. (2006) 'Measuring the effects of file-sharing on music purchases', *Journal of Law and Economics*, **49**(1), 63–90.

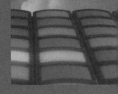

# INDEX

*NB:* Entries in bold indicate a glossary entry